The Origins of Genocide

This year the United Nations celebrated the 'Convention on the Prevention and Punishment of the Crime of Genocide', adopted in December 1948. It is time to recognize the man behind this landmark in international law. At the beginning were a few words: "New conceptions require new terms. By 'genocide' we mean the destruction of a nation or of an ethnic group". Rarely in history have paradigmatic changes in scholarship been brought about with such few words. Putting the quintessential crime of modernity in only one sentence, Raphael Lemkin (1900-1959), the Polish Jewish specialist in international law, not only summarized the horrors of the National Socialist Crimes, which were still underway, when he coined the term "genocide" in 1944, but also influenced international law. As the founding figure of the UN Genocide Convention Lemkin is finally getting the respect he deserves. Less known is his contribution to historical scholarship on genocide. Until his death, Lemkin was working on a broad study on genocides in the history of humankind. Unfortunately, he did not manage to publish it. The contributions in this book offer for the first time a critical assessment not only of his influence on international law but also on historical analysis of mass murders, showing the close connection between both.

This book was published as a special issue of the *Journal of Genocide Research.*

Dominik J. Schaller is Editor of the Journal of Genocide Research and lecturer and researcher at the University of Heidelberg, Germany.

Jürgen Zimmerer is Editor of the Journal of Genocide Research. He is also Reader in International History and Director of the Centre for the Study of Genocide and Mass Violence at the University of Sheffield.

The Origins of Genocide

Raphael Lemkin as a historian of mass violence

Edited by Dominik J. Schaller and
Jürgen Zimmerer

Routledge
Taylor & Francis Group
LONDON AND NEW YORK

First published 2009 by Routledge
2 Park Square, Milton Park, Abingdon, Oxon, OX14 4RN

Simultaneously published in the USA and Canada
by Routledge
711 Third Avenue, New York, NY 10017

Routledge is an imprint of the Taylor & Francis Group, an informa business

First issued in paperback 2013

Typeset in Times by Value Chain, India

British Library Cataloguing in Publication Data
A catalogue record for this book is available from the British Library

ISBN13: 978-0-415-48026-0 (hbk)
ISBN13: 978-0-415-85130-5 (pbk)

CONTENTS

Notes on contributors

Tanya Elder, Montefiore Medical Centre/Harry M. Zimmerman, MD Archives, New York.

Myriam Gessler, University of Berne, Switzerland.

Michael A. McDonnell, University of Sydney, Australia.

A. Dirk Moses, University of Sydney, Australia.

Dominik J. Schaller, University of Heidelberg, Germany.

Daniel Marc Segesser, University of Berne, Switzerland.

Dan Stone, Royal Holloway, University of London, UK.

Anton Weiss-Wendt, Brandeis University, Waltham, MA, USA.

Jürgen Zimmerer, University of Sheffield, UK.

INTRODUCTION

The Origins of Genocide – Raphael Lemkin as a Historian of Mass Violence

DOMINIK J. SCHALLER and JÜRGEN ZIMMERER

> "An analysis of the laws and decrees promulgated by the Nazis and their puppet governments in the conquered areas of Europe has been made by Dr. Raphael Lemkin, a Polish lawyer now in this country, in a book called 'Axis Rule in Occupied Europe'. The book published Wednesday, contains 674 pages. Columbia University Press is distributing it."[1]

This simple abstract, published in the *New York Times*, shows that Lemkin's contemporaries did not realize immediately how deeply and significantly *Axis Rule in Occupied Europe* would influence both international law and the social sciences. The new term and concept of 'genocide' was not even mentioned in this laconic text. Only a few years later, international lawyers and observers of the Nuremberg Trials had to conclude that expressions like 'mass murder', 'Germanization' or 'crimes against humanity' were neither adequate nor sufficient to characterize the acts of violence committed by the Nazis during the second World War. Most specialists in international law agreed that a more specific term was needed and soon recognized that Lemkin's idea of genocide could be a useful framework for the analysis and punishment of the persecution and annihilation of the European Jewry. Waldemar Kaempffert, science editor of the *New York Times*, for example, proclaimed that 'genocide is the new name for the crime fastened on the Nazi leaders'. What is more, Kaempffert understood the global and temporal scope of Lemkin's concept:

> Attempts at the wholesale extermination of a population and the transmutation of its culture had been made before and after Rome reduced Carthage to ruins. The wars waged by the Crusaders and Mohammedans of old were largely wars of extermination. The Turks in their time did their best to destroy the Armenians. It was to identify such crimes that Professor Lemkin coined the word genocide.[2]

The adoption of the 'Convention on the Prevention and Punishment of the Crime of Genocide' by the United Nations General Assembly on 9 December 1948 marked the breakthrough of Lemkin's concept. However, Lemkin's wish that the UN Convention would effectively and sustainably prevent further genocides from occurring did not come true. Due to the political constellations determined by the Cold War, the Genocide Convention had not been more than a statement of intent. The superpowers would have had the means at their disposal to prevent or punish the crime of genocide, but they preferred not to meddle in the domestic affairs of their respective allies. Rather, they concentrated on denouncing acts of mass violence perpetrated by the opposing side. It was the end of the bipolar world order that led to a diminishing of the deadlock that had made the Genocide Convention a rather dysfunctional tool. The appointment of the ad hoc tribunals for the wars in former Yugoslavia and the mass murder of the Tutsi in Rwanda in 1993 and 1994 respectively, as well as the adoption of the Rome Statute on the establishment of the International Criminal Court (ICC) in July 2002, reflected the newly gained significance and acceptance of the Genocide Convention. Finally, on 2 September 1998, the first verdict ever on the count of genocide was handed down, as the International Criminal Tribunal for Rwanda (ICTR) found Jean Paul Akayesu, the former mayor of the Rwandan town of Taba, guilty as charged. And in July 2008, the Chief Prosecutor of the ICC decided to charge the Sudanese president Omar Hassan al-Bashir with genocide because of the latter's role in the organization of the atrocities committed in Darfur.[3] If the pre-trial chamber of the ICC confirms the charges by its prosecutor this would be the first genocide indictment of a current head of state.

The growing importance of the Genocide Convention coincides with an increasing general interest in the man who coined the term genocide. After his death in 1959, Lemkin and his work were forgotten for decades. It was the institutional establishment of genocide studies in the mid-1990s that led to a rediscovery of the self-proclaimed 'founder of the Genocide Convention'. Although genocide researchers revere Lemkin as the pioneer of their discipline, and name libraries and human rights awards after him, historical scholarship on his biography and work is still in its infancy. So far, only one comprehensive biography has been written.[4] What is still largely forgotten is the fact that Lemkin was not only a campaigner for the UN convention but also a historian of genocide. Large parts of his oeuvre have not yet been examined, let alone published.[5] The contributions in this volume offer for the first time a critical assessment not only of his influence on international law but also of his historical studies on mass violence, showing the close connection between the two.

After all, who was Raphael Lemkin? And what made him develop a new concept for the analysis of a special form of collective violence and relentlessly struggle for a new international law aimed at the prevention and punishment of the worst form of human rights abuse?

Raphael Lemkin and the Genesis of the UN Genocide Convention

Lemkin was born in 1900 in Bezwodene, a town in then Eastern Poland, into a family of farmers. According to his own testimony, Lemkin had been sensitive to the suffering of ethnic groups from his early days onwards. In his unpublished autobiography, entitled 'Totally Unofficial', Lemkin stated how the novel *Quo Vadis* had had a lasting impact on his thinking and his career, and on the way he – as a Jew – had identified with the fate of the persecuted Christians:

> In my early boyhood, I read Quo Vadis by Henry Sienkiewicz – this story full of fascination about the sufferings of the early Christians and the Romans' attempt to destroy them solely because they believed in Christ. Nobody could save them, neither the police of Rome nor any outside power. It was more than curiosity that led me to search in history for similar examples, such as the case of the Hugenots, the Moors of Spain, the Aztecs of Mexico, the Catholics in Japan, and so many races and nations under Genghis Khan. The trail of this unspeakable destruction led straight through modern times up to the threshold of my own life. I was appalled by the frequency of the evil, by great losses in life and culture, by the despairing impossibility of reviving the dead or consoling the orphans, and above all, by the impunity coldly relied upon the guilty.[6]

Lemkin stated that the analysis of mass violence made him become a lawyer, because he 'thought that this profession would best qualify, [him] for [his] task of making the destruction of groups of human beings punishable'.[7] These passages are typical of the expressive and pathetic style of his autobiographical writing. Although his unpublished memoirs are not a reliable source regarding the stages of his career, they shed light on his self-understanding.

What is true is that the fate of the Anatolian Armenians during the first World War, especially the inability of the victorious Allies to prosecute the leading Young Turks, shocked the young Lemkin deeply. In the wake of this experience he concluded that an international law against the wholesale extermination of ethnic and religious groups had to be created. In order to achieve this goal, Lemkin was willing to limit state sovereignty, which most legal philosophers and practitioners of international law rejected: 'But sovereignty of states implies conducting an independent foreign and internal policy, building of schools, construction of roads, in brief, all types of activity directed towards the welfare of people. Sovereignty cannot be conceived as the right to kill millions of innocent people.'[8]

After obtaining his doctorate in 1926, Lemkin rose to become a renowned expert on international law and a leading advocate of the protection of minorities. In order to strengthen the security of national, religious and racial minorities, Lemkin proposed, at the Fifth International Conference on the Unification of Criminal Law in Madrid (1933), the establishment of two additional statutory offences in international law: 'vandalism' and 'barbarism' were to be included in the domestic criminal law of the 37 participant states. By 'vandalism', Lemkin meant the deliberate destruction of the cultural heritage of a specific group; by 'barbarism', the suppression and extermination of members of a racial, religious or social group. However, the congress rejected Lemkin's proposals.

After the outbreak of the second World War, Lemkin was confronted with persecution on a very personal level. He had to leave Poland after the German invasion in 1939 and fled via Sweden to the United States, where he taught at Duke University and at Yale before working for the Board of Economic Warfare.[9]

The far-reaching indifference of the US-American public towards the murder of the European Jews depressed and motivated Lemkin at the same time. An international treaty for the protection of ethnic and religious minorities, signed by the Allies and neutral states, might prevent the National Socialists from fulfilling their plan, he hoped naively:

> It was still possible to save at least a part of the people. The Allies still had an access to the parliaments of most of the nations of the world at that time. A treaty naming genocide a crime could still be enacted and applied by many parliaments. And then a warning had to be issued to Hitler concomitantly with the treaty. The warning would say that the protection of the very existence of nations is the main aim of the Allies.[10]

Restlessly, Lemkin looked for the necessary support for the creation of such a treaty. But the unsuccessful lobbying wore him down, and he himself described impressively how he suffered from his helplessness and inability to win politicians and opinion-makers over to his cause. In addition, he was worried about his remaining family in Poland:

> My nights at these times turned into nightmares. Dreams came often incessantly and compellingly. I saw my parents in my dreams very realistically. The worst, however, were the visions which came in a half-sleepy stage. During one of them, I saw the interior of a train. A drab light was falling on people sitting on valises. Among them was my mother with a stony face. Next to her was a small boy. Who was he? I recognized the dark coat of my mother, her high forehead, her eyes were saying nothing. Her mouth was silent ice. Where was she going? Was it her last journey? ... My health was deteriorating ostensibly and friends made an appointment for me to see a doctor.[11]

Nevertheless, Lemkin never abandoned his idea of an international law against the murder of peoples. In 1944, he published his famous *Axis Rule in Occupied Europe*, both a compilation of documents on and a lucid analysis of the German policy of occupation and destruction in Europe.[12] In this work Lemkin introduced the term 'genocide' for the first time, giving a name to what British Prime Minister Winston Churchill had called 'a crime without a name'.[13] The neologism 'genocide', meant, as he defined it

> the destruction of a nation or of an ethnic group. … Generally speaking, genocide does not necessarily mean the immediate destruction of a nation, except when accomplished by mass killings of all members of a nation. It is intended rather to signify a coordinated plan of different actions aiming at the destruction of essential foundations of the life of national groups, with the aim of annihilating the groups themselves. The objectives of such a plan would be the disintegration of the political and social institutions, of culture, language, national feelings, religion, and the economic existence of national groups, and the destruction of the personal security, liberty, health, dignity, and even the lives of the individuals belonging to such groups. Genocide is directed against the national group as an entity, and the actions involved are directed against individuals, not in their individual capacity, but as members of the national group.[14]

Furthermore, genocides – according to Lemkin – have to be understood as processes:

> Genocide has two phases: one destruction of the national pattern of the oppressed group; the other, imposition of the national pattern of the oppressor. This imposition, in turn, may be made upon the oppressed population which is allowed to remain, or upon the territory alone, after removal of the population and the colonization of the area by the oppressor's own nationals.[15]

Lemkin hoped that after the end of the war, the statutory offence of genocide would be included in the charges brought by the International Military Tribunal (IMT) against the National Socialist war criminals; but this was not the case. Specialists in international law soon recognized that the legal concept of 'crimes against humanity' and its linking with war was problematic for the future punishment of systematic persecution and massacres committed by a government during peacetime against an ethnic or religious group among its own national population. Consequently, it would hardly be suitable as a means of protection for minorities. New paradigms were called for in international law.

In April 1947, therefore, the General Secretary of the United Nations Trygve Lie commissioned Raphael Lemkin, the Romanian Vespasian V. Pella (1897–1960), who was President of the International Association of Penal Law, and the French law professor and former judge at the IMT Henri Donnedieu de Vabres to prepare a draft of an international criminal code against genocide.

Lemkin's original concept of genocide constituted the basis of a possible draft, but the three experts on international law took differing views with respect to some crucial points. Lemkin deemed the deliberate destruction of a group's culture, for instance, by banning use of a language or destruction of religious and historical monuments to be a form of genocide as well, something his two colleagues regarded as an inadmissible extension of the term genocide. With the exception of the forced transfer of children into a different group, Pella and de Vabres did not consider forms of forced assimilation as being genocidal.

On 9 December 1948, the UN General Assembly eventually passed the final version of the Genocide Convention, which Lemkin, Pella and de Vabres had agreed on, by a vote of 55 : 0 : 0. The Convention came into effect on 12 January 1951, after being ratified by 20 countries as well.

Despite all his efforts for an international law against genocide and for the ratification of the UN Convention, Lemkin never won adequate recognition. In 1959 he died impoverished and isolated.

Raphael Lemkin as a Historian of Genocide

As Lemkin stated in his unpublished autobiography, the destruction of the Ottoman Armenians made a lasting impact on him and reinforced his interest in mass violence. Up until his death he had been working on a broad study of genocides in the history of humankind. Although his manuscripts on the Armenian Genocide and on the Holocaust have been touched upon in recent years, the real significance of his unpublished works has been widely neglected.[16]

The contributions in this volume lead to some significant insights and to a re-evaluation of Lemkin: the author of *Axis Rule in Occupied Europe* is not 'only' the 'founder of the genocide convention', as Lemkin liked to address himself, but also the 'father of genocide research'.

Two observations may highlight the insights which are to be won by a closer look at Lemkin's writings. In the emerging debate on colonialism and genocide, Lemkin is often referred to as a theorist of a genocide concept in which the European settlement of the various 'New Worlds' is not dealt with. Several authors have gone to great lengths to prove that genocide is a concept that can be applied to colonial situations. A debate has also arisen about the application of the term genocide to cultural destruction. For Lemkin the answer was obvious. It was not only cases where the perpetrators tried to eliminate a targeted group physically and in whole that constituted genocides: 'The disintegration of the political and social institutions, of culture, language, national feelings, religion, and the economic existence of national groups, and the destruction of the personal security, liberty, health and dignity'[17] were also central. Consequently, Lemkin attached great importance to the phenomenon of colonialism in his concept of genocide, as McDonnell, Moses and Schaller highlight in their articles in this volume.[18] It is therefore not surprising that Lemkin himself wrote extensively on the destruction of indigenous peoples in the Americas and on atrocities committed by Europeans in Africa.

The Articles in this Volume

Given the decades of neglect, not all aspects of Lemkin's work could be covered in this volume. Daniel Marc Segesser and Myriam Gessler (chapter 1) show how important the issue of the punishment of war crimes was after the end of the first World War and how politicians and jurists alike discussed it in a controversial manner. The trials in Leipzig and in Constantinople, where alleged war criminals from Germany and the Ottoman Empire had been judged, had not been satisfactory at all. Jurists were therefore looking for a new way to deal with war criminals in the future. Segesser and Gessler describe how the young Raphael Lemkin entered into this discussion, and examine who influenced him and how his concept relates to the ideas of others.

The purpose of Tanya Elder's contribution (chapter 2) is to further expose Raphael Lemkin through the lens of his archival collections. Elder provides genocide researchers with a useful and meticulous roadmap to Lemkin's unpublished works.

Michael A. McDonnell and A. Dirk Moses (chapter 3) not only prove that Lemkin regarded many instances of European–Indigenous encounters in the Americas as genocidal, but analyse in detail Lemkin's methodology. By contrasting new historical insights with Lemkin's perception they also identify some flaws in his description, mainly resulting from a much too naive reliance on Las Casas. Lemkin's quality as a historian is also questioned by Dominik J. Schaller (chapter 4). He shows in his contribution that Lemkin partly relied on untrustworthy sources in his manuscripts on the colonial war in 'German South West Africa' and on the Belgian atrocities in the Congo. In addition, Schaller discusses Lemkin's ambivalent view of European colonialism in Africa.

As Dan Stone shows in chapter 5, the study of colonial genocides provided Lemkin with a conceptual framework for understanding the German policy of occupation and extermination during the second World War. Lemkin was, of course, not the only person writing on the genocide of the Jews at this time, but he was innovative in noting that the murder of the Jews was just one aspect of a broad Nazi plan to ethnically restructure Eastern Europe.

The way Lemkin interpreted Stalinist Terror also seems to be problematic. Anton Weiss-Wendt (chapter 6) states that the discussion of the ethnic deportations in the Soviet Union was mainly part of the evolving Cold War and that Lemkin had resorted to anti-communism to convince the US administration to ratify the UN Genocide Convention. By insisting on the term genocide while describing the deportations of ethnic minorities in the Soviet Union, Lemkin wanted to demonstrate to US opinion-makers the relevance of the Genocide Convention, Weiss-Wendt argues. Nevertheless, Weiss-Wendt acknowledges that Lemkin was probably the first scholar to introduce a comparative method into the study of genocide.

The contributions in this volume are not based on a *unité de doctrine* nor are all the important papers by Lemkin on various genocides in the history of humankind covered; only a small part of Lemkin's historical scholarship is discussed. But the editors hope that this collection of articles will provoke fruitful discussions and stimulate further research on Lemkin as a historian of mass violence.

Notes and References

1 *New York Times*, 17, November 1944, 17.
2 *New York Times*, 20, October 1946, E13.
3 A summary of the Chief Prosecutor's application for warrant of arrest against al-Bashir can be found on the website of the ICC: http://www.icc-cpi.int/library/organs/otp/ICC-OTP-Summary-20081704-ENG.pdf (last accessed 19 January 2009).
4 John Cooper, *Raphael Lemkin and the Struggle for the Genocide Convention* (London: Palgrave Macmillan, 2008).
5 An exception is the publication and analysis of Lemkin's paper on Tasmania. See A. Dirk Moses and Dan Stone (eds), *Colonialism and Genocide* (London: Routledge, 2006), 66–100.
6 Raphael Lemkin, 'Totally Unofficial' [manuscript, without date], New York Public Library, Manuscript and Archives Division, The Raphael Lemkin Papers, Box 2: Bio- and Autobiographical Sketches of Lemkin.
7 Ibid.
8 Ibid., p. 13.
9 See Samantha Power, *"A Problem from Hell": America and the Age of Genocide* (London: Flamingo, 2003), 23–6.
10 Lemkin, 'Totally Unofficial', chapter VIII, 4.
11 Ibid., 8.
12 Raphael Lemkin, *Axis Rule in Occupied Europe* (Washington DC: Carnegie Endowment for International Peace, 1944).
13 Leo Kuper, *Genocide: Its Political Use in the Twentieth Century* (New Haven: Yale University Press, 1981), 12.
14 Lemkin, *Axis Rule*, 79.
15 Ibid.
16 Steven L. Jacobs, *Raphael Lemkin's Thoughts on Nazi Genocide: Not Guilty?* (Lewiston: Edwin Mellen Press, 1992). Steven L. Jacobs, 'Raphael Lemkin and the Armenian Genocide', in Richard Hovannisian (ed.), *Looking Backward, Moving Forward: Confronting the Armenian Genocide* (New Brunswick: Transaction, 2003), 125–35.
17 Lemkin, *Axis Rule*, 79.
18 See also John Docker, 'Raphael Lemkin's History of Genocide and Colonialism', Paper for United States Holocaust Memorial Museum, Center for Advanced Holocaust Studies, February 2004, http://www.ushmm.org/conscience/analysis/details/2004-02-26/docker.pdf (last accessed 19 January 2009) and the contributions in A. Dirk Moses (ed.), *Empire, Colony, Genocide: Conquest: Occupation, and Subaltern History in World History* (New York: Berghahn, 2008).

Raphael Lemkin and the international debate on the punishment of war crimes (1919–1948)

DANIEL MARC SEGESSER and MYRIAM GESSLER

When World War I ended in 1918 the issue of the punishment of war crimes was central, not only to many members of the governments of the victorious allies, but also to many jurists who had already worked on the topic during the war.[1] David Lloyd George, Prime Minister of Great Britain at the time, won the election immediately after the end of the war with the slogan "Hang the Kaiser" and Benjamin Clemenceau, Prime Minister of France, insisted that Germany would have to pay for the war and that those responsible not only for war crimes but also for the outbreak of the war would have to be punished. All of this finally resulted in articles 227 to 230 of the Versailles Treaty that were, with the exception of the article relating to the former Kaiser, almost literally also incorporated into the treaties with Austria, Hungary, Bulgaria and the Ottoman Empire. These articles were the work of the so-called Responsibilities Commission set up by the Preliminary Peace Conference[2] and of the council of four, which had decided on the final wording of these articles. Within the commission as well as among the four leading statesmen of the Paris Peace Conference there had been no full agreement on the fact what a war crime exactly was and as to whether the unleashing of a war was to be considered a war crime or not.[3] This was not surprising as the term "war crime," used for the first time in 1872 by Johann Caspar Bluntschli in his *Modern International Law of Civilised States* to describe the crimes of franc-tireurs in the Franco-German War,[4] had not been frequently used before the beginning of World War I and was therefore only loosely defined. Consequently, the commission set up a list of crimes which it considered as criminal breaches of the laws and customs of war. Amongst them were classical violations of the Hague and Geneva Conventions, but also many crimes that have since been called crimes against humanity, such as massacres, systematic terrorism, deliberate starvation of civilians, enforced prostitution, forced labour of civilians or the internment of civilians under inhuman conditions.[5]

Jurists, publicists, diplomats and members of governments were not able to agree as to what exactly a war crime was. Almost all of them—at least amongst jurists of allied countries—agreed, however, that war crimes were punishable offences against the laws and customs of war.[6] Most jurists also agreed on the fact that the trials in Leipzig and Constantinople, where a number of alleged war criminals from Germany and the Ottoman Empire had been judged and some of them even found guilty, had been far from satisfactory.[7] It was therefore important that a new way be found to deal with war criminals in the future, a way which would be considered neither victor's justice nor too lenient as in the case of trials in Leipzig and Constantinople, but would be based on a truly international criminal law.[8] It was into this discussion that the young Raphael Lemkin entered, when he began his studies at the law school of the University of Lwow in the newly created state of Poland. According to his own testimony crimes that the list of the responsibilities commission counted among war crimes were one of the reasons for him to choose to study law in general and especially criminal law. Although the persecution of Jews in the western provinces of Tsarist Russia, probably also close to his home town of Bezewodene, would have been close at hand,[9] Lemkin was much more attracted to the fate of the Armenians, this probably due to the publicity given to the Armenians in Russian propaganda during the war. Lemkin's interest in the Armenian question was further raised, at least according to his own testimony, by the trial of Soghomon Tehlirian, who had assassinated the former grand vizier of the Ottoman Empire, Taalat Pasha.[10] All this raises the question as to the development of the international debate on possible future sanctions for war crimes during the interwar period and World War II. It shows how Raphael Lemkin tried to participate in these debates. Lemkin having studied law and criminal law as well as philology[11] raises the question as to how far Lemkin was influenced by the differing methods of law and philology.

Raphael Lemkin and the international debate on war crimes in the interwar period

Already before the failure of the system of Versailles to come to terms with the issue of the punishment of war crimes became clear, there were voices amongst academics who demanded that an international criminal law, which was found to be missing or at least to be incomplete, should be created or improved. In 1920 Maurice Travers, a French jurist and lawyer from Paris, published the first volume of a multi-volume work on international criminal law. He criticized the way the system of Versailles was dealing with the issue of the punishment of war crimes and demanded that a precise legal basis should be laid, before any further trials for war crimes could be held.[12] On a proposal of the Belgian minister of state and professor of natural and international law at the University of Louvain, Édouard Descamps, the Advisory Committee of Jurists of the League of Nations recommended the creation of an international court of justice to deal with crimes constituting a breach of the international public order or the universal law of nations—amongst which Descamps ranked war crimes as well as the crime to wage war.[13] Descamps' proposal had not met with universal approval within the Advisory Committee. Some had criticized that only national courts had the right to punish such crimes, while others such as Lord Phillimore claimed that only war crimes could be punished, while waging war could not be considered a crime.[14] The Council of the League of Nations wanted to refer the matter to international organizations of law, but the Assembly decided that the time was not yet ripe for the matter, not least because the majority of its delegates believed that there was no such thing as international criminal law.[15]

Although the Descamps resolution, as it later became known, failed, it became the starting point for the debate on the punishment of war crimes in the interwar period. The first to take up the ideas of Descamps was Hugh H. Bellot, a British lawyer and secretary-general of both the International Law Association and the Grotius Society. Bellot, who had actively fought for the idea of the punishment of war criminals during World War I,[16] took up the idea of Lord Phillimore and proposed the creation of an international criminal court to judge war crimes. At the 31st meeting of the International Law Association in Buenos Aires in 1922 he criticized the war crimes trials held in Leipzig as unsatisfactory and claimed that this was due to the fact that the trials had been held in national courts. Further trials in national courts would only lead to conflicting judgements and would always bear the stigma of national prejudice, something which was detrimental to the principle of justice. Therefore, an international criminal court to judge war criminals—but not those responsible for making war—had to be created.[17] Bellot's proposal did not meet with universal approval at the meeting of the International Law Association in Buenos Aires, but a majority of the members present asked Bellot to present a detailed proposal.[18] Bellot submitted his revised proposal, which concentrated on the punishment of war crimes and offences contrary to the laws of humanity, at the 33rd meeting of the International Law Association in Stockholm in 1924. After a lively debate the plenary session of the conference referred Bellot's proposal to an international committee of jurists for redrafting.[19] After a few changes—amongst them a widening of the jurisdiction of the proposed court to other international crimes such as the breaching of international treaties or the violation of punishable international obligations—the proposal was finally accepted by a majority of the members at the 34th meeting of the International Law Association in Vienna in 1926.[20] After the deaths of Hugh Bellot in 1928 and Lord Phillimore in 1929 the activities of the International Law Association on the punishment of war crimes almost came to a standstill. Wyndham Bewes, who succeeded Bellot as secretary-general of the International Law Association, was not able to bring the idea up again in future meetings of the organization and preferred to continue his activities within other frameworks such as the Association Internationale de Droit Pénal.[21]

While English-speaking authors, such as Bellot and Phillimore, had dominated the debate on the punishment of war crimes with their common law background in the early 1920s, the lead passed on more and more to jurists with a legal background dominated by Roman law. Proposals for the punishment of international crimes—amongst them war crimes as well as aggressive war, the abuse of diplomatic privileges, common crimes committed during an occupation or the spreading of false news endangering peace—were made at the meetings of the

Interparliamentary Union in 1924 and 1925 in Berne and Washington, DC. They did, however, not come from English-speaking jurists, but from Rumanian jurist Vespasien Pella, Professor of Criminal Law at the University of Jassy.[22] English-speaking academics began to move away from the issue of the punishment of war crimes—and the crime of making war, if they accepted the existence of such a crime—and concentrated more and more on the outlawry of war without further reference to the issue of punishment.[23] While the debates within the Interparliamentary Union did not make much progress in the years between 1926 and 1931,[24] the debate shifted more and more to jurists, who gathered at meetings of or organized by the Association Internationale de Droit Pénal, an organization largely dominated by specialists of criminal law from France, Belgium, Spain and some of the new Eastern European countries, who were strongly influenced by legal teaching from France.[25] Amongst the leading figures of the Association Internationale de Droit Pénal were Vespasien Pella from Rumania, Henri Donnedieu de Vabres and Jean-André Roux from France, Henri Carton de Wiart from Belgium, Megalos Caloyanni from Greece and Emil Stanislaw Rappaport from Poland. Although they did not all completely agree on all aspects of the punishment of international crimes, their main aim was the same: to create a truly international criminal law which would make it possible to punish international crimes, amongst which aggressive war was for many of them the most important.[26]

Raphael Lemkin finished his legal studies with his doctorate at the University of Lwow in 1926 and the following year began to teach criminal law at the Free University of Warsaw. In 1928 he was appointed prosecuting attorney for Warsaw.[27] In this context Lemkin met Emil Stanislaw Rappaport, Professor of Criminal Law at the Free University of Warzaw and Judge at the Court of Review in Warsaw. Rappaport was the president of the Polish Commission for International Juridicial Cooperation and Vice President of the Association Internationale de Droit Pénal.[28] The collaboration of the two men resulted amongst other things in the new Polish Criminal Code of 1932 and the publication of a commentary on the new law together with Janusz Jamontt.[29] They were also both interested in comparative criminal law as the publication lists of the two men show.[30] It is therefore not surprising that Lemkin also joined the Polish Commission for International Juridicial Cooperation and the Association Internationale de Droit Pénal at some time after 1927.[31] He was not a very active member of these two organizations, but it seems clear from all indications available that he supported the main line taken by Pella and Rappaport to find ways to punish international crimes—among them especially aggressive war—by way of international criminal law, an international criminal court or national criminal legislation.[32]

In 1927 the Polish Commission for International Juridicial Cooperation organized the first international conference for the unification of criminal law in Warsaw. The proposal for such a conference had come at the first general meeting of the Association Internationale de Droit Pénal from Pella, who became the secretary-general of the conference, which was in turn presided over by Rappaport. At least officially Lemkin did not participate in the conference, but it is nevertheless possible that he attended some of the meetings.[33] The conference discussed a number of topics of criminal law and international criminal law. In this context Rappaport and the Polish Commission for International Juridicial Cooperation proposed that not only aggressive war, but also the propaganda for aggressive war should be considered an international crime and that the Warsaw Conference should name a commission to make proposals for a possible implementation of the proposal on the diplomatic level.[34] The conference accepted Rappaport's proposal. Amongst other things it also discussed the issue of *delicta juris gentium* and declared the offences of piracy, counterfeiting of coins, trade in slaves, trade in women and children, intentional use of instruments capable of producing public danger, trade in narcotics and traffic in obscene publications, crimes punishable anywhere under the principle of universal jurisdiction.[35] At the following international conferences for the unification of criminal law in Brussels in 1930 and Paris in 1931 the issue of the intentional use of instruments capable of producing public danger was again taken up. Some delegates from Eastern European countries proposed to subsume acts of terrorism under this heading, but others, amongst them Rappaport and Lemkin, opposed such a decision. Finally, the conference of Paris decided to refer the issue to a commission, which included Lemkin as one of its members.[36] The commission presented its findings at the fifth international conference for the unification of criminal law in Madrid in 1933. A first report was presented by Jean-André Roux, the secretary-general of the Association Internationale de Droit Pénal. He proposed to concentrate on the aspect of terrorism and to try to fix minimal penalties in national criminal law for this offence.[37] Lemkin did not agree with Roux. In his report submitted to the conference of Madrid he pointed to the fact that it was not only necessary to fight terrorism on an international level, but that there were other crimes that had to be dealt with by means of the principle of universal jurisdiction, a principle promoted by Pella, Donnedieu de Vabres and Rappaport.[38] To Lemkin it was clear that the principle of universal jurisdiction could not be applied to all violations of international law. Only violations that were considered "so particularly dangerous as to present a threat to the interests, either of material nature or of a moral nature, of the entire international community"[39] could be considered crimes that should be judged anywhere according the principle of universal jurisdiction. Lemkin then referred to the decisions taken by the international conferences for the unification of criminal law in Warsaw, Brussels and Paris and pointed to the fact that terrorism did not constitute a legal concept, but rather embraced a large variety of different criminal acts. Lemkin therefore pleaded for a return to the original concept of the intentional use of instruments capable of producing public danger, which was to include acts of barbarity, acts of vandalism, provocation of catastrophes in and international interruption of international communications as well as the propagation of human, animal or vegetable contagions. Further into his proposal Lemkin also pointed to violations of human rights, acts of extermination and the destruction of culture and works of art as violation, which had to be punished everywhere independently of the location of such acts. Lemkin proposed an international convention to ensure the repression of all these offences.[40]

In the debate on the reports of Roux and Lemkin the former proposed to concentrate on the issue of terrorism, because it had become a crime of an international dimension and because it was not clear whether the intentional use of instruments capable of producing public danger could really be considered delicts in terms of international criminal law.[41] Lemkin's report was therefore dropped from the agenda of the commission and not taken up in the full meetings of the conference. From the official documents of the conference it seems that Lemkin was not personally present at the conference, which may be one of the explanations why there was almost no opposition to dropping Lemkin's report. Rappaport, who was unable to attend the meetings of the commission dealing with the reports of Roux and Lemkin, did not voice any criticism to the dropping of Lemkin's report, although he had been critical of the proposals made at Brussels and Paris. Probably this was due to the moderate version of the proposals the commission made in relation to terrorism.[42] Lemkin did not take up the subject again before the beginning of World War II, probably also because of the fact that terrorism became the dominant topic within the Association Internationale de Droit Pénal and the League of Nations after the murder of Yugoslav King Alexander and French Foreign Minister Louis Barthou in Marseilles on October 9, 1934.[43] Although the Association Internationale de Droit Pénal had already set up a commission of which Rappaport was a member, to deal with the issue,[44] the League of Nations decided to set up its own commission, which was, however, presided over by the president of the Association Internationale de Droit Pénal, Henri Carton de Wiart. Furthermore, Vespasien Pella was elected reporter of the commission and prepared several drafts for a convention for the international repression of terrorism and the creation of an international criminal court.[45] The draft conventions that were finally adopted by an international conference in 1937 did, however, not nearly go as far as Pella originally would have wished and neither included the crime of aggressive war nor war crimes, as they had been defined by the responsibilities commission in Versailles and accepted by Pella in 1925.[46]

Although Lemkin and Rappaport participated at the sixth international conference for the unification of criminal law, which dealt with the issue of terrorism in Copenhagen in 1935,[47] neither of them took a prominent part in the formulation of the conventions for the repression of terrorism and for the creation of an international criminal court. Nor did Poland sign any of the conventions, although it had been represented at the conferences by Tytus Komarnicki and Lucien Bekerman.[48] Neither Rappaport nor Lemkin came back to the issues of aggressive war or acts of barbarism, before the beginning of World War II. While Rappaport became a victim of the German crimes in Poland and would therefore not come back to the issue before the end of the war, Raphael Lemkin became involved in the American efforts to pursue the war criminals of the new world war.[49]

The debate on the punishment of war crimes during World War II

When in September 1939 the German forces attacked Poland Raphael Lemkin was drafted into the Polish Armed Forces and wounded. He nevertheless managed to escape first to Lithuania and then to Sweden, where he lectured for 18 months at the law faculty of the University of Stockholm, mainly on the topic he had been dealing with lately, finance law. At the same time he began to collect German laws and decrees with respect to subject peoples and accumulated hundreds of papers, which would later form the core of the documentation of his study *Axis Rule in Occupied Europe*. Early in 1941 he was offered a contract with the law school of Duke University, not least due to his friendship with Professor Malcolm McDermott, whom he had met when the latter was serving as visiting scholar at the universities of Warsaw and Cracow. Travelling through the Soviet Union Lemkin finally arrived in the United States in the late summer of 1941.[50]

Although the war had not cut off his relationship with McDermott, he had lost contact with all those with whom he had worked in the interwar period. Rappaport had remained in Poland and was therefore not able to continue his work. Vespasien Pella was in Rumania, an ally of Hitler Germany, and did also not contribute any further studies to the issues of war crimes and aggressive war before the end of the war. The same was also true of Henri Donnedieu de Vabres, who remained in Vichy France after the fall of Paris in 1940. The net of the Association Internationale de Droit Pénal had broken down with the beginning of the war, not to be restored before 1945/1946.[51] Others began to dominate the debate on the punishment of war crimes, which from the beginning did not only concentrate on the classical war crimes, but also on aggressive war and crimes that would later be called crimes against humanity. It was, however, only after the fall of France that the debate really began, although German barbarities in Poland became known to the public in France and Britain from the beginning of the war in 1939. Ernst Joseph Cohn, an exiled German academic, who lived and taught in Britain, was one of the first to address the issue of the punishment of war crimes. He called for war crimes trials in the countries of the victims, while opposing the inclusion of violations of international obligations—such as aggressive war in violation of the Briand–Kellogg treaty—into the category of war crimes, because such a proposal was "too far from practical politics and constitutes therefore an unnecessary burden for the whole plan."[52] Others disagreed with Cohn. The London International Assembly, an unofficial body of scholars created under the auspices of the League of Nations Union by Viscount Robert Cecil and other academics, such as Hans Kelsen and Albert Levy, stressed the fact that aggression was considered an international crime and that therefore the authors of the war had to be punished.[53] Others, such as Sheldon Glueck or George A. Finch, agreed with Cohn and argued against trials for the aggressors under international law, contending that the effort would only confuse the much clearer issue of liability for classical war crimes committed during the war.[54] On the other hand, Glueck and to a lesser degree also Finch argued that not only crimes in contravention to the Hague and Geneva Conventions should be punished, but also crimes such as mass slaughter, the crimes against the Jews and generally speaking all violations of the principles of criminal law observed in civilized states.[55] This view was also supported by other jurists such as Manfred Lachs from the University of Cracow, Georg Lelewer, an exiled Austrian specialist on military law, Vaclav Benes, the nephew of the exiled president of Czechoslovakia, or Aaron Naumovitch Trainin, Professor of Criminal Law at the University of Moscow.[56] Further topics discussed amongst jurists were the problems of the jurisdiction for the punishment of war crimes (and possibly further war-related crimes), of superior orders, of the principle of *nullum crimen, nulla poena sine lege* or of the legitimacy of the aerial bombardment of civilian centres.[57]

There were of course different levels on which the debate took place. While government leaders were reluctant to take up the issue due to the fear of reprisals against their prisoners of war, some members of Parliament, especially in Great Britain, tried to bring it up in their respective chambers. Unofficial bodies such as the London International Assembly and the International Commission for Criminal Reconstruction and Development played an important role as well. The most important body, however, was the United Nations War Crimes Commission, which was finally created in 1943, almost a year after its creation had been announced.[58] Furthermore, leading journals especially in the fields of international law, criminal law and political science as well as some books published by important authors such as Hans Kelsen, Sheldon Glueck or Aaron Naumovitch Trainin played an important role, especially in order to press certain points upon which no decision had yet been reached.[59] There was an almost general agreement amongst all the authors that those responsible for war crimes had to be punished. Only very few authors were sceptical and criticized the idea of war crimes trials.[60]

Raphael Lemkin and the issue of war crimes and genocide, 1940–1945

Soon after Raphael Lemkin's arrival in the United States the country found itself involved in war as a consequence of the Japanese attack on Pearl Harbour. This changed Lemkin's situation dramatically, having been called by the US Army to teach classes on military government at Charlottesville, Virginia. Furthermore, the Board of Economic Warfare drafted him as a consultant. Lemkin never joined the international debate on the punishment of war crimes before 1945, probably because of his heavy workload, the fact that he had lost his scholarly network and his determination to publish the documentation he had been collecting since the beginning of World War II.[61] In 1944 his book *Axis Rule in Occupied Europe* was finally published and welcomed by most reviewers as a stunning indictment of the crimes committed by all Axis governments and military during the war.[62]

When the Division of International Law of the Carnegie Endowment of International Peace decided to publish Lemkin's book, it did so with the aim on the one hand to show the differences between the occupation policy of the Allies and that of the Axis powers, not least by quoting American occupation laws of the past. On the other hand, the Carnegie Endowment wanted to give the "liberators of Nazi-occupied Europe" an idea of possible modes and agencies of redress in order to repair the damage that had been done to persons and property. Only after such a reparation had been done could a peaceful world founded upon law and order be rebuilt.[63] Lemkin was convinced that many of his potential readers were inclined to believe that the Axis regimes could not possibly be as cruel and ruthless as they had been told so far. It was therefore important to show the readers that the occupation of large parts of Europe had been marked by grave outrages against humanity and international law as well as against human rights, morality and religion and that the occupants had not even refrained from using law to commit their crimes. The publication of a collection of occupation laws was essential, Lemkin believed, for a clear understanding of the Axis regimes.[64] To a large extent Lemkin's book was therefore a collection of those laws and decrees, which he had collected from the time he had arrived in Sweden. It was supplemented by a synthesis of the techniques of occupation and an analysis of the regime in each occupied country. Although Lemkin made it clear that he would also deal with the other Axis countries, his main focus was on Germany, since this country had been and was the leader and main organizer of what Lemkin called a system of occupation, to which the reader was introduced in the first part of Lemkin's book. Dealing with administration, police, law, property, finance and labour, Lemkin wanted to show his reader how the German authorities had organized their occupation of large parts in violation of international law and that, following the example set by Bethmann–Hollweg in 1914, they had used a unilaterally utilitarian conception of law—law is what is useful to the German nation—to give the impression of a legal behaviour.[65]

In the major part of the first section of his book Lemkin continued to work along the lines that had dominated the interwar debate in the Association Internationale de Droit Pénal. He not only discussed crimes committed as part of an occupation policy by the police or military authorities as most others authors did, but he also included aspects of property, finance and labour, which were not commonly discussed when dealing with the possible punishment of crimes committed during the war. At that point of his analysis, however, Lemkin introduced a new concept, which would influence not only the debate of the years to come on international law, but also on political and social science as well as on history.[66] Starting out by saying that "new conceptions require new terms,"[67] Lemkin introduced the term "genocide" and then went on to describe techniques of genocide in various fields. Of course Lemkin did not claim to introduce a new category of crime. His aim was rather to include a number of crimes that had so far be described by various terms into one category. He therefore referred to the work of several authors of the past such as James Wilford Garner's study on *International Law and the World War* or the report of the Responsibilities Commission of the Paris Peace Conference as well as his proposal of 1933,[68] but he refrained from mentioning any occurrence of genocide in the past apart from wars of extermination that for Lemkin had ended at the latest with the Thirty Years' War.[69] Lemkin's focus was clearly on the crimes he was documenting in the third part of his book and he recommended that the proposal he had made in 1933 should be taken up again and genocide be prohibited by an international treaty as well in time of war as in time of peace. Lemkin did not call for an international criminal court to punish genocide, but rather demanded an agency vested with specific powers—which Lemkin did not specify—to make sure that genocide and other crimes of occupation would be prevented in the future. National courts should, however, be competent to try offenders for genocide according to the legal principle of universal jurisdiction.[70] In his book Lemkin does not give any reasons for his introduction of the term genocide. At the beginning of his chapter on genocide he said that new conceptions require new terms, but later on made it clear that the concept was not really as new as he claimed at the beginning. Although there is no final proof, the authors of this article believe that it may be that Lemkin decided to introduce the concept of genocide not least because he was aware of the fact that it would be difficult to demand the prevention and punishment of such a crime, if it was just included amongst others under the heading of the intentional use of instruments capable of producing public danger that had been used in the debate within the Association Internationale de Droit Pénal and International Conferences for the Unification of Criminal Law.

The second part of Lemkin's *Axis Rule in Occupied Europe* contains studies of occupation of 17 countries or part of countries. In these chapters Lemkin gives an overview of the administration, the judiciary, criminal law, issues dealing with private property, public finance, labour and genocide legislation.[71] In his third part, which makes up more than half of the book, Lemkin then publishes documents relating to the laws of occupation, i.e. statutes, decrees and other legal documents, all listed by countries in which they were published.[72] The issue of the punishment of those responsible is almost not touched upon in Lemkin's book, because he believed that he would not be able to address the issue exhaustively. To Lemkin there was more to redress than just the punishment of those responsible for international crimes, as there were many political, economic, legal and moral considerations that would need to be addressed in this context. Hitler and the Nazis were not the only ones responsible for the gruesome crimes committed during the German and Axis Occupation of Europe. The German people voluntarily assisted Hitler in the scheme of world domination. Therefore, the United Nations would be faced with the tremendous task of destroying what Lemkin called an "amalgamation of master-race mythology and aggressive technology."[73] For Lemkin, whose plan for a post-war Germany went even further than the ideas of the Henry Morgenthau,[74] it was clear that the aggressive industrial potential of the German economy had to be reduced and transformed into a more peaceful economic pattern marked by agriculture combined with a new theory of master morality, international law and true peace.[75] Although Lemkin came up with the new concept of genocide, the main aim of his study was not conceptual, legal or historical. In its major parts it was a documentation of the legal background of the crimes committed by Axis government members and military forces during World War II. Although Lemkin was a lawyer by training he did not speak much about the legal consequences of the crimes committed by Axis leaders, officers and soldiers. Trials for war crimes or for genocide were not on Lemkin's agenda in *Axis Rule in Occupied Europe*. Neither was the book meant to be an analysis of genocide in its historical or legal context. Lemkin's main aim was to document the crimes that had been committed during World War II, not least in order to use them later on as the basis for his further work on international criminal law, which he assumed he would resume at the end of the war.

Nuremberg and the genocide convention

Towards the end of the war the international debate on the punishment of war crimes centred on the question as to whether the main German war criminals were to be punished by summary execution—a plan supported by Churchill and Morgenthau—or by way of a trial before an international criminal court of whatever sort—a plan, which had the support of the majority of academics as well as of the American Secretary of State for War, Henry Stimson.[76] Lemkin only joined the debate when the decision to hold war crimes trials had almost been taken. He argued that Hitler and his associates were just common criminals that had to be tried in allied military courts.[77]

Although the Allies had finally agreed on the principle of war crimes trials in April 1945, there was much work ahead in setting up such trials. In America Supreme Court Justice Robert H. Jackson was named head of the American delegation for a conference in London in August 1945, where the Allies finally agreed on a charter for an International Military Tribunal.[78] Lemkin, who had successfully influenced the American delegation's view on the concept of criminal organizations,[79] joined the American prosecution team for the war crimes trials in Nuremberg and became one of the legal advisors to US Chief Prosecutor Jackson. Lemkin continued to work hard and hoped to have the concept of genocide included into the indictment against the major war criminals, as the British delegation had allegedly opposed the concept in London, saying that it was not found in the Oxford Dictionary.[80] Lemkin succeeded this time,[81] but the court did not take up the concept in its verdict, which was a great disappointment for Lemkin.[82] His determination to get his concept inscribed in international law was, however, not broken. Already in spring 1946 he published an article in the *American Scholar*, in which he tried to explain why it was necessary to introduce the concept of genocide into international criminal law and to set up an international convention for the prevention and punishment of genocide.[83] Furthermore, he tried to renew his contacts with the Association Internationale de Droit Pénal and published two articles in a special number of the association's journal devoted to the future of international criminal law after World War II.[84] His aim now was to show the people concerned that genocide was a danger for peace and that it exerted "an immediate and direct detrimental effect upon countries other than those in which it is practiced."[85] In the consequence he worked very hard within the United Nations to have genocide accepted as an international crime and to set up an international convention on the prevention and punishment of genocide. On December 9, 1948, Lemkin finally reached his aim, when the UN General Assembly accepted the convention by a unanimous vote.[86]

Conclusions

When in 1945 the major German war criminals were put on trial at the International Military Tribunal, the charter of the tribunal as well as the indictment were concerned with three crimes: crimes against peace, war crimes and crimes against humanity. All three of these categories had been discussed in the interwar period and Raphael Lemkin had participated in this debate both as member of the Polish Commission for International Juridicial Cooperation and the Association Internationale de Droit Pénal. On the one hand, Lemkin joined the call of Vespasien Pella and his colleague Emil Stanislaw Rappaport to create instruments to punish aggressive war as well as the propaganda for aggressive war on an international level according to the legal principle of universal jurisdiction. On the other hand, both Rappaport and Lemkin were rather sceptic when the conferences for the unification of criminal law in Brussels and Paris tried to narrow the concept of the intentional use of instruments capable of producing public danger to acts of terrorism. Only Lemkin, however, presented an alternative proposal. After this proposal had been defeated neither Lemkin nor Rappaport participated in the efforts of the Association Internationale de Droit Pénal to set up conventions for the prevention of terrorism and the creation of an International Criminal Court. World War II separated the two men that had worked together for about a decade. While Rappaport remained in occupied Poland, Lemkin escaped to the United States. During the war it was Lemkin's aim to collect as much information as possible on the German system of occupation. On the one hand, Lemkin's aim was legal, as he believed that Hitler and his associates had to be punished as common criminals. His documentation was meant to support any indictment brought up in this context. Lemkin, however, also believed that the German crimes had to be documented for history, in order to prevent such crimes from happening again in the future and in order to work as an argument for the future codification of international criminal law. Lemkin's work was therefore the work of a lawyer and a philologist at the same time. It is in this context that Lemkin developed the concept of genocide. Whether this was done on purpose or by accident is not quite clear, but Lemkin had created a new and powerful catchword for jurists as well as for philologists. After the UN General Assembly had voted the Genocide Convention, Lemkin was found with tears in his eyes in the Assembly chamber, to a large extent probably because of his family that had been killed during the Holocaust.[87] Perhaps there was another reason: Lemkin seemed to have reached his aim and finally it was the concept of genocide that was taking the place of the concept of the intentional use of instruments capable of producing public danger formulated at the Warsaw Conference of 1927. Genocide now seemed to take the place as the most dangerous crime, a place that in the debate on international criminal law of the interwar period had first been occupied by the issues of war crimes and aggressive war and then by the concept of terrorism.

Notes and References

1 Daniel Marc Segesser, "The international debate on the punishment of war crimes during the Balkan Wars and the First World War," *2004 Annual Meeting Session Papers of the American Historical Association* (Ann Arbor: UMI, 2004).

2 For its report, see: Commission on the Responsibility of the Authors of the War and the Enforcement of Penalties, "Report presented to the Preliminary Peace Conference," *American Journal of International Law*, Vol 14, 1920, pp 95–154.

3 Gary Jonathan Bass, *Stay the Hand of Vengeance: The Politics of War Crimes Tribunals* (Princeton: Princeton University Press, 2000), pp 75–80, 83–88, 135–136; James F. Willis, *Prologue to Nuremberg: The Politics and Diplomacy of Punishing War Criminals of the First World War* (Westport, CT: Greenwood Press, 1982), pp 65–86, 177–181.

4 Johann Caspar Bluntschli, *Das moderne Völkerrecht der civilisirten Staaten*, 2nd edn (Nördlingen: Beck'sche Buchhandlung, 1872), pp 358–359.

5 Commission on the Responsibility, op cit, pp 114–115; United Nations War Crimes Commission (hereafter UNWCC), *History of the United Nations War Crimes Commission* (London: HMSO, 1948), pp 34–35. On the terminology, see: Gerry J. Simpson. "War crimes: a critical introduction," Timothy L. H. McCormack and Gerry J. Simpson, eds, *The Law of War Crimes: National and International Approaches* (The Hague: Kluwer Law International, 1997), pp 1–30; Howard S. Levie, "Violations of human rights in time of war as war crimes," Yoram Dinstein and Mala Tabory, eds, *War Crimes in International Law* (The Hague: Martinus Nijhoff, 1996), pp 123–127; M. Cherif Bassiouni, *Crimes Against Humanity in International Criminal Law*, 2nd revised edn (The Hague: Kluwer Law International, 1999), pp 60–82.

6 Segesser, op cit.

7 On the Leipzig trials, see: Gerd Hankel, *Die Leipziger Prozesse: Deutsche Kriegsverbrechen und ihre strafrechtliche Verfolgung nach dem Ersten Weltkrieg* (Hamburg: Hamburger Edition, 2003). On the trials in Constantinople, see: Taner Akçam, *Armenien und der Völkermord: Die Istanbuler Prozesse und die türkische Nationalbewegung* (Hamburg: Hamburger Edition, 1996).

8 Hans-Heinrich Jescheck, *Die Verantwortlichkeit der Staatsorgane nach Völkerstrafrecht: Eine Studie zu den Nürnberger Prozessen* (Bonn: Ludwig Röhrscheid Verlag, 1952), p 89. A closer analysis of the debate will be included into the forthcoming Habilitationsschrift of Daniel Marc Segesser on the international debate on the punishment of war crimes, 1872–1945.

9 On the Russian persecution of Jews during their retreat from advancing German forces, see: Peter Gatrell, *A Whole Empire Walking: Refugees in Russia during World War I* (Bloomington: Indiana University Press, 1999), pp 16–26; Mark Levene, "Frontiers of genocide: Jews in the Eastern war zones, 1914–1920 and 1941," in Panikos Panayi, ed., *Minorities in Wartime: National and Racial Groupings in Europe, North America, and Australia during the Two World Wars* (Oxford: Berg, 1993), pp 92–98; Ulrich Sieg, "Judentum," in Gerhard Hirschfeld, Gerd Krumeich and Irina Renz, eds, *Enzyklopädie Erster Weltkrieg* (Paderborn: Schöningh, 2003), p 599.

10 New York Public Library: Raphael Lemkin Papers 1947–1959, Series V: Writings—Autobiography, pp 17–18. See also Steven L. Jacobs. "Lemkin and the Armenian genocide," in Richard G. Hovannisian, ed., *Looking Backward, Moving Forward: Confronting the Armenian Genocide* (New Brunswick: Transaction, 2003), p 126, and Gatrell, op cit, pp 150–154.

11 William Korey: "Raphael Lemkin: 'the unofficial man'," *Midstream*, Vol 35, No 5, 1989, p 46.

12 Maurice Travers, *Le Droit Pénal International et sa Mise en Oeuvre en Temps de Paix et en Temps de Guerre*, 5 vols (Paris: Receuil Sirey, 1920–1922), Vol 1, pp 61–66 and Vol 4, pp 618–619.

13 See Document 4a in Benjamin B. Ferencz, *An International Criminal Court: A Step toward World Peace—A Documentary History and Analysis*, 2 vols (London: Oceana, 1980), Vol 1, pp 193–224; Jescheck, op cit, p 90; Heiko Ahlbrecht, *Geschichte der völkerrechtlichen Strafgerichtsbarkeit im 20. Jahrhundert* (Baden-Baden: Nomos-Verlagsgesellschaft, 1999), pp 46–47.

14 Ferencz, op cit, pp 202–210; Jescheck, op cit, pp 90–91.

15 Ahlbrecht, op cit, p 48; Ferencz, op cit, pp 239–243; Jescheck, op cit, p 91.

16 Hugh H. Bellot, "War crimes and war criminals," *Canadian Law Times*, Vol 36, 1916, pp 754–768, 876–886; ibid, "War crimes and war criminals," *Canadian Law Times*, Vol 37, 1917, pp 9–22; ibid, "War crimes: their prevention and punishment," *Transaction of the Grotius Society*, Vol 2, 1917, pp 31–55; ibid: "War crimes, their prevention and punishment," *Nineteenth Century and After*, Vol 80, 1916, pp 636–660.

17 Hugh H. Bellot, A Permanent International Criminal Court, International Law Association, *Report of the Thirty-First Conference (Buenos Aires 24th August–30th August 1922)* (London: Sweet&Maxwell, 1923), pp 63–80.

18 Bellot, op cit, pp 80–86.

19 Amongst the critics of Bellot were Graham Bower, Charles-Henry Butler, Ludwik Erlich, John Hinkley and John Fischer Williams, as well as James Leslie Brierly, who although present did not voice his criticism in Stockholm. International Law Association, *Report of the Thirty-Third Conference (Stockholm September 8th to 13th, 1924)* (London: Sweet&Maxwell, 1925), pp 93–110 and James Leslie Brierly, "Do we need an International Criminal Court?" *British Yearbook of International Law*, Vol 8, 1927, pp 81–88.

20 International Law Association, *Report of the Thirty-Fourth Conference (Vienna August 5th to 11th, 1926)* (London: Sweet&Maxwell, 1927), pp 106–225, 279–309; Hellmuth von Weber: *Internationale Strafgerichtsbarkeit* (Berlin: Ferd. Dümmlers Verlag, 1934), pp 11–14; Jescheck, op cit, pp 93–97.
21 Jescheck, op cit, pp 97, 113–114; Weber, op cit, p 14.
22 Ahlbrecht, op cit, pp 49–50; Jescheck, op cit, pp 112–113; Weber, op cit, p 47.
23 Jescheck, op cit, pp 74–75. See also: Quincy Wright, "The outlawry of war," *American Journal of International Law*, Vol 19, 1925, pp 76–103 and Vilho Harle, "The implementation of peace ideas: the case of outlawry of war," *History of European Ideas*, Vol 10, 1989, pp 677–688.
24 Ahlbrecht, op cit, p 50; Jescheck, op cit, p 113.
25 Jescheck, op cit, p 97; Association Internationale de Droit Pénal, "Projet d'une Association Internationale de Droit Pénal," *Revue Internationale de Droit Pénal* (hereafter *RIDP*), Vol 1, 1924, pp 1–2.
26 For an overview, see: Jescheck, op cit, pp 97–110 and Weber, op cit, pp 14–47. A more detailed analysis of the debate will be given in the forthcoming Habilitationsschrift of Daniel Marc Segesser on the international debate on the punishment of war crimes, 1872–1945.
27 Korey, op cit, p 46.
28 Georges Sliwowski, "Le Président Emile Stanislas Rappaport," *RIDP*, Vol 36, 1965, pp 13–19; Alozjy Zebrowska, "Rappaport Emil Stanislaw," in *Polski Slownik Biograficzny*, Vol 30 (Wroclaw: Zaklad Narodowy Imienia Ossolinskich Wydawnictwo Polskiej Akademii Nauk, 1987), pp 586–589.
29 Janusz Jamontt, Raphael Lemkin and Emil Stanislaw Rappaport, eds, *Kodeks Karny r. 1932*, 2 vols (Warzaw: Bibljoteka Prawnicza, 1932).
30 For Lemkin, see: www.preventgenocide.org/lemkin/bibliography.htm (November 11, 2004), for Rappaport, see: Sliwowski, op cit, pp 15–17.
31 It is not clear when Lemkin exactly joined the two organizations, but in 1930 he already occupied the position of secretary to the Polish Commission for Criminal Legislation. Simon Sasserath, ed., *Actes de la IIIe Conférence Internationale pour l' Unification du Droit Pénal (Bruxelles, 26–30 Juin 1930)* (Brussels: Office de Publicité, 1931), p 11.
32 There is only one article in which Lemkin himself discussed part of this problem, but there are no indications that he disagreed with Pella and Rappaport: Raphael Lemkin, "La Protection de la Paix par le Droit Pénal Interne," *RIDP*, Vol 35, 1938, pp 95–126.
33 Michel Potulicki, ed., *Actes de la Ière Conférence d' Unification du Droit Pénal (Varsovie, 1er–5 Novembre 1927)* (Paris: Librairie du Recueil Sirey, 1929), pp 1–7.
34 Potulicki, op cit, pp 38–41.
35 Potulicki, op cit, pp 59–67, 116–130.
36 Sasserath, op cit, pp 43–48, 114–117, 173–175, 194; Henri Donnedieu de Vabres, ed., *Actes de la IVe Conférence Internationale pour l' Unification du Droit Pénal (Paris, 27–30 Décembre 1931)* (Paris: Librairie du Recueil Sirey, 1933), pp 48–68, 133–152, 253–264.
37 Jean-André Roux, "Terrorisme," in Manuel López-Rey, ed., *Actes de la Vème Conférence Internationale pour l' Unification du Droit Pénal (Madrid 14–20 Octobre 1933)* (Paris: A. Pedone, 1935), pp 42–47.
38 Henri Donnedieu de Vabres, *Les Principes Modernes du Droit Pénal International* (Paris: Recueil Sirey, 1928), pp 135–166; Vespasien Pella, *La Criminalité Collective des États et le Droit Pénal de l' Avenir* (Bucarest: Imprimérie de l' État, 1925), pp 157–159; Emil Stanislaw Rappaport, *Le Problème de l' Unification Internationale du Droit Pénal* (Warzaw: Revue Pénitentiaire de Pologne, 1929), pp 19–21.
39 Raphael Lemkin, "Les Actes constituant un danger general (interétatique) considerés comme delits du Droit des Gens," in López-Rey, ed., op cit, pp 48–56. For an English translation, made by James T. Fussell, see: www.preventgenocide.org/lemkin/madrid-1933-english.htm (November 11, 2004). A short version of Lemkin's proposal was also published in German: Raphael Lemkin, "Akte der Barbarei und des Vandalismus als delicta juris gentium," *Internationales Anwaltsblatt*, Vol 6, 1933, pp 117–119.
40 Lemkin, op cit, p 56.
41 López-Rey, op cit, pp 241–242.
42 López-Rey, op cit, pp 16–20, 143, 243; Donnedieu de Vabres, op cit, p 145.
43 Jescheck, op cit, pp 117–120; UNWCC, op cit, p 440; Timothy L. H. McCormack, "From Sun Tzu to Sixth Committee: the evolution of an international criminal law regime," McCormack and Simpson, eds, op cit, p 54. On the *Association International de Droit Pénal*, see: Jean-André Roux, "Le Projet de Convention Internationale pour la Répression des Crimes présentant un Danger Public," *RIDP*, Vol 12, 1935, pp 99–130 and Quintiliano Saldaña, "Le Terrorisme," *RIDP*, Vol 13, 1936, pp 26–37.
44 Megalos Caloyanni, "Commission de Rédaction d' un Projet concernant les Infractions et leurs Sanctions," *RDIP*, Vol 12, 1935, pp 337–347.
45 Ferencz, op cit, pp 269–371; Jescheck, op cit, p 118.

46 Vespasien Pella, "Plan d'un Code Répressif Mondial," *RIDP*, Vol 12, 1935, pp 348–369; ibid, op cit, pp 240–257, 271–277; Ferencz, op cit, pp 373–398; Jescheck, op cit, pp 118–120.
47 Charles B. Ingwersen and Henrik Sachs, eds, *Actes de la VIème Conférence Internationale pour l'Unification du Droit Pénal (Copenhague 31 Août–3 Septembre 1935)* (Paris: A. Pedone, 1938), pp 147–209, 369–413.
48 Ferencz, op cit, pp 378, 387–388, 397–398.
49 On Rappaport, see: Sliwowski, op cit, pp 16–17 and Zebrowska, op cit, p 588; on Lemkin, see: Korey, op cit, pp 46–47.
50 Korey, op cit, p 46.
51 Jean-André Roux, "Editorial," *RIDP*, Vol 17, 1946, pp 1–2; Emil Stanislaw Rappaport, "Vingt Ans Après," *RIDP*, Vol 17, 1946, pp 3–5; Simon Sasserath, "Le Président Vespasien Pella," *RIDP*, Vol 23, 1952, pp 12–13; Dominique Gros, "Le Statut des Juifs et les Manuels en Usage dans les Facultés de Droit (1940–1944)," in Philippe Braud, ed., *La Violence Politique dans les Démocraties Européennes Occidentales* (Paris: Éditions L'Harmattan, 1993), pp 144–152.
52 Ernst Joseph Cohn, "The problem of war crimes to-day," *Transactions of the Grotius Society*, Vol 26, 1941, p 141. Cohn had presented his ideas to the *Grotius Society* on May 29, 1940.
53 UNWCC, op cit, pp 99–101; Hans Kelsen, *Peace through Law* (Chapel Hill: University of North Carolina Press, 1944), pp 71–75; Albert Levy, "The law and procedure of war crimes trials," *American Political Science Review*, Vol 37, 1943, pp 1067–1068.
54 Sheldon Glueck, *War Criminals: Their Prosecution and Punishment* (New York: Alfred A. Knopf, 1944), pp 37–38; George A. Finch, "Retribution for war crimes," *American Journal of International Law*, Vol 37, 1943, pp 81–88. See also William B. Simons, "The jurisdictional bases of the International Military Tribunal at Nuremberg," in George Ginsburgs and Vladimir N. Kudriavtsev, eds, *The Nuremberg Trial and International Law* (Dordrecht: Martinus Nijhoff, 1990), pp 45–50.
55 Glueck, op cit, pp 37–45, 56–62; Finch, op cit, pp 85–88.
56 Manfred Lachs, *War Crimes: An Attempt to Define the Issues* (London: Stevens & Sons, 1945), pp 100–101; Georg Lelewer "The definition of war crimes," *Central European Observer*, Vol 21, 1944, p 116; Vaclav Benes, "The question of the definition of war crimes," *Central European Observer*, Vol 20, 1943, p 282; Aaron Naumovitch Trainin, *Hitlerite Responsibility under Criminal Law* (London: Hutchinson, 1945), pp 37–42, 71–78.
57 Daniel Marc Segesser, "On the road to total retribution? The international debate on the punishment of war crimes, 1872–1945," in Roger Chickering, Stig Förster and Bernd Greiner, eds, *A World at Total War: Global Conflict and the Politics of Destruction, 1937–1945* (Cambridge: Cambridge University Press, 2005), pp 362–370; Arieh Kochavi, *Prelude to Nuremberg: Allied War Crimes Policy and the Question of Punishment* (Chapel Hill: University of North Carolina Press, 1998), pp 95–171; Bass, op cit, pp 147–203.
58 UNWCC, op cit, pp 87–118; Jescheck, op cit, pp 121–137; Kochavi, op cit, pp 27–62.
59 Segesser, op cit, pp 364–370, 372.
60 Jescheck, op cit, pp 137–140; Segesser, op cit, pp 367–368.
61 Korey, op cit, p 46.
62 Raphael Lemkin, *Axis Rule in Occupied Europe: Laws of Occupation—Analysis of Government—Proposals for Redress* (Washington, DC: Carnegie Endowment of International Peace, 1944), reviewed by Arthur Leon Horniker in *Military Affairs: Journal of the American Military Institute*, Vol 9, No 1, 1945, pp 69–73, by John Mervyn Jones in *British Yearbook of International Law*,Vol 22, 1945, pp 313–314, by Arthur K. Kuhn in *American Journal of International Law*, Vol 39, 1945, pp 360–362, by Vlastimil Kybal in *Annals of the American Academy of Political and Social Science*, Vol 239, 1945, pp 190–192, by Ramsay Moran in *Virginia Law Review*, Vol 31, 1945, pp 730–733, and Melchior Palyi in *American Journal of Sociology*, Vol 51, 1946, pp 496–497.
63 Foreword of George A. Finch to Lemkin, op cit, pp vii–viii.
64 Lemkin, op cit, p ix.
65 Lemkin, op cit, pp x–xi, 7–78.
66 See Myriam Gessler, "Die Singularität des Holocaust und die vergleichende Genozidforschung: Empirische und theoretische Untersuchung zu einem aktuellen Thema der Geschichtswissenschaft," unpublished Lizentiatsthesis, University of Berne, Berne, 2000, pp 20–22.
67 Lemkin, op cit, p 79.
68 James Wilford Garner, *International Law and the World War*, 2 vols (New York: Longmans, Green, 1920); Commission on the Responsibility, pp 95–154; Lemkin, op cit, pp 48–56.
69 Lemkin, op cit, p 79–82.
70 Ibid, pp 90–95.
71 Ibid, pp 99–264.
72 Ibid, pp 267–635.

73 Ibid, p xiv.
74 On Morgenthau's ideas for a post-war Germany, see: Bass, op cit, pp 157–169; Bernd Greiner, *Die Morgenthau-Legende: Zur Geschichte eines umstrittenen Plans* (Hamburg: Hamburger Edition, 1995), pp 169–184; Gerhard L. Weinberg, *A World at Arms: A Global History of World War II* (Cambridge: Cambridge University Press, 1994), pp 795–797.
75 Lemkin, op cit, pp xiii–xiv.
76 Kochavi, op cit, pp 201–217; Segesser, op cit, p 372.
77 Raphael Lemkin, "The legal case against Hitler," *The Nation*, Vol 160, No 8, 1945, pp 205–207, 268–270; ibid, "Genocide—a modern crime," *Free World*, Vol 9, No 4, 1945, pp 39–43. On the debate on war crimes trials in early 1945, see Kochavi, op cit, pp 201–222.
78 William B. Simons, "The jurisdictional bases of the International Military Tribunal at Nuremberg," in George Ginsburgs und Vladimir N. Kudriavtsev, eds, *The Nuremberg Trial and International Law* (Dordrecht: Martinus Nijhoff, 1990), pp 41–45; Bradley F. Smith, *The American Road to Nuremberg: The Documentary Record 1944–1945* (Stanford: Hoover Institution Press, 1982), pp 142, 212–220; Kochavi, op cit, pp 222–230.
79 Robert E. Conot, *Justice at Nuremberg* (London: Weidenfeld and Nicholson, 1983), pp 11–12.
80 Korey, op cit, p 47; Bernhard F. Hamilton, *A Note on Professor Lemkin's Work in London Culminating in the Nuremberg Indictment of October 18, 1945* at www.genocidewatch.org/LKF/18oct2000.htm (November 5, 2004).
81 Count 3 (A) of the Indictment. See: www.yale.edu/lawweb/avalon/imt/proc/count3.htm (November 5, 2004). In the German text the word Genocide was translated as "Massenmord," of which the equivalent in English would be "mass murder": *Der Prozess gegen die Hauptkriegsverbrecher vor dem internationalen Militärgerichtshof: 14. November 1945—1. Oktober 1946*, 42 vols (Nuremberg: International Military Tribunal, 1947–1949), Vol 1, p 47.
82 Korey, op cit, p 47; Jacobs, op cit, p 133.
83 Raphael Lemkin, "Genocide," *American Scholar*, Vol 15, No 2, 1946, pp 227–230.
84 Raphael Lemkin, "Genocide: a new international crime: punishment and prevention," *RIDP*, Vol 17, 1946, pp 360–370; ibid, "Le Genocide," *RIDP*, Vol 17, 1946, pp 371–386. The latter was a French translation of Lemkin's chapter on genocide from *Axis Rule in Occupied Europe*.
85 Lemkin, op cit, p 363.
86 Korey, op cit, pp 45, 47. On the genesis of the Genocide Convention, see: William Schabas, *Genocide in International Law* (Cambridge: Cambridge University Press, 2000), pp 51–81.
87 Korey, op cit, p 45.

What you see before your eyes: documenting Raphael Lemkin's life by exploring his archival Papers, 1900–1959

TANYA ELDER

> There's a serious risk that a commemoration of Raphael Lemkin's work will not become an act of remembering, but an act of forgetting, obliterating what was so singular about his achievement. (Michael Ignatieff[1])

"What? What? So What? What?" These words, along with "Why? Why, Why, Why?" are scribbled in the margins of notes of Raphael Lemkin's unfinished work, "Totally unofficial: the autobiography of Raphael Lemkin." More than once the refrain of "So What? What?" is written in pencil throughout Lemkin's papers,[2] seemingly used as a refrain that pushed him to continue a difficult, uphill battle with statesmen, lawyers, the general public, and most of all, himself, in order to define, inform, and abolish the act of genocide.

"So what?" This question seems to have bothered Lemkin enough to devote the greater part of his life, actively beginning in 1933 and progressing earnestly in 1941, in answering the question for civilization. So what if a populace is destroyed; how does that affect another people? So what if a culture is lost, and why should one care?

The general public, through no fault of Raphael Lemkin's, is oblivious of him. Mention the word "genocide," a term Lemkin created to express "the use or a user of deliberate, systematic measures such as killing, bodily or mental injury, unlivable conditions, prevention of births, calculated to bring about the extermination of a racial, political, or cultural group or to destroy the language, religion, or culture of a group," and the greater majority would not know that the word was born in 1943, nor that it was a hybrid of Greek and Latin.[3] The public may be able to tell you that acts of genocide had happened throughout history, but none would surmise that no specific word existed for this crime prior to the Jewish Holocaust or possibly for some, that such crimes actually occurred prior to World War II.

Historians specializing in Jewish studies with a focus on the Holocaust, or other topics of population murder and conflicts such as the Armenian genocide, may know of Lemkin, but rarely consult his archival papers.[4] A lawyer may know of his name through his writings on international law or currency exchange or possibly from the strong opposition by the American Bar Association to treaties such as the one that Lemkin produced out of the UN, the Convention for the Prevention and Punishment of Genocide. A psychologist, sociologist, or anthropologist who studies the cause and affect of mass murder may know of him in regards to those areas were his studies of the history of genocide and these disciplines might converge, but then again, probably not. Possibly a political scientist studying the efficacy of grassroots campaigns like the one Lemkin undertook to persuade over 58 countries to ratify an international treaty such as the Convention? Maybe a painter or rose cultivator might know of books he wrote on these subjects? There is no clue to these books in his archival documents, though he wrote on both subjects in his early years.[5] No full-length biography of meaning, besides that of a Holocaust revisionist, has yet been written about him.[6] However, without Lemkin, we would not be able to name, let alone comprehend, what Winston Churchill called "a crime without a name."[7]

In 1982 and 1999, Steven Schnur and Steven L. Jacobs, respectively, wrote articles chronicling newly unearthed or compiled collections of Lemkin archival documents, including correspondence, articles, manuscripts, notebooks, and photographs. These articles formed a basic catalog of how the documents were acquired or highlighted a "first look" at the materials within the collections. The purpose of this article is to further expose Raphael Lemkin through the lens of his archival collections, to see what Lemkin saw before his eyes and was determined to make others see as well. While many professions would benefit from knowing more about Lemkin's archival papers, it is of prime importance that those involved in Genocide Studies know about them, so as to act as visionaries to expand on his work. It is hoped that this study will provide a roadmap to his collections for that purpose.[8]

Raphael Lemkin was a man who devoted the greater part of his short life to answering the question, "So what?" As the "premier pioneering scholar of 'Genocide Studies'" and self-proclaimed "Founder of the Genocide Convention," Lemkin forcibly created a pathway through a dark tunnel of mankind's cruelty and came out at the opposite end to inform everyone of the path *not to follow*. If mankind actually paid attention to the signposts that Lemkin left behind, we might have averted tragedies like the recent genocidal nightmares of Cambodia, Bosnia, Rwanda, Darfur, and others.

Raphael Lemkin was born on June 24, 1900,[9] in the Bialystok region of Bezwondene, Poland, located in imperial Russia at his birth and eventually known as Volkovysk, Belarus. He grew up with a penchant for languages, history, and the law. He studied philology and philosophy and eventually became a lawyer, working for the Prosecutor's office in Warsaw from 1929 to 1934. While a prosecutor, he helped to codify the laws of the new Polish Republic, wrote on Jewish law, and in 1933, a paper based on his concept of "barbarity" and "vandalism" (mass slaughter and cultural destruction) was read at the Madrid League of Nations conference. The Nazi Party, representing Germany and in attendance at the meeting, ridiculed the work, and in 1934, Lemkin was forced to leave his position as a prosecutor by the pro-Hitler Polish government. From 1934 to 1939 he practised privately, taught family law at Tachkemoni College in Warsaw, and attended numerous conferences on international law to promote his concepts. By 1939, Lemkin acknowledged the impending doom that was about to hit Europe and decided it would be best to leave. His mother, a significant influence on his life, urged him to escape in order that he could continue his work regarding barbarity and vandalism. Contacts helped him to Sweden, where he lectured on international monetary exchange, and he eventually travelled eastward via the USSR to America, where he joined the faculty of Duke University Law School in 1941. When the US joined the war, Lemkin travelled to Washington as an advisor to the Foreign Economic Administration's Bureau of Economic Warfare, and later, as part of the War Department, he became an advisor on foreign affairs, which included advising US Chief Justice Robert Jackson at the Nuremberg Tribunals.

In 1943, Lemkin compiled numerous Nazi legal decrees that he had collected while in Sweden, and first proposed and defined the word *genocide* in a volume entitled *Axis Rule in Occupied Europe*. After the war, Lemkin stalked the halls of the newly formed United Nations in an effort to persuade the UN to adopt the Convention for the Prevention and Punishment of Genocide, which passed in 1948. From there, Lemkin fought vigorously in the defence of his Convention in the face of real and perceived threats to its existence. Lemkin grew increasingly obsessed with promoting his new word, and educating the public on its meaning. He wrote drafts of an autobiography and a definitive history of genocide through the ages, but ill health, exhaustion and destitution took its toll and he died of a heart attack at his publisher's office in August 1959. His personal papers were collected from his home after his death, but they and a few other collections remained orphans. Eventually the collections were donated to three separate archives, but they languished for another 40 years until a new interest in Lemkin's work emerged.[10]

By known donation dates, the "first" collection of 2.8 linear feet (seven boxes) are documents that reside at the Jacob Rader Marcus Center of the American Jewish Archives (AJA) located at Hebrew Union College in Cincinnati, Ohio. The papers contain materials spanning the years of 1942–1959. This portion of Lemkin's papers were donated in two parts: by a cousin, Dr Robert Lemkin, a dentist from Long Island, NY, in April 1965 and were added to by Rabbi David Saperstein of the Union of American Hebrew Congregations in November 1983.[11]

According to historian Jim Fussell, the documents that Robert Lemkin donated were originally from Raphael's apartment and packed up after his death in 1959 by Elias Lemkin, his brother who lived in Montreal along with his son, Saul, and Robert Lemkin. Lore has it that Raphael Lemkin's apartment was crammed from floor to ceiling with books and documents; but according to Saul, this was not the case. Saul noted that there was not much in the apartment and that a few valises of items were packed. Family photographs and personal items were taken to Montreal by Elias Lemkin while the documents of Raphael were taken by Robert Lemkin to Long Island. Saul Lemkin relayed to Fussell that the personal items in Montreal were subsequently destroyed in a fire about 10–15 years later.[12]

The second collection of 7.5 linear feet or 12 boxes, donated in 1975, was given to the American Jewish Historical Society (AJHS), then located in Waltham, MA. These documents primarily cover the years of 1944–1952 (a few are from 1941–1943). An article and NYPL exhibit program about Lemkin were later added. The records of the AJHS provide conflicting information regarding acquisition: accession records report that Harvey Ladin donated the records on October 1, 1975, while the collection's shelf card says that Isaiah Spector donated the records, with no date given. Mr Fussell provides some information regarding the mysterious dual donation. Mr Spector, a furrier, and his wife were friends of Lemkin's while he worked at Yale, and Lemkin often stayed at their Connecticut home. In 1951, Mr Lemkin left his position as a teacher of international law at Yale and the documents remained with the Spectors. Mr Ladin was the founder and first President of the Jewish Historical Society of New Haven, and the Spectors may have given Ladin the documents. It is not clear why the documents were transferred from Ladin to the AJHS. The documents moved to the AJHS at the Center for Jewish History in New York when the Society relocated its primary facilities from Massachusetts to New York in 2001.[13]

The third collection of papers consists of 2.5 linear feet (the five boxes are on microfilm) and spans the years of 1946–1959, though most of the documents are largely undated. Alexander Gabriel, a friend of Lemkin's, donated the papers to the New York Public Library (NYPL), Archives and Manuscripts Division. Gabriel was a journalist for the Transradio News Agency and covered the United Nations. An email from the NYPL relayed that Gabriel acquired these papers from two of the numerous typists Lemkin retained over the years, and that Gabriel had stored these documents in his UN office. No date was given as to when Gabriel acquired these papers. However, according to Schnur, Gabriel was present when Lemkin's apartment was cleared and that's how Gabriel acquired the documents. The two stories converge when Fussell reports that Gabriel attempted to donate the documents to Robert Lemkin as well as the Dag Hammerskold Library in New York. Mr Fussell reports that the documents were offered for sale to historian and friend of Lemkin, William Korey, but he refused to buy them. Gabriel ultimately donated the documents to the New York Public Library in 1982.[14]

Other collections contain materials relating to Raphael Lemkin, but no other significant collection is solely dedicated to his papers. Steven Jacobs at the University of Alabama has a complete set of photocopies or microfilm of the three collections, but they are not original documents.[15]

The collections can be divided into three periods of Lemkin's life: (1) "Establishing the groundwork to creating the word: 1900–1944," (2) "Toward the Genocide Convention, 1945–1948," and (3) "Defense, dissemination, research, and instruction, 1949–1959." Though separated by venue, the three collections share an extraordinary amount in common, from types of documents, to overlapping documents, to threads of information that begin in one collection and ventures on to another. The three collections primarily detail Lemkin's life after he escaped from Poland and there are no personal affects such as photographs, birth certificates or mementos prior to 1941, except for two publications, one from 1933 and another from 1941.[16] The remaining documents related to his life span the years of 1941–1959, the bulk of which cover 1947–1958.

In terms of the first phase of Lemkin's life, "Establishing the groundwork to creating the word, 1900–1944," because there is so little extant documentation such as correspondence or personal memorabilia, this portion of Lemkin's life is more difficult to document. There are no known photographs of his mother, Bella, or father, Joseph, or the Lemkin brothers, Raphael, Elias and Samuel as children or their homestead.[17] The greater portion of what we know about Lemkin from 1900 to 1944 (and in particular his life prior to leaving Europe in 1941) is relayed in the incomplete autobiography begun about 1951 and housed at the New York Public Library.

He recalls in his autobiography (a story which reached the level of lore in various articles written about him) that in 1913 at the age of 12, he first came across the concept of mass killing for religious reasons while reading Henryk Sienkiewicz' *Quo Vadis*, a look at the life of Roman emperors that included scenes of Christians being thrown to the lions.[18] However, there was more to it than this incident, including learning of the slaughter of the population in distant Armenia by Turkish forces and the pogroms and wars between Russia and Germany that occurred near his home, driving his family into the forest and eventually causing the death of Raphael's youngest brother, Samuel, of pneumonia and malnourishment.[19] Being Jewish in this part of the world was not easy, and certainly living between warring entities did not help matters. According to Lemkin, he was a sensitive loner of a child, easily influenced by world events.

The biggest influence of his life was his mother, a woman who home schooled her children and spoke several languages, was a painter, and studied philosophy. Lemkin's mother was highly educated and had an extensive collection of books, but was married to a farmer.[20] This dichotomy of an educated mother and farmer father was somewhat incongruous, and Lemkin did not refer to these early childhood circumstances in his autobiography.

In some ways, Lemkin created a framework of his early life with few witnesses, in which he provided a myth of himself upon which to stand as the founder of the Genocide Convention. In fact, because of this seeming self-creation, certain myths of his life were perpetuated, such as his claim in numerous venues that he personally presented his 1933 work defining "barbarity" and "vandalism" at the Madrid League of Nations conference and the notion that he was injured while hiding in the forests of Poland during the resistance.[21] Even the year of Lemkin's birth is a matter of dispute, as some records and articles claim that he was born in 1901 as opposed to 1900. Jim Fussell and documentation at the AJHS dispute this claim and points to Lemkin's year of birth as 1900.[22]

In some ways, Lemkin opened himself up to the later attack of James J. Martin, a Holocaust denier from the Institute of Historical Review, who deconstructed Lemkin's life in his publication *The Man Who Invented "Genocide": The*

Public Career and Consequence of Raphael Lemkin.[23] This book, what Samantha Powers calls a "nominal biography," attempted to spawn suspicion over the details of Lemkin's life, steadfastly using quotation marks around the word "genocide" (as in "so-called genocide") and slyly wondering how Lemkin managed to make his way from Poland to Sweden to America. Martin has no endnotes in his "biography," but one doubts that he had access to Lemkin's autobiography, as Lemkin does explain to some extent how all of this actually happened. Lemkin may have opened the door to some revisionism or confusion, but Martin busted the door down, insinuating that Lemkin was an agent provocateur used by the Allied Powers to advance the "theory" of genocide, Holocaust, and Germany's implication in the murder of millions of Jews as well as Slavs, gypsies, homosexuals, Soviet POWs, political dissidents, and the mentally ill during World War II. Martin also overlooked the fact that Lemkin's idea of genocide reached far beyond the Jewish people. Jews may have suffered the largest and most systematic of abuses, but genocide, to Lemkin, reached back to antiquity through to the modern era and affected scores of people.

But, as Lemkin would say, "So what?" that he may have embellished the early part of his life in order to create a greater public interest over the issues of genocide. Did this embellishment (or non-correcting of the journalistic record) ultimately mean that what Lemkin wanted to convey to the world did not merit relevance? Or did Lemkin realize that even after the horror of the Holocaust, that unless one brings an excitement to bear on why a man such as Lemkin would devote his life to preventing genocide that people would not care unless there was an exciting tale to tell? In fact, some publishers later rejected Lemkin's autobiography and his proposed *History of Genocide* for these very reasons. For instance, his autobiography proposal to Simon and Schuster brought the following reply: "My reservations about the manuscript (apart from the subject) are two: it never really tells the reader the mechanics of getting a passionate conviction transformed into international law except in terms of personal magnetism, midnight walks around Lake Leman, etc. I'm afraid that after the English was cleaned up some of the charm of the story might be lost" or "This is a very important story, but it is told so simply that the reader occasionally forgets how great the issue is . . . If Lemkin does not win the Nobel prize, I think the audience for such a book would be very small. I know several relatively well-read college students who not only have never heard of Lemkin but could not define genocide."[24]

What a vicious cycle this created: few knew who Lemkin was because Lemkin had not won the Nobel Prize, and neither the autobiography nor the *History of Genocide* were exciting enough to be published and yet genocide itself was not exciting enough to warrant publication because it had not been heard of. If ever Lemkin's refrain of "So What?" applied, it certainly applied to this twisted form of publishing logic.

So, taking into account that the documentation on Lemkin's early life is lacking, and that what we mostly know is from Lemkin himself, are there other collections or materials that shed light on his early years? The answer is yes, but the documentation is still slim and some of it conjectural.

In regards to his young life in Poland, there is little information to be found. From his autobiography, we do know that at least four things seems to have affected Lemkin the most: (1) his mother, (2) the Armenian genocide, (3) *Quo Vadis*, and (4) the pogroms and wars that ravaged his home and led to his brother's death. His autobiography contains anecdotes of farm life and his recollections concerning some events, but consists mostly of childhood memories. In regards to his family home, records may exist recalling the town where his family hailed from, but probably little else. One might look at specialized collections such as the YIVO Institute for Jewish Research at the Center for Jewish History or the Center's Genealogy department for data on the area or relatives of the family. Living family members may provide some more information, though these members may be too far removed to provide concise information. It will be interesting to see how new biographies dealing with Lemkin's life hone in on his childhood.

As Lemkin approached his college years, he decided to study philology. According to his autobiography, he developed a passion for language from his mother, and learned several languages including Yiddish, Polish, French, English, German, Spanish and Russian by the time he was a teenager. In 1919 he entered the University of John Casimir in Lwow, Poland, to study philology, went on to the University of Heidelberg in Germany to study philosophy, then back to John Casimir for law school. Records pertaining to his grades or career at these schools may still be extant. Several papers from his law school days are known, mostly written on the criminal codes of Soviet Russia and fascist Italy, fiscal law and the organization of the legal record as regards to the Jewish people.[25]

After law school, Lemkin took a position as a public prosecutor from 1929 until 1934. If there are records concerning the prosecutor's office of Warsaw during these years, and if they survived the war, and later, Communist occupation, one might find out how Lemkin's law career prevailed in the form of briefs or correspondence. This period is particularly interesting as Lemkin began to formulate his opinions on genocide, spurred on, he noted, by the massacre of Christians in Iraq in 1933 and the rise of the Hitler regime. He presented several papers beginning in 1931 and culminating in 1934 that spoke about terrorism, "barbarity" and "vandalism" (along with others concerning various penal codes).

The document that prompted his early departure from the prosecutor's office (besides a growing anti-Semitism in the Polish government), was *Acts Constituting a General (Transnational) Danger Considered as Offences Against the Law of Nations*. The pamphlet proposed an international conference and convention to enact laws that barred acts against mankind, in the forms of barbarity, what Lemkin described as acts of extermination directed against the ethnic, religious or social collectivities whatever the motive (political, religious, etc.) or vandalism, "An attack targeting a collectivity [in] the form of systematic and organized destruction of the art and cultural heritage in which the unique genius and achievement of a collectivity are revealed in fields of science, arts and literature." An English version of this document can be read online, and the AJHS contains a copy of the original French version. Documentation regarding the 1933 conference can be found at the League of Nations archive located in Geneva, Switzerland.[26]

After his dismissal from the Prosecutor's office, Lemkin went into private practice and continued writing in earnest regarding penal codes, international crime, and barbarity and vandalism. Jim Fussell reports that Lemkin also contributed a sporadic advice column on the law that appeared in the Warsaw Yiddish newspaper, *Haynt* (*Today*), copies of which are located at the YIVO archives. In 1938 Lemkin met Duke University law professor Malcolm McDermott. Lemkin and McDermott collaborated on the English translation of *The Polish Penal Code of 1932* and *The Law of Minor Offenses*, two volumes that Lemkin had worked on earlier in his career. Ultimately, this contact would help Lemkin escape from Europe and obtain a position at Duke. Lemkin explains in his autobiography how this connection as well as connections with his French publisher, his father's brother who lived in America, and other contacts made over his career, helped him to Sweden, through Russia and Japan to the United States in 1941.[27]

In Sweden between 1940 and 1941, Lemkin lectured at Stockholm University and delivered a paper (in Swedish, which he learned during his time there) on "Exchange control and clearing," a continuation of his work, *The Regulation of International Payments*, written in 1939 (proofed by Lemkin while waiting in Lithuania for clearance to Sweden). Records or correspondence at Stockholm University, or correspondence with his publisher, the legal publishing house of A. Pedone (Paris), may be available.

During his stay in Sweden he persuaded government officials to provide him with Nazi law directives, and he accumulated a thick set of documents, which would later form the basis of *Axis Rule in Occupied Europe* as well as "Recording on military government in Europe." The latter translation was compiled by Lemkin during his tenure at Duke, and was then transferred to the School of Military Government when Lemkin went to work for the Bureau of Economic Warfare. A printed collection of these documents is located at the AJA.[28]

Cleared for immigration by the US in 1941, Lemkin began a long trek across the Soviet Union to Japan, eventually travelling from Yokohama to Vancouver, Canada, to Washington State. His autobiography consistently offers glimpses of Lemkin's personal inclination to deeply appreciate beautiful places and objects, and shows a touch of his humour as well. Arriving in Kyoto, he could have travelled to Tokyo with acquaintances he had met on the crossing, but ever the loner, Lemkin decided to visit Yokohama instead. He was captivated with the architecture he saw there and walked into a kimono shop. Lemkin said,

> One robe took me prisoner. I looked at it for a long while, finally deciding I could not buy it because of its cost. I left the shop, then re-entered and spent more time looking at the robe. I left again, with a heavy heart, still thinking about "my" kimono. Finally, capitulating to its beauty and craftsmanship, I entered the shop for a third time and bought it—or rather, the robe bought me. My capture by the vivid Japanese colors was a symbol to me of my temporary surrender to this foreign culture, a surrender everyone who travels will understand.

There is no indication as to the fate of this treasured possession, but Lemkin's keen sense of other countries and peoples helped in his work. As he developed his later campaigns, he always saw the issues from that particular culture's side—whether he had personally visited the country or not. In this case, a handwritten note appears at the top of the chapter, "Impact & Japanese mentality and policy." The chapter opened with a graphic account of the hostilities in Japan between the Japanese people, European Catholics and Japanese converts to Christianity during the seventeenth century.[29]

Lemkin arrived in Durham, North Carolina, in April 1941. Within days, he was delivering lectures on the state of Europe, and he continued translating the Nazi decrees he brought with him and added to the collection with visits to the Library of Congress. Some of this material was used in a paper delivered to the American Bar Association on "Totalitarian control over foreign economies."[30] Lemkin's autobiography offers an account of his time at Duke, but no documents were found in the collection directly relating to his tenure at the university, and the Duke Archives does not contain material relating to Lemkin except for a biographical file.

He received a note from his parents in June 1941, very short, very cryptic: "We are well. We hope you are happy. We are thinking of you."[31] It was the last time that Lemkin heard from them. Though he established contact with his relatives in Chicago, New York, Connecticut and Canada, he did not cling to them for familial comfort. In fact, all three collections contain letters from family members asking why he would not write back to them. This problem of not writing to family did not stop with relatives. Lemkin was also notorious when it came to friends (and debtors). The collections contain many instances of family and friends begging Lemkin to write back to them or at least let them know how he was faring in terms of his health.

For the remainder of his time at Duke, Lemkin taught classes, gave lectures, formulated his plans, and established contacts with government officials. After the US entered the war, Lemkin decided that his services would best be used in Washington. Through contacts and his work on the economic impact of war and monetary exchange, Lemkin was able to secure a position with the Board of Economic Warfare, and in the summer of 1942, moved to DC. Limited information on his time at the Board is available. At one point, Lemkin enquired as to any pension that he may be entitled to, and the War Department wrote back that as a consultant, he was not entitled to one. A search of the US National Archives and Records Administration or Army Archives may turn up documents and lectures.

In Washington he began in earnest on *Axis Rule*, his compilation of accumulated Laws of Occupation, adding to it an analysis of occupation, and wrote a 92-page general analysis of "German techniques of occupation." Lemkin penned nine specific chapters on Nazi occupation: the "Administration," "Police," "Law," "Courts," "Property," "Finance," "Labour," "Treatment of Jews," and ultimately, the ninth chapter, on "Genocide." Lemkin had finally been able to culminate the first part of his life . . . the birth of the word. Unfortunately, no notes, drafts, or documentation besides the Axis laws he brought with him from Sweden have been found in his archival papers. However, Lemkin does explore his thinking behind the creation of the word in a draft of *History of Genocide*, including the significance of new words, how they are made, the meaning of genocide, and words as moral judgments.[32]

On January 21, 1945, a full-page review of *Axis Rule in Occupied Europe* appeared on the front page of the *New York Times Book Review*. Lemkin had finally created a name for a crime that previously had none. Now began the fight to have the world acknowledge the name and the concepts behind the word.

The second phase of his life, "Toward the Genocide Convention, 1945–1948," proves to be much easier to document from his archival papers and therefore will be divided up differently than chronologically driven "Birth of the word, 1900–1944." Each major event of Lemkin's life during 1945–1948 can be divided into separate segments; each segment corresponds with papers spread over three collections.

The major events of Lemkin's life during these three hectic and stressful years were the Nuremberg Trials, the Lake Success Resolution, passage of the Genocide Convention (Geneva and Paris), lobbying (including the US Committee for a Genocide Convention), and the start of both the ratification of the Genocide Convention and the *History of Genocide*. (The last three events actively continued over to the next phase of Lemkin's life, but for purposes of this article, ratification and *History of Genocide* will be discussed in phase three of Lemkin's life, "Defense, dissemination, research, and instruction, 1950–1959.")

Lemkin left his consultant position (paid at $25 per day) at the Board of Economic Warfare in 1944, and became an advisor on foreign affairs for the War Department. He had just published a somewhat successful (if not profitable) book, began developing the groundwork for his next book, the *History of Genocide*, and wrote several articles on genocide. In 1945, he left DC for Germany and the Nuremberg Trials.

Nuremberg Tribunals and Hitler

Lemkin's papers do not hold a large resource of material regarding the Nuremberg Tribunals. The AJHS collection primarily has documents from this time period (1945–1946), but contains few documents on the Trials. There are only two distinct instances of material regarding the Trials at the AJHS: (1) a paper by a student that compared and contrasted the "Nuremberg Trial and the Genocide Convention" and (2) a folder of law notes by Lemkin on the relation of the Convention and the Trials. Barely any correspondence is included on the subject, and the same phenomenon occurs in the NYPL papers, with only two instances of materials relating to the Nuremberg Principles in regards to the Draft Code of Offences Against the Peace and Security of Mankind.[33]

The AJA collection has more materials on this subject, including a long deposition of witnesses, a fragment of a trial transcript and voluminous research notes from "Biffy" to Lemkin. Biffy was a researcher for Lemkin in Europe in 1949. Lemkin asked her to visit the French-Jewish historian, Leon Poliakov.

She sent Lemkin two unnamed (and lost) articles by Poliakov on the rescue or attempted rescue of Jews through intermediaries, researched information on the Final Solution, and Poliakov recommended the book *Hitler's Professors* by Max Weinreich. Poliakov recommended that Case 8 of the Nuremberg Trials on the idea of Germanism, of building the race and promulgating it, would be applicable to Lemkin's work and his ideas on the construction of race. Poliakov also recommended Felix Kersten's book describing his occupation as Himmler's doctor, as well as *La Fin de Hitler* by Trevor Roper, and the anthology of documents *Le Pitre* of Rousset. Biffy also pointed out that Poliakov had two boxes of photographs which included images of "piles of corpses, shoes, glasses, clothing, etc., of victims—shrunken skulls and paintings on human skin and of a jar of soap made from human beings."[34]

This folder contains a rather long synopsis of Biffy's findings as she poured through the Nuremberg Trial records looking for testimony attributing persons to the murder of Jews and others and accounts of death methods and experiments conducted. These reports are filed under the titles of "Psychology of genocidist"; "Slave labor"; "Cultural genocide"; "Youth movement"; "Techniques"; and "Nazi principles" (racism, pangermanism, war, lebensraum, and totalitarianism as incorporated into the National Socialist program). Included is a 57-page paper, "The Nazi case," on the conditions and reasoning leading to genocide (premeditation), science and machinery (organization), techniques, Jews as an example, psychology of victims, genocidists, of people (German), after effects, and conclusion—an eyewitness account.

A small treasure trove of Lemkin-related material regarding the Nuremberg Trials is housed at the Columbia University Law School Archives. The collection contains documents from the years of 1938–1947, though it is mostly material not directly produced by Lemkin and is in English, German, and Polish. The documents, used as background for his work as a trial advisor, contain a few boxes of articles, transcripts, affidavits, case files, German and Polish government directives, some handwritten notes by Lemkin and Chapter 9: "Genocide," of *Axis Rule in Occupied Europe* (1944). In general, this collection and a portion of the AJA collection are the only ones that hold material regarding Lemkin's work at the Nuremberg Trials. The University of Connecticut holds one document from the Thomas Dodd Papers regarding comments produced by Lemkin on the "Significance of the concept of genocide in the trial of war criminals."[35]

Lemkin's travels to Germany for the Trials began on a bittersweet note. Lemkin found that his brother, Elias, along with his wife and two sons, had survived the war. Elias and his family had been expatriated to a factory town near the Urals by the Russians and were separated from the larger part of their family, including their mother and father. There is some discrepancy concerning the number of Lemkin's relatives who perished (ranging from 40 to 70), but most accounts state that between 47 and 49 members of the Lemkin family perished. There is a limited amount of correspondence from his brother from the date of the reunion, all in Yiddish and mostly pleas asking for help in leaving Europe (which they did in 1948), help finding employment, and asking why Raphael did not write to them.[36]

Finally, Steven Jacobs points out that included in Lemkin's papers is an unpublished manuscript entitled "Nazi genocide," containing 267 pages of various proceedings and law reports of the Trial and war criminals, excerpts on the "Nazi conspiracy" and the "Nazi war against the Jews," and "The black book." Another document, entitled the *Hitler Case*, gives an outline for a book documenting Hitler's influence on science and philosophy, geopolitical aims, the techniques of the crime, the internationalization of genocide, and ends with an analysis of the war's aftermath. "The *Hitler Case* and the Nazi genocide" provides a compilation of evidence against the Nazi regime's extermination of the Jews and other peoples. Both documents use the Nazi's own words against them and may have been informed by Biffy's study and Lemkin's collection of Axis directives and certainly, Nuremberg Trial testimony. Steven L. Jacobs edited "Nazi genocide" in 1992.[37]

Lake Success Resolution/Genocide Convention (Geneva and Paris)

After the Nuremberg Trials, Lemkin quickly attended two European conferences, one in Cambridge and the other in Paris, both of which failed to adopt resolutions on genocide. In September 1946, he fell ill and spent time in a military hospital. He heard a radio broadcast concerning the first session of the UN General Assembly. Still sick, he left the hospital and travelled to Lake Success, New York, where the first session was taking place.

The Lake Success Resolution of 1946 paved the way for the Genocide Convention of 1948, but not much in the way of documentation on the Resolution is included in his papers. There are some draft documents or notes of what could be the 1946 Resolution, but they are mostly fragments of type- and handwritten notes, and none are clearly delineated as 1946. The earliest document is dated November 12, 1946, and is a Sixth Committee US Delegation Resolution relating to the codification of the Principles of the International Law by the Charter of the Nuremberg Tribunal. A draft entitled "Discussion on genocide in the legal committee," dated November 22, 1946, 11:00 A.M., with two copies of the Resolution of November 12, 1946, and a draft Press Release round out the materials found on this subject.[38]

The collection that has the most documentation regarding the Genocide Convention itself is that of the AJHS. This includes official United Nations printings of both the Geneva and Paris sessions including: Delegate Statements; Economic and Social Council Committee Proceedings; General Assembly Proceedings and Resolutions; Non-Governmental Agencies Petitions and Communications; Press Releases; Sixth Committee, General Assembly Proceedings and Reports (*Journal of United Nations*, including one from 1946), and the most comprehensive document of all, the *Sixth Committee*, *Official Records of the 3rd Session of the General Assembly*, Part 1, Summary Record of Meeting, spanning the dates of September 21–December 10, 1948. The Convention for the Prevention and Punishment of Genocide was adopted on December 9, 1948.[39]

Lemkin wrote or dictated voluminous drafts of materials regarding the Convention, including notes for articles, draft texts, resolutions, and memoranda, and his autobiography. A few notes are in shorthand and presumably were written by one of several typists or secretaries. Certainly there are many items that are not in Lemkin's hand, and as a hard and fast rule, one should be careful in assuming that all of the handwriting is his. Notes scribbled on the back of correspondence are the best indication of his writing style. Compare these notes to the handwritten notes, and one can begin to acquire an eye for which handwriting belongs to him. Most of these notes are in English, but some are occasionally in Polish or French.[40]

The AJHS devotes a section to the various writings found about the Convention, including early versions of the Convention text, statements and memoranda by Lemkin and government officials, essays, articles and clippings by or about Lemkin, interviews and radio broadcast transcripts. The AJA also has a section that follows a similar pattern of scripts of radio programs, resolutions and memoranda. The NYPL papers have a much smaller proportion of items of this nature, with more memoranda than resolution drafts, including writings on the explanation and evolution of the Convention, and the implementation on the next steps of the Convention.[41]

Each collection has statements from organizations or individuals urging the passage or ratification of the Genocide Convention. Types of speeches and memoranda include those before the Sixth Committee discussing changes to the Convention (Sardar Bahadur Kahn, Member of the Pakistan Delegation to the UN General Assembly in Paris, October 12, 1948: "In my view, Mr. Chairman, genocide should be condemned no matter by what manner of means it may encompass…"); statements urging ratification before various Senates including the US Senate (Jacob Blaustein's "The eyes of the world are watching…": plea to the Senate for the ratification of the Convention, January 23, 1950: "Even in our century, on every occasion genocide has been committed, other countries have done nothing more than send notes of protest."); and memorandums outlining the objections of countries such as China or the Soviet Union ("Memoranda to the reservations of the U.S.S.R., Byelorrusia, and the Ukraine concerning Article 9 of the Genocide Convention" of February 1950: "… the Russian reservation goes too far … and its final result is to prevent any case to be brought before the court …").[42]

The correspondence from this period is quite impressive and ranges over the three collections. As a lobbyer, Lemkin was brilliant. When it came to genocide or the Genocide Convention, he was quick to write long and complicated passages in letters on the law as he saw it in regards to genocide. He could easily jot down a note to a statesmen, journalist or mere acquaintance asking for help in persuading a President or Prime Minster to lend an ear to ratification, or request a synopsis of how ratification of the Convention was going in their country. Lemkin would also ask advice on addressing dignitaries or enquire about a country's government, history or customs. For example, on January 17, 1950, Djalel Abdoh wrote to Lemkin with the correct form of address for the Shah of Iran and other government officials at Lemkin's request.[43] It was these types of special touches that won many people over to his cause.

At times some letters would be mere copies with interchangeable addresses, as are letters located at the NYPL, written to 26 individual countries. The correspondence—spanning the years of the resolution and ratification—was carefully targeted to its audience and focused on countries that had not yet ratified the Convention, were about to ratify the Convention, or whose governments had ratified and Lemkin requested their help in speaking with their neighbours. Some folders contain letters in response to queries from Lemkin and include references to the inner working of governments. However, other items appear within these folders, such as a 15-page letter (in Spanish) concerning Gerard Viau of the Dominican Republic, who had been executed in Haiti sometime after 1948, during an era of political unrest between the two countries. This letter may have been sent to Lemkin as an example of the political climate of the Dominican Republic at the time. Nevertheless, as an illustration of an effective grassroots lobbying effort, Lemkin was a master at communicating with delegates and officials, though there were many times he pushed them away with his insistence and persistence.[44]

Lobbying and the US Committee for a Genocide Convention

Lobbying consisted of a three-tier attack: correspondence, petitions, and the US Committee for a UN Genocide Convention, a non-governmental organization (NGO)-related committee formally organized in 1948 for the purpose of ratifying the Convention, with its primary goal being to act as a public face for Lemkin, his theories and strategies.[45]

The US Committee for a UN Genocide Convention was born out of the National Council of Christians and Jews, an NGO that Lemkin had considerable contact with, as with other NGOs. However, the Council, which coordinated with the Committee for an International Convention, was an "indispensable handmaiden to Lemkin's efforts." Attorney James Rosenberg, Council co-Chairman Henry Noble MacCracken, and Willard Johnson, Council secretary, headed this Committee. Their mission was to publicize the definition of genocide, petition and urge the Economic and Social Council of the UN to vote favourably on the Convention and to generally support the Convention through other organizations. In turn, the Committee recruited prominent persons for the cause. Prior to the US Committee, Lemkin worked directly with authors Pearl Buck, Gabriel Mistral, and Aldous Huxley, among others.[46]

The AJHS holds a considerable amount of the correspondence that came out of this committee. In addition, this collection holds letters from Mistral and Buck, along with a draft manifesto by Buck. There are minutes of meetings, a PR kit and member lists. The University of Minnesota Social Welfare History Archives, which holds the archives of the National Council of Christians and Jews, houses additional information and correspondence, though only a few specific folders are named "Genocide Convention." Some letters regarding the Committee are spread throughout the AJA and the AJHS correspondence, and one folder at the NYPL is labelled "U.S. Committee for a United Nations Genocide Convention, 1948–1952." Correspondence with other organizations that Lemkin communicated with can be found throughout the correspondence files of all three collections.[47]

Through the efforts of the US Committee, Lemkin was able to rally a worldwide network of people connected to the National Council in the form of NGOs, which Lemkin and the Committee used to generate petitions representing millions of people. Though this petition material is very monotonous, the strength of this effort is noticeable. For instance, a compiled petition submitted to the UN in September 1948 listed by country each supporting agency and numbers of members in that agency. This petition was compiled from other petitions located within the collection, including those with brief endorsements and form petitions, with a member signing on behalf of an organization. Ultimately, the final compiled petition represented "approximately one-tenth of the world's population" or "166 organizations from twenty-eight countries of over 200 million persons." With such grassroots backing, along with the persistence and annoyance of Lemkin (and despite the objections of or demands to change the language of the Convention text from Great Britain, the Soviet Union, and China) there was little chance that the Convention would fail. The UN Convention for the Prevention and Punishment of Genocide was unanimously passed on December 9, 1948. The United States, the country that Lemkin pinned many hopes on, was the first to sign the maiden treaty of the United Nations. Lemkin had looked past the statesmen, and went straight to the people. It would be the work of statesmen that would ultimately disappoint him.[48]

The third and final phase of Lemkin's life, "Defense, dissemination, research, and instruction, 1949–1959," began on a high note—he had achieved a major goal and fulfilled his task from 1933—but still, there was, in Lemkin's mind, a long way to go. And he was right. The last ten years of Lemkin's life found him in a continuous battle of defending what Michael Ignatieff calls the moral imagination and singularity of his achievement—his ability to name—prior to anyone else, the horror that befell not only the Jewish people, but to people and collectivities who came before and who would come after them. Lemkin attempted to single-handedly rescue humanity from the horror that he termed genocide. Such a grandiose task could easily destroy a person; such determination could readily turn one into a "dreamer" or a "fanatic"—as diplomats called Raphael Lemkin—depending on how they viewed him and his work.[49]

Defence of his vision took a two-part form: achieving ratification by Senates and Parliaments in record time and fending off attacks, in the guise of incorrect application or criticism from UN delegate countries, rival bills, or fringe groups. Dissemination propelled him to speak on the issue of genocide to anyone and everyone who would listen, forcibly, if needed. Research drove him to pour over case after case of genocide-related abuse, preparing a definitive work on method and atrocity. Instruction led him to write about his life as an example to others, to educate the public, and teach new and seasoned lawyers about genocide and how to stop it, if not with the conscience, then by the law.

Defence

After the passing of the Convention in December 1948, Lemkin, still in Paris, became viciously ill. While doctors could not pinpoint the exact cause of Lemkin's illness (more than likely high blood pressure mixed with exhaustion), he delivered his famous line when asked what had stricken him. His reply: "Genociditis, exhaustion from work on the Genocide Convention." After three weeks, he returned to New York by ship. He walked along the ship's deck, and watched the waves that "seemed to be angry without reason. I did not dare to make comparisons in order to avoid what would remind me of the past . . . Instinctively, I was defending myself against something which, as I thought, almost destroyed me in Paris. I was girding myself for the struggle ahead."[50]

If Lemkin were suffering from genociditis, the symptoms were an "unflagging determination," "ceaseless striving," a broken heart, the weight of the world, and a hidden, seething anger that was driving him, not necessarily without reason, but certainly to the edge.[51] Once back in New Haven, he barely rested as he began to push countries to ratify the Convention as soon as possible. In order for the treaty to go into effect, ratification by at least 20 UN signatory nations were due no later than December 31, 1949. Lemkin wanted more than 20 countries to sign as soon as possible, especially his adopted country of the United States.

In New York, from January to March 2, 1949, the US Committee for a Genocide Convention did not meet. During these months, Lemkin was intermittently ill, missing appointments, but still corresponding. US Representative Emanuel Cellar, a Convention supporter, wrote requesting clarification on several points of the Convention for an article he was penning for the *American Bar Association Law Journal*.[52] Cellar asked a series of nine questions, which he himself answered in the letter. Several of these questions would prove to be stumbling blocks to US ratification, including the questions of whether a charge of genocide could be brought against a signatory country in the case of "a mob for a lynching, say, in Mississippi?" and if so would the US agree to extradite the citizens involved for trial in another country? Cellar also asked whether individuals, groups and associations in the US could bring charges against the US (or groups and individuals in the US) in a foreign country's court. Cellar admitted, "The answer is yes. That is quite serious. That may involve yielding of some sovereignty."

The US Committee had members of its Legal Advisory Committee familiarize itself with constitutional and legislative questions about the Genocide Convention and the International Covenant on Human Rights, noting in particular the response of Frank Holman, President of the American Bar Association (ABA), saying that he did not favour approval of any human rights legislation that infringed on the workings of the US Bill of Rights. Since a bill of rights was a document between a people and their government, the UN, under human rights legislation, would have to interfere in the workings of Member States in order to determine when international rules had been violated, then to take action to correct and punish.[53]

Correspondence relating to the ABA can be found in all three collections, but is concentrated in the AJA collection, since that collection spans a greater period of time (until 1959). The AJHS collection also contains correspondence regarding the ABA, but as the correspondence only goes to 1951, this collection must be used in correlation with the other two collections. The AJHS also holds ABA debate transcripts and addresses from 1949 on the subject of the Convention. The NYPL collection has the most limited amount of correspondence. Law-related articles from the ABA and other organizations can also be found in all three collections, with the concentrated items in the AJA and the AJHS collections. The law-related articles take the form of pro and con articles from lawyers, printed publications from various organizations, and comments. One unique item from the AJA collection is a US Committee for a Genocide Convention pamphlet urging the ratification of the treaty.[54]

Several student papers are located in the AJHS collection that focus on international treaty law and US state statutes that contain provisions "similar to genocide." One paper, from Sterling Fellow Stephen Gorove (who went on to pioneer law in regards to human activity in space), writes on "'Mental harm' in the genocide convention and its relation to similar concepts in American jurisprudence."[55]

Correspondence in relation to the ratification of countries outside of the US is concentrated in the NYPL collection, though it mostly consists of form letters. (These are the same correspondence files described earlier in *Lake Success Resolution/Genocide Convention (Geneva and Paris).*) All three collections contain statements, press releases, and speeches on ratification, with the most concentrated of these in the AJA. The AJA holds a "Statement by Raphael Lemkin on final ratification of the Genocide Convention" in which he credited the ultimate ratification of the Convention to members of the press, especially the UN correspondents who "did the most remarkable job in explaining the complicated issue to the world." Lemkin believed that this was the first instance in which newspapermen played an important part in producing international law.[56]

Another attack strategy on the Convention came in the form of Soviet Union and Chinese attempts to strip the Convention of wording, to use the Convention against the US (see *We Charge Genocide*), and the attempts by the Chinese to manipulate the wording of the Convention in translation from English to Chinese. The NYPL has a folder of documentation outlining the history of the destruction of Chinese religious groups, including Catholics, Muslims, and Buddhists, and China's attempt to revise the Convention text so that the destruction of a family of two or three would be termed genocide. A letter from Carsun Chang (Zhang Junmai) in reference to the Chinese-language revisions can be found at the AJA; the NYPL has a detailed UN guide to the English text and Chinese translations. The NYPL also holds a document that is aimed at France's attempt to "destroy" the Genocide Convention to "avoid responsibility for genocide in Algeria" (circa 1957).[57]

Human rights legislation

Prior to and during the American Bar Association's adamant stance against the Convention, Lemkin had to deal with human rights treaties: the Universal

Declaration on Human Rights and the Code of Offenses Against the Peace and Security of Mankind. Lemkin perceived these treaties as threats or attempts to undermine the strength of the Convention, even though Lemkin acknowledged that the Convention had some holes as written. Lemkin simply stated in one memo that "The Genocide Convention became wrapped up in a spider web of misunderstanding, political intrigue, and believe it not, communist subversion."[58]

The perceived attacks on the Genocide Convention, from the drafting of human rights legislation (beginning in 1948) and the criticism from individuals, lawyers, and law associations in the United States, were fierce at the start of 1949. Some who knew Lemkin were perplexed at his vehemence against the language of human rights-related UN bills. In actuality, Lemkin was perplexed that a set of declarations with no legal enforcement could actually trump the legal precedent of the Genocide Convention. Whereas one declared that "no persons should be deprived of his life" and should not "be subjected to torture or to cruel, inhuman or degrading treatment or punishment," the Convention actually outlawed the taking of human life en masse and made the crime punishable and technically enforceable.[59] The collections contain numerous memos drawn up in defence of the Convention against these two human rights documents. Of special note in the AJA collection is the correspondence of 1951, which is concentrated mostly on the defeat of the Human Rights Convention.

We charge genocide

The question of Blacks in America was a tricky subject for the Genocide Convention. On one hand, the subject was used as a wedge by the Soviet Union against the United States in relation to human rights violations. On the other hand, the issue was an example of a "fringe group" misapplying the Convention. Could the US be charged with genocide due to its treatment of Blacks in America, say, in regards to, lynching? Cellar answered this question in his letter to Lemkin of February 26, 1949. "The lynchers do not seek to destroy a racial group—the negroes. Usually, only a small segment of negroes is involved. The Whites seek to intimidate the Blacks. Reference is not to isolated cases like lynching but to the collective action aimed at destroying a whole group . . ." A student paper located at the AJA, "The Genocide Convention and race relations," discusses the matter and argues that even though "whites may desire to eliminate the Negro [in America], there is no intent to do so." The intent of the White, argued Richard D. Gillam, was to force the Negro to remain in his place through scare tactics, not to systematically destroy the race, which was extremely intertwined with the White populace.[60]

It was on the nature of scare tactics and discrimination that Oakley C. Johnson (teacher, author, social activist, and member of the Communist Party of America)[61] wrote to Lemkin in response to a *New York Times* Op-ed ("Nature of genocide," June 14, 1953). Johnson stated that for the most part, Lemkin's Op-ed was convincing except in the discussion of "fright" and "discrimination." On the topic of fright and genocide, Johnson stated that it was not the case of

White Americans frightening one Black American, but a case of terrorizing a whole race of people who were coloured. Johnson argued that Lemkin's suggestion, "Genocide is a *rare* crime of *great* magnitude," seemed to imply that unless all persons of a race were destroyed, then one could argue that the "Nazis did not commit genocide after all, since there are several million Jews still living!" Lemkin argued in the Op-ed that Blacks had conditions of increasing prosperity and progress in the US, to which Johnson primarily said, well, so had the Jews in Europe; could not genocide be applied to the Negroes in America? On discrimination, Johnson asked if discrimination against all the "individuals in a well-defined racial group" led to resistance, and if that resistance is put down by "laws, police, and courts" that is "consciously calculated to enforce 'white supremacy'" leading to anguish in the racial group, "isn't there a potential element of genocide in it?" Johnson was not confusing discrimination with genocide, as Lemkin contended in the Op-ed, but that discrimination is a factor in genocide.

Lemkin's answer to the query was not found in the collection, but a document entitled "Background paper: United States statement on the Civil Rights Congress publication 'We Charge Genocide'" can be found at the AJA. The paper claims that the "We Charge Genocide" group was a Communist front whose angle was leveraging the Convention against the US and away from the Soviet Union. Johnson was a contributor to "We Charge Genocide." Nonetheless, the points that Johnson brought up were relevant and needed to be asked in regards to Blacks in America and other places, such as South Africa. However, as Lemkin noted in 1953, "Genocide implies destruction, death, annihilation, while discrimination is a regrettable denial of certain opportunities of life. To be unequal is not the same as to be dead."[62] It can be said, however, that the issue of racism did undermine the authority of the United States in the world when it came to issues of racial equality.

Dissemination

Lemkin sought to disseminate information on genocide in two ways: by highlighting contemporary genocides of his time (notwithstanding the Holocaust, and along with the Armenian genocide), and through publicity in the form of articles, radio addresses, interviews, and tours. In the first instance, highlighting any current atrocity would, he hoped, connect the public to the reality of genocide, and in the second instance, people had to be educated about genocide as no one would really talk about genocide unless they were forced to. After the Holocaust, it was difficult for the world in general, and Americans in particular, to speak about what happened in Germany as the Allied Powers' alliances crumbled.

Contemporary events in Algeria, Korea, Greece, China, Hungary, Czechoslovakia, Bulgaria, India, Pakistan, Chechnya and the Baltic States are featured in one way or another in the collections. Lemkin teamed up with Lithuanian groups, among others, to highlight modern-day oppression and cases of genocide. At the AJA, statements linking genocide with the ground situation in some of the above-mentioned countries can be found, while both the AJA and the AJHS have pamphlets regarding a 1951 exhibit Lemkin was an advisor on, "Communism Exterminates Nations: Exhibit of Genocide in Lithuania." More pamphlets and journals including several copies of the *Lithuanian Bulletin* are found at the AJHS. Two documents from the Free Algeria Front of the National Liberation Delegation from 1957 are of note: a statement by Jean Paul Sartre, "Make peace before it is too late" and "Genocide in Algeria," a presentation of the case of genocide against France to the 11th Session of the UN General Assembly. The NYPL files mentioned earlier in regards to lobbying correspondence also contain instances of contemporary genocide cases and other hot issues, including a 1949, seven-page confidential memo draft translation on the "Present political situation existing in Latin America in general and in particular reference to communism in the Latin American policy of the United States."[63] Various instances of correspondence regarding contemporary genocide can be found throughout the collections, as well as in the research notes for the *History of Genocide*.

Much of the push for ratification can be found in the articles by and about Lemkin during this time. He had become something of a minor star, and he took the limelight in stride, with the purpose of promoting ratification and the Convention. The publications of the three collections hold rich documentation from magazines, newspapers, and radio broadcast transcripts of and by Lemkin.[64] A screenplay and a radio play were written about him. The radio play, broadcast on NBC on May 1, 1949, dramatized Lemkin's life from youngster to coiner of the word to powerhouse behind the passing of the Convention. It ended with a sweeping call from Judge Joseph Sherbow of the Supreme Court Bench of Baltimore, Maryland, announcing that the fight was not yet over, and that 20 nations were required to make the Convention an international law.[65]

In regards to audiovisual material relating to Lemkin, there is only one that is known to exist, a statement by Lemkin on the Genocide Convention dated December 23, 1947.[66] There may, however, be other recordings of Lemkin that have yet to be unearthed. He appeared on various news programs around the world, and some of the recordings mentioned in the collection can possibly be tracked down by an intrepid researcher, particularly if a program was distributed through a major broadcasting company in the United States or abroad.

Research—History of Genocide

Lemkin's masterpiece, what should have been the crowning achievement of his life's work, was *The History of Genocide*. Unfortunately, due to the nature and subject of the work, publishing houses would not fund its publication. In addition, Lemkin had failed to win the recognition of the Nobel Peace Prize, an event that would have continued to hold him in the spotlight. Four years of intense publicity, from 1948 to 1952, ended as the US would not ratify the Convention, and the Korean War created an isolationist period in American history.

How many volumes this work was to be completed in varies. One letter, written on February 13, 1951, from the Littauer Foundation, said the study was to be in two volumes, though others cite three volumes, and still others, four. Generally, one volume was intended as a general volume on genocide, while two–three additional volumes were to focus on genocide in ancient, Middle Age, and modern, time periods.[67] More than likely, the book expanded as time went on and Lemkin accumulated a wealth of material.

All three collections have extensive research summations of genocide-related incidents through history. On the whole, hired researchers or student assistants wrote the summations. Lemkin, however, seemed to work backwards; he wanted researchers to find evidence of atrocities in some cases, and then theories would be applied later. One researcher complained: "ordinarily on undertaking a work of this kind, one would have a theory on why people commit genocide and in the light of that theory the fact would be interpreted. So far, I am groping in the dark ... I do not have an overall idea which would guide me to interpret certain happenings ..." On the whole, correspondence between Lemkin and the researchers was amiable, but there was at least one instance of a researcher complaining of non-payment for his services and threatening to publish materials researched for Lemkin on his own in lieu of payment. In other cases, long-term friendships arose, including one with Miriam Milleren, who would be helpful to Lemkin for the remainder of his life.[68] Correspondence regarding the research begins in 1947.

The earliest parts of the research are numerous index cards and essays found at the AJHS. These cards, as well as the essays, are too numerous to catalog here. In general, excerpts of books, pamphlets, or journals were recorded on the cards that gave evidence of genocide-related abuses, along with their bibliographic sources. The essays also had excerpts from research works, but took more of a narrative form. There are 21 sets of index cards and over the three collections, 55 essays on genocide incidents. The NYPL has the actual manuscripts written by Lemkin, including outlines and descriptions of the project (the AJHS has early correspondence about the project), an introduction to Part 1, and chapters on "Genocide in sociology, psychology, anthropology, and economics," along with the "Impact on the culture," "Genocide as socially approved behavior," "Psychological scars" and "International law." Bibliographic references abound throughout these essays, and a long list of books Lemkin held overdue from the Yale Library shows a wide range of sources that Lemkin used for his work. The references are an excellent bibliographic resource on pre-mid-twentieth century sources.[69]

Another source of materials for *History of Genocide* are journals and pamphlets found within the collection (used for historical purposes as well as contemporary issues) and the most intriguing of these are on the Armenian genocide. The AJHS collection has several rare documents (*La Suppression des Arméniens* by René Pinion, 1916, *Mémoires d'une Déportée arménienne* by Madam P. Captanian, 1919, and *Rapport du Comité Américain de New-York sure les Atrocités commises en Arménie*, 1915) on the subject, as well as Blue Books from the Armenian Youth Federation of America, and "What do the Armenians want?" by James G. Mandalian from 1946. This last pamphlet states that the recent war had given publicity to certain events (i.e. the Holocaust), but that the "Armenian case is an old case and a forgotten case which is being revived." It goes on to illustrate the history of Armenians, their grievances, and how Armenians contributed in World War II. A July 7, 1946 "Program of the voice of Armenia" bulletin honouring the Armenian struggle rounds out this excellent collection of pamphlets. A charge sheet, evidence, and testimony against Misshak Torlakian (sp), accused of assassinating Behbouth (sp) han Djevanshire, in Constantinople, circa 1921 is located at the AJHS. The trial testimony seems to be part of a military tribunal and Djevanshire may have been a member of the Azerbaijan government, killed by Torlakian, an "Ottoman," or Turkish subject. The microfilm contains part testimony and part handwritten documents, possibly by Lemkin commenting on the case.[70]

Reading through this material is an exercise in pain and horror, as instance after instance of cruelty and punishment are catalogued through the sources. It is too bad that publishers did not see fit to publish the work, but it is not difficult, when reading through the material, to understand why they would be reluctant to do so in the 1950s. Ultimately, the cataloguing of cruelty is somewhat too difficult to bear.

Instruction

Lemkin sought out opportunities to teach young people (as well as his law students) about genocide and the Genocide Convention. In 1954, he was asked to be a guest lecturer on the New York Times Youth Forums, with the topic of "Can the Genocide Pact stop barbarism?" The forum was a question–answer session, with Lemkin creating a series of questions for the young adults to answer. The ten sets of questions focused on the history of the Convention, the definition of the words "Convention" and "Pact," and questions on who ratified the Pact and how many countries had signed on. Other questions asked what issues blocked the US from ratifying; did discrimination count as an act of genocide; and how is domestic legislation against genocide developed? These questions were rather intense for a teenage audience, but excellent in teaching on the Convention.[71]

When Lemkin gave a law school course on genocide, he always engaged his students in discussion by keeping them within the scope of the problem and then "almost casually [dropping] a thought which they would grab vividly like a ball in a basketball game." He said that they understood and approved of the humanitarian aspects of the Convention, but could not see the implications of genocide in "terms of cultural losses." Lemkin noted that their minds grasped the procedural aspects of the crime and not the substantive aspects. Lemkin also stressed the interdisciplinary concepts of psychology, sociology, anthropology and economics when he taught on genocide.[72]

Totally unofficial

Another form of instruction was to be the publication of his autobiography. Though the autobiography cannot be termed "instructional" in the classic sense of the word (in reality, the *History of Genocide* was much more of an "instructional" document), "Totally unofficial: the autobiography of Raphael Lemkin" was to introduce the world to the creator of the term genocide and in turn, bring a wider audience to bear on the issue of genocide, to expose the author and the issue. And its publication would have brought some form of relief for Lemkin, hopefully in the form of funds to sustain his life.

The NYPL collection has all of the materials regarding "Totally unofficial," including multiple drafts of chapters and handwritten drafts of those chapters. Lemkin revised the outline a number of times, but primarily it consisted of about 12 chapters at around 450 pages, from childhood to an illness that Lemkin suffered in 1951. Publishers wrote that the language was too simple, the story did not have much dynamic action, and the grammar needed shoring up, but when it comes to reading the actual pages at the NYPL, one wonders what the publishers were thinking. Yes, the childhood details were too long and Lemkin didn't explain (or didn't remember) the things that really mattered, like how his educated mother and farmer father met and fell in love. He didn't really go deeply into what drove him on toward the Convention, but then again, maybe he didn't know, or it was too much of a psychological wound to delve deeply into. Whatever the case, Lemkin's autobiographical pages are actually interesting to read and, with the proper editor, would have made a good read. It's too bad that he didn't live long enough to complete the work, or didn't win the Nobel Peace Prize so that he could finally relax a bit, and possibly have a little garden with some roses in it.

Conclusion

Oh heart don't stop beating
in a fleeing to end it all
I wish to see my roses
bloom in my garden again
Stop this cutting pain
Delay eternity's call
(written on the back of a note, March 15, 1957[73])

Lemkin's personal life

To say the least, Raphael Lemkin's life was bitter and seldom sweet. He won a few major awards, including the Cuban Grand Cross Carlos Manuel de Cespedes, but the award that would bring him and his concepts the most recognition, the Nobel Peace Prize, eluded him. There is no indication on why the Nobel organization did not award him the Prize. The reasons may rest in several complicated realms; genocide itself was waning in the public eye and few people wanted to talk about the horror of WWII; anti-Semitism may have played a part; Lemkin's reputation of "dreamer" or "fanatic" may have caused the Nobel Committee to shun him. Awards were reserved (not given) in the years of 1955–1956, the primary years that Lemkin was nominated. Whatever the reason, Lemkin's personal life, though filled with friends (and more than a few enemies), was lonely and desolate and his life's work was only superficially recognized by the world during his lifetime.

Women fell in love with him, but time and again he shunned them, even so much so that intermediaries had to warn him of their wrath. Miriam Milleren, wrote Lemkin in 1948: "For a long time now she had been writing in this vein. Every letter to me since she [Trudy] went abroad has contained some nasty phrase the like of which I showed you the day Masaryk died . . . As a result of all this, she was telling all who were acquainted with you of the unscrupulous character of Dr. Lemkin."[74] Family members begged him to write them back, and complained that they had not heard from him and were worried about his health.

As a younger man, Lemkin cultivated roses and painted. As an older man with no time on his hands, these hobbies were put aside. The only indication of his penchant for art can be found in a few pen and ink drawings located at the AJHS.[75]

William Cohen said, "He was very warm to those close to him." Looking through his more personal letters and autobiography shows his humour and his gratitude to those who remained close with him but they also portray a very driven and dedicated man, who pushed those same people away. Why he did this may rest in the psychological traumas he experienced in his life and his sense of responsibility, literally, to the world. He went hungry day after day, and worked a feverish schedule. Creditors hounded him, attempting to get blood out of a stone. Rejection letters for his books flowed onward from 1956. He was sick again and again, and had limited time for rests or vacations or love. He thought about genocide day and night. Raphael Lemkin's entire life and the concept of genocide are incredibly and irrevocably intertwined. He literally died of genociditis, exhaustion from working on genocide.

A final word: Lemkin's lost papers?

On March 7, 1950, Lemkin, who had moved from Washington, DC to New Haven, received a letter from the Merchants Transfer and Storage Company. They informed him that the storage unit holding many of his possessions, transferred there by Milleren from a former apartment while Lemkin was in Europe more than a year prior, would be closed due to a non-payment of $39.40 and the possessions auctioned at their next sale.[76]

According to an undated *Washington Post* article, one Joseph J. Blondell, who had attended the auction at C. G. Sloan and Co., recognized Lemkin's name from the news and bought the papers for a $12 bid, with the intent of returning them to Dr Lemkin. The article said that the papers consisted of documents relating to "the Nazis' heinous plans for annihilating Jews." The *Post* put Blondell in contact with an appreciative Lemkin, who promised to repay the fee that Blondell paid for the papers and move the documents. There is no record of Lemkin retrieving the papers.[77]

On July 8, 1957, Milleren wrote to Lemkin saying that she had gone to "inspect your papers . . . And as I looked over the collection and repacked some in new cartons, I couldn't help wondering if these boxes might not contain things you have forgotten you have that could be of value to your work. It's nine years since you last saw these papers. You probably haven't the vaguest memory of what is here." Miriam complained that over a year prior Lemkin had said he would make arrangements to move the papers, but he had not written nor spoken with her since then. It is not known whether the documents were eventually given back to Lemkin before his death or whether they were lost or destroyed. If the papers did relate to "the Nazis' heinous plans," then these documents might have related to Lemkin's work on the Nuremberg Trials and possibly *Axis Rule in Occupied Europe*. Maybe the kimono that so captivated Lemkin in 1941 might have been included within the boxes or valises as well.[78]

In response to the *Post* in 1950, Lemkin said of the papers, "They are of great sentimental value to me. They're not worth much money now, I guess, just documents, you know. But perhaps, who knows, after I am dead, someday they may be worth something."

Now that Lemkin has passed away and his papers are "worth something," he would probably still say, "So what? So now what?"

Acknowledgements

Bob Sink, Chief Archivist, Center for Jewish History; Lyn Slome, Head Archivist, American Jewish Historical Society at the Center for Jewish History; Kevin Profitt, Head Archivist, Jacob Rader Marcus Center of the American Jewish Archives; Jim Fussell; Sherry and George Haley; Stanislav Pejša, Greg Naranjo and Bridget Conley at the United States Holocaust Memorial Museum; Professor Steven Jacobs; Christopher M. Laico, Archivist, Arthur W. Diamond Law Library, Columbia University Law School; and David Klaassen, Archivist, Social Welfare History Archives, University of Minnesota.

Collection key

The following is a list of archival repositories included in this collection, along with their identifying acronym:

AJA—MC-60	Raphael Lemkin Papers, Jacob Marcus Rader Center of the American Jewish Archives, Cincinnati, OH
AJHS—P-154	Raphael Lemkin Collection, American Jewish Historical Society at the Center for Jewish History, New York, NY
COL—AWD-CLS	Raphael Lemkin (Collection)—Nuremberg Tribunal Materials, Arthur W. Diamond Law Library, Columbia University, New York, NY

DODD—MSS1994006587	Thomas Dodd Papers, Personal Notes and Comments, Thomas J. Dodd Research Center, Archives and Special Collections, University of Connecticut, Storrs, CT
JM	Jewish Museum, New York, NY
LEAGUE	League of Nations Archives, Geneva Switzerland
NYPL	Raphael Lemkin Papers, Manuscripts and Archives Division, New York Public Library, New York, NY
SOCIAL	National Council of Christians and Jews, Social Welfare History Archives, University of Minnesota, Minneapolis, MN
UN—PF 12, Track 3	Prof. Lemkin—Statement on Genocide, United Nations Archives, Sound Recordings, New York, NY (located at JM)
USHMM	United States Holocaust Memorial Museum, Washington, DC
YIVO	YIVO Institute for Jewish Research at the Center for Jewish History, New York, NY

Notes and References

1 Michael Ignatieff, lecture on Raphael Lemkin's "Moral imagination," United States Holocaust Memorial Museum, December 13, 2000, http://www.ushmm.org/conscience/events/ignatieff/ignatieff.php.

2 Charles Howard Allen, Jr to Lemkin, October 18, 1950, verso, handwritten notes by Lemkin, Raphael Lemkin Papers, Box 1, Folder 1, MC-60, Jacob Marcus Rader Center of the American Jewish Archives (AJA), Cincinnati, OH. Allen had forwarded to Lemkin a newly published pamphlet entitled "International crime and the U.S. Constitution," and wrote that the document contained an "exhaustive legal discussion to date contending that the United States does *not have the power to ratify* the United Nations [Genocide] Convention." Lemkin may have been bothered by this statement, as he hoped his new homeland would ratify the Convention as an example to others. He scribbled, "So what now? Now? Now? Now? Now? Now? SO WHAT? What? What? What?" and a series of three "What's" are struck out. Biographical Sketch, pp 4–5 (one of several drafts), Raphael Lemkin Papers, Reel 2, Box 1, Folder 33, New York Public Library (NYPL), New York. Lemkin had a particularly difficult time writing his autobiography, as it (1) dredged up old memories, (2) was a matter of life and death as to its publication, in terms of what funds and recognition it could bring for himself and for the cause of promoting the new concept of genocide, and (3) he was constantly ill and penniless. His publisher pushed for more emotion, while he struggled with the English vernacular and pondered what it meant to him having read Henryk Sienkiewicz' *Quo Vadis* as a young man, the book that started him on a tortured path of mass killing. The book's title is written several times, along with "Why? Why," "So what?" "So [not] what?" along with "Australia," "caracter assasination [sic]," "Delegate," "Russian delegate" and "I never gave one exclusive interview." Notes—Unsorted, Reel 5, Box 4, Folder 2, NYPL. A series of handwritten notes appear, written again in conjunction with his autobiography, "What? What? What? What? So What? What?"

3 Raphael Lemkin, *Axis Rule in Occupied Europe: Laws of Occupation—Analysis of Government—Proposals for Redress* (Washington, DC: Carnegie Endowment for International Peace, 1944). Jim Fussell relates that the word is used in the preface dated November 15, 1943, earlier than the publication date of 1944. Elizabeth Nowinsky, a friend of Lemkin's, wrote that she saw the word defined as such in the 1950 addenda of *Webster's New International Dictionary*, 2nd edn, p 6, and goes on to say that "This work is also entered and defined in *Webster's New Collegiate Dictionary* although the definition is, of necessity, a shorter one." Elizabeth Nowinsky to Lemkin, February 15, 1950, Reel 1, Box 1, Folder 1, NYPL. The word itself is a combination of the Greek *genos* or race, and Latin *cide*. Lemkin also considered the word ethnocide, consisting of the Greek word "ethnos"—nation—and "cide." More information on the publishing of *Axis Laws* might possibly be found at: the Carnegie Corporation of New York Records, Rare Book and Manuscript

Library, Columbia University Libraries, Series III: Grants, Grant Files 1911–1988, Carnegie Endowment for International Peace, http://www.columbia.edu/cu/libraries/indiv/rare/guides/Carnegie/index.html.

4 Steven L. Jacobs, "The papers of Raphael Lemkin: a first look," *Journal of Genocide Research*, Vol 1, No 1, 1999, pp 105–114. Jacobs mentions that the number of people who have consulted the Lemkin papers over four decades "have been very, very few" (p 112). Records had been rarely accessed at the American Jewish Historical Society, while Kevin Profitt, archivist at the American Jewish Archives, notes that in the last two years, interest in the Lemkin papers has increased. The publication of Samantha Powers' book *"A Problem from Hell": America and the Age of Genocide* (New York: HarperColllins, 2002) may have increased awareness, while both the AJHS and the AJA have recently put their collection finding aids online. AJHS: http://www.cjh.org/academic/findingaids/AJHS/nhprc/Lemkin02-03.html; AJA: http://www.huc.edu/aja/Lemkin.htm. At the AJHS as of December 2004, the Lemkin collection has been accessed by researchers at least 11 times since the finding aid went online in March 2003. No records of access prior to March are available. The majority of the inquiries have been from researchers located outside of the United States. The NYPL has yet to put an accessible finding aid for their collection on the Internet.

5 Powers, p 79.

6 Currently, several biographies are in the works, including one by Jim Fussell, of the Prevent Genocide organization. Mr Fussell is an expert on Lemkin, as well as historical and contemporary instances of genocide. His website, www.preventgenocide.org, is a repository of articles and laws on genocide, and contains several Lemkin publications, including Chapter 9 on genocide in the hard-to-find book Lemkin wrote, *Axis Rule in Occupied Europe*. The only full-length book regarding Lemkin was published by a Holocaust revisionist, Dr James Joseph Martin, *The Man Who Invented Genocide: The Public Career and Consequence of Raphael Lemkin* (Torrance, CA: Institute for Historical Review, 1984). Samantha Powers did much to bring Lemkin back into the light, as the first several chapters of her book recount Lemkin's life and work.

7 Testimonial Luncheon Statement, January 18, 1951, Reel 2, Box 1, Folder 34, NYPL. In a statement given by Lemkin at a luncheon in his honour hosted by the New York Region of the American Jewish Congress at the Hotel Pierre in NY, Lemkin said that during WWII he heard a radio broadcast given by Churchill in which he stated that the Nazis "commit[ed] a crime without a name." This, according to the testimonial, led him on the search for the word genocide. Lemkin often referred to this story. Powers notes that Churchill did not directly "refer to the extermination of Europe's Jewry (which Churchill did not mention) but to the Germans' 'methodical, merciless butchery' of the Russians" (p 523).

8 Steven Schnur, "Unofficial man: the rise and fall of Raphael Lemkin," *Reform Judaism*, Vol 11, No 1, 1982, pp 9–11, 45; Steven L. Jacobs, "The papers of Raphael Lemkin: a first look," *Journal of Genocide Research*, Vol 1, No 1, 1999, pp 105–114. Jacobs called Lemkin the premier genocide studies scholar and says that "his research, his writing, and his thinking may very well open doors to our own work and energize and stimulate us even more, not only in our own scholarly pursuits, but in our moral commitment to eliminate the very acts which are our concern" (p 111). Lemkin often referred to himself in correspondence and campaign letters as the "Founder of the Genocide Convention."

9 There are differences of opinion concerning his birthdate. See endnote number 22.

10 Information was derived from the following: (E) Offices Held, Book Proposal, undated, pp 6–7; Raphael Lemkin Papers, Reel 1, Box 2, Folder 1, NYPL; Collection Guides to the AJA and AJHS Lemkin Papers; Jacobs, p 106; Powers, Chapters 2–4.

11 Schur's article "Unofficial man: the rise and fall of Raphael Lemkin," from *Reform Judaism*, chronicles the Robert Lemkin donation and somewhat, the Saperstein donation. There is conflicting information between Schnur's accounts of how a portion of the documents came to the NYPL, and there are two versions of the story. Samantha Powers, as reported by William Korey (Powers, p 157), says that Robert Lemkin approached Korey after reading an article on his cousin written by Korey; Schnur says that Korey suggested to Robert that he donate the documents to the AJA; see endnote number 14 for an additional account. Schnur may have confused the three collections.

12 Access and Provenance Note, An Inventory to the Raphael Lemkin Papers, Manuscript Collection No 60, AJA, p 1. Anecdotal information relayed from Greg Naranjo of the USHMM regarding documents destroyed in a fire. Information was also provided or confirmed by Jim Fussell in an interview regarding the provenance of the collections conducted on Tuesday, November 9, 2004. According to Schnur, Maxwell Cohen recalled that the one room that Lemkin lived in contained "several international awards and a number of honorary degrees in odd places and memoranda prepared for foreign ministries and ambassadors with respect to the Genocide Convention ... There were five hundred books, each which had been read, underlined, and interlineated ... at the insistence of the Landlord, Cohen and several of Lemkin's students hastily emptied the one-room apartment, carting the papers to Robert Lemkin's basement." Schnur, p 45, notes that Maxwell Cohen, a friend of Lemkin's, and Robert Lemkin were present, but does not mention that Elias and Saul Lemkin were present. Possibly Elias and Saul came after the apartment had been initially cleared of items.

13 Guide to the Raphael Lemkin Collection, P-154, AJHS, p 7. The AJHS collection remained largely unprocessed, until 2003. The author of this paper, an archivist, reprocessed and created a new finding aid (guide) to the collection. The author had never heard of Raphael Lemkin, nor had any knowledge of the creation of the word genocide. Jim Fussell provided anecdotal information to the author regarding Mr Ladin and Mr Spector. The added article is William Korey's "Raphael Lemkin: 'The unofficial man'," *Midstream*, June–July 1989. Korey's hard-to-find *An Epitaph for Raphael Lemkin* (New York: Jacob Blaustein Institute for the Advancement of Human Rights, 2001), donated by the American Jewish Committee, will be added to the collection.

14 Email from NYPL Manuscripts and Archives Division, November 2004 led to the Steven Schnur article regarding the AJA and NYPL acquisitions. Schnur, p 45, writes that: "Alexander Gabriel then offered ... to transfer the essential records to the Dag Hammerskjold Library ... [but] the library had refused the papers because of their disorganized condition ..." After the Hammerskjold refused the documents, Gabriel may have then transferred them to his office, though the NYPL says the documents were given to Gabriel by former secretaries of Lemkin's; Fussell interview, November 9, 2004.

15 For access to the four collections, please contact the archives or the compiled collection custodian.

16 Any artefacts prior to 1941 that Lemkin may have retained were more than likely destroyed in the fire that Saul Lemkin recalled to Jim Fussell or lost when Lemkin was unable to retrieve trunks stored at a Washington, DC storage unit. Though the records were saved, there is no indication that Lemkin personally retrieved them.

17 There are living members of Lemkin's family located in Canada and the US, but none were contacted for this article. There may be some photographic evidence still housed with them, but it is doubtful, as related by Fussell and Saul Lemkin. Family photographs taken in the 1950s of Elias Lemkin and his two sons can be found at the AJHS, Box 1, Folder 15.

18 Jim Fussell related that in 1951, when Lemkin was writing his autobiography, the film version of *Quo Vadis*, starring Robert Taylor, Deborah Kerr and Peter Ustinov, was released, and Lemkin may have been attempting to link his past passion with a present icon of the era.

19 Powers, p 21.

20 Powers, p 20.

21 Powers, p 522. Powers notes that William Korey in *Epitaph for Raphael Lemkin* (pp 11–12) states that Lemkin did not attend the conference and Lemkin wrote in his autobiography that he did not attend the Madrid conference; Korey corrected the record by way of Stephen Jacobs. See Chapter 2 of autobiography. In addition, there are numerous newspaper articles that claim that Lemkin was injured in the leg either during the resistance or while travelling from Poland to Sweden. Lemkin did not write about this incident in his autobiography.

22 The AJHS collection contains two documents that point to 1900 as Mr Lemkin's year of birth. One is his War Department identification and a *Who's Who* entry sent to Lemkin for his approval. Identity Cards, Raphael Lemkin Collection, Box 1, Folders 2 and 12, AJHS. Library of Congress authority files also point to 1900, and the Prevent Genocide website (www.preventgenocide.org/lemkin/birthdate) says a 1952 Social Security card application records 1900. Lemkin's gravestone also bears the year of birth as 1900. Even William Korey contradicts himself between 1989's *Midstream* article and *An Epitaph for Raphael Lemkin*.

23 James Joseph Martin, *The Man Who Invented "Genocide": The Public Career and Consequences of Raphael Lemkin* (Torrance, CA: Institute of Historical Review, 1984).

24 Unnamed Simon and Schuster editor to Lemkin, Reel 1, Box 1, Folder 2, NYPL.

25 A bibliography of Lemkin's writings can be found at http://www.preventgenocide.org/lemkin/bibliography.htm. Jim Fussell has compiled this list using the catalogs of the University of Warsaw, the Library of Congress, and Raphael Lemkin's papers. Fussell writes that the complete list of Lemkin books and articles "includes items on comparative penal codes, international offenses and jurisdiction in domestic penal codes, family law (including juvenile and divorce law), expert witnesses in the judicial process, tax and amnesty law, international private law (conflict of laws), currency and exchange control law, law of wartime occupation, and lastly international public law (focused specifically on genocide)."

26 The English version can be read at http://www.preventgenocide.org/lemkin/madrid1933-english.htm, and the French version can be found at the AJHS, Box 1, Folder 11. A curator located at the United States Holocaust Memorial Museum conveyed that one of their researchers had travelled to Geneva to ascertain the Lemkin documents located there, though a report of their findings was not available.

27 Writings—Autobiography, Reel 2, Box 1, Folders 36, 40–43, NYPL.

28 "Recording on military government in Europe," compiled by Raphael Lemkin, School of Military Government, Raphael Lemkin Papers, MC-60, Box 6, Folder 1, AJA.

29 Lemkin autobiography, p 87, Chapter 5, Reel 2, Box 1, Folder 36, NYPL.

30 In 1937, Lemkin met law librarian John Vance, at the Congress of Comparative Law. Vance worked at the Library of Congress and introduced Lemkin to Colonel Archibald King of the Military Division of the War Department. Chapter 6, "Totally unofficial," Reel 2, Box 1, Folder 36, NYPL.

31 This note is possibly located at the AJHS, Raphael Lemkin Collection, Box 1, Folder 4. The note is dated May 25, 1941, and consists of short notes front and back, one from his father, the other from his mother. There are several accounts from articles concerning what happened to Lemkin's parents and brother, and Lemkin briefly speaks about the fate of his parents in Chapter 7 of his autobiography, though he never found out precisely how they perished.

32 For a summary on *Axis Rule in Occupied Europe* and the full text of Chapter 9, see: http://www.preventgenocide.org/lemkin/AxisRule1944-1.htm. The Axis laws were signed over to the Bureau of Economic Warfare on December 7, 1942. The School of Military Government at Charlottesville, VA, printed *Readings on Military Government in Europe*, located in Box 6, Folder 1, AJA; "Part I: the new word and the new idea," Reel 3, Box 2, Folder 1, NYPL.

33 AJHS, Box 6, Folders 7 and 9; NYPL, Reel 5, Box 3, Folders 3–4 (Threats to the Genocide Convention) and Reel 6, Box 4, Folder 7; AJA has some correspondence on the Nuremberg Trials, Box 1, Folder 13.

34 Biffy to Lemkin, February 16, 1949, Box 1, Folder 8, AJA.

35 Deposition of witnesses at the Nuremberg Trials, 1945–1946; reprint of trial transcript (fragment), Box 5 Folders 1–2, AJA; Raphael Lemkin (Collection)—Nuremberg Tribunal Materials, AWD-CLS, Columbia University Law Library Archives, Columbia University, New York. (Fussell notes that this collection may have been left at a friend of Lemkin's apartment or with someone who worked for him); "The significance of the concept of genocide in the trial of war criminals," by Raphael Lemkin, Thomas Dodd Papers, Box/Folder 387:8580, Thomas J. Dodd Research Center, University of Connecticut.

36 Correspondence at AJHS is filed by year; AJA, by last name (though Elias's letters in Yiddish are filed in Unidentified, Box 2, Folder 19); NYPL has the least amount of correspondence of the three collections, but some personal letters (Reel 1, Box 1, Folder 31). Other NYPL correspondence is filed by year, Reel 1, Box 1, Folder 1.

37 "Nazi genocide" (Untitled Manuscript) and *Hitler Case*, Box 7, Folders 12 and 13, AJA; Jacobs, Steven L., ed., *Raphael Lemkin's Thoughts on Nazi Genocide: Not Guilty?* (Lewiston, NY: Edwin Mellen Press, 1992); Jacobs, p 110.

38 Notes and Drafts, Handwritten, Misc., Box 6, Folder 6; Sixth Committee, General Assembly Proceedings, 1946–1947, Box 4, Folder 2; "Discussion on genocide in the legal committee," November 22, 1946, 11:00 A.M. and Resolutions of 12 November 1946, Box 6, Folder 11; Draft Press Release, Box 7, Folder 1, AJHS. An undated (possibly September 23, 1947) memorandum for Mrs Pandit, addressed to Vijaya Lashmi Pandit, is located in Box 2, Folder 5, AJHS.

39 Subseries 2: United Nations, Box 2, Folder 13, Boxes 3–4, AJHS. Box 4, Folder 7 contains a photo of Lemkin amid a roomful of the Ad-Hoc Committee on Genocide delegates, April 5, 1948, AJA.

40 Notes and Drafts, Handwritten, Misc., Box 6, Folder 6, AJHS. Handwritten (and typed) material at the NYPL can be found in the Writings—Autobiography and Writings—Genocide (Reel 2, Box 1, Folders 35–43; Reel 2, Box 2, Folders 1–16.) There are also several notebooks at the NYPL: Reel 5, Box 4, Folders 1–3. One may belong to Alexander Gabriel.

41 Genocide Convention—Writings, Box 5–Box 7, Folders 1–4, AJHS; Box 3 and Box 4, AJA; Printed Material, Reel 6, Box 4 and Box 5, NYPL.

42 AJHS: Delegate Statements, 1947–1948, Box 2, Folder 13; Jacob Blaustein, "The eyes of the world are watching," Box 6, Folder 12, p 9; "Memoranda to the reservations of the U.S.S.R., Byelorussia, and Ukraine concerning Article 9 of the Genocide Convention," Box 6, Folder 12, AJHS; AJA, Box 4, Folder 4–5. Quote is from "Memoranda on Genocide Convention," Reel 5, Box 3, Folder 1, NYPL.

43 Djalel Abdoh to Lemkin, January 17, 1950, Box 1, Folder 1, AJA.

44 Argentina–Venezuela Correspondence, Reel 1, Box 1, Folders 3–30; General Correspondence, Reel 1, Box 1, Folders 1–2; NYPL. The AJHS collection is in three correspondence sections: Personal Correspondence (Box 1, Folders 4–10); Genocide Convention: Lemkin Correspondence, 1945–1951 (Box 1, Folders 18–19 and Box 2, Folders 1–5) and US Committee for a UN Genocide Convention Correspondence, 1947–1951 (Box 2, Folders 7–12). The AJA correspondence contains letters about genocide or the Convention, though all correspondence, including personal, is included in one series (Boxes 1 and 2). The Viau letter is in Spanish. See also Printed Matter, Gerard Viau Incident, undated, Folder 15, Kurt Fisher/Haitian History Collection, Schomburg Center for Research in Black Culture, New York Public Library, New York for more information.

45 Korey, p 48. Korey mentions an initial proposal for the Committee, possibly "Emergency proposal for the creation of an international committee for the adoption of the United Nations Convention on the crime of genocide" in footnote 98, p 119. The AJHS collection has been reorganized since Korey wrote in

2001. Documents have been shifted. This document now resides in Box 2, Folder 12 of the Lemkin papers at the AJHS.

46 Korey, 48. AJHS: Buck, Pearl S., Correspondence and Proposed Manifesto, Box 1, Folder 17; Lemkin Correspondence, 1948 Box 1, Folder 19 (includes letters to Buck from Count Bernadotte of the International Red Cross and Chilean author Eduardo Bello who wrote, "Yesterday on looking at the black board with the news of the end of Gandhi, I had the impression that every one of us is a part in the whole of Human kind," February 1948).

47 US Committee for a UN Genocide Committee Correspondence, 1947–1921, Box 2, Folders 7–11; ... Membership List and Minutes, undated, 1948–1949, Box 2, Folder 12, AJHS; US Committee for a US Genocide Convention, 1948–1952, Reel 1, Box 1, Folder 3, NYPL. Printed matter can be found at: AJA, Box 3, Folder 3; AJHS, Box 14, Folder 6.

48 A Petition Respectfully Submitted to the General Assembly of the United Nations, September 1948, Box 3, Folder 9, AJHS; Petitions to the UN General Assembly to adopt the Genocide Convention, Box 4, Folder 1, AJA. Korey, p 52. The Universal Declaration of Human Rights was approved by the General Assembly on December 10, 1948. The Draft International Covenant on Human Rights resumed in Committee in May 1949.

49 Korey, p 36, quoting Lawrence J. LeBlanc, *The United States and the Genocide Convention* (Durham NC: Duke University Press, 1991), p 19. LeBlanc wrote that "dreamer" and "fanatic" were the two words used most by diplomats in describing Lemkin.

50 Powers, p 60 as recalled from Lemkin's autobiography, Reel 2, Box 1, Folder 37, p 61 of several drafts, NYPL.

51 Korey, p 44, the Genocide Convention was adopted partially by Lemkin's "ceaseless striving and unflagging determination."

52 US Committee ... Notice of Meeting, February 23, 1949, Box 2, Folder 12; Cellar to Lemkin, February 26, 1949, Box 2, Folder 1, AJHS.

53 Law Association Journals, "Documents for Study" American Bar Association, February 1949, Box 11, Folder 1, AJHS. Additional Law Association Journals may be found in Box 11, Folder 2.

54 Though archivists do not favour the artificial combining of collections, it is worth noting that the Jacobs compilation contains all correspondence in one place. It is not known how this collection is organized. Pamphlets and articles: Box 3, Folders 3–5, AJA; Box 4, Folder 9, NYPL (and other materials interspersed in the Printed Material series); Box 5, Folders 3–4, 7, 9–10, Box 7, Folder 4; Box 10–Box 11, AJHS. A draft of a US Committee brief in support of the Convention can be found in Box 2, Folder 12. ABA Debate Transcript and Address, 9/49, Box 5, Folder 2, AJHS.

55 US Law and the Genocide Convention Essays, Stephen Gorove, "Mental harm," Box 7, Folder 4, AJHS. It is not clear whether Mr Gorove was a student of Lemkin's or merely sending him a summary of a monograph he had written.

56 Box 4, Folders 3–5, AJA; Box 1, Folder 34, NYPL.

57 Chinese Revisions, Box 3, Folder 5; Chinese Text Translation, Box 4, Folder 2; France, Algeria, and the Convention, Box 3, Folder 4, NYPL; Chang to Lemkin, Box 1, Folder 3; Box 3, Folder 5, AJA.

58 "The truth about the Genocide Convention," Box 3, Folder 1, NYPL.

59 Article 3 of the Universal Declaration on Human Rights would later read, "Everyone has the right to life, liberty and security of person."

60 Cellar to Lemkin, ibid; "The Genocide Convention and race relations," by Richard D. Gillam, Jr, p 42, Box 4, Folder 6, AJA.

61 Johnson's archival papers can be found at the NYPL Schomberg and SUNY Stony Brook University.

62 "Background paper: United States statement on the Civil Rights Congress publication 'We Charge Genocide,'" Box 4, Folder 7, AJA. Powers, p 75.

63 Statements and Speeches, 1949–1957, Box 4, Folder 4, Box 3, Folder 1, Algeria: Box 4, Folder 4 and Box 5, Folder 5, AJA; Box 11, Folder 5, Box 12, Folders 1–3, AJHS. See also Box 3, Folder 4 for French attempts to weaken the Convention in regards to Algeria, and Reel 1, Box 1, Folder 25, "Peru," NYPL.

64 AJHS: Box 1, Folders 1–2; Box 5, Folders 3–7, 9–11; Box 6, Folders 1, 3, 8; AJA: Box 3, Folder 1–5; Box 4, Folder 2; NYPL, Box 4, Folder 4, 9.

65 "Portrait of dedication," *The Eternal Light*, NBC, May 1, 1949, Box 1, Folder 3; Mittler, Leo Screenplay, "Genocide," Box 6, Folder 3, AJHS.

66 UN Casebook "Genocide Convention Chapter XXI, 1949." A copy of this program is in the National Jewish Archive of Broadcasting at the Jewish Museum in New York (Archive No T316). Mr Ernest Gross—Genocide (November 1948); Mr B. Ikramullah (Pakistan)—Def. Genocide (October 7, 1948); Dr W. J. Digman (Australia)—Genocide (October 6, 1948); Mr E. Wikborg (Norway)—Genocide (October 11, 1948); Dr Alfano Ricardo—Genocide (October 6, 1948); Prof. Lange (Poland)—Genocide (October 8, 1948); Prof. Emile Giraud—Genocide (July 24, 1948 (French)); and Memo from Lake Success #7—Human Rights (November 13, 1948).

67 Starr to Lemkin, February 13, 1951, Box 8, Folder 11. Korey, p 85, cites three volumes; Powers, p 77, cites four volumes.
68 Anonymous to Lemkin, June 9, 1949, Box 2, Folder 1; Kurt Grossman to Lemkin, September 17–October 21, 1947, AJHS.
69 Yale Library to Lemkin, May 23, 1949, Box 1, Folder 7, AJHS. The *Hitler Case* and "Nazi genocide" (Untitled Manuscript) are included as part of the research essays at the AJA.
70 Turkey–Armenia Publications, 1915–1919, 1946–1948. Box 12, Folder 3, Turkish–Armenian Trial Transcript, Box 9, Folder 23, AJHS.
71 *The New York Times* Youth Forum Study Outline, Box 3, Folder 2, NYPL.
72 "Climbing a mountain again" (The Years of Trial), Autobiography, Box 1, Folder 38, NYPL.
73 Poem, verso, Hamparian to Lemkin, March 15, 1957, Box 2, Folder 1, AJA.
74 Milleren to Lemkin, June 13, 1948, Box 1, Folder 6, AJHS.
75 Medical Papers, Position Appointments, Final Grades and Drawings, Box 1, Folder 13, AJHS.
76 Merchants Storage to Lemkin, Box 1, Folder 8, AJHS. Milleren had written to Lemkin on September 13, 1948 that she had to leave Washington, DC, and did not know what to do with documents and books. They had lived in the same boarding house in DC.
77 Robert E. Baker, "Owner will regain genocide documents," *Washington Post*, undated, Box 5, Folder 7, AJA.
78 Milliren to Lemkin, July 8, 1957, Box 2, Folder 8, AJA. If these were given to Gabriel, the NYPL might have that record in their files, but donor records are usually confidential.

Raphael Lemkin as historian of genocide in the Americas

MICHAEL A. MCDONNELL and A. DIRK MOSES

Introduction

That Raphael Lemkin (1900–1959) was keenly interested in colonial genocides is virtually unknown. Most commonly, and erroneously, he is understood as coining the term genocide in the wake of the Holocaust of European Jewry in order to reflect its features as a state-organized and ideologically-driven program of mass murder.[1] An inspection of his unpublished writings in New York and Cincinnati reveals that this is a gross distortion of his thinking.[2] In fact, the intellectual breakthrough that led to the concept of genocide occurred well before the Holocaust. Already in the 1920s and early 1930s, he had begun formulating the concepts and laws that would culminate in his founding text, *Axis Rule in Occupied Europe* (1944), and in the United Nations convention on genocide four years later.[3] It is a signal failure of genocide studies scholars in North America in particular, where the field has been primarily based until recently, that they have neglected his manuscripts sitting on their doorstep, preferring to regard themselves as fellow "pioneers of genocide studies," although there is surely one pioneer, namely, Raphael Lemkin.[4] Rather than investigate what he actually meant by the term and its place in world history, the field has rejected or misunderstood his complex definition and engaged instead in comparative study of twentieth century mass killing and totalitarianism, all the while claiming Lemkin as a legitimating authority.[5]

Contrary to the weight of this scholarship, what Lemkin's manuscripts reveal is that early modern and modern colonialism was central to his conception of genocide. Indeed, the very notion is colonial in nature because it entails occupation and settlement. The link is made plain by Lemkin in his description of genocide on the first page of the salient chapter of *Axis Rule*:

> Genocide has two phases: one, destruction of the national pattern of the oppressed group: the other, the imposition of the national pattern of the oppressor. This imposition, in turn, may be made upon the oppressed population which is allowed to remain, or upon the territory alone, after removal of the population and the *colonization* of the area by the oppressor's own nationals.[6]

Mass killing, by contrast, is *not* intrinsic to genocide; it can occur without executions or gassings.[7] The proposition that scholars who think that genocide is a synonym for the Holocaust need to entertain is that Lemkin regarded the latter as a consequence of Nazi imperialism and colonialism in Europe. The Holocaust and German *imperium* between 1939 and 1945 was for him a continuation of the genocidal occupations that have characterized colonialism through the ages—to be sure, in an extremely radicalized, bureaucratic mode.[8] This viewpoint, reinforced by renewed attention to the section on imperialism in Hannah Arendt's *Origins of Totalitarianism*, is now finding support in the literature.[9] To be sure, Lemkin conducted his systematic studies of colonial genocides in the later 1940s and 1950s, that is, after he had articulated the concept of genocide in 1944, but in all likelihood he was well aware of colonialism and critiques of it well before World War II.[10] What is important to note, however, is that although Lemkin probably regarded the genocide of European Jewry as the most extreme genocide in history, he assessed the extra-European cases of colonial genocide in terms of that concept's *generic* attributes rather than project the Holocaust back into history as the ideal type with which to categorize previous genocides.[11]

If Lemkin's definition of genocide as colonial has been studiously ignored by the literature, Australian, German, and English scholars interested in imperial history have now begun to implement it in their research on the destructive dimensions of colonialism.[12] But Lemkin not only provided conceptual guidance to later scholars; he wrote about these colonial cases himself. In "Part III: modern times" of a projected global history of genocide from antiquity to the present, he wrote, *inter alia*, on the following cases: "1. Genocide by the Germans against the Native Africans"; "3. "Belgian Congo"; "11. Hereros"; "13. Hottentots"; "16. Genocide against the American Indians"; "25. Latin America"; "26. Genocide against the Aztecs"; "27. Yucatan"; "28. Genocide against the Incas"; "29: Genocide against the Maoris of New Zealand"; "38. Tasmanians"; "40. S.W. Africa"; and finally, "41. Natives of Australia."[13] Then, in a "Report on the preparation of a volume on genocide," dated March–May 1948, a less ambitious project comprising ten chapters, two of which covered extra-European colonial cases: "2. The Indians in Latin America" and "10. The Indians in North America (in part)." The Holocaust, a term Lemkin never used, was not included, although the Armenians and Greeks in Turkey were, as well as the Early Christians, and the Jews of the Middle Ages and Tsarist Russia.[14] To continue to deny, as many "founders of genocide studies" deny, that he regarded colonialism as an integral part of a world history of genocide is to ignore the written record.

Unfortunately, this written record is incomplete. Although the unpublished manuscript that lists the 41 cases Lemkin examined contains handwritten notes indicating a "good," "fair," and sometimes even "duplicate" copy of the chapters listed above, only some of them are contained in the three Lemkin collections. Thus we only have the notes of Lemkin (or, rather, of his research assistant) on the "American Indians," and the chapters on the New Zealand Maoris and Natives of Australia are nowhere to be found as yet.[15] But we do have copies of his chapters, ranging between 17 and 32 double-spaced typed, unnumbered pages, on the Incas of Peru, the Mayas of the Yucatan peninsula, and the Aztecs of Mexico, as well as a general analysis he called "Spain colonial genocide." We are in a position, then, to investigate how Lemkin worked as a historian for some of the Americas. What we find is that he regarded the concept of genocide as perfectly adequate to analyse the complex processes of colonialism, but that his adherence to certain sources and perspectives blinded him to aspects of the Spanish case. We conclude by highlighting the tension between genocide scholarship and modern historiography of Native Americans generally, and propose that the former learn from the latter's insights.

Lemkin's research

The notes Lemkin and/or his research assistant took—at least those that are extant—are uneven, even anecdotal, and drawn from a disparate and limited range of popular and scholarly sources. They follow no clearly discernible methodology. For North America, there are only note cards, which are scattered, and episodic—ranging from King Philip's War in Massachusetts in 1676, to the battle of Wounded Knee on the Plains in the 1870s. For the most part, the notes are drawn from Edward Channing's monumental, though very general work, *A History of the United States*, Vols I–V (New York: Macmillan, 1929). He also used John Halkett, *Historical Notes Respecting the Indians of North America* (London: A Constable, 1825) to compare British and French policies, Grant Foreman, *Indian Removal: The Emigration of the Five Civilized Tribes of Indians* (Norman: University of Oklahoma Press, 1932) for Indian removal, and John Collier, *The Indians of the Americas* (New York: W. W. Norton, 1947) on the nineteenth century Plains Indians Wars and on the treatment of California Indians. For primary sources, he drew on the extensive appendix of official documents in Charles J. Brill, *Conquest of the Southern Plains* (Oklahoma City: Golden Saga, 1938), as well as the treaties listed in James Truslow Adams, *Dictionary of American History*, five volumes (New York: C. Scribner's Sons, 1940) and Charles C. Royce, comp., *Indian Land Cessions in the US* (Washington, DC: Government Printing Office, 1899). Significantly, Lemkin and/or his research assistant took many notes from J. Clarence Webster, ed., *The Journal of Jeffery Amherst: Recording the Military Career of General Amherst in America from 1758 to 1763* (Toronto: Ryerson Press, 1931). Like contemporary scholars, Lemkin was clearly intrigued by reports that Amherst had authorized the deliberate distribution of smallpox infested blankets among Indians.[16]

For the Aztecs and New Spain, Lemkin took most of his notes from F. A. MacNutt, *Fernando Cortes and the Conquest of Mexico, 1485–1507* (New York: Putnam, 1909), George C. Vaillant, *Aztecs of Mexico* (Garden City, NY: Doubleday, Doran, 1941), and Collier's *Indians of the Americas*. For the Yucatan Peninsula and the Maya, Lemkin mainly consulted Arnold Channing and F. J. Tabor Frost, *The American Egypt* (New York: Doubleday, Page, 1909), and Frans Blom, *The Conquest of Yucatan* (Boston: Houghton Mifflin, 1936). For the Incas and Peru, Lemkin notes that his chief source was William H. Prescott,

History of the Conquest of Peru (London: Dent, 1916; originally published 1847), and again, Collier's more general work, *The Indians of the Americas.*

For the essays he wrote on Spanish America, however, Lemkin drew mainly upon the work of Spanish witness Bartolomé de las Casas, derived mainly from Marcel Brion's, *Bartolomé de las Casas: "Father of the Indians"* (New York: E. P. Dutton, 1929), which Lemkin notes was his chief source for Spanish colonial genocide, and Francis Augustus MacNutt, *Bartholomew de las Casas: His Life, His Apostolate, and his Writings* (New York: Putnam, 1909). Indeed, for the bulk of his text on Spanish America in general, and the Incas, Aztecs, and Maya in particular, Lemkin cites Las Casas. For Lemkin, Las Casas was one of the few heroes of American colonialism and the sole authority on Spanish cruelties. As he wrote, Las Casas' "name has lived on through the centuries as one of the most admirable and courageous crusaders for humanity the world has ever known." "And in his famous work on conditions in the Indies," Lemkin concluded, "he has collected all the gruesome facts of genocide which he met with and bitterly indicted the vicious Spanish colonial administration." Lemkin let Las Casas speak for him: "[Las Casas' account] has come down to us as one of the most shocking monographs on genocide." His text thus follows Las Casas closely both in tone and evidence, although the structure and analysis is, in the last instance, his own.[17]

Lemkin's method and analyses

Because Lemkin regarded genocide as "an organic concept of multiple influences and consequences," he did not limit his investigation to "one branch of science."[18] He proceeded interdisciplinarily, utilizing categories from sociology, political science, demography, economics, psychology, and law. Accordingly, the chapters are not descriptive narratives, but tightly structured analyses organized under the following headings. Here is Lemkin's outline of the template he used in each chapter. These are his words:

1. Background-historical.
2. Conditions leading to the genocide: fanaticism (religious, racial), irredentism (national aspirations), social or political crisis and change, economic exploitation (e.g. slavery), colonial expansion or military conquest, accessibility [sic.] of victim group, evolution of genocidal values in genocidist group (contempt for the alien, etc.), factors weakening victim groups.
3. Methods and techniques of genocide:
   - physical—massacre and mutilation, deprivation of livelihood (starvation, exposure, etc. often by deportation), slavery—exposure to death.
   - biological—separation of families, sterilization, destruction of foetus.
   - cultural—desecration and destruction of cultural symbols (books, objects of art, loot, religious relics, etc.), destruction of cultural leadership, destruction of cultural centers (cities, churches, monasteries, schools, libraries),

prohibition of cultural activities or codes of behavior, forceful conversion, demoralization.

4. The genocidists: responsibility, intent, motivation, feelings of guilt, demoralization, attitude towards victims, opposition to genocide within genocidist group.
5. Propaganda: rationalization of crime, appeal to popular beliefs and intolerance, sowing discord (divide and rule), misrepresentation and deceit, intimidation.
6. Responses of victims:
   - active: submission (suicide, hiding, etc), escape, disguise, (planned) emigration, political subordination, assimilation, resistance, demoralization
   - passive (emotional mental): terror, conceptions of genocidist and his crimes. submission, escape, resistance, attitude towards genocidists; disguise, demoralization.
7. Responses of outsider groups: opposition to genocide, indifference to genocide, condonement [sic.] of genocide, collaboration in genocide, demoralization (exploitation of genocide situation), fear as potential victims.
8. Aftermath: cultural losses, population changes, economic dislocations, material and moral deterioration, political consequences, social and cultural changes.[19]

The lead-up to genocide

In the event, Lemkin did not utilize every heading in each chapter he wrote, attending first and foremost to the historical evidence he found. He commenced each chapter with a brief survey of the indigenous peoples, describing their culture, society, and vulnerability to European penetration. Although not blind to their faults—"Mexico was ruled by a covetous and tyrannical conqueror, Montezuma ... [who] ... had subjected many formerly independent people who served as oppressed vassals to the Aztec"[20]—Lemkin generally praised the virtues of these American civilizations. Despite tyranny, the Aztecs possessed a "fairly democratic government," "Commerce was highly developed," "Much land had been reclaimed from the sea by careful water controls," they "were highly skilled in arts and crafts," and so on.[21] The Incas received still further praise: their culture "is one of the most remarkable in history, both for artistic as well as socio-political achievement."[22] For all that, the Mayas stood "on a higher plane culturally" because of their "picture writing which was highly stylized."[23] In the narrative structure of these chapters, these halcyon, introductory depictions are meant to stand in stark contrast to the abject condition of the surviving indigenous people in the sombre concluding section, the "Aftermath."

The attention then shifts to the Spanish conquerors. Lemkin described the sixteenth century expeditions in a page or two before proceeding to analyse the "Conditions leading to genocide." Lemkin himself generalized about them:

> As for the conditions leading to the discovery and conquest of Yucatan by the Spanish, they are more or less identical with those leading to Spanish conquest elsewhere after Columbus.

> Desire for the riches of the new continent, for glory and adventure drew the conquistadors to the American shores.[24]

The situation was exacerbated in Peru, "Because of the many hardships of the expedition and the unsurpassed riches which were eventually found."[25] Another common feature was the Spanish assumption that they had a right to the territory and its riches, so much so that resistance by the Indians was regarded as treacherous and thus crushed with brutal force. As we will see, the quelling of resistance was a major feature of what Lemkin called "physical genocide." Another feature that led to a radicalization of the Spanish was an honour code that did not countenance failure, and a "necessity to hold out despite almost insurpassable [sic.] difficulties": the conquerors exhibited "rapacity and ruthlessness against kindly natives" once they were "within reach of what they had striven for."[26]

The Indians were no match for the conquistadors. The Aztecs had made themselves so unpopular by their tyranny that the Spanish—"after all a small troop of worn-out strangers in a rugged country full of enemy peoples"—could enlist the "active cooperation of Indian vassal tribes" against them.[27] More generally, superstition and religion issued in a dangerously welcoming attitude to the Europeans. Awe was inspired by their strange mode of transport (horses), steel armour, and arabesques. "Later this awe increased to stupefied subjection when the violation of the idols and the emperor's person did not bring down the wrath of the gods."[28] The Mayan civilization was already in decline when the Spanish arrived, riven by civil war and economic difficulties, but Lemkin did not regard this weakness as decisive.

> While conquest by the small Spanish forces was usually difficult and dangerous, it is most likely that the Spanish with their horses and superior weapons would eventually have conquered the country, whether it had been internally weak or not.[29]

The genocides

Lemkin then laid out the "methods of genocide." The first was physical, typically massacres. These were of three sorts. Preemptive strikes were carried out by Pizarro in 1532 after he entered the city of Caxamalca, and by Cortes in Cholula, in order to intimidate the locals, and to forestall attack by them. Fear of being overwhelmed by the far more numerous Indian forces was an important factor, Lemkin observed.[30] The second sort of massacre was the putting down of rebellions. Killing took the form of reprisal actions: "For every Christian killed during the fighting brutal reprisals were taken and many hundreds of Indians were massacred. Some governors and captains simply had populations massacred without ceremony." Captured locals suffered a worse fate: "Indian captives of the Spanish were frequently tortured and killed. This was not the exception among the cruder soldiers but was looked upon as a matter of course by soldiers and officers alike."[31] In form, such massacres resembled the third type: gratuitous exhibitions of violence for their own sake.

> Massacre of defenseless Indians did not stop with the completion of the conquest. During the bloody days of Spanish colonial rule, Spaniards used to amuse themselves by hunting down the natives with bloodhounds for sport or to train their dogs for game.[32]

Outright killing or murder was not the only physical method of genocide. Lemkin also counted the "deprivation of livelihood," by which he meant "genocidal slavery." In the case of the Incas, he identified the Spanish instrumentalization of indigenous practices of labour service to effectively work the locals to death. Or they taxed "the strength of the Indians to the utmost and beyond, and they did not afford them any protection whatsoever."[33] He was aware that the Spanish crown had attempted to protect the Indians by instituting a system of "encomiendas," but they became "a cloak for continual exploitation and slavery" because the stipulated conditions were ignored by colonial authorities.[34] Lemkin was appalled by the loss of life:

> The population of San Juan and Jamaica fell from 600,000 to 200 in 40 years (op. cit. 118). In the Bahamas the population fell from 50,000 to nearly zero. The population of Nicaragua was almost entirely wiped out; In 14 years more than 600,000 had died as beasts of burden (op. cit. 121). The supposedly impartial historian Jomara claims that by 1553 there was not a single Indian left in Cuba. Another authority claims that 20,000 were wiped out there (op. cit. 23) Just within a few months, 7,000 children died of hunger. Las Casas claim the total Indians killed in Spanish America as more than 20 million (op. cit. 26). This number does not include those that died from overwork, the slaves who were killed in the mines, or the Indians killed during active combat, nor the caciques or prisoners who were executed (Ibid.).[35]

The second method of genocide was biological. This is the method that had the most direct implications for women because it bore on the natural reproduction of family and therefore group life. Mass rapes and the separation of children from their parents fell under this rubric.

> Indian women were not only violated indiscriminately but also carried off to fill the harems of the Spanish colonists (Brion, 39). The fact the exhausted slave mothers were often unable to nurse their babies, also contributed to the death of the race (Ibid). Children were not infrequently carried off by the Spanish (25).[36]

Slavery also affected procreation and so was included as a form of biological genocide. "As the men were slaves were used as porters and miners, and the female ones as cooks and mistresses (op. cit. 54), the separation of families was concomitant with slavehunting."[37] The harems affected the Incas' ability to reproduce. "Between this forceful removal of Indian girls and the undermining of the health of the male slave, the biological continuity of the Peruvian people must have been greatly jeopardized."[38]

Lemkin had more to say about the cultural genocide of the Indigenous peoples of Latin America. Since his thinking of this method of genocide has been widely misunderstood, it is worth attending to closely.[39] He identified six forms of cultural genocide: destruction of leadership, forced conversion, prohibition of cultural activities, destruction of religious and cultural symbols, destruction of cultural centres, and looting. The destruction of local elites, and indeed leaders like Montezuma, was designed to decapitate the enemy in order to render it more easily conquerable. The humiliating execution of such political rulers, such as the Inca emperor, "revealed to the people that a power stronger than that of the Incas had now control of their country and that the dynasty of the Children of the Sun with all its cultural and religious implications had now passed away for ever (op. cit. 302)."[40] Lemkin summarized the situation by relying on Las Casas: "According to Las Casas, one chief after the other, one kind after the other was killed by the Spanish. Caciques were burned everywhere; the kings of Mabua, Buacagar and Darien, of Maguana, Xaragua and Higuey perished as a result of the Spanish genocide (120, Brion)."[41] Religious leaders were also targeted: "In order to prevent the maintenance of tribal religion and culture, the Mayan nobles and priests were either killed outright by the Spanish military or forced to flee (Blum 83)."[42]

Although Lemkin praised the efforts of the clergy to learn the locals' languages and protect them from the depredations of the Spanish soldiers, he held the latter responsible for "A subtle kind of cultural genocide" in the "Spanish missions which abounded in Mexico, California, Louisiana and elsewhere." Indians may not have been converted by force—conversion by coercion was a clear case of cultural genocide—but by virtue of baptism belonged to the Church and thereby became "virtual prisoners" of the missions and the violence enforcement of their discipline.[43] They were separated from their people and its culture. With the same logic, Lemkin suggested that Cortes' refusal to accept unbaptized girls as gifts by the Spanish was tantamount to cultural genocide because "Indian etiquette required the acceptance of gifts offered. The Indians could not take back the girls they offered as gifts without seeming offensive [sic.] according to their customs; thus they were obliged to consent to their baptism," although Lemkin speculated that Cortes may not have intended this outcome, concerned as he may have been with the Christian purity of this men.[44] Clearly, the intention rather than simply the effect mattered for Lemkin.

Closely related to forced conversion was the prohibition of cultural activities. In his only discussion of the method, Lemkin is not entirely clear on whether its effects must be physical to qualify as genocidal. Thus the substitution of the healthy Maya drink, the *balche*, with "Spanish intoxicants," which had the predictable effects on the health of the Indians, is a case of cultural policies having a biological consequence. No such effect was immediately obvious, although in retrospect predictable, from the manifold restrictive measures imposed by the friars on their unhappy "converts." Because these kind of regulations are so common in colonial contexts around the world, the proclamation of Tomas Lopez warrants reproduction in full. If they were culturally genocidal in nature, as Lemkin suggested, then many of the heavy handed assimilation policies of policies of colonizing powers fall under this rubric.

The control of residence and travel (to facilitate indoctrination)
Prohibition of native rites and assemblies
Establishment of one church in each town within 2 years
Establishment of a school for the teaching of the catechism and the necessity for baptism to

> be built by the town; attendance required
> The punishment of the relapsed converts
> The control of marriages (none to marry more than once; no native marriage customs, no secret marriages, monogamy)
> Children not be given heathen names
> All to attend church regularly and to follow all Christian rites
> No tattooing, devination
> Command to care for the sick, "so lacking in charity are the Indians"
> No slavery allowed for the Indians; caciques (chiefs) may have accredited servants
> No banquets to be held of more than 12 persons and then only on special occasions such as weddings
> Dancing only in the daytime
> Ancient drinks prohibited
> Towns to be built in Spanish style with a market place and racial segregation
> Dress regulated
> All bow and arrows burnt to prevent hunting; caciques were allowed some for emergencies.[45]

The next method of cultural genocide was the Spanish violation of cultural symbols, by which he meant the plundering of sacred sites out of greed. "In the capital of Peru, Cuzco, the Spanish soldiers stripped off the rich ornaments from the royal mummies in the temple of Corichancha. They even violated the sepulchres and deprived them of their dead and their wealth (Prescott, 316)."[46] Christian outrage at heathen practices was also a factor. Thus

> Cortes was the idol smasher par excellence. He ordered crosses to be erected in the villages. In one city he commanded his soldiers to ascend the temples and cast down the idlos [sic.] which were then burned in the public square under protest of the governor (MacNutt, 100, also 30).[47]

The destruction of cultural centres entailed both the laying waste of villages, towns and cities, as well as the despoliation of temples and pyramids. "At Kalisco, the Spanish boasted of having burned 300 villages to the glory of God and kind (op. cit. 123)." In both cases, he emphasized that Spanish institutions replaced the Indigenous ones. They destroyed Aztec cities "and built Spanish cities on their ruins." In Peru, "The Spanish friar of the expedition, Father Valverde, began his career as Bishop of Cuzco by erecting a monastery on the ruins of the House of the Sun, the great temple." With perhaps unintended irony, he observed that "The former House of the Virgins of the Sun was transformed into a Catholic nunnery."[48]

Only the Incas receive a separate section on loot. Lemkin appeared to want to make two points; that the looting impoverished the country and that it destroyed unique material culture. Thus "The Indian goldsmiths were required to melt down all the previous and bejewlled [sic.] articles of gold that poured into Spanish headquarters." Generalizing for the Spanish colonial genocide, he wrote, "Looting and pillaging of Indian wealth was so general that it seems almost banal to mention it. Frequently the Indians would be threatened with violence lest they [not?] reveal their treasure to the Spanish. Usually, the conquerors took the treasures and then the lives of the Indian owners (Brion, 33)."[49] We revisit the issue of cultural destruction when we discuss his discussions of the "Aftermath" of the genocide below.

The genocidists

Lemkin's attempt to attribute responsibility for these crimes presents the scholar with an important insight into how he reasoned about colonial genocides. After all, the cases he was covering here were not centrally controlled instances of focused extermination like the Holocaust. How does he deal with the key category of intent in such a diffuse and uncoordinated process? His approach was to focus directly on what he called the specific "genocidists" and to discuss them in terms of their "responsibility," "intent," "motivation," and "demoralization," as well as their "attitude towards the victim," and any "opposition from within." Generally, the colonists were to blame:

> With few exceptions ... the colonists of New Spain were guilty of genocide and firmly resolved to frustrate all efforts at stopping it. They profited by the ownership of slaves and since even the governors were slave-holders they could not be induced to enforce the royal orders against slavery and other abuses ... the colonists were guilty on all counts.[50]

The military officers and their troops were "the enforcers of genocide" by virtue of "the brutal reprisals against rebellious Indians." Even here, though, Lemkin was careful to differentiate. Writing of the massacre of the Cochuah and Chemtual in Yucatan, he noted, "To what extent higher military or governmental authorities sanctioned this genocide is difficult to say; Don Francisco de Montejo, at least, was not involved in the above atrocities, but condemned them in vain (25)."[51] Non-state actors were also guilty. The colonists "endorsed and commanded such action," Lemkin observed of the killing. Sometimes, they "perpetrated massacre themselves."[52] Indigenous collaborators with the Spanish in Mexico were likewise guilty: "The allied Indians helped in the massacre and general pillage at Chochula; they could not be restrained by the Spanish though apparently this was attempted (Bonte, 58)."[53]

A striking feature of the analysis is the distinction Lemkin draws between the Spanish king in Madrid and the "wealthy colonists" who intrigued at court in order to prevent any humanitarian interference in their exploitation of the "new world." Their greed, he is effectively arguing, corrupted all involved in the governance of the colonies. He reserves particular opprobrium for those who should have intervened on behalf of the Indians.

> The royal administrators of the Spanish colonies were perhaps the most responsible for the crimes, since they had the power and duty to interfere on the basis of royal orders. However, they were slaveholders themselves and thus did more than merely condone genocide.[54]

Responsibility could be vicarious. Thus Pizarro, a commander in Peru under Cortes, had forbidden his soldiers from violating buildings and the population of Cuzco; but they did so anyway. Afterwards, Pizarro supervised the division of the spoils, whose theft he ultimately sanctioned. "While it seems from the evidence, that certain of the most scandalous acts of genocide were not immediately traceable to Pizarro's initiative, the commander of the Peruvian expedition has received the blame, which of course is his due by virtue of his position."[55]

Lemkin also identified those responsible for cultural genocide. Clergy who had imposed forced conversion were guilty of cultural genocide. Father Valverde's inducement to the Inca monarch to convert before execution was regarded by Lemkin in these terms. The inquisitorial actions of Church figures in removing Indians from towns and destroying their religious icons in *auto de fes* was roundly condemned.[56] He was certainly aware that many clergy had protected Indians against the soldiers, but his point was that different techniques of genocide—physical/biological and genocide—need not be perpetrated by the same agents or with the same motives.

So much for responsibility; what about "intent," and how did it differ from the next section called "motivation"? This is how Lemkin put it:

> Just as in all cases of Spanish colonial genocide, we might correlate certain motives with certain intent. When the intent was wilfull destruction of the group of the culture, as in the Caxamalca massacre of the destruction of the emperor, expedience (as in these two cases) or religious fanaticism are often the motives involved. When, however, the intent was merely self-gratification with complete disregard for the group or culture thus victimized, as in the slaughter of the llamas or the widespread loot, greed or the desire for power is often the main motive.[57]

This statement is not very helpful because it borders on circularity; if the intent is self-gratification, the motivation must be greed or power. In his other examples, he tries to distinguish between the two more sharply. Thus fear, religious fanaticism, or "the craze for gold," motivated certain massacres, but the intent was to "take possession of it ['the empire of Peru'] as their lawful territory and to convert the Peruvians to the true faith (214)."[58] The intent, then, was the officially proclaimed will of the Spanish crown such as the proclamation to the Mayans about the Spanish right to their country. "If you do not ['recognize the Church and his Majesty the king as your rulers'], we will war on you, take your wives and children away, dispose of your property and harm you as much as we can 'as to vassals who will not obey and refuse to receive their lord ...' (160)."[59] But Lemkin was not naïve. He regarded the stated intentions of the Spanish as "a mere fiction" because the pre-emptive massacres committed by Cortes were obviously "intended."[60] Seemingly inconsistent, he wrote that the "motivation" of the Spanish in killing "rebellious Indians," was the "self-righteous attitude towards the Indians as Spanish property."[61] So were their actions intended or motivated? It is unclear, but it probably does not matter.

What was clear is the depravity of the Spanish, above all, the soldiery. Lemkin discussed them in the sections entitled "Demoralization," by which he meant their moral degeneration. As adventurers, these men probably possessed few ethical scruples to begin with, and the "moral standards of Europe and more especially of Spain in the 16th century were not high in comparison with contemporary ones," but the circumstances in the colonies, above all, the prospect of enormous riches and Eurocentric contempt for the indigenous culture, led them to atrocities.[62]

> Long after the conquest demoralization not only persisted but became part of the conqueror's and colonists [sic.] behavior. In his eyes, what he did had probably ceased to be anything dishonorable. Only in that way can we comprehend the blood-thirstiness of the Spaniards who amused themselves by hunting Indians with dogs, or their licentiousness as they collected harems of Indian girls . . .[63]

The great distance from Spain made restraint of the colonists all but impossible. "The restricting influence of church, family, community, crown were absent and they could for once revel in feelings of omnipotence."[64] Not that the Church in the "new world" was able to successfully resist corruption either. "The religious foundations and fraternities . . . were often more interested in their exploitation of the Indians than their conversion (466)."[65]

What about those Spanish who opposed the treatment of the Indians? The Spanish government, Lemkin noted, never authorized general slavery, and tried to ameliorate the conditions of the indigenous peoples by a system of "encomiendas" that would aid in their protection and conversion to Christianity. Pope Paul II promulgated bulls against slaveholders. Like Queen Isabella, King Charles V sympathized with the plight of the Indians. He also sided with Las Casas, who became his chaplain. A court faction backed "the humane crusader," but equally the "Council of the Indies" thwarted him.[66] Such tension was evident in the colonies themselves. Thus the friars often inveighed against the treatment of the Indians by the colonists, and took pains to learn their languages, thereby gaining their trust. The Church's insistence that the Indians observe religious services and receive religious instruction earned the ire of the Spanish secular authorities. Padre Olmedo apparently chastised Cortes for forced conversions from the first. The judicial murder of the Inca monarch was similarly opposed by a number of officers.[67] In the end, however, the efforts of Las Casas, who was defamed as an "enemy of Spain," and his supporters amounted to little in the face of the "the general corruption and demoralization at court and in the colonies."[68]

Lemkin was particularly interested in the Spanish rationalizations of their policies and behaviour. In the main, they pointed to the barbarism and savagery of the Indians to justify their rule: human sacrifice, cannibalism, the bloody tactics of battle, their supposed stupidity, superstition, and so on. Explicitly following Las Casas in his controversy with the "pro-genocide historian," Sepulveda, Lemkin doubted the credibility of such claims. Were European claims of cultural superiority sustainable in any event? "Ignored in all these stories is the fact that the Indians possessed a high degree of culture themselves in such places as Yucatan, Mexico and Peru; and that among them vice was not greater perhaps even smaller than in Spain (op. cit. 16)."[69] The barbarians were the Spanish, he wanted the reader to believe.

Perhaps the most significant rationalization of the Spanish colonial genocide was the Spanish claim, based on the theory of universal monarchy, that they were legally entitled to the Americas, and therefore resistance to them was illegitimate, indeed, that it was rebellion that could be violently quashed. Unlike uncritical supporters of western expansion, he did not take this claim on face value. How were the natives to understand the Spanish arrogation of their land? Lemkin was asking. The reading of the Spanish proclamation of sovereignty, whether natives were present or understood it, "seemed quite sufficient, in the eyes of the Spaniards, to produce obedience and justify genocide (see Intro. xi)."[70] The Spanish assumption was ultimately a pretext to kill, a posture inherited by subsequent English thinkers such as John Locke, who wrote that rebellious natives had

> declared war against all mankind, and therefore may be *destroyed as a lion or tiger, one of those wild savage beasts with whom men can have no society or security.* And upon this is grounded that great law of Nature, "Whoso sheddeth man's blood by man shall his blood be shed." Also Cain was so fully convinced that every one had a right to destroy such a criminal, that, after the murder of his brother, he cries out, "Every one that findeth me shall slay me," so plain was it writ in the hearts of all mankind.[71]

Lemkin was effectively arguing that occupations and settlements conducted on such terms—that is, without recognition of indigenous rights and subsequent negotiations—were bound to issue in genocide because resistance was as inevitable as its brutal suppression.[72] In this regard, it may be significant that many of his research notes taken on Native North American conflicts and massacres begin with some kind of Indian uprising. More noteworthy still is that he observed that Hitler regarded the Russian partisan warfare as but a pretext to "eradicate everyone who opposes us."[73]

The victims

As to the victims, despite violent resistance by some, like the Yucatans, the Incas, who put up "heroic resistance" and even once defeated the Spanish, and also the Aztecs, who "revealed the fearlessness and tenacity of the Mexicans,"[74] submission was the prevalent response. Basing his explanation on the testimony of Columbus and Las Casas, Lemkin remarked of the indigenous peoples that their behaviour could be explained "partly because of the typically gentle personality and partly because the Indians were too defenseless to resist the Spanish conqueror and slave-holder."[75] Their belief in the quasi-divine status of the Europeans was a particular impediment to military preparedness. All too often, the outsiders were feted and invited into the heart of the polities where they could decapitate the indigenous regime.

Such a posture did not preclude strategies of escape, such as later absconding from missions, but sometimes they evinced hopelessness, like the collective suicides of villages as the conquistadors approached. Other communities rose in rebellion upon "severe and brutal provocation," but invariably they were "brutally suppressed."[76] Despite such acts of defiance, Lemkin's view was that the Indians were doomed. By quoting at length his bleak summaries of what he called the

"Aftermath" of colonialism, we can see how he viewed the relationship between genocide and culture, and the nature of culture itself.

> The long range after math [sic.] of Spanish conquest was the enslavement of the native population and the *supplantation* of Spanish Christian culture on the ruins of the once high Maya culture. During the long centuries of Spanish exploitation and cruelty the Maya Indians lost their old vitality and personal qualities. The noble character to which even Spanish historians have paid tribute (Arnold and Frost, 331) was crushed out of the Mayas under the oppressive system of "haciendas" (slavery). The Indians gradually became so cowed that they lost all sense of discontent and all desire for resistance (ibid.) Their lives were a long drudgery and humiliation. Sexual abuse of even the youngest girls by the boys of the masters and the master themselves became a matter of course. The Indians even forgot how to object to this supreme insult (op. cit. 332). They have learned how to creep up to their masters after being whipped and to kiss their hand in slavery subservience (op. cit. 333) . . . While the condition of the Indians has been improving since then, under a more progressive Mexican administration, their lot is still hard and their *cultural heritage has been irrevocably lost.* 1,000,000 Indians still speak Maya dialect today. They still till the land as their forefathers had done but they have lost their civilized habits, their remarkable skills and knowledge long ago. (Blom, 83–8)[77]

> After the conquest, Aztec civilization was dead (Vaillant, 265). While at first the conversion of the Indians had only been intended, the colonial exploiters followed on the heals of the conquistadors to exploit and enslave the Indians (ibid.) The death of Indian Mexican culture was gradual but sure (op. cit. 267). Crushed under their labor on the haciendas and in the mines, the Indians, their customs and beliefs, their whole way of life [sic.]. Only the Indian racial type persevered until this day (op. cit. 269).[78]

These quotations reveal three significant features of Lemkin's thinking on genocide and colonialism. The first is that he regarded the extinction of the culture as genocide. It did not require the entire physical extermination of the victims, only the elimination of the culture-bearing strata. As he wrote elsewhere, the "permanent crippling" of a people was tantamount to genocide.[79] The second feature is that he equated culture with high culture, because it is synonymous with national, as opposed to local, peasant, consciousness. In this regard, his comments are reminiscent of his observations about the Nazi attacks on the culture of the victims during the Second World War. "Side by side with the extermination of 'undesirables' went a systematic looting of artworks, books, the closing of universities and other places of learning, the destruction of national monuments."[80] For him, they were part and parcel of the Germans' genocidal policies. (We consider the problem of focusing on high culture as the bearer of group consciousness in the final section.) Finally, Lemkin wanted to show that the conquerors not only destroyed the indigenous culture but replaced it with their own, just as he postulated in *Axis Rule* in relation to the German wartime occupation of Europe. There, we recall, he posited that "Genocide has two phases: one, destruction of the national pattern of the oppressed group: the other, the imposition of the national pattern of the oppressor." In fact, what the manuscripts of Spanish Latin America reveal is that he regarded genocide as comprising an ensemble of policies and practices that attack the "foundations of national life," as he did in relation to the Nazis. The crucial difference between the two cases, however, is that there can be no question of a "coordinated plan" in the American instance. But for Lemkin, genocide had taken place there all the same. Such a plan was actually unnecessary to establish in premodern colonial contexts. Destruction occurred without one. The intention to destroy was evident in particular situations at the local and regional level. Genocide could be said to have occurred there and then, perpetrated by identifiable Spaniards.

Lemkin as researcher

Lemkin's account of the Spanish colonial genocide is problematic. Indeed, we need to stress here that Lemkin's account, based so heavily on Las Casas, cannot be taken at face value. Anthony Pagden, in an introduction to one of the more recent editions of Las Casas' *A Short Account of the Destruction of the Indies*, reminds us that Las Casas wrote to inform, but also to persuade: "It was in the most immediate, most transparent sense of the word, an exercise in propaganda." His account was above all, a petition—a petition for justice. It was also part of a formal debate in the early sixteenth century over the legitimacy of Spanish claims to Indian labour—a debate of which Lemkin was aware.[81] Thus while many of the stories Las Casas told may have been true, others had clear classical antecedents and were part of a "recognizable rhetorical strategy for arousing wonder in the reader." As were the numbers he so often cites, which often ran into the indeterminate but impressive sounding "teeming millions." As Pagden quite conclusively shows, the exaggerated and horrific tales of destruction, and constant inflation of numbers was meant "only to impress upon the reader the literal magnitude of the event." Las Casas, the witness, wanted to unveil the "truth" about what was happening in the New World. Given this context, Las Casas has to be used in a more critical fashion.[82]

Though Lemkin's uncritical over-reliance on Las Casas might make him a poor social historian, his rehabilitation of Las Casas in the aftermath of the Second World War was not, it turns out, unusual. For while Las Casas' account of the Spanish in the Americas may have originally fuelled the rise of the "Black Legend"—a Protestant-inspired distortion of Spanish imperial ventures—from the sixteenth to the eighteenth centuries, an antithetical, equally polemical "White Legend" had taken deep root by the mid-twentieth century. The turn away from the "Black Legend" began in the second half of the nineteenth century. Though as always there was considerable diversity and ambivalence in English scholarship on the Spanish colonial empire, the monumental histories written by the gentlemen-scholars of nineteenth century America began to move away from a general emphasis on Spanish atrocities and ferocious conquests to take a more romantic view of Spanish imperialism. Though the literature still reflected strong anti-Spanish, anti-Catholic prejudices, the influence of Social Darwinism towards the end of the nineteenth century also meant that "even the inferior Spanish variant of white civilization had a role in the [civilizing] mission" of the "superior white race among the lesser breeds." In this scholarship, Las Casas was often depicted, at best, as a well-meaning but misguided and naïve figure. At worst, he was accused of purposefully and wilfully distorting and exaggerating the facts of Spanish imperialism.[83]

The historical debate over the Spanish colonial system and Las Casas grew more intense in the first few decades of the twentieth century. His controversial status was inspired in part by social and political upheavals in both Spain and Spanish America, but also resulted from a more heated discussion of imperialism in general. Interestingly, the rise of America's own empire in the Caribbean and the Pacific (including a victory against Spain, and the violent suppression of native rebels in the Philippines) helped ensure a prominent place for American scholars in rehabilitating Spain's colonial reputation, which reached its height in the aftermath of Franco's victory in Spain. The proponents of the new "White Legend" brought a professionalism to their studies of the Spanish colonial experience, and a relativism that tended to shy away from overt moral judgments (at least of condemnation). As one chronicler of the historiography has put it, Spanish and American historians after 1898 took a "hardboiled" approach that regarded colonial conquest and exploitation as unfortunate but inevitable, and a tendency to assess Spanish colonial policy and practice from the standpoint of Spanish rather than Indian interests. Instead of ignoring Las Casas' over-inflated claims, more confident scholars of the inter-war period took them on and even justified Spanish atrocities. One reputable scholar, Arthur S. Aiton, went so far as to defend reports that Antonio de Mendoza, the first Viceroy of New Spain, had punished Indians during the Mixton War by blowing them from cannons and setting dogs upon them. Aiton, assuming a relativist posture reflecting the mood of the 1920s and 1930s, argued that it was after all "a matter of opinion, admirably expressed by Mendoza," when he claimed that the punishments were necessary as "a lesson in order to strike fear into the Indians."[84]

Significantly, Lemkin may have written in deliberate reaction to this drift in historical scholarship. Though there is no clear evidence that Lemkin read any of the new professional historians (such as Aiton, Bernard Moses, Edward Gaylord Bourne, and Lesley B. Simpson), he did read and rely on one of the older, more romantic proponents of the White Legend, William H. Prescott. Prescott's monumental *History of the Conquest of Peru* (1916; originally published 1847) was Lemkin's chief source for his work on the Incas. But though Prescott assumed a tone of "judicious impartiality," his pro-Spanish leanings were clear. And like other romantic historians such as Parkman, his work asserted a triumphant Christianity and civilization over Indian heathenism and savagery. Though he often gave his Indian subjects a romantic, even heroic character, it was clear that he believed they were doomed to extinction in the face of an expanding superior white civilization. Prescott, then, was neither sympathetic to Las Casas nor the Black Legend. Lemkin, however, plundered his work for evidence while challenging his condemnation of Las Casas.[85]

If this was Lemkin's intention, he was not alone. Lemkin's work was part of a more general post-Second World War historiographic turn away from apologetic and pragmatic interpretations of colonialism and empire, and back towards a more explicit critique of Spanish policy and a more favourable orientation toward Las Casas in particular.[86] Such a movement was evident in the rapid rehabilitation of Las Casas and his reputation. Ironically, White Legend revisionists such as Bailey W. Diffie and Lewis Hanke began this trend when they co-opted Las Casas as representative of Spanish benevolence in their imperial endeavours. The resurrection of Las Casas, however, reached its apotheosis in a very different postwar climate with critical reappraisals such as Juan Friede and Benjamin Keen's edited collection, *Bartolomé de las Casas in History: Toward an Understanding of the Man and His Work* (Dekalb, IL: Northern Illinois University Press, 1971). In a celebratory preface, they noted that in the post-Second World War period, Las Casas' reputation stood higher than ever before, mainly because of his teachings on the unity of mankind, the principle of self-determination, and the right of men to the satisfaction of their elementary and cultural needs—all of which, they asserted, had acquired a new relevance with the defeat of fascism, and the liquidation of colonialism which was predicated on "anti-Lascasian" principles of racism and the right of the strong to dominate the weak. "It is, therefore, a time of full vindication of Las Casas and his ideals," they concluded.[87]

At the same time, however, Lewis Hanke also precipitated a broader movement to put Las Casas and his life and work into historical context, as well as to trace Las Casas' contributions to anthropology, political science, and other fields outside of history. Today, Las Casas is still a popular historical figure for analysis, but few scholars use Las Casas as a primary source for accounts of the Spanish conquest, at least not without careful qualification and corroboration. Most commentators would agree with Pagden's assessment of Las Casas, and recognize that his work was a polemic, written as part of a dialogue among Spanish Colonial administrators and missionaries, and as an early contribution to an ongoing western critique of and debate over colonialism.[88]

Lemkin, Disease, and "biological genocide"

Significantly, Lemkin's reliance on Las Casas blinded him to one of the most significant findings emerging in the 1930s and 1940s—that the population of Indians in the Americas declined precipitously after contact with Europeans because of newly introduced diseases.[89] In Lemkin's account, based on Las Casas, "biological genocide" consisted of exhausted slave mothers not able to nurse their children, and the separation of families by slavehunters. And yet it was not as if he was unaware of the impact of disease in colonial contexts. Writing on Tasmania, he observed that "Many natives died of the white men's diseases. A great many deaths may be laid to the door of the civilizing process which clothed these people of the outdoors who had grown hardy and strong living a life in the open and were suddenly deprived of their physical exercise, and made to live in houses."[90] But only in one place in the American writings, in his discussion of the demographic decline of the Mayans, does he mention disease, observing that "The losses in population were attributable to smallpox, and cruelties to 'reduce revolts.'"[91]

This neglect is puzzling. Though historians were certainly not conscious of the immense magnitude of the death toll caused by diseases that most accept today, most historians were at least dimly aware that diseases had taken some kind of heavy toll. As early as 1883, Hubert H. Bancroft had downplayed the numbers of Indians lost to Spanish cruelties, and even forced removals, but stressed "the effect of climatic changes on persons suddenly transferred from a warm district to cold and rugged mountain regions." And even deaths from these climatic changes, he asserted, were comparatively small when juxtaposed with the "great ravages" that resulted from "diseases following the new civilization, such as small-pox, measles, and probably syphilis."[92]

As Lemkin wrote, scholars were introducing more precision in their calculations and, perhaps more importantly, beginning to challenge the early low estimates of the numbers of Indians in the Americas. Until the mid-1940s, the Indian population of the Americas, north and south, was estimated from the accounts of early colonists and officials and most scholars believed them to be very low. Disputes centred on which reports to regard most, until at the University of California, Berkeley, Sherburne F. Cook began a collaboration with Lesley Byrd Simpson and then Woodrow Borah and developed more reliable calculations both of native populations at the time of the arrival of Europeans and subsequent depopulation rates. Cook, for example, wrote in 1946 of the "Incidence and significance of disease among the Aztecs and related tribes" and acknowledged even then that "for many years students of epidemiology and sociology have recognized the importance of diseases introduced from Europe in the New World," and that the "profound dislocations in population and in economic life caused by smallpox, measles, and similar maladies can scarcely be overestimated." Eventually, Cook, along with others, including Woodrow W. Borah and Lesley B. Simpson, dramatically confirmed the general claims of Las Casas of large pre-conquest Indian populations and catastrophic population decline after the conquest. But whereas Las Casas was all too ready to attribute this decline to Spanish atrocities, the new studies that suggested up to perhaps 90% of many indigenous populations were wiped out by newly introduced European diseases within the first decades after contact. Such claims have so far withstood the test of time.[93]

Given these conclusions, we are left with the question: what would Lemkin have made of the relationship between disease and genocide had he known what we now know about disease and demography? In view of the centrality of intention to genocide, we would expect him to fasten on instances of deliberate infection, like that of Amherst, and to ascribe the balance of cases to the regrettable though non-genocidal consequences of human contact. Certainly, that is the view of some historians who deny a genocidal character to colonialism and western expansion. Steven T. Katz, for instance, is prepared to acknowledge that "sheerly as a matter of quantity the Indian catastrophe [between the sixteenth and nineteenth centuries] is unparalleled."[94] But, in Katz's view, there was nothing that could be done to save the hapless natives, vulnerable as they were to the new pathogens. In fact, the Europeans, like missionaries, did much to keep them alive. There can be no question of genocide.

> When mass death occurred among the Indians of America, and it did occur, it was almost without exception caused by microbes, not militia ... that is, this depopulation happened unwittingly rather than by design, even transpiring in direct opposition to the expressed and self-interested will of the white empire-builder or settler.[95]

This kind of reading is wont to blame the indigenous peoples for their own demise and to regard them as victims of an inevitable process for which no one is responsible: "by being unable to unwilling to change their mores," opined a medical historian in one case, "Hawaiians committed themselves to continuing mortality."[96]

It is highly doubtful that Lemkin would have agreed with this viewpoint because of its undifferentiated approach to the evidence of agency on the part of the Europeans. Given what he wrote about "biological genocide"—the interdiction of procreation by slavery, harems, and so on—he would concur with those who see greater complexity in the causes of the demographic catastrophe. Indeed, it is really the degree to which Europeans exacerbated the spread of deadly diseases that is perhaps the key issue at stake. An initial problem is that, despite extensive research, we do not know for certain how much destruction disease wrought in particular places, and exactly how and why they did so. The evidence simply does not always exist.[97] What we do know is that diseases often struck in certain circumstances created by the European invaders, making its impact far greater that it would have been otherwise. Slave labour camps, for instance, were particularly lethal sites of contagion, as were missions.[98] Disease and "purposeful genocide" cannot be separated so neatly.

Then there was the fact that European action—massacres, expropriation of land, and the like—radically inhibited population recovery after the ravaging of disease.[99] The demographic disaster cannot just be attributed to smallpox and outright killing at "first contact," but also to the subsequent stifling of opportunities for indigenous reproduction. Consequently, as David E. Stannard insists, "the near-total destruction of the Western Hemisphere's native people was neither inadvertent nor inevitable." The picture that emerges is that population decline issued from an ensemble of causes in which human agency was a key component.

> Although at times operating independently, for most of the long centuries of devastation that followed 1492, disease and genocide were interdependent forces acting dynamically—whipsawing their victims between plague and violence, each one feeding upon the other, and together driving countless numbers of entire ancient societies to the brink—and often over the brink—of total extermination.[100]

Without active European intervention, then, the impact of disease would have been far less. This is a proposition that extends rather than negates the

Las Casasian account, and is one, the evidence suggests, with which Lemkin would have concurred.

Genocide and historiography

The stakes are high among those scholars interested in the issue of genocide in the Americas. On the one hand, many regard the application of the term to a case where the major cause of death is largely unintentional (disease) as misleading and mischievous. On the other, historians and social scientists like Stannard and Russell Thornton go so far as to deploy the loaded term "holocaust."[101] So do Native American activists and those who write in their name.[102] Indeed, they counter the claim of uniqueness of the Jewish Holocaust, such as that made by Steven T. Katz, by invoking that privileged status for the American experience: "The destruction of the Indians of the Americas was, far and away, the most massive act of genocide in the history of the world," insists Stannard, while Ward Churchill avers that "The American holocaust was and remains unparalleled, both in terms of its magnitude and the degree to which its goals were met, and in terms of the extent to which its ferocity was sustained over time by not one but several participating groups."[103] Weighing up genocides against another in this way was not how Lemkin proceeded.[104] Given these polemics, it is not surprising that very few practicing historians working on Native American history use the concept of genocide to further their work.

That is not the only reason why the concept is not prevalent in the historiography. Its implication of cultural or racial destruction and the connotation of finality do not sit well with current trends in the social history of indigenous peoples in the Americas that stress Native American persistence and continuity. For Lemkin, and indeed many others who have followed him in attempting to categorize European–Native relations as genocidal, Indians in the Americas could only be victims of European imperialism.[105] While Lemkin and the Berkeley School reflected a more critical stance towards Spain's Indian policies, the Indians themselves for the most part remained passive objects, viewed through the eyes of those that punished, enslaved, or killed them. Indeed, Lemkin and other post-Second World War scholars who were sympathetic to the Indians generally practiced a "victim" history that emphasized the "death" of native cultures, whether through outright physical destruction, or overwhelming acculturation to European "civilization." If Lemkin's work reflected a general postwar disillusionment with self-reinforcing justifications of colonialism, past and present, his aims and interpretive strategy prevented him from fully embracing another emerging historiographical trajectory in the postwar period: towards Indians of the Americas as subjects of historical study, as dynamic historical actors and participants, and as highly adaptive and syncretic peoples.

Even as Lemkin wrote, serious work on Indians in the Spanish colonial period as a distinct unit of study had been underway for at least a few years. Such studies have often been said to have begun with Charles Gibson's *Tlaxcala in the Sixteenth Century*, published in 1952. But several other interesting studies were also available to Lemkin, though not, it seems, taken up. These include the seven volume *Handbook of South American Indians* by Julian H. Steward *et al.*, eds (Washington, DC, 1946–1959), in which Volume II, published in 1946, contains long essays by John Howland Rowe and George Kubler on Inca society on the arrival of Europeans and through the colonial period, based on Indian chronicles, early Spanish accounts, and some archaeological findings. Also neglected by Lemkin were the pioneering works by Ralph L. Roys, *The Indian Background of Colonial Yucatan* (Washington, DC, 1943), and France V. Scholes *et al.*, *The Maya Chontal Indians of Acalan-Tixchel: A Contribution to the History and Ethnography of the Yucatan Peninsula* (Washington, DC, 1948). Significantly, works such as Gibson's *The Aztecs under Spanish Rule* (1964) that took an Indian perspective often vindicated Las Casas' views as they explored in more systematic detail the harshly exploitative Spanish labour and tribute systems. But taking an Indian perspective has also forced scholars to recognize and explore Native American strategies of survival and ultimately, their persistence.[106]

In the years since Lemkin wrote, Gibson's pioneering work especially, but also the influence of anthropologists in the post-Second World War period, has helped radically revise the history of Indians in the Americas. Interdisciplinary approaches, most significantly the combination of historical and anthropological approaches in the newly created field of "ethnohistory," have flourished, and native American historiography has exploded in all kinds of different directions. Most notably for our purposes, however, this trend has included a tendency to adopt a pro-Indian stance, viewing Indians as dynamic agents of history rather than as passive victims of Spanish rule or even a wider and inevitable acculturation process. For example, historians are much more likely now to distinguish between the many different Native American groups that Europeans encountered (rather than "Indians"), to portray the European invasion in terms of small groups of difficult-to-control ethnic European groups inserting themselves into dynamic power struggles and complex relationships between many small groups of difficult-to-control ethnic Indian groups, and to portray the conquest of the Aztec and Inca civilizations as the substitution of one aggressive, expanding, exploitative imperial elite for another.[107] Moreover, though much of this literature has stressed Indian resistance to Spanish and European pressures, scholars have also begun to recognize the degree to which Indians creatively adapted to the arrival of newcomers on their shores, noting the marked continuity and persistence in adaptive strategies between pre- and post-1492 native communities and from there throughout the long encounter with Europeans.[108] Lemkin's single-minded focus on high or elite culture blinded him to the continuity of folk cultures that persisted just as they changed.

This new scholarship highlights an inner tension or dilemma within the field (and perhaps a tension between the focus of those interested in Native American social history, and scholars interested in the history of genocide): whether to focus on and emphasize Indian agency, adaptation, resistance, persistence, and continuity, *or* to highlight the undeniable magnitude of the physical and cultural destruction of Native peoples. By fixating on the genocidal dimensions of the

European invasion, we are forced—like Lemkin—to take a more European-centred approach to indigenous history. We follow the story over the shoulders of European conquistadors, settlers, and soldiers who brought disease, dislocation, and death. We focus on the numbers killed, the cultures destroyed, and the tragedy of contact, colonization, and conflict between different peoples. What we lose in this story is a much richer and nuanced tale of Indian agency and dynamism as diverse groups reacted in different and creative ways to the new challenges presented by the arrival of Europeans. We lose focus on those who individually and collectively adapted to the new circumstances, exploited new opportunities, and ultimately survived. And yet by stressing successful "adaptations" and "negotiations" are we not thereby losing a sense of the human tragedy that accompanied European settlement in the Americas?

A closer look at the chronology reveals that this may only be a question of emphasis and narrative strategy, and not an either/or situation. During the long colonial period, at least, Europeans were rarely able to impose themselves so wholeheartedly on Native Americans in a one-sided way. In the most (in)famous example of European penetration, the conquest of New Spain, the Spanish essentially did what the previous Mexican people had done: inserted themselves at the top of an imperial hierarchy and tried to manipulate it to their advantage. They were supported by some constituent parts of that empire, and opposed by others. Even where they "dominated" there was still much room for "negotiations" because numerically the Spanish could never impose their full will on such vast numbers. Moreover, despite initial losses from the brutality of the Spanish conquest, and despite much larger losses in population due to diseases, the cultural and social history of New Spain and the racial politics of Mexico today would simply not support the genocide thesis, at least not for the whole population and whole historical experience.[109]

The situation was not qualitatively different in North America. As Richard White shows in his book *The Middle Ground*, the vast majority of Native Americans before 1800 were not subject to "European domination," whether physical or cultural. In the colonial period in North America, "negotiations" between Indian tribes and different European groups took place all of the time, indeed in all instances where there was not outright conflict—which was relatively and surprisingly small—or deaths from diseases. Many Native Americans became particularly adept at playing off different imperial powers, and threatening military and trade alliances when they could not get what they wanted from one power. After 200 years of settlement, Europeans "dominated" only a tiny area along the eastern seaboard extending into the continent about 200 miles, and not from want of trying. Of course, some Indian groups had been conquered, or worse, but often even these, we are now learning, were dispersed, integrated into other communities, and are now re-emerging, a process that had been underway among Indians well before the Europeans arrived.[110]

Thus while recognizing the destructive nature of many European–Indian relations, to apply the label of genocide to *all* European–Indian interactions, at least before 1800, is to deny the historical experience of perhaps the majority of indigenous peoples living in North America. The "New Indian history" has taught us that we need to take into account a great deal more nuance and subtlety when thinking about "the" Native American experience in the Americas. After all, the "Indian" in the Americas was a fictional European construction. Ignoring the diversity of historical experiences among different Native American groups is to perpetuate this fiction and commit another kind of destructive act.

Even as he regarded European history as spreading humanistic norms of international law around the globe, Lemkin urged his contemporaries not to regard western expansion in uncritical terms. Occupations of foreign peoples often destroyed or permanently crippled them, that is, they were genocidal. And yet, today it is difficult to follow him in every respect. His equation of culture with high culture meant that he saw its extinction where we can see creative cultural adaptations, if under difficult circumstances. Genocide scholarship needs to pay heed to the extraordinary insights won by modern historiography. Survival and renewal are also part of the story. This does not mean abandoning the Lemkian viewpoint that the terms and structure of European occupation were often arrogant and genocidal. Nor does it mean abandoning the idea that the new settler societies in the Americas gave rise to new nations that often and at different times exacerbated, sanctioned, and legitimated the "eliminationist logic" of these settler democracies.[111] If the Indigenous people possessed agency, so surely did the Europeans, and historians are entitled to identify those responsible for destructive policies and practices.

Notes and References

1 This misunderstanding of Lemkin and his definition is pervasive. It is evident regularly even on the pages of this journal, e.g. Stuart D. Stein, "Conceptions and terms: templates for analysis of holocausts and genocide," *Journal of Genocide Research*, Vol 7, No 2, 2005, p 171.

2 Most of Lemkin's papers are contained in three places: the Manuscripts and Archive Division of the New York Public Library, 42nd Street, Manhattan, New York; the American Jewish Historical Association, 15 West 16th Street, Manhattan, New York 10011; and the Jacob Rader Marcus Center of the American Jewish Archives, 3101 Clifton Avenue, Cincinnati, Ohio 45220-2488. Lemkin's writings discussed in this article are drawn from all three institutions. A number of files pertaining to the Genocide Convention and Lemkin are contained National Conference of Christians and Jews collection held at the Social Welfare History Archives, University of Minnesota. Steven L. Jacobs of the University of Alabama reports that he has been cataloguing and editing 20,000 pages of Lemkin's papers for imminent publication: Jacobs, "Afraid to call genocide genocide? Reflections on Rwanda and beyond," in Robert S. Frey, ed., *The Genocidal Temptation* (Dallas: University Press of America, 2004), p 69. See also his Introduction to Raphael Lemkin, *Raphael Lemkin's Thoughts on Nazi Genocide: Not Guilty?*, Steven L. Jacobs, ed. (Lewiston: Edwin Mellen Press, 1990), pp xv–xvii.

3 He had been fascinated and disturbed by the persecution of human cultural groups since boyhood, and had been indignant that the great powers had not persecuted the architects of the Armenian genocide. See A. Dirk Moses, "The Holocaust and genocide," in Dan Stone, ed., *The Historiography of the Holocaust* (Houndsmills: Palgrave Macmillan, 2004), pp 533–555.

4 Samuel Totten and Steven L. Jacobs, eds, *Pioneers of Genocide Studies: Confronting Mass Death in the Century of Genocide* (Westport, CT: Greenwood Press, 2002). An autobiographical fragment of Lemkin is reproduced as Chapter 19. Incredibly, he appears as just one among 25 other "pioneers." Here the complaint of Israel Charny is apposite: "Even more regrettable are those scholars who, patently, are more concerned with *their* ideas and with *their* political standing in academia or the community than with a commitment to all human lives." Charny, "Foreword," in Alan S. Rosenbaum, ed., *Is the Holocaust Unique? Perspectives on Comparative Genocide* (Boulder, CO: Westview Press, 1996), p xi.

5 For example, Frank Chalk and Kurt Jonassohn, eds, *The History and Sociology of Genocide* (New Haven: Yale University Press, 1990); Helen Fein, "Revolutionary and antirevolutionary genocides: a comparison of state murders in democratic Kampuchea, 1975 to 1979, and in Indonesia, 1965 to 1966," *Comparative Studies in Society and History*,Vol 34, No 4, 1993, pp 796–823; Barbara Harff, "Genocide as state terrorism," in Michael Stohl and George A. Lopez, eds, *Government Violence and Repression* (Westport, CT: Greenwood Press, 1986), pp 166–187; idem, "No lessons learned from the Holocaust? Assessing risks of genocide and political mass murder since 1955," *American Political Science Review*, Vol 97, 2003, pp 57–73.

6 Raphael Lemkin, *Axis Rule in Occupied Europe* (Washington, DC: Carnegie Council, 1944), p 79. Emphasis added.

7 Ibid. emphasis added: "Generally speaking, genocide does not necessarily mean the immediate destruction of a nation, *except when* accomplished by mass killing of all the members of the nation. It is intended *rather* to signify a coordinated plan of different actions aimed at destruction of the essential foundations of the life of national groups, with the aim of annihilating the groups themselves. The objective of such a plan would be the disintegration of the political and social institutions, of culture, language, national feelings, religion, and the economic existence of national groups, and the destruction of personal security, liberty, health, dignity, and the lives of individuals belonging to such groups." Israel Charny's understandable plea that all mass murders must be genocide has no foundations in Lemkin's thought: Charny, "Toward a generic definition of genocide," in George Andreopolous, ed., *Genocide: Conceptual and Historical Dimensions* (Philadelphia: University of Pennsylvania Press, 1994), pp 64–94.

8 The view that the Holocaust can only be understood in the context of the German occupation of Europe as a whole has been enjoined by German scholarship on the basis of massive archival research. See Ulrich Herbert, "Extermination policy: new answers and questions about the history of the 'Holocaust' in German historiography," in Herbert, ed., *National Socialist Extermination Policies* (New York and Oxford: Berghahn Books, 2000), pp 1–52; Christian Gerlach, "Some recent trends in German Holocaust research," in Jeffry M. Diefendort, ed., *Lessons and Legacies: New Currents in Holocaust Research*, Vol VI (Evanston: Northwestern University Press, 2004), pp 285–299.

9 Jürgen Zimmerer, "Kolonialer Genozid? Vom Nutzen und Nachteil einer historischen Kategorie für eine Globalgeschichte des Völkermordes," in Dominik J. Schaller *et al.*, eds, *Enteignet,Vertrieben, Ermordet: Beiträge zur Genozidforschung* (Zürich: Chronos, 2004), pp 109–129; idem, "The birth of the *Ostland* out of the spirit of colonialism: a postcolonial perspective on the Nazi policy of conquest and extermination," *Patterns of Prejudice*, Vol 39, No 2, 2005, pp 202–224; A. Dirk Moses, "Conceptual blockages and definitional dilemmas in the 'racial century': genocides of indigenous people and the Holocaust," *Patterns of Prejudice*, Vol 36, No 4, 2002, pp 7–36; Enzo Traverso, *The Origins of Nazi Violence* (New York and London: The Free Press, 2003); Benjamin Madley, "From Africa to Auschwitz: how German South West Africa included ideas and methods adopted and developed by the Nazis in Eastern Europe," *European History Quarterly*, Vol 33, No 3, 2005, pp 429–464. In an independent line of research, the German scholars Götz Aly and Susanne Heim have been arguing the Holocaust had its origins in a "territorial solution" to the "Jewish question" in east-central Europe in the context of Nazi plans for a more general "ethnic reordering" of the region for German settlers: Aly and Heim, *Architects of Annihilation: Auschwitz and the Logic of Destruction* (London: Phoenix, 2002). See now David Furber, "Near as far in the colonies: the Nazi occupation of Poland," *International History Review*, Vol 26, No 3, 2004, pp 541–579; an overview of the Nazi occupation and the Holocaust in Poland is Dieter Pohl, "War, occupation, and the Holocaust in Poland," in Stone, ed., *The Historiography of the Holocaust*, pp 88–119.

10 The critiques of colonialism by Franceso de Vitoria were well known to international lawyers in this period. See Andrew Fitzmaurice, "Anti-colonialism in western political thought: the colonial origins of the concept of genocide," in Moses, ed., *Genocide and Colonialism*.

11 Lemkin wrote of the "common elements of one generic notion" of the concept: Lemkin, *Axis Rule in Occupied Europe*, p 80. A striking case of such a retrospective projection is Steven T. Katz, *The Holocaust in Historical Context* (Oxford: Oxford University Press, 1994).

12 Tony Barta, "Relations of genocide: land and lives in the colonization of Australia," in Isidor Wallimann and Michael Dobkowski, eds, *Genocide and the Modern Age* (Westport, CT: Greenwood Press, 1987), pp 237–252; idem, "Discourses of genocide in Germany and Australia: a linked history," *Aboriginal History*, Vol 25, 2001, pp 37–56; idem, "Mr. Darwin's shooters: on natural selection and the naturalizing of genocide," *Patterns of Prejudice*, Vol 39, No 2, 2005, pp 116–137; Norbert Finzsch, "'It is scarcely possible to conceive that human beings could be so hideous and loathsome': discourses of genocide in eighteenth- and nineteenth-century America and Australia," ibid, pp 97–115; Jürgen Zimmerer and Joachim Zeller, eds, *Völkermord in Deutsch-Südwestafrika: Der Kolonialkrieg (1904–1908) in Namibia und seine Folgen* (Berlin: Links Verlag, 2003); Dominik Schaller "'Ich glaube, dass die Nation als solche vernichtet

werden muss': Kolonialkrieg und Völkermord in 'Deutsch Südwest Afrika', 1904–1907," *Journal of Genocide Research*, Vol 6, No 3, 2004, pp 395–430; Ann Curthoys and John Docker, "Introduction—genocide: definitions, questions, settler colonies," *Aboriginal History*, Vol 25, 2002, pp 1–15; A. Dirk Moses, ed., *Genocide and Settler Society: Frontier Violence and Stolen Indigenous Children in Australian History* (New York and Oxford: Berghahn Books, 2004); idem, ed., *Genocide and Colonialism* (New York and Oxford; Berghahn, forthcoming); Dan Stone, "White men with low moral standards? German anthropology and the Herero genocide," *Patterns of Prejudice*, Vol 35, No 2, 2001, pp 33–45; Richard H. King and Dan Stone, eds, *Imperialism, Slavery, Race, and Genocide: The Legacy of Hannah Arendt* (Oxford and New York: Berghahn Books, forthcoming). The American Ward Churchill's publications, such as *A Little Matter of Genocide* (San Francisco: City Light Books, 1997), seem to us to be anything but dispassionate and sober considerations of the salient issues, and are not part of this recent research trend.

13 Raphael Lemkin "Description of the project," Lemkin Collection, New York Public Library, Reel 3, Box 2, Folder 1. The chapter on Tasmania has been edited and commentated by Ann Curthoys: Raphael Lemkin, "Tasmania," *Patterns of Prejudice*, Vol 39, No 2, 2005, pp 170–196; Ann Curthoys, "Raphael Lemkin's 'Tasmania': an introduction," ibid, pp 162–169.

14 American Jewish Historical Association, Raphael Lemkin Papers, P-154, Box 10, Folder 8.

15 John Docker analyses these notes and argues that Lemkin extended his definition of genocide in light of his postwar studies of colonialism in "Are settler societies inherently genocidal? Rereading Lemkin," in Moses, ed. *Genocide and Colonialism.*

16 Lemkin and/or his research assistant consulted a greater range of sources for North America than Spanish America and wrote more notes. They are contained at the American Jewish Historical Association, P-154, Box 8, Folder 12. Lemkin may have worked up the North American notes in an essay, but so far, no such text has surfaced. If he did not in the end summarize his thoughts on North American Natives, it may have been because he had no contemporary chronicler (such as Las Casas, see below) to sum up the historical experience of what amounted to several hundred nations over three hundred years. Other sources that Lemkin used to different degrees include S. F. Cook, *The Conflict Between California Indians and White Civilization* (Berkeley and Los Angeles: University of California Press, 1943); Clark Wissler, *Indians of the United States* (New York: Doubleday, Doran, 1940); Clark Wissler, "Population changes among the Northern Plains Indians," *Yale University Publications in Anthropology*, No 1, 1936; Almon Wheeler Lauber, *Indian Slavery in Colonial Times within the Present Limits of the United States* (New York: Columbia University, 1913); F. H. Hodge, ed., *Handbook of American Indians* (Washington, DC: Bureau of American Ethnology, 1907–1910); C. Hale Sipe, *The Indian Wars of Pennsylvania* (Harrisburg, PA: Telegraph Press, 1929); Lewis Merian *et al.*, *The Problem of Indian Administration* (Baltimore: Institute for Government Research, Johns Hopkins University Press, 1928). For the most recent evaluation of Amherst and the smallpox debate, see Elizabeth A. Fenn, "Biological warfare in eighteenth-century North America: beyond Jeffrey Amherst," *Journal of American History*, Vol 86, No 4, 2000, pp 1552–1580.

17 Raphael Lemkin, "Spain colonial genocide," AJHS, P-154, Box 8, Folder 12.

18 Raphael Lemkin "Description of the project," Lemkin Collection, New York Public Library, Reel 3, Box 2, Folder 1.

19 Raphael Lemkin, "Revised outline for genocide cases," AJHS, P-154, Box 8, Folder 11.

20 Raphael Lemkin, "Aztecs," AJHS, P-154, Box 8, Folder 12.

21 Ibid.

22 Raphael Lemkin, "Incas," Jacob Rader Marcus Center of the American Jewish Archives, Collection 60, Box 7, Folder 7/1.

23 Raphael Lemkin, "Yucatan," AJHS, P-154, Box 8, Folder 12. Plainly, Lemkin subscribed to notions of civilization development common among European intellectuals at the time, although it is important to recall his firm commitment to the inherent value of all cultures and civilizations. The purpose of his activism was to protect them from destruction.

24 Ibid.

25 Lemkin, "Incas."

26 Ibid.

27 Lemkin, "Aztecs."

28 Lemkin, "Incas."

29 Lemkin, "Yucatan."

30 Lemkin, "Aztecs."

31 Lemkin, "Spain colonial genocide."

32 Lemkin, "Incas."

33 Ibid.

34 Lemkin, "Spain colonial genocide."

35 Ibid.
36 Ibid.
37 Ibid.
38 Lemkin, "Incas."
39 William A. Schabas, *Genocide in International Law: The Crime of Crimes* (Cambridge: Cambridge University Press, 2000), pp 179f.
40 Lemkin, "Incas."
41 Lemkin, "Spain colonial genocide."
42 Lemkin, "Yucatan."
43 Lemkin, "Spain colonial genocide."
44 Lemkin, "Incas."
45 Lemkin, "Yucatan."
46 Lemkin, "Incas."
47 Lemkin, "Aztecs."
48 Lemkin, "Spain colonial genocide"; "Aztecs"; "Incas."
49 Lemkin, "Incas"; "Spain colonial genocide."
50 Lemkin, "Spain colonial genocide."
51 Lemkin, "Yucatan."
52 Lemkin, "Spain colonial genocide."
53 Lemkin, "Aztecs."
54 Lemkin, "Spain colonial genocide."
55 Lemkin, "Incas."
56 Ibid; Lemkin, "Yucatan."
57 Lemkin, "Incas."
58 Ibid;
59 Lemkin, "Yucatan."
60 Lemkin "Aztecs."
61 Lemkin, "Yucatan."
62 Lemkin, "Spain colonial genocide."
63 Lemkin, Incas."
64 Lemkin, "Spain colonial genocide."
65 Ibid.
66 Ibid.
67 Lemkin, "Yucatan"; idem, "Aztecs"; idem, "Incas."
68 Lemkin, "Spain colonial genocide."
69 Ibid.
70 Lemkin, "Yucatans." On the theory of universal monarchy, see Anthony Pagden, *Lords of All the Worlds: Ideologies of Empire in Spain, Britain, and France, c. 1500–1800* (New Haven: Yale University Press, 1995), Chapter 2.
71 John Locke, *Two Treatises on Civil Government* (London: Routledge, 1884), p 196f; emphasis added. For an analysis of the English reception of the Spanish debates on colonialism, see Andrew Fitzmaurice, *Humanism and America* (Cambridge: Cambridge University Press, 2003).
72 Lemkin, "Aztecs."
73 Lemkin, *Raphael Lemkin's Thoughts on Nazi Genocide*, pp 196f.
74 Lemkin, "Incas"; idem, "Aztecs."
75 Lemkin, "Spain colonial genocide."
76 Ibid.
77 Lemkin, "Yucatan." Emphasis added.
78 Lemkin, "Aztecs."
79 Raphael Lemkin, "Genocide as crime under international law," *American Journal of International Law*, Vol 41, No 1, 1947, p 147.
80 Lemkin, *Raphael Lemkin's Thoughts on Nazi Genocide*, pp 299, 303.
81 Lemkin, "Spain colonial genocide."
82 See Anthony Pagden, "Introduction," in Nigel Griffin, ed., *A Short Account of the Destruction of the Indies* (London: Penguin Books, 1992), pp xxxi–xxxii.
83 See Keen, "Approaches to Las Casas," pp 33–34, 34–35. Cf. Marshall C. Eakin, "Latin American history in the United States: from gentlemen scholars to academic specialists," *The History Teacher*, Vol 31, No 4, 1998, pp 539–561, who notes that scholars of this ilk at the end of the nineteenth century were trying to move away from the general emphasis on the black legend, i.e. that the Spanish had systematically

annihilated native populations through a cruel and ferocious conquest in the sixteenth century. Among the revisionists were Edward Gaylord Bourne (1860–1908) who taught at Yale and wrote *Spain in America* (1904), as well as Lesley Byrd Simpson, at Berkeley, who wrote *The Encomienda in New Spain: Forced Native Labor in the Spanish Colonies, 1492–1550* (Berkeley: University of California Press, 1950). Such scholars (Eakin, "Latin American History," p 541) downplayed by the Black Legend by taking a pragmatic approach to colonial conquest and exploitation that saw it as inevitable. The revisionist program continued well into the 1950s. Cf. Benjamin Keen, "The Black Legend revisited: assumptions and realities," *Hispanic American Historical Review*, Vol 49, 1969, pp 703–719.

84 See Keen, "Approaches to Las Casas," p 40; Arthur S, Aiton, *Antonio de Mendoza, First Viceroy of New Spain* (Durham: Duke University Press, 1927), pp 85, 158n. Keen notes that the revisionist movement in the US was paralleled in Spain and Spanish America, and the three movements reinforced each other. Spanish revisionist historians, for example, repeatedly acknowledged their North American colleagues for their help in undermining the Black Legend. Two years after Franco's victory in Spain had helped enshrine the White Legend as the official version of Spanish colonialism, P. Alvarez Rubiano noted the pioneering efforts of the "North American historical school" in tearing down the "weak foundations of the 'Black Legend'" in his article "Importancia politico-social de las mercedes de 1549 concedidas a los labradores de Tierra Firme," *Revista de Indias*, Vol 2, No 5, 1941, p 133; see Benjamin Keen, "Main currents in United States writings on colonial Spanish America, 1884–1984," *Hispanic American Historical Review*, Vol 65, No 4, 1985, p 663. Keen (p 662) also points to Herbert E. Bolton's role in sustaining the "White Legend": "Bolton ignored or minimized the negative, coercive aspects of mission activity just as he ignored the predatory aspect of military conquest. In effect, he offered a 'white man's burden' defense of Spanish colonialism."

85 J. F. Kirk, ed., 3 vols (Philadelphia, 1873), I: pp 375–378. In his *History of the Conquest of Mexico*, Prescott even asserted that Las Casas exaggerated and distorted his accounts, and that his statistics "came from Las Casas's heart rather than his head." Prescott thought it would have been better had Las Casas' *Brief Account* never been written. Prescott was, it seems, engaged in some distortions himself. See James D. Cockcroft, "Prescott and his sources: a critical appraisal," *Hispanic American Historical Review*, Vol 48, 1968, pp 59–74. Prescott thought Las Casas was misguided and too fixed on the idea of the Indian as a persecuted victim. Critical views of Prescott were emerging even as Lemkin wrote. As early as 1959 David Levin included him as a main protagonist in an analysis and critique of nineteenth century romantic historians. See David Levin, *History as Romantic Art: Bancroft, Prescott, Motley, and Parkman* (Stanford: Stanford University Press, 1959). Lemkin also used the work of F. A. MacNutt, who, like Prescott, thought Las Casa was naïve, and who praised Spanish monarchs for their good intentions and "wise laws." MacNutt, *Bartholomé de Las Casas* (New York: Putnam, 1909), pp 172–173. Most major scholars that Lemkin might have drawn from were highly critical of Las Casas. See, for example, Lesley B. Simpson, *The Encomienda in New Spain: Forced Indian Labor in the Spanish Colonies, 1492–1550* (Berkeley: University of California Press, 1929), p x. Though Simpson (ibid, p x; cf. Keen, "Main currents," pp 664–665) would later soften toward Las Casas in his 1929 monograph, like Bourne he blamed Las Casas for having led astray whole generations of historians with distorted and exaggerated accounts of Spanish cruelties.

86 See Keen, "Main currents."

87 Juan Friede and Benjamin Keen, *Bartolomé de las Casas in History: Toward an Understanding of the Man and His Work* (Dekalb, IL: Northern Illinois University Press, 1971), p xii; cf. Keen, "Introduction: approaches to Las Casas, 1535–1970," p 3; Bailey W. Diffie, *Latin American Civilization: Colonial Period* (Harrisburg, PA: Stackpole, 1947); Lewis Hanke, *The Spanish Struggle for Justice in the Conquest of America* (Philadelphia: University of Pennsylvania Press, 1949); idem, *Aristotle and the American Indians* (Chicago: H. Regnery, 1959).

88 Lewis Hanke, *The Spanish Struggle for Justice in the Conquest of America* (Philadelphia, PA: University of Pennsylvania Press, 1949); Fitzmaurice, "Anti-colonialism in western political thought." The Black Legend and Las Casas still have admirers and proponents. See, for example, Wilbur R. Jacobs, "Columbus, Indians, and the Black Legend hocus pocus," *American Indian Culture and Research Journal*,Vol 17, No 2, 1993, pp 175–187.

89 Las Casas' neglect of disease has also been noted by David Noble Cook and W. George Lovell, eds, *"Secret Judgments of God": Old World Disease in Colonial Spanish America* (Norman, OK: University of Oklahoma Press, 1991), p 241.

90 Lemkin, "Tasmania," p 188.

91 Lemkin, "Yucatans."

92 Hubert H. Bancroft, *The History of Mexico*, 6 vols (San Francisco: History Co., 1883–1888), Vol 3: p 738.

93 Sherburne F. Cook, "Incidence and significance of disease among the Aztecs and related tribes," *Hispanic American Historical Review*, Vol 26, 1946, p 320; John Kicza, "The social and ethnic historiography of

colonial Latin America: the last twenty years," *William and Mary Quarterly*, Vol 45, 1988, pp 470–471; Sherburne F. Cook and Leslie Byrd Simpson, *The Population of Central Mexico in the Sixteenth Century* (Berkeley: University of California Press, 1948); Woodrow Borah and Sherburne F. Cook, *The Population of Central Mexico in 1548: An Analysis of the Suma de Visitas de pueblos* (Berkeley: University of California Press,1960); idem, *The Indian Population of Central Mexico, 1531–1610* (1960); idem, *The Aboriginal Population of Central Mexico on the Eve of the Spanish Conquest* (Berkeley: University of California Press, 1963); Woodrow W. Borah, *New Spain's Century of Depression* (Berkeley: University of California Press, 1951). The extensive literature is registered by Kenneth F. Kiple and Stephen V. Beck, "Introduction," in idem, eds, *Biological Consequences of European Expansion, 1450–1800* (Aldershot: Ashgate Varorium, 1997), xv–xxix.

94 Katz, *The Holocaust in Historical Context*, p 91.

95 Steven T. Katz, "The uniqueness of the Holocaust: the historical dimension," in Alan S. Rosenbaum, ed., *Is the Holocaust Unique? Perspectives on Comparative Genocide* (Boulder, CO: Westview Press, 1996), p 21.

96 O. A. Bushnell, *The Gifts of Civilization: Germs and Genocide in Hawai'i* (Honolulu: University of Hawaii Press, 1993), p 270.

97 Francis J. Brooks, "Revising the conquest of Mexico: smallpox, sources, and populations," *Journal of Interdisciplinary History*, Vol 24, No 1, 1993, pp 1–29; Alfred W. Crosby, "Hawaiian depopulation as a model for the Amerindian experience," in Terence Ranger and Paul Slack, eds, *Epidemics and Ideas: Essays on the Historical Perception of Pestilence* (Cambridge: Cambridge University Press, 1992), p 175; idem, *The Columbian Exchange: Biological and Cultural Consequences of 1492* (Westport, CT: Greenwood, 1972); idem, *Ecological Imperialism: The Biological Expansion of Europe, 900–1900* (New York and Cambridge: Cambridge University Press, 1986).

98 Sheldon Watts, *Epidemics and History: Disease, Power and Imperialism* (New Haven and London: Yale University Press, 1997), pp 84, 91; David E. Stannard, "The politics of genocide scholarship," in Rosenberg, ed., *Is the Holocaust Unique?* p 179.

99 David E. Stannard, "Disease and infertility: a new look at the demographic collapse of native populations in the wake of western contact," *Journal of American Studies*, Vol 24, No 3, 1990, pp 325–350.

100 David E. Stannard, *American Holocaust* (New York and Oxford: Oxford University Press, 1992), p xii.

101 Katz, *The Holocaust in Historical Context*; Stannard, *American Holocaust*; Russell Thornton, *American Indian Holocaust and Survival: A Population History Since 1492* (Norman, OK: University of Oklahoma Press, 1987). An insightful analysis of the uniqueness claims of the Holocaust is Dan Stone, *Constructing the Holocaust* (London: Vallentine Mitchell, 2003).

102 Churchill, *A Little Matter of Genocide*; M. Annette Jaimes, "Sand Creek: the morning after," in M. Annette Jaimes, ed., *The State of Native America* (Boston: South End Press, 1992), 1–12.

103 Stannard, *American Holocaust*, p x; Churchill, *A Little Matter of Genocide*, p 4; cf. Thornton, *American Indian Holocaust and Survival*, p xvi.

104 A non-polemical comparison of the evils involved in the Holocaust, slavery and experience of the Native Americans written in the spirit of Lemkin is James P. Sterba, "Understanding evil: American slavery, the Holocaust, and the conquest of the American Indians," *Ethics*, Vol 106, 1996, pp 424–448.

105 For example, Benjamin Madley, "Patterns of frontier genocide, 1803–1910: the Aboriginal Tasmanians, the Yuki of California, and the Herero of Namibia," *Journal of Genocide Research*, Vol 6, No 2, 2004, pp 167–192.

106 See James Lockhart, "The social history of colonial Spanish America: evolution and potential," *Latin American Research Review*, Vol 7, No 1, 1972, pp 6–45. Lockhart (pp 24f.) notes that such was the impoverished state of knowledge about Indian social history in the 1950s that Gibson had to start from scratch, took methods and sources from Latin American history as it had developed, and ended up writing an institutional-jurisdictional history, with economic overtones.

107 See especially Keen, "Main currents," pp 671–673; Neal Salisbury, "The Indians' old world: Native Americans and the coming of Europeans," *William and Mary Quarterly*, Vol 53, 1996, pp 435–458; Claudio Saunt, *A New Order of Things: Property, Power, and the Transformation of the Creek Indian, 1733–1816* (New York and Cambridge: Cambridge University Press, 1999); Karen Spalding, "Social climbers: changing patterns of mobility among the Indians of colonial Peru," *Hispanic American Historical Review*, Vol 50, 1970, pp 645–664; William B. Taylor, *Drinking, Homicide, and Rebellion in Colonial Mexican Villages* (Stanford: Stanford University Press, 1979); Karen Spalding, *Huarochirí: An Andean Society under Inca and Spanish Rule* (Stanford: Stanford University Press, 1984); Steven Stern, *Peru's Indian Peoples and the Challenge of Spanish Conquest: Huamanga to 1640* (Madison: University of Wisconsin Press, 1983); Camilla Townsend, "Burying the white gods: new perspectives on the conquest of Mexico," *American Historical Review*, Vol 108, No 3, 2003, pp 659–687. For a recent review of some of the general contours of these histories, see Philip J. Deloria, "Historiography," in Philip J. Deloria and Neal Salisbury, eds, *A Companion to North American Indian History* (Oxford: Blackwell, 2002).

108 See especially Neal Salisbury, "The Indians' old world," and Philip J. Deloria, "Historiography," in Philip J. Deloria and Neal Salisbury, eds, *A Companion to North American Indian History* (Oxford: Blackwell, 2002). Cf. Peter Iverson, "American Indian history as a continuing story," *The Historian*, Vol 66, No 3, 2004, pp 524–531.

109 See, for example, Michael Mann's account of Spanish–Mexican relations in *The Dark Side of Democracy: Explaining Ethnic Cleansing* (Cambridge: Cambridge University Press, 2005), pp 76–78.

110 Richard White, *The Middle Ground: Indians, Empires, and Republics in the Great Lakes Region, 1650–1815* (Cambridge: Cambridge University Press, 1991). Cf. Salisbury, "The Indians' old world," and especially Daniel Richter, *Facing East from Indian Country: A Native History of Early America* (Cambridge, MA: Harvard University Press, 2002).

111 Patrick Wolfe, *Settler Colonialism and the Transformation of Anthropology* (London: Cassell, 1999); Mann, *The Dark Side of Democracy*, pp 83–98.

Raphael Lemkin's view of European colonial rule in Africa: between condemnation and admiration

DOMINIK J. SCHALLER[1]

The Polish-Jewish specialist in international law Raphael Lemkin (1900–1959) was not "only" an influential jurist but also a historian, a fact that has been ignored by most genocide researchers up to now. Due to financial problems, deteriorating health, and lack of interest by publishers, Lemkin did not manage to complete and bring out his broad study on genocides from antiquity to the twentieth century which he had been working on for many years. A look at his unpublished manuscripts reveals that Lemkin's historical scholarship was not only dedicated to well-known cases such as the fate of European Jewry or the persecution and murder of the Anatolian Armenians. Many of his unpublished works deal with atrocities committed by European colonialists and settlers in the various "New Worlds." How has Lemkin's intensive preoccupation with colonialism to be adequately understood?

When Raphael Lemkin defined his neologism "genocide" for the first time, he emphasized that this term does not exclusively describe the immediate destruction of an ethnic or a religious group.[2] Rather, he understood genocides as processes and distinguished between two phases, "one destruction of the national pattern of the oppressed group; the other, imposition of the national pattern of the oppressor."[3] And Lemkin specified that this imposition "may be made upon the oppressed population which is allowed to remain, or upon the territory alone, after removal of the population and the colonization of the area by the oppressor's own nationals."[4] Colonialism, thus, plays a central role in Lemkin's concept of genocide.[5] And it was the study of colonial mass murders that provided him with a conceptual framework for analysing the German policy of occupation and extermination in Eastern Europe during World War II.[6]

The question whether the term "genocide" can be applied to cases of extremely bloody suppression of indigenous resistance or even to the colonial situation in general is discussed controversially in the historiography of colonialism. The political and legal explosiveness of this issue becomes apparent if one recalls the increasing number of claims for restitution by the descendants of victims from European colonialism or the trans-Atlantic slave trade.[7] Much attention has recently been paid to the claims of the Herero in Namibia.[8] With the exception of a few stubborn revisionists, most historians finally describe the murder and the enslavement of the Herero by German colonialists 1904–1908 as genocide.[9] Politicians, however, avoid the use of the term "genocide" to classify the events of 1904 in then "German Southwest Africa" if at all possible. Such a confession, they fear, would result in a surge of similar lawsuits against former colonial powers. Philip Musolino, one of the lawyers of the Herero, supports this view: "I don't think there's any doubt, to be candid about it, that, if this case [of the Herero] succeeds, other lawyers and other ethnic groups are going to look at the overall colonial era in Africa. I suspect that events in the Congo would be of interest to historians and as a result to lawyers with respect to similar claims."[10]

Indeed, historians have turned their attention to Belgian colonial rule in the so-called "Congo Free State." But they have a lot of difficulty in classifying the atrocities committed by the Belgians. Although Adam Hochschild, whose publication *King Leopold's Ghost* has heavily influenced the public discussion, admits that the "killing in the Congo was of genocidal proportion," he does not consider it to be a "real" genocide since King Leopold's aim was not the extermination of all the Congolese or of any particular tribes in the Congo.[11] Regardless, some historians speak in a rather undifferentiated way of "the Congo holocaust."[12]

That the UN Convention on the Prevention and Punishment on Genocide does not necessarily require that there be an attempt to exterminate a targeted group physically or in whole is often ignored in these discussions.[13] Similarly ignored have been Lemkin's concept of genocide and his unpublished works on colonial genocides. It is the aim of this article to remedy this neglect by examining how Raphael Lemkin understood the murder of the Herero and Belgian colonial rule in the Congo. Furthermore, Lemkin's attitude towards European colonialism in general and his perception of Africans will be in the centre of interest.

Lemkin on the murder of the Herero

Two typewritten manuscripts on German colonialism and the war of extermination against the Herero 1904–1908 are to be found in Lemkin's unpublished works.[14] Both are undated, but must have been written in the early 1950s.

Lemkin was not well informed about the cultural, socio-economic, and political conditions that determined the life of the Herero in Namibia. For example, the widespread stereotyped idea of the Herero as the outstanding cattle-breeder turns up in Lemkin's manuscripts: "The Hereros' almost exclusive diet of milk and meat made them vitally dependent on their large herds of cattle, for which they had a worshipful devotion. The cattle were believed to belong to the Hereros' ancestors, and as such, were considered sacred, for the Hereros were ancestor worshipers."[15] With regard to his analysis of the colonial war between the Herero and the German Schutztruppe (colonial troops), Lemkin's sources are even more questionable: he relied almost completely on British reports and sources whose aim was to discredit Germany as a responsible and competent colonizer.

Although the European powers had agreed before World War I that their colonial possessions should remain unaffected in case of war, the victorious Allies decided to seize German overseas territories all the same. This procedure was justified with the argument that the Germans were, unlike the British and French, not able to advance the peoples with whom they were entrusted.[16] In the British "Blue Book" of 1919, German rule in Namibia was excoriated:

> As a colonist, the German in South-West Africa, speaking generally, has been a failure. ... When he arrived here he found the natives both rich and comparatively numerous. His sole object seemed, as soon as he felt strong enough, to take the fullest advantage possible of the simplicity of these people and despoil them utterly. When the process did not, by means of the system of trading that sprang up, which in itself was often but a thinly disguised form of chicanery and knavery, go quickly enough, rapine, murder, and lust were given full play with the disastrous results of which we see evidences every day around us.[17]

For British observers and commentators one reason for this "failure of German colonialism" was the inadequate training of German officials who were said to be completely out of their depth in the colonies.[18] Lemkin shared this assumption, and stated that "the German administration was generally carried out by poorly qualified officials."[19] For Lemkin, the cruelty and excesses of violence by German officials and soldiers in the colonies were the consequence of a wrong system of rule:

> In the German colonies no attempt was made to respect native tribal customs or to invest the chiefs with their former dignity and authority. The chiefs were deprived of their privileges and the only authority permitted them was that delegated to them by the German officials, such authority being solely used for the purpose of recruiting forced labour. If the chiefs failed to cooperate in everything demanded of them, they were systematically ill-treated, flogged and imprisoned, even for the most trivial offenses.[20]

The system of "indirect rule" as practised by the British colonial administrations would have been much more humane and could have prevented from outrages, Lemkin believed.[21] But he turned a blind eye to the political realities in German Southwest Africa: up to 1904, the German governor in Namibia depended heavily on cooperation with indigenous chiefs like Samuel Maharero and Hendrik Witbooi.[22] When Lemkin noted that "the Germans introduced the Prussian military system into their rule of the African colonies, a system of cruelty and oppression," he obviously overestimated the power of the German colonial administration in Namibia.[23] In fact, until 1904–1905, the colonial infrastructure in Southwest Africa was rather poor due to the unwillingness of the German chancellors to invest huge sums in their overseas territories.[24] Whether the ruthless treatment of the "rebellious" Herero in the colonial war of 1904–1908 can be traced back to a specific form of German military culture ("Prussian militarism" in Lemkin's words) is livelily discussed in historiography.[25] But it was rather the helplessness of German officials and the insufficiently equipped Schutztruppe as well as the fear of loosing the control in the colony completely that contributed to a "cumulative radicalization" and led to the genocidal war against the Herero.[26] Lemkin's stereotyped image of the Germans as cold-blooded and ruthless militarists ("Prussian militarism was founded on the principles of terror and power"[27]) was certainly influenced by his own traumatic experiences with Nazi Germany during World War II and by contemporary discourses on the nature of German militarism.[28]

Although Lemkin has never used the term "genocide" in his papers to describe the murder of the Herero, there can be no doubts that he regarded his concept of genocide perfectly applicable to the events of 1904–1908. His assessment of the German colonial war in Namibia ("After the rebellion and von Trotha's proclamation, the decimation of the Hereros by gunfire, hanging, starvation, forced labour and flogging was augmented by prostitution and the separation of families, with a consequent lowering of the birthrate"[29]) features the crucial criterions of his definition of genocide:

> Genocide does not necessarily mean the immediate destruction of a nation, except when accomplished by mass killings of all members of a nation. It is intended rather to signify a coordinated plan of different actions aiming at the destruction of essential foundations of the life of national groups, with the aim of annihilating the groups themselves. The objectives of such a plan would be disintegration of the political and social institutions, of culture, language, national feelings, religion, and the economic existence of national groups, and the destruction of the personal security, liberty, health, dignity, and even the lives of the individuals belonging to such groups.[30]

Until recently, the Herero's coping with the far-reaching consequences of the genocide has not been dealt with adequately. The expression "silence of the graveyard" has usually been used to describe the socio-economic and cultural situation of the Herero in post-genocide Namibia.[31] That the Herero had undergone a remarkable process of social and national restructuring was unknown to Raphael Lemkin.[32] He just saw the Herero as helpless victims whose fate was sealed for all time. Moreover, he believed the Herero were committing "race suicide." This theory was very popular at the time of Lemkin and had been promoted by Willem Petrus Steenkamp:

> There exists in South-West Africa a widespread belief that the declining birthrate amongst the Herero is due to a nation-wide determination for committing national or race suicide. This resolution was soon taken after the German conquest, because as a race they could not reconcile themselves to the idea of subjection to Germany and thus loss of independence. ... Having nothing left to exist for as a nation any longer, national suicide was started by birth control of a rigorous nature and artificial abortion."[33]

Believing in this theory, Lemkin specified the method of the Herero to kill themselves: "[The Herero] learned to make a very strong beer called Kari, which means 'the drink of death', brewed from potatoes, peas, sugar and yeast. This drink made the natives wild and afterwards, unconscious for hours. Kari, drunk by the Herero women as well as the men, had a most weakening and exhausting effect on their productive powers."[34] This theory of "race suicide" is highly problematic. The historian Gesine Krüger is absolutely right when she points out that this myth has to be understood as an attempt to blame the Herero women for the fatal consequences of the genocide, namely, the lowering of their birthrate.[35]

Lemkin on the Belgian Congo

In Lemkin's eyes, the imposition of Belgian colonial rule in the Congo and the forced labour of the indigenous population that went with it was an unambiguous genocide. He estimated that 75% of the Congolese population was "wiped out in the space of a few years."[36] His unpublished manuscript on the Belgian Congo is not only interesting in this regard but also reveals Lemkin's perception of Africans. Although he made it very clear that he considered the colonial administration ("from the humble employee of the rubber companies to the King of the Belgians"[37]) to be guilty of the murder and the enslavement of the Congolese, he emphasized that atrocities had usually been committed by Africans themselves who were in the pay of the Belgians. These "native militia" were described by Lemkin as "an unorganized and disorderly rabble of savages whose only recompense was what they obtained from looting, and when they were cannibals, as was usually the case, in eating the foes against whom they were sent."[38] The Belgian system of exploitation only worked thanks to the readiness of some "natives" to support the colonizers, Lemkin believed:

> An ingenious system was devised by the rubber companies . . . Sentries were chosen for their savage characters, and killed and tortured the natives according to the barbaric customs prevalent among primitive peoples, and also in terror of the punishment that would be inflicted on them by the white agents should they fail to collect the required amount [of rubber].[39]

Moreover, Lemkin has stated the spread of diseases and the destruction of traditional indigenous institutions had been above all the result of the native mercenaries' activities:

> The sentries introduced gross and wholesale immorality, broke up family life, and spread disease throughout the land. Formerly native conditions put restrictions on the spread of disease and localized it to small areas, but the black Congo soldiers, moving higher and thither to districts far from their wives and homes, took the women they wanted and ignored native institutions, rights, and customs.[40]

It is acknowledged that Europeans could not have ruled their overseas territories without indigenous collaboration.[41] Therefore, Lemkin is right when he highlights the role of Congolese colonial troops during the period of Belgian rule. But tracing the cruelties in the Congo back to the alleged inborn savagery of the indigenous population is inappropriate and racist.

Concluding remarks

The human rights activist and "father of the genocide convention," Raphael Lemkin, decidedly condemned the bloody suppression of the indigenous resistance in Namibia by the Germans and the excessive exploitation of the Congo by the Belgians. Nevertheless, his critique was not directed at European colonialism in general. On the contrary, Lemkin has been an enthusiastic advocate of colonialism and he considered the "civilization" of the Congo and other parts of Africa by Europeans to be a necessary task. Quite a favourable view of King Leopold II's alleged philanthropic plans to bring peace and prosperity to Central Africa has been taken by him: "Almost all of the hundred articles drawn up at the Brussels Conference were admirable and had they been enforced the natives of the Congo would have benefited immeasurably."[42]

The way Lemkin has perceived Africans can only be described as racist. In his manuscripts, Africans are portrayed as either weak-willed and helpless victims or as bloodthirsty cannibals.[43] His obvious lack of ethnographic knowledge made him misunderstand Africa as "the heart of darkness." Besides, his attitude that Africans themselves have to be blamed for their fate is more than problematic and questions the value of his historical scholarship.

Do these findings diminish Lemkin's significance and reputation? When he was writing, racist views were common and colonial thinking was still widespread; and since he was a child of his time it would be anachronistic to judge him too harshly. Nevertheless, uncritical worship of Lemkin's personality that is quite common among many genocide researchers today is highly questionable as well.

Notes and References

1 I would like to thank Dirk Moses (University of Sydney) for valuable comments on an earlier draft of this article.

2 Raphael Lemkin, *Axis Rule in Occupied Europe* (Washington, DC: Carnegie Endowment for International Peace, 1944), p 79.

3 Ibid.

4 Ibid.

5 For a more detailed discussion of this observation, see the contribution of Michael A. McDonald and A. Dirk Moses in this volume.

6 See Dan Stone's contribution in this volume. The question of continuities between colonial genocides and the Holocaust is hotly debated. See, for example, Jürgen Zimmerer, "The birth of the *Ostland* out of the spirit of colonialism: a postcolonial perspective on the Nazi policy of conquest and extermination," *Patterns of Prejudice*, Vol 39, No 2, 2005, pp 202–224; Birthe Kundrus, "Von den Herero zum Holocaust? Einige Bemerkungen zur aktuellen Debatte," *Mittelweg 36. Zeitschrift des Hamburger Instituts für Sozialforschung*, Vol 14, No 4, 2005, pp 82–91; Dominik J. Schaller, "Kolonialkrieg, Völkermord und Zwangsarbeit in 'Deutsch-Südwestafrika'," in idem *et al.*, eds, *Enteignet-Vertrieben-Ermordet. Beiträge zur Genozidforschung* (Zürich: Chronos, 2004), pp 147–232. See further the contributions in A. Dirk Moses, ed., *Genocide and Colonialism* (New York: Berghahn, forthcoming).

7 Elazar Barkan speaks in this connection of a "new international moral." See idem, *The Guilt of Nations—Restitution and Negotiating Historical Injustice* (New York: Norton, 2000). Michael J. Bazyler has shown how the successful outcome of litigations against Swiss banks and German companies have inspired other victim groups. See idem, "Lex Americana. Holocaust litigation as a restitution model for other massive human rights abuses," in Schaller, *Enteignet*, pp 349–394.

8 See Jürgen Zimmerer, "Entschädigung für Herero und Nama," *Blätter für deutsche und internationale Politik*, Vol 50, No 6, 2005, pp 658–660; Janntje Böhlke-Itzen, *Kolonialschuld und Entschädigung. Der deutsche Völkermord an den Herero 1904–1907* (Berlin: Brandes & Apsel, 2004).

9 See, for example, Jürgen Zimmerer and Joachim Zeller, eds, *Völkermord in Deutsch-Südwestafrika. Der Kolonialkrieg (1904–1908) in Namibia und seine Folgen* (Berlin: Ch. Links, 2003); Larissa Förster *et al.*, eds, *Namibia-Deutschland. Eine geteilte Geschichte. Widerstand, Gewalt, Erinnerung* (Köln: Rautenstrauch-Joest-Museum, 2004).

10 Philip M. Musolino in an interview with Dr Joachim Zeller, Berlin, March 4, 2003. I thank Joachim Zeller for providing me with the recording of this discussion.

11 Adam Hochschild, *King Leopold's Ghost—A Story of Greed, Terror and Heroism in Colonial Africa* (Boston: Houghton Mifflin, 1999), pp 2, 25.

12 See, for example, Georges Nzongola-Ntalaja, *The Congo from Leopold to Kabila. A People's History* (London: Zed Books, 2002), p 20.

13 A rare exception is Robert G. Weisbord who has stated that "injury, physical or mental, and the creation of unbearable conditions, as well as killing, qualify as genocide." Weisbord strictly opposes the view of Hochschild and concludes that "in the case of the Congo all these techniques were employed." See idem, "The king, the cardinal and the pope: Leopold II's genocide in the Congo and the Vatican," *Journal of Genocide Research*, Vol 5, No 1, 2003, pp 35–45, p 35.

14 The first manuscript is incomplete, without title and consists of 17 pages. It is solely dedicated to the fate of the Herero: Jacob Rader Marcus Center of the American Jewish Archives Cincinnati, the Raphael Lemkin Papers, Box 6, Folder 12 (hereon cited as Lemkin, "Herero"); the other paper is longer (52 pages) and entitled "The Germans in Africa." The suppression of the so-called "Maji-Maji Rebellion" in Tanzania and the "Duala Massacres" in Cameroon is also covered in it: Jacob Rader Marcus Center of the American Jewish Archives, Cincinnati, the Raphael Lemkin Papers, Box 6, Folder 9.

15 Lemkin, "Herero," p 2.

16 For a discussion of this argument and its consequences for the decolonization process after World War II, see Jürgen Zimmerer, "Von der Bevormundung zur Selbstbestimmung. Die Pariser Friedenskonferenz und ihre Auswirkungen auf die britischen Kolonialherrschaft im südlichen Afrika," in Gerd Krumeich, ed., *Versailles 1919: Ziele-Wirkungen-Wahrnehmung* (Essen: Klartext-Verlagsgesellschaft, 2001), pp 145–158.

17 Union of South Africa, *Report on the Natives of South-West Africa and their Treatment by Germany. Prepared in the Administrator's Office, Windhuk, South-West Africa, January 1918* (London: His Majesty's Stationery Office, 1918), p 9. Despite of the propagandist intention of the editors the "Blue Book" is an interesting source. It has recently been re-edited and commented: Jeremy Silvester and Jan-Bart Gewald, eds, *Words Cannot Be Found. German Colonial Rule in Namibia. An Annotated Reprint of the 1918 Blue Book* (Leiden: Brill, 2003).

18 Evans Lewin, for example, stated: "Unfortunately the majority of Germany's colonial administrators have not been gifted with ... tact and ability.... Without entering into unnecessary details regarding German administration it may be stated broadly that it was altogether too inflexible and rigid [...], and that it lacked the broader instinct of compromise which has so frequently saved British administrators from errors that might have led to disastrous results." Idem, *The Germans and Africa. Their Aims on the Dark Continent and How They Acquired their African Colonies* (London: Cassell and Company, 1915), pp 111–112.

19 Lemkin, "Herero," p 4.

20 Lemkin, "Germans in Africa," p 18.

21 The concept of "indirect rule" goes back to the British colonial official Lugard. According to this concept the colonial administration should exercise of the colonized peoples through traditional indigenous institutions. See Frederick John D. Lugard, *The Dual Mandate in British Tropical Africa* (London: Blackwood, 1922).

22 For the so-called "System Leutwein," see Helmut Bley, *Kolonialherrschaft und Sozialstruktur in Deutsch-Südwestafrika 1894–1914* (Hamburg: Leibniz-Verlag, 1968), pp 18–185; Jan-Bart Gewald, *Herero Heroes. A Socio-Political History of the Herero of Namibia 1890–1923* (Oxford: James Currey, 1999), pp 29–140; see also Governor Leutwein's own contemporary report: Theodor Leutwein, *Elf Jahre Gouverneur in Deutsch-Südwestafrika* (Berlin: Mittler & Sohn, 1906).

23 Lemkin, "Germans in Africa," p 49.

24 In 1890, Bismarck even had concrete plans to give up the whole colonial project. See Horst Gründer, *Geschichte der deutschen Kolonien* (Paderborn: Schöningh, 2000), p 80.

25 See, for example, Isabel V. Hull, *Absolute Destruction. Military Culture and the Practices of War in Imperial Germany* (Ithaca and London: Cornell University Press, 2005).

26 The expression "cumulative radicalization" was first used by the German historian Hans Mommsen to describe the genesis of the National Socialists' "Endlösung." Jan-Bart Gewald emphasizes the radicalization process of 1904 in his work. See idem, *Herero Heroes*, pp 141–191.

27 Lemkin, "Germans in Africa," p 49.

28 For the criticism of Prussian militarism in Germany, see Nicholas Stargardt, *The German Idea of Militarism. Radical and Socialist Critics 1866–1914* (Cambridge: Cambridge University Press, 1994). Especially the atrocities committed by Germans against Belgians during World War I have contributed to this discourse in Great Britain. See John Horne and Alan Kramer, *German Atrocities, 1914. A History of Denial* (New Haven: Yale University Press, 2001).

29 Lemkin, "Herero," p 16.

30 Lemkin, *Axis Rule*, p 90.

31 See Horst Drechsler, *Südwestafrika unter deutscher Kolonialherrschaft. Der Kampf der Herero und Nama gegen den deutschen Imperialismus (1884–1915)* (Berlin (DDR): Akademie Verlag, 1966), p 260.

32 For the national restructuring of the Herero, see Jan-Bart Gewald, "Die Beerdigung von Samuel Maharero und die Reorganisation der Herero," in Zimmerer and Zeller, *Völkermord in Deutsch-Südwestafrika*, pp 171–179; Gesine Krüger, *Kriegsbewältigung und Geschichtsbewusstsein. Realität, Deutung und Verarbeitung des deutschen Kolonialkriegs in Namibia 1904 bis 1907* (Göttingen: Vandenhoeck & Ruprecht, 1999).

33 Willem Petrus Steenkamp, *Is the South-West African Herero Committing Race Suicide?* (Cape Town: Unie-Volkspers, 1944), p 8. For the contemporary social-Darwinist discourse on the "natural dying out" of human races, see Patrick Brantlinger, "Dying races: rationalising genocide in the nineteenth century," in Jan Nederveen Pieterse and Bhikhu Parekh, eds, *The Decolonization of Imagination: Culture, Knowledge and Power* (London: Zed Books, 1995), pp 43–56.

34 Lemkin, "Herero," p 16.

35 Krüger, *Kriegsbewältigung*, p 145.

36 New York Public Library, Manuscripts and Archives Division, the Raphael Lemkin Papers, Box 3, the Belgian Congo, p 10. Estimates of the death toll in the Congo vary to a high degree since the first census of the indigenous population was only made in 1924. Most historians estimate that the population of the Congo has halved during the period of Belgian rule because of slave labour and diseases. See Jean Stengers and Jan Vansina, "Western Equatorial Africa: King Leopold's Congo, 1886–1908," in John D. Fage and Roland Oliver, eds, *Cambridge History of Africa, Volume 6: c.1870—c.1905* (Cambridge: Cambridge University Press, 1985), pp 315–158.

37 Lemkin, "Congo," p 88.

38 Ibid, p 9.

39 Ibid, p 89. Lemkin also pointed out that the German rule in Africa had been based on the same principle: "The African natives have always been divided into two categories: The peacable and the warlike, and the Germans turned this situation to their own advantage. The warrior tribes were turned into tools of the German army and were thoroughly trained, ferociously disciplined, and given practically unlimited power over all other natives. The word of a German soldier was always believed rather than that of a subject native, and thus the native soldiers were free to tyrannize over their fellows, giving fee rein to their savage lust for murder and rapine." Lemkin, "Germans in Africa," p 49.

40 Lemkin, "Congo," p 26.

41 See Ronald Robinson, "Non European foundations of European imperialism: sketch for a theory of collaboration," in Roger Owen and Bob Sutcliffe, eds, *Studies in the Theory of Imperialism* (London: Longman, 1972), pp 117–141; Jürgen Osterhammel, *Kolonialismus. Geschichte. Formen. Folgen* (München: C. H. Beck, 1995), pp 70–76.

42 Ibid, p 10.

43 See, for example, Lemkin, "Congo," pp 9, 25.

Raphael Lemkin on the Holocaust

DAN STONE

> For the moral point of this matter is never reached by calling what happened by the name of "genocide" or by counting the many millions of victims: extermination of whole peoples had happened before in antiquity, as well as in modern colonization. It is reached only when we realise that this happened within the framework of a legal order and that the cornerstone of this "new law" consisted of the command "Thou shalt kill," not thy enemy but innocent people who were not even potentially dangerous, and not for any reason of necessity but, on the contrary, even against all military and other utilitarian considerations. The killing program was not meant to come to an end with the last Jew to be found on earth, and it had nothing to do with the war except that Hitler believed he needed a war as a smoke screen for his non-military killing operations; those operations themselves were intended to continue on an even more grandiose scale in time of peace. (Hannah Arendt[1])

Raphaël Lemkin (1901–1959) is, after many years of obscurity, well known today as the man who coined the term "genocide" and whose tireless campaigning led to the framing and adoption of the UN Convention on Genocide in 1948. He is, in other words, remembered as a human rights campaigner and international jurist. As a historian he has been neglected. Yet his work was based on substantial historical scholarship, since only with reference to mass killings throughout history, from ancient times to his own day, was Lemkin able to formulate clearly the notion of "genocide" to his own and, eventually, others' satisfaction. Lemkin did not restrict the definition of his term so that it referred solely to the murder of the Jews in Nazi-occupied Europe; his interest in the nullification of peoples emerged in his teenage years, around the time of the Armenian genocide.[2] But it was the genocide of the Jews, above all, that provided him with the main impetus for his research and for his campaign to have the crime of genocide incorporated into international law. This article will examine what Lemkin knew about the genocide of the Jews—not yet called the "Holocaust"—as he was writing his book *Axis Rule in Occupied Europe* (1944), and ask to what extent his analysis of the situation as presented in that book and his other writings on Nazi Germany have stood the test of time. Given the size and sophistication of the historiography of the Holocaust, it would be tedious merely to measure Lemkin's achievement against what scholars now know. Yet I will argue that Lemkin's insights into the persecution of the Jews under Nazi rule, though partial, were largely accurate and able to grasp the extraordinariness of what was transpiring in a way that few other commentators managed at the time.

In order to understand the conceptual framework through which Lemkin understood what we now call the Holocaust, a lengthy quotation from *Axis Rule* is necessary. Here Lemkin sets out what is meant by the term "genocide":

> Genocide is effected through a synchronized attack on different aspects of life of the captive peoples: in the political field (by destroying institutions of self-government and imposing a German pattern of administration, and through colonization by Germans); in the social field (by disrupting the social cohesion of the nation involved and killing or removing elements such as the intelligentsia, which provide spiritual leadership—according to Hitler's statement in *Mein Kampf*, "the greatest of spirits can be liquidated if its bearer is beaten to death with a rubber truncheon"); in the cultural field (by prohibiting or destroying cultural institutions and cultural activities; by substituting vocational education for education in the liberal arts, in order to prevent humanistic thinking, which the occupant considers dangerous because it promotes national thinking); in the economic field (by shifting the wealth to Germans and by prohibiting the exercise of trades and occupations by people who do not promote Germanism "without reservations"); in the biological field (by a policy of depopulation and by promoting procreation of Germans in the occupied countries); in the field of physical existence (by introducing a starvation rationing system for non-Germans and by mass killings, mainly of Jews, Poles, Slovenes, and Russians); in the religious field (by interfering with the activities of the Church, which in many countries provides not only spiritual but also national leadership); in the field of morality (by attempts to create an atmosphere of moral debasement through promoting pornographic publications and motion pictures, and the excessive consumption of alcohol).[3]

It may seem strange at first to see listed side by side the mass murder of population groups and the promotion of pornography and alcohol consumption. For some scholars, it is already unacceptable to mention the mass murder of the Jews in the same breath as that of other groups. Yet, Lemkin employed a logic that is clear in his explanation of what constitutes genocide. Genocide, according to Lemkin, does not simply mean mass murder—this remains a common misconception today; the UN Genocide Convention is quite clear on this point—but can be brought about by various means. "Generally speaking," Lemkin writes:

> genocide does not necessarily mean the immediate destruction of a nation, except when accomplished by mass killings of all members of a nation. It is intended rather to signify a coordinated plan of different actions aiming at the destruction of essential foundations of the life of national groups, with the aim of annihilating the groups themselves. . . . Genocide has two phases: one, the destruction of the national pattern of the oppressed group; the other, the imposition of the national pattern of the oppressor.[4]

Indeed, although in the 1930s Lemkin used the term "extermination" before he coined his neologism,[5] it was likely, he argued in 1945, that "the machine gun" would be used "as a last resort" rather than as the first instinct of the oppressor.[6] The recent revival of interest in prosecuting genocide has also led courts to interpret the Convention along the same lines.[7] The destruction of human groups, the crime that came to be known as genocide, and the destruction of cultural and artistic works of these groups, which came to be known as cultural genocide, were originally termed by Lemkin the new crimes of barbarism and vandalism.[8] The latter, to Lemkin's regret, was not explicitly incorporated into the UN Genocide Convention.[9]

Lemkin's definition of genocide, the way in which he helped frame the UN Convention on Genocide, and the subsequent uses to which that convention have been put, are not, however, the main concerns of this article. Bearing in mind his definition, it will analyse Lemkin's writings on Nazism and the Holocaust. Although *Axis Rule in Occupied Europe* was Lemkin's crowning achievement, it is important to note that he wrote several other studies of Nazism: one untitled, full-length manuscript that was envisaged as a section of his projected three-volume history of genocide, published in 1992 by Steven Jacobs; and an unpublished (and probably unpublishable) manuscript, a sketchy first draft entitled "The Hitler case."[10] Each contributes to our understanding of Lemkin's position, and reveals the extent to which his insights adumbrated later historiographical concerns.

Yet Lemkin, it is important to remember, was not writing as a historian. His methodology was not one that would be regarded today as satisfactory for producing significant contributions to the historiography of Nazism and the Holocaust. Rather, he saw his studies as contributions to jurisprudence and international law, in particular to defining and explicating the crime of genocide. In undertaking this task, though, Lemkin necessarily studied and categorized past events in some detail. Even more important, when writing about Nazism in particular, Lemkin was writing about events that were either still ongoing (*Axis Rule*) or were in the very recent past (*TNG*, *HC*). This makes his achievement in identifying many of the issues that were to become central to later historiography all the more striking. It also means, however, that his writings were not written as historical narratives, nor even as systematic analyses of the nature of the Nazi regime. They are, rather, detailed guides through the mass of evidence compiled at the Nuremberg Trials supplemented by Lemkin's stress on legal matters and his tantalizingly brief comments.

What is immediately striking about Lemkin's interpretation of Nazi genocide—as the epigraph from Arendt indicates—is the fact that law lies at its centre. Law was, unsurprisingly, key to Lemkin's thinking, and most of *Axis Rule* is devoted to setting out the legal framework of the German occupation regime, analysing decrees and the nature of the administration. In his *Thoughts on Nazi Genocide* this insistence on law led Lemkin to overemphasize the importance of Hans Frank, leading Nazi lawyer and later General Governor of Poland (the General Government was the part of central Poland occupied by Germany but not incorporated into the Reich). The space that Lemkin devoted to Frank is understandable in terms of Lemkin's legal approach, but does not accurately reflect Frank's (comparative lack of) importance in the regime, especially where Jewish policy was concerned.[11]

Lemkin's emphasis on Frank is a reminder that he was writing before the mass of historical research on the Third Reich and the Holocaust that exists today.

Unsurprisingly, then, Lemkin did not always get things right. In the same way that the judges at Nuremberg refused to believe that no gassings took place at Dachau, Lemkin was under the impression that Bergen–Belsen was an extermination camp, which it was not. Similarly, he placed more emphasis on the Wannsee Conference of January 20, 1942 than most historians would do today, seeing it—quite understandably—as the moment at which the "final solution" was decided on.

These errors are forgivable, if one considers the fact that Lemkin, like other early scholars of Nazism, relied primarily on the documents gathered at the Nuremberg Trials for his information. These had not yet been examined in the kind of depth that would clarify the nature of the various institutions and decision-making procedures in Nazi Germany. Nor, as courtroom documents, were they arranged in order to facilitate the work of historians. Nevertheless, through his own substantial reading and working through the documents available to him, Lemkin identified a number of key issues. These merit further examination, since they remain central to debates on the nature of Nazism and the Holocaust.

The first of these is what is now referred to as "political religion," a formula that has been used in recent years (especially since the end of the Cold War and the return to popularity of totalitarianism theory) to explain the appeal of both fascism and communism. It is intended to suggest that what motivated followers of these ideologies was less to do with rational choice and more to do with a kind of need for community and devotion in a modernized world in which "traditional" forms of affiliation had broken down. Anthropologists, and anthropologically-minded historians and philosophers, especially, have indicated how the rituals, structures, and rhetoric of these regimes gave rise to forms of emotional attachment that liberal parliamentary regimes rarely generate.[12] As Lemkin noted: "modern technical means alone do not explain the Nazi enigma. It is an enigma how a highly civilized nation like the Germans could have been led to acquiesce in a regime of oppression and murder" (*TNG*, p 189). And he went on to provide an explanation that accords well with the findings of those who employ the idea of Nazism as "political religion": "We find a leader, bewitched by his own twisted conviction and an enormous power to bewitch others. We find a small clique of followers, imbued by the same fanatical spirit and willing to execute his orders, and we find a large mass of people who follow blindly or remain indifferent, except for few who either go into exile or underground" (*TNG*, pp 189–190). Even the genocide committed by Nazi Germany could be seen, according to Lemkin, as part of a spiritual or sacred project to revitalize the German *Volk*, or bring about its salvation: "Germany has transformed an ancient barbarity into a principle of government by dignifying genocide as a sacred purpose of the German people."[13] But he added a more prosaic explanation, one that accorded well with the idea of totalitarianism that was current as he was writing in the 1950s: "crime committed by the State in a regime in which a state and party are one, and in which popular control is prevented by the absence of freedom of thought, freedom of expression and free election is, from the point of view of the criminal, the easiest to commit" (*TNG*, p 287).

Having written these words, though, Lemkin appears to contradict them when he goes on to describe the killings themselves. The notion of genocide as a "sacred purpose" does not necessarily imply that its perpetrators act in a frenzy or out of bloodlust,[14] but it still comes as something of a surprise when Lemkin writes that "Almost the most frightening aspect of the Nazi mass murders is the cold, scientific manner in which they were committed" (*TNG*, p 226). With these words, Lemkin appears to anticipate the arguments of the functionalist historians of the 1970s and 1980s, such as Martin Broszat and Hans Mommsen, although the notion of "factory-line murder" was also commonplace in the early studies of the Holocaust. Léon Poliakov, for example, devoted a whole chapter of his pioneering study, *Harvest of Hate*, to "the industry of death," and opened it by asserting that "German technical genius made it possible to set up an efficient and rationalized industry of death within a few months."[15] But Lemkin also seems to foreshadow the "ordinary men" debate of the 1990s,[16] noting that "The striking fact emerged at Nuremberg and at the subsequent trials that most of the defendants had come from good homes, had had good education and somehow continued to convey the impressions of normal good citizens. They did not look like fiends and they used the words 'good' and 'bad' as if they had the same meanings for them as for their listeners" (*TNG*, p 229). This combination of cold-blooded, scientifically-planned mass murder being carried out by men who were in all respects thoroughly unremarkable (save, in a rather circular way, that they were perpetrators of genocide) appears to sit uneasily with the view put forward by Lemkin of Nazism as a radical racist ideology to which its followers adhered as if it were a deeply-held faith. But Lemkin, writing before these historiographical debates that were to follow, provides little in the way of analysis in order to unite these potentially contradictory explanations.

There are other instances where Lemkin anticipates later historiographical concerns. For example, he devoted considerable space to discussing the role of the *Wehrmacht*, a subject that was far from popular at the time he wrote his manuscript *Thoughts on Nazi Genocide*, and which still has the power to provoke strong emotions, as the storm in Germany over the *Wehrmachtsausstellung* recently revealed. Lemkin quotes the infamous directives given by von Reichenau and von Brauchitsch in 1941, and asserts unequivocably that "The Army cooperated closely in the wholesale slaughter of Jews" and that "Even where the Wehrmacht did not actually participate in the killings, they assisted by arresting Jews and turning them over to the Einsatzgruppen" (*TNG*, p 274). In the 1950s, when most western governments were busy finding reasons to exculpate leading Wehrmacht generals leaving them fit to fight the Cold War against the common communist enemy, these were brave words.

In another instance, Lemkin refers to a subject that has only very recently been investigated in detail by historians: the plunder of Jewish property. Historians have for decades written about the economic isolation of the Jews in Germany, and have discussed in outline the process of "Aryanization." But recently there have been studies of Aryanization on a local level that reveal the extent of complicity of ordinary citizens (in buying goods at "Jew markets," for instance).[17] Similarly, the continent-wide scale of the robbery of Jewish-owned art and property has come under close scrutiny of late.[18] Key to this enormous process of robbery, which was a Europe-wide and not solely a German effort, was the *Einsatzstab Rosenberg*, an outfit that has only been researched in any detail very recently by historians such as Martin Dean and Frank Bajohr. In the chapter of *TNG* entitled "Losses" (again, note the legal framework), Lemkin noted the importance of this unit. Although Lemkin clearly knew little about it and offers little information other than the fact of its existence, he nevertheless showed that he was able to identify certain aspects of the Nazi genocidal machine—by virtue of the fact that he was interested in processes other than simply killing—that have started to occupy historians only in the post-Cold War context of understanding the massive complicity that underwrote what previously was seen as solely a German undertaking. Lemkin noted in the context of the *Einsatzstab Rosenberg* that "Side by side with the extermination of 'undesirables' went a systematic looting of artworks, books, the closing of universities and other places of learning, the destruction of national monuments" (*TNG*, p 299). Again, it is because Lemkin had a concept of cultural genocide that he was as sensitive to these aspects of Nazi occupation as he was to the mass murder they committed.

There are then several themes in Lemkin's work that connect with recent trends in the historiography of the Holocaust: the "return of ideology"; the role of the Wehrmacht and agencies other than the SS in the genocide; the theft of Jewish property across Europe; Nazism as a "political religion"; the genocide of the Jews being only one aspect of Nazi ambitions where "population policy" was concerned; the links between Nazi genocide and other genocides. But it is the last two that mark Lemkin's real achievement as a historian of the Holocaust.

On population policy, the favour with which Lemkin's work is currently viewed is soon explained. Lemkin set out quite clearly that Nazi genocide was one of the most clear-cut examples of stated intention that one could hope to find: "Seldom in history has a murderer so cynically announced his intentions as did the Nazis. With them, murder was neither defense nor did they try to masquerade it in any way. They intended to do away with the Jews, the Gypies, the 'inferior' races like the Poles and other Slavs—with the exception of the strong, dumb workhorses" (*TNG*, p 154). But he understood what we know as the Holocaust only in the broader context of Nazi demographic plans: "The Nazis were out to eliminate not only groups of people like the Jews, but to destroy all the inhabitants of an area, along with all their cultural manifestations, in order to create 'space' for their own people" (*TNG*, p 168); "Genocide was not restricted to extermination of the Jewish people or the Gypsies. It was applied in different forms to Yugoslavia, to the non-German inhabitants of Alsace-Lorraine, to the people of the Low Countries and of Norway. The technique varied from nation to nation, from people to people. The long-term aim was the same in all cases" (*TNG*, p 171). The example of the Holocaust, then, which many scholars see as unique, suggested to Lemkin by contrast not only that mass killing is not the only way to carry out genocide but also that "genocide" rather than "mass killing" is the more helpful category. Thus he subsumed the attacks on the various occupied people of

Europe under that term, without seeing the different approaches to those peoples taken by the Nazis as of prime importance.[19] Nazi policies as a whole led Lemkin to argue, at the very start of *Axis Rule*, that "The picture of coordinated German techniques of occupation must lead to the conclusion that the German occupant has embarked upon a gigantic scheme to change, in favour of Germany, the balance of biological forces between it and the captive nations for many years to come" (*AR*, p xi).

The most significant aspect of his analysis of Nazi genocide is the fact that at every turn Lemkin does not distinguish between the fate of the Jews ("the Holocaust") and that of other victims of Nazism; rather, he sees Nazi genocidal policy as a unitary phenomenon, although he does distinguish between "racial genocide" such as characterized the genocide of the Jews and the Gypsies, and "national genocide," as was committed with the aim of acquiring Polish, Russian, and Ukrainian territory (*HC*, pp 1–2). For example, when discussing the establishment of extermination camps and slave labour plants Lemkin notes that "These two plans were inconsistent because a Jew consigned to the gas chamber was a worker lost and because the conditions in which slave workers were forced to live ensured that they would not be fit to work for very long." Lemkin does not see the fate of the Jews as somehow "special" or separate from broader Nazi ambitions of reshaping Europe's demography through radical measures of extermination, expulsion and forced resettlement. Similarly, Lemkin devotes considerable space to the fate of Soviet POWs under the Third Reich (*TNG*, pp 99–102) and civilians (*TNG*, pp 102–110).

Lemkin's picture of the Holocaust, then, was one that was based on immensely detailed knowledge of the occupation regimes, especially their legal frameworks. He relied heavily on official Third Reich publications, such as the *Reichsgesetzblatt* (Reich legal code) and corresponding publications from German-occupied and Axis lands, such as the Romanian *Monitorul oficial* or Vichy France's *Journal officiel de la République Française*. Many of the characteristics of Nazi rule that Lemkin identified have become key to the historiographical debates that have raged ever since. But perhaps Lemkin's most original contribution, and one that is really only now being appreciated, is his inclusion of the murder of the Jews in a wider policy for the demographic reshaping of Europe. Historians such as Götz Aly, Debórah Dwork and Robert Jan Van Pelt have shown the extent to which the genocide of the Jews was part of a broader plan for the "resettlement" of ethnic Germans and the expulsion or murder of millions of Slavs, as encapsulated in the *Generalplan Ost* (General Plan East). Where Lemkin does not adumbrate contemporary concerns is in his failure to see the attack on the Jews as driven by a radical ideology. Rather than seeing racism as central to Nazism, he argued, in the manner of Franz Neumann, that "race theory served the purpose of consolidating internally the German people" (*HC*, p 2).[20] Today historians accept that the murder of the Jews was not the full extent of the Nazis' ambitions, but they understand that there are good reasons why the Jews were targeted first and most tenaciously, and equally that the Jews held a special place in the Nazi *Weltanschauung*. Nevertheless, Lemkin's contribution to the historiography of the Holocaust lies in his incorporation of the genocide of the Jews in the broader framework of Nazi population policy. As he noted at the start of *The Hitler Case*, "The Nazi plan of Genocide was related to many peoples, races, and religions, and it is only because Hitler succeeded in wiping out six million Jews, that it became known predominantly as a Jewish case" (*HC*, p 1).

Lemkin wrote more about the Holocaust than about any other genocide. But it is vital to bear in mind that, just as he did not separate the fate of the Jews from that of Nazism's other victims, so he did not single out the genocide of the Jews as falling into a separate category (as some historians today distinguish "Holocaust" from "genocide"). His comments on the Holocaust make sense only in the light of Lemkin's detailed studies of other genocides, from examples in antiquity to the annihilation of the indigenous Tasmanians to Armenia. Indeed, these earlier genocides provided Lemkin with a conceptual framework for understanding German actions: that of colonialism. Given the extent to which scholars today are pursuing the links between colonialism, genocide, and the Holocaust, it is striking to read Lemkin writing decades ago that

> Nazi Germany embarked upon a gigantic plan to colonize Europe, and since there are no free spaces local populations had to be removed in order to make room for Germans. Nazi Germany did not have a fleet to protect overseas colonial possessions. Moreover Germany had never [sic] good experiences in the past with overseas colonization. It was thus much simpler to colonize the European continent. (*HC*, p 1)

He placed more emphasis on Alfred Rosenberg than many other historians did or still do (for the obvious reason that he, like Frank, was not the real wielder of power in the Nazi empire), and noted especially Rosenberg's imperialist ambitions. Lemkin had a personal connection to the Holocaust in a way that he did not with the other events he studied; this, the extremity of the Holocaust, and the simple facts of where and when he wrote mean that the Holocaust loomed large in his oeuvre. But it did so in order that Lemkin could formulate a broad theory and definition of genocide, in which the Holocaust served as a prime example, not as an exception. Numerous scholars have raised objections to Lemkin's and, subsequently, the UN Convention's definition of genocide—for being both too narrow and too broad—but in this context it suffices simply to note that for Lemkin the genocide of the Jews illustrated not a "unique" occurrence but a phenomenon that had a long and ignoble history.

However, Lemkin was of course not the only person writing on the genocide of the Jews at this time. Although, as many historians have noted, the first decade or so after the war was marked by a striking silence on the issue where professional historians were concerned—in contrast to the efforts of survivor groups to produce memoirs and *Yizker-Bikher*, or mainstream society to find ways of not talking about it—there were nevertheless some attempts made to open a scholarly discussion of what was naturally still a raw and emotionally-debilitating open wound. Indeed, Lemkin himself relied heavily on the works of some of these scholars, such as Max Weinreich and Joseph Wulf, in his own research.

For example, the publications of the New York-based Institute of Jewish Affairs are proof that it was possible, from the late stages of the war onwards, to produce balanced and clear assessments of what was occurring under Nazi rule without underestimating the extent of the catastrophe. Gerhard Jacoby's 1943 discussion of the occupation of the Czech lands is a case in point. Like Lemkin, Jacoby relied heavily on a legal framework in order to make sense of what was going on. And he did not shrink from portraying the extent of the Jews' suffering. Much of the book is taken up with a sophisticated rendering of the gradual process of the appropriation of Jewish property and the deprivation of the Jews' legal existence in Bohemia and Moravia, leading step by step to the "complete physical extinction" of the Jews, "in full accord with the example of Germany itself."[21] Jacoby provides an in-depth analysis of the decrees and various offices involved in this process and notes the "legal" organization of a "racial state": "The Nazi masters of the Protectorate did not neglect the final steps of liquidating the Jews of Bohemia–Moravia 'legally', as well as in fact." But he finally also notes the inevitable failure of the racial principle for ordering society: "The racial caste state could not form the basis of an organized society; Nazism could accomplish only organized annihilation."[22] In 1943 this understanding of the centrality to Nazism of race and law as intertwined principles was quite an original insight. Lemkin was not the only one to make it.

Nor was he the only one to articulate with clarity what was happening to the Jews, and why. It has been well established that in the liberal democracies, the idea that the Jews were being exterminated was hard to grasp, both because of the history of World War I terror propaganda, and because (according to some historians) the targeting of particular groups for no reason other than their membership of that group ran counter to the "liberal imagination." The publications of the IJA sought to dispel these comforting thoughts, and to drive home the racist principles on which Nazism lay, and the consequences to which this state-initiated racism had led. In his study of the persecution of the Jews, Boris Shub, the editor of the IJA, spoke in a most unambiguous way about the annihilation of the Jews, and argued that "Only about 8 percent of the Jewish dead [of 3,000,000] have fallen in actual warfare. The other died because they were Jews." And he put forward a description that comes close to Lemkin's notion of "cultural genocide":

> Finally, for the 3,300,000 who may still be alive, even the spiritual consolation of their faith and their way of life has been ruthlessly assaulted. Their schools have been closed down, their libraries, museums and other cultural treasures plundered, their synagogues destroyed or desecrated. And with each day of continuing war, the threat of total extermination, so often voiced by Hitler and his lieutenants, comes closer to fulfilment.[23]

After the war too, the foundations were laid for later Holocaust historiography, by the pioneering works of Philip Friedman, Gerald Reitlinger, Léon Poliakov, Joseph Tenenbaum, Samuel Gringauz, and others. In this respect, Lemkin was not the only trailblazer. But all of these other scholars identified a Jewish tragedy and not a general Nazi policy of genocide of which the Holocaust was part.

Lemkin was of course quite correct to note that the Nazi assault on the Jews was only one part of the occupation regime, albeit "one of the main objects of German genocide policy" for they "are to be destroyed completely."[24] The extent of the persecution of Romanies, Poles, Yugoslavs, Russians, Serbs and other nationalities by the Germans is horrifying and has rightly become a significant part of the historiography of the Second World War. Where Lemkin challenges contemporary orthodoxy is in his implication that the notion of a "Holocaust" as a specifically Jewish tragedy makes no sense, because the genocide of the Jews was just one aspect of a broad Nazi demographic plan based on extreme racial fantasies. Most historians of the Holocaust would probably respond by noting that Lemkin's portrayal does not sufficiently indicate the depth of feeling, the passionate belief, held by the leading Nazis, that the Aryan struggle against the Jewish *Gegenmensch* held the key to Germany's redemption. As early as 1935 Aldous Huxley noted that "in Nazi Germany, the *sacramentum*, or oath of allegiance, has taken on all the religious significance it had in Rome under the Empire. The dictator's name and title, like those of the emperor, are used liturgically, as though they had the force of magic spells."[25] Central to this Nazi *Heilsgeschichte* were the Jews, for their force was the one thing in the way of the Germans attaining salvation.

But this is of a different order of analysis. The "metaphysical" position held by the Jews in Nazi ideology certainly differentiated them from Nazism's other victims. But from the legal point of view of prosecuting a criminal regime for committing crimes against humanity, there is no difference between the death of a Jew and a Catholic Pole. Whether or not the treatment of the occupied territories of eastern Europe constitutes genocide or not is debatable; there seems little evidence that the Nazis intended to seek the destruction of the Poles or Ukrainians as such, as opposed to reducing their numbers and leaving the remaining population in the position of slaves. But there is plenty of evidence for the commission of cultural genocide; after all, Hitler, Himmler and Frank were agreed that the Poles—like other Slavic populations—should not be in a position to do more than write their own names and make basic calculations. Given the current historiographical trend that sees the Holocaust as on a continuum (albeit an extreme variant) with earlier, especially colonial genocides, and given our understanding of the Nazis' grand population policy plans, Lemkin's challenge—to view the genocide of the Jews not as *sui generis* but as one, if unusually significant, part of Nazi genocide, and as one, albeit extreme variant of genocide—remains to be satisfactorily addressed by historians of the Holocaust and by comparative genocide scholars.

Notes and References

1 Hannah Arendt, "Personal responsibility under dictatorship" (1964), in Jerome Kohn, ed., *Responsibility and Judgment* (New York: Schocken Books, 2003), p 42.

2 See Steven L. Jacobs, "Raphael Lemkin and the Armenian genocide," in Richard G. Hovannisian, ed., *Looking Backward, Looking Forward: Confronting the Armenian Genocide* (New Brunswick: Transaction, 2003), pp 125–135.

3 Raphaël Lemkin, *Axis Rule in Occupied Europe: Laws of Occupation, Analysis of Government, Proposals for Redress* (Washington, DC: Carnegie Endowment for International Peace, 1944), pp xi–xii.
4 Lemkin, *Axis Rule*, p 79.
5 Henry R. Huttenbach, "From the Editor: towards a conceptual definition of genocide," *Journal of Genocide Research*, Vol 4, No 2, 2002, pp 172–173.
6 Raphaël Lemkin, "Genocide—a modern crime," *Free World*, Vol 4, 1945, online at: www.preventgenocide.org/lemkin/freeworld1945.htm
7 For example, in the case of the Bosnian Serb Nikolai Jorgić, the Federal Constitutional Court of Germany (*Bundesverfassungsgericht*) said that "the statutory definition of genocide defends a supra-individual object of legal protection, i.e. the social existence of the group [...] the intent to destroy the group [...] extends beyond physical and biological extermination [...] The text of the law does not therefore compel the interpretation that the culprit's intent must be to exterminate physically at least a substantial number of the members of the group." Cited in William A. Schabas, "National courts finally begin to prosecute genocide, the 'crime of crimes'," *Journal of International Criminal Justice*, Vol 1, No 1, 2003, p 58.
8 Raphaël Lemkin, "Acts constituting a general (transnational) danger considered as offences against the law of nations" (1933), online at: www.preventgenocide.org/lemkin/madrid1933-english.htm (originally written in French and presented in absentia at the International Conference for the Unification of Criminal Law, Madrid, October 1933); idem, "Genocide as a crime under international law," *American Journal of International Law*, Vol 41, No 1, 1946, pp 145–151.
9 As Lemkin wrote in his unpublished autobiography, "Totally unofficial man" (1958), "I defended it [i.e. cultural genocide] successfully through two drafts. It meant the destruction of the cultural pattern of a group, such as the language, the traditions, the monuments, archives, libraries, churches. In brief: the shrines of the soul of a nation. But there was not enough support for this idea in the Committee. ... So with a heavy heart I decided not to press for it." Cited in John Docker, *Raphael Lemkin's History of Genocide andColonialism* (Washington, DC: United States Holocaust Memorial Museum, 2004), p 3. See also Schabas, "National courts," pp 58–59; Matthew Lippman, "A road map to the 1948 Convention on the Prevention and Punishment of Genocide," *Journal of Genocide Research*, Vol 4, No 2, 2002, pp 183, 189.
10 Steven L. Jacobs, ed., *Raphael Lemkin's Thoughts on Nazi Genocide: Not Guilty?* (Lewiston: Edwin Mellen Press, 1992), henceforth referred to in the text as *TNG*. Raphaël Lemkin, "The Hitler case" (unpublished ms), henceforth referred to in the text as *HC*. I am very grateful to Steven Jacobs for providing me with a copy of "The Hitler case."
11 For the most recent work, see Martyn Housden, *Hans Frank, Lebensraum and the Holocaust* (Basingstoke: Palgrave Macmillan, 2003). For a good discussion of law in the Nazi racial state, see Claudia Koonz, *The Nazi Conscience* (Cambridge, MA: Belknap Press of Harvard University Press, 2003), Chapter 7.
12 As, for example, in the writings of Lucie Varga, Eric Voegelin, Bronislaw Malinowski, Norbert Elias, and Eric Wolf. For a discussion, see Dan Stone, *Responses to Nazism in Britain, 1933–1939: Before War and Holocaust* (Basingstoke: Palgrave Macmillan, 2003), pp 37–42; idem, "Nazism as modern magic: Bronislaw Malinowski's political anthropology," *History and Anthropology*, Vol 14, No 3, 2003, pp 203–218.
13 Lemkin, "Genocide—a modern crime," p 3.
14 See Dan Stone, "Genocide as transgression," *European Journal of Social Theory*, Vol 7, No 1, 2004, pp 45–65.
15 Léon Poliakov, *Harvest of Hate* (London: Elek Books, 1956 [orig. French 1953]), p 182.
16 That centres on Christopher R. Browning, *Ordinary Men: Reserve Police Battalion 101 and the Final Solution in Poland* (New York: HarperCollins, 1992) and Daniel Jonah Goldhagen, *Hitler's Willing Executioners: Ordinary Germans and the Holocaust* (London: Little, Brown, 1996). For a discussion of the sub-discipline of "perpetrator studies" that this debate has engendered, see Jürgen Matthäus, "Historiography and the perpetrators of the Holocaust," in Dan Stone, ed., *The Historiography of the Holocaust* (Basingstoke: Palgrave Macmillan, 2004), pp 197–215.
17 For a discussion, see Frank Bajohr, "Expropriation and expulsion," in Stone, ed., *The Historiography of the Holocaust*, pp 52–64.
18 See, for example, Avi Beker, ed., *The Plunder of Jewish Property during the Holocaust: Confronting European History* (New York: New York University Press, 2001); *Confiscation of Jewish Property in Europe, 1933–1945: New Sources and Perspectives: Symposium Proceedings* (Washington, DC: United States Holocaust Memorial Museum, 2003).
19 See *TNG*, Chapter 3, pp 153–176.
20 Franz Neumann, *Behemoth: The Structure and Practice of National Socialism* (London: Victor Gollancz, 1942). Neumann argued (p 107) that "racism and Anti-Semitism are substitutes for the class struggle. ... The internal political value of Anti-Semitism will, therefore, never allow a complete extermination of the Jews. The foe cannot and must not disappear; he must always be held in readiness as a scapegoat for all the evils originating in the socio-political system."

21 Gerhard Jacoby, *Racial State: The German Nationalities Policy in the Protectorate of Bohemia–Moravia* (New York: Institute of Jewish Affairs of the American Jewish Congress and World Jewish Congress, 1943), p 220.
22 Ibid, pp 244, 269.
23 Boris Shub, ed., *Hitler's Ten Year War on the Jews* (New York: Institute of Jewish Affairs of the American Jewish Congress, World Jewish Congress, 1943), pp 301, 302.
24 Lemkin, *Axis Rule*, pp 78, 81.
25 Aldous Huxley, "Emperor-worship up to date" (1935), in David Bradshaw, ed., *The Hidden Huxley* (London: Faber and Faber, 1994), p 193.

Hostage of Politics: Raphael Lemkin on "Soviet Genocide"

ANTON WEISS-WENDT

This article summarizes Raphael Lemkin's views on Stalinist terror. To follow Lemkin's train of thought, I consider the evidence he had, the importance he attached to it, and the ends to which he used that evidence. I argue that the discussion of the ethnic deportations in the Soviet Union was part and parcel of the evolving Cold War. Raphael Lemkin resorted to anticommunism to convince the US administration to ratify the Genocide Convention, which was essentially his creation.

As the United Nations General Assembly was preparing to vote on the resolution against genocide, Lemkin approached the Soviet delegation through Jan Masaryk, the Czechoslovak Foreign Minister. Lemkin conveyed to the Soviets that the resolution was not a conspiracy against them. As a result, nobody in the Soviet bloc opposed the resolution, which was unanimously adopted on December 11, 1946.[1] Five years later, however, Lemkin was claiming that the Soviet Union was the only country that could be indicted for genocide.[2] How to explain such a dramatic transition?

Lemkin's concept of genocide covered Stalinist deportations by default. That concept, as outlined in his book *Axis Rule in Occupied Europe*, differed significantly from the wording of the UN Genocide Convention. Lemkin identified several forms of genocide: political, social, cultural, economic, biological, physical, religious, and moral. He interpreted genocide as an intention to annihilate a group of the population by destroying essential foundations of life such as: social and political institutions, culture, language, national feelings, religion, economic means, personal security, liberty, health, dignity and, finally life itself.[3] Such a broad interpretation of the crime would make just any instance of gross human rights violation genocide. Indeed, from today's perspective, several cases that Lemkin deemed "genocidal" back in 1944 (for example: German policy in occupied Luxemburg, Alsace-Lorraine, or Slovenia) did not amount to actual genocide. Despite the fact that the UN Genocide Convention only deals with physical and biological destruction of life, Lemkin stuck to his original interpretation of genocide.

Raphael Lemkin had numerous encounters with Soviet power. In 1926 and 1928, Lemkin published two works in which he analysed the Soviet Penal Code. The Soviet and Nazi delegations walked away from the memorable 1933 Madrid conference when Lemkin's proposal to ban what he then called the crimes of vandalism and barbarism was read. Andrei Vyshinsky, Soviet Deputy Foreign Minister and Chief Prosecutor at the infamous purge trials of 1936–1938, argued that by proposing to make the crime of barbarism punishable under international law the capitalist world intended to intervene in the affairs of the Soviet Union.[4] The two met at the International Military Tribunal in Nuremberg, where Lemkin unsuccessfully lobbied for charging the Nazi leadership, among other crimes, with genocide. The next meeting took place in the United States; as the Head of the Soviet Delegation to the United Nations, Vyshinsky took part in the drafting of the Genocide Convention. It does not mean though that Lemkin had a grudge against Stalin regime or that he was watching closely the developments in the Soviet Union in the 1930s and early 1940s. In fact, Lemkin spoke about Stalinist terror for the first time only in 1949.[5] That might have something to do with the quantity and quality of information coming from behind the iron curtain.

Not even at the time of Lemkin's death in 1959 did the western world have a clear picture of the extent of political purges and ethnic deportations carried out by the Stalin regime. Most, if not all, information came from the recent emigrants from East Central Europe and from occasional journalist accounts. The evidence thus acquired was ridden with inaccuracies, exaggerations, and sometimes distortions. That was also the only kind of information Lemkin had at his disposal. Lemkin tended to substitute the word "Soviet" for Russian, implying that ethnic Russians benefited from deportations.[6] Lemkin used to talk about the "Russian practice of genocide," which he explained through the Soviet fear of encirclement.[7] He contended that the Russians decided to destroy a quarter of the population of East Central Europe for they were incapable of "digesting a great number of people belonging to a higher civilization."[8] According to Lemkin, genocide was taking place in almost all East Central European countries. As a proof, he referred to the Vatican Radio broadcast from July 1950 that announced 10,000 priests missing in the territories overtaken by the Red Army. With regard to the Baltic States, Lemkin claimed that substitute husbands were imported from Siberia for the destitute widows whose spouses had been deported![9] An article in *Pravda* from spring 1941 supposedly exposed the Soviet intent to commit genocide against the Baltic people; the article cited the Russian Tsar Peter the Great who claimed a mistake for letting the inhabitants of the Baltic area stay there.[10] In the midst of the Cold War, fabulous stories like these found a receptive audience worldwide.

Lemkin subscribed to the then fashionable theory of totalitarianism, which capitalized on similarities between Soviet and Nazi terror. As Ray Madden, a Republican Congressman, stated in a radio interview: "Victims of Stalin equal to victims of Hitler plus all tyrants."[11] Director of Anti-Defamation LeagueBenjamin Epstein took it even further, arguing that by fomenting anti-Semitism the Soviet authorities were currying favour with German neo-Nazis.[12] According to Lemkin, communists succeeded in applying techniques of genocide against the Baltic peoples because the Nazis had previously decapitated the political and intellectual leaderships of Estonia, Latvia, and Lithuania.[13] Needless to say, Lemkin's facts, as it often happened, were incorrect.

Lemkin was particularly sensitive to the persecution of Jews. He argued that anti-Semitic propaganda in the Soviet Union has matched the efforts of Streicher and Goebbels. The local population could be easily provoked to participate in a large-scale genocide, Lemkin said, for the Russian soil was saturated with the blood of hundreds of thousands of Jews.[14] In his interpretation, anti-Jewish pogroms and the conscription of Jewish teenagers into the active military service (which back then lasted 25 years) in the nineteenth-century Russian Empire was nothing less than a precursor of genocide. Lemkin contended that in 1949 and 1950 the Soviet authorities carried out a mass deportation of Jews from the western borderlands to Siberia. Lemkin drew that conclusion from the observation that some friends and relatives of the Soviet Jews received back their letters, marked "addressee not found." In addition, Lemkin called upon the western democracies to declare the Soviet Union guilty of inciting its satellites to commit genocide. According to Lemkin, in 1951 Hungary and Rumania started deporting their Jews, who were allegedly seen performing drainage work in the marshes along the Danube River.[15] Finally, he mentioned Czechoslovakia and the infamous Slansky trial.

At Stalin's instigation, state president Klement Gottwald initiated a purge within the Czechoslovak Communist Party. The most prominent among the 14 defendants that stood trial in November 1952 was Rudolf Slansky, secretary general of the Czechoslovak Communist Party. The Prague trial specifically targeted Jewish intellectuals and functionaries, who were accused of fomenting a "Trotskyist–zionist–titoist–bourgeois–nationalist conspiracy." Slansky and eleven other individuals were sentenced to death by hanging. Purge trials in Czechoslovakia continued even after Stalin's death, but the distinctive anti-Semitic tone was dropped.[16] Lemkin insisted that Czechoslovakia violated Article 2 of the Genocide Convention by committing the following acts: murdering innocent Jews; administering drugs to extort confessions; inciting genocide by distributing posters that read "hang the Jews."[17] The charges that Lemkin laid against Czechoslovakia were based on an article in the *New York Times*.

The last paragraph of the above-mentioned statement indicates where Lemkin was getting with his allegations of "communist genocide against the Jews." The present anti-Jewish campaign, Lemkin argued, was not an isolated phenomenon. Other nations under the Soviet control were subject to genocide as well. The nations in Asia and Africa should understand that communists would destroy them, too, unless all potential victims of Soviet genocide unite under the guidance of the free world.[18] It seems as if Lemkin borrowed his arguments from the then official doctrine of the US government; it was not coincidental.

To understand the kind of political rhetoric that Lemkin was increasingly using, one needs to go back to the period following the adoption of Genocide Convention in December of 1948. To make the Genocide Convention a binding treaty required at least 20 signatures. To acquire those 20 ratifications turned out to be more difficult than anybody would expect. Lemkin worked tirelessly addressing foreign governments, public figures, and nonprofit organizations. That made one journalist proclaim Lemkin "the UN's most persistent salesman." To convince individual countries to ratify the convention, Lemkin often resorted to political rhetoric. In other words, Lemkin told his counterparts what they wanted to hear. He did so by discussing from the perspective of genocide historical grievances that one country or another had. Thus, he urged Japan to ratify the treaty by drawing attention to the plight of Japanese prisoners of war in China and the Soviet Union. In his letter to the Mayor of Dublin, Lemkin used the Irish famine of 1845–1850 as a reference point. In a memo prepared for the West German Parliament, Lemkin emphasized that the Genocide Convention covered the millions of ethnic Germans who have been expelled from East Central European countries. To secure the Austrian signature, Lemkin reminded State President Karl Renner that in his book, *Axis Rule in Occupied Europe*, he treated Austria as a victim of Hitler's aggression rather than as a Nazi ally.When advising Catholics to press their Senators on ratification, Lemkin spoke of the destruction of the Catholic religious groups behind the iron curtain. With the delegates of the Women's Commission in Chile he spoke about the plight of Greek children.[19]

Lemkin scored a personal victory when the Genocide Convention went into effect on January 12, 1951. The United States, however, had repeatedly refused to ratify the Genocide Convention. Among the reasons were concerns about sovereignty, general distrust of the UN, growing xenophobia, and anticommunism.[20] At the UN General Assembly meeting in Paris in December 1951, the Civil Rights Congress (listed by the US Attorney General as a subversive communist organization) urged delegates to investigate charges that US treatment of blacks violated the Genocide Convention. The Civil Rights Congress summarized its findings in a book called *We Charge Genocide*.[21] At the same meeting, Eleanor Roosevelt, acting chief of the American delegation, received the question whether the US should bring up genocide charges against the Soviet Union, as urged by émigrés of East European descent. In response, Roosevelt said: "How could you prove it? I am not sure you can prove that. Unless you can prove it, there is no use bringing it up."[22]

By ratifying the Genocide Convention or by indicting the Soviet Union for genocide, the United States would have exposed itself to similar allegations. In accordance with the basic principle of American diplomacy, the US opposed anything that the USSR favoured.[23] The fact that the Soviet Union ratified the treaty (in May 1954) ruled out a possibility of any serious discussion in the United States regarding the future of the Genocide Convention. The American Bar Association, an influential organization with a strong anti-Soviet agenda, felt apprehensive of frivolous allegations of genocide if the United States ratified the convention, and therefore recommended against it.[24] Lemkin realized that without the participation of the United States, the Genocide Convention remained a dead letter. In his desperate attempt to resuscitate the treaty, Lemkin resorted to what he, correctly, recognized as the defining feature of American foreign and domestic policy at that time—anticommunism.

Lemkin went after the Soviet Union (also after Stalin's death) under the guise of Article 1 of the Genocide Convention that talked about prevention of genocide. Consider, for example, Lemkin's position on the Korean War. Lemkin urged to counteract the Soviet propaganda in Asia by demonstrating that the Soviet Union (Lemkin used the word "Russia") destroyed small nations rather than liberate them. To prove it, Lemkin argued for similarities of genocidal methods applied by the Soviet Union in the Baltic and Korea. Lemkin warned that a wave of genocide was bound to come in Cambodia, Laos, and Vietnam, the countries that "were given away to the communists in direct violation of the spirit of the Genocide Convention."[25]

Lemkin encouraged the United States to sponsor a UN special committee to investigate Soviet genocide. By indicting the Communist leaders, Lemkin argued, the United Nations would render "a verdict of which history will be proud":

> The great and historic importance of the Genocide Pact lies in the fact that it permits us to meet the present Communist barbarity not on the level of a discussion of "dialectical materialism" of Karl Marx but on the level of common criminality of an Al Capone and his like.[26]

Lemkin's efforts were futile. As William Korey wrote, "exploitation of cold war symbols, including a vituperative anticommunism, did not win Lemkin the politically meaningful rightwing support he sought."[27] The United States did not ratify the Genocide Convention until after the ideological confrontation with the Soviet Union started fading away in the late 1980s, 29 years after Lemkin's death.

At the time when Lemkin and his ideas found little support in government offices, East European ethnic communities became Lemkin's most trusted allies. The 12 million émigrés of East European descent in the United States let their voice be heard through numerous ethnic-based organizations. Passionate in their negation of communism, those organizations were eager to see the Soviet dominance in Eastern Europe ended and their native countries free. The émigrés immediately incorporated the new term into their political lexicon. A little known fact: the very first charge of genocide submitted to the UN originated in the Lithuanian, Latvian, and Estonian legations-in-exile in Washington. In November 1947, that is, a year before the Genocide Convention was officially adopted, representatives of the three former Baltic States appealed to the General Assembly to indict the Soviet Union for genocide against their respective nations.[28] In November 1951, representatives of the so-called Captive European Nations appealed to the US Secretary of State Dean Acheson urging him to place an investigation of Soviet genocide on the agenda of the UN General Assembly. The motion was supported by 116 Republican Congressmen, who argued that by keeping those nations alive they would prevent the Soviet Union from unleashing World War III.[29] The émigrés realized that they could not afford the time to collect evidence attesting Soviet genocide. The further the delay with the indictment of the Soviet Union before the bar of the UN, the less the political impact.[30] The suppression of democracy in Hungary in 1956 was deemed "genocide," and so were arrests and deportations of ethnic Lithuanians. The number of people deported by the Soviets from Lithuania was estimated anywhere between 500,000 and one million, that is, about ten times more than the actual number.

Lemkin was actively involved with émigré organizations: he attended their meetings, participated in their lobbying campaigns, and even edited their public appeals. For example, on December 20, 1954, the Assembly of Captive European Nations adopted a resolution which had the following line: "Communist puppet governments have suppressed all freedoms and all human rights." Lemkin augmented that sentence by adding: "By resorting to genocide they are threatening our civilization and weaken the forces of the free world."[31] For his planned three-volume *History of Genocide* Lemkin intended to write a chapter on Soviet repression in Hungary. The chapter was to be drawn from the "UN report" on the Soviet invasion of the country.[32]

At a certain point, Lemkin decided to quit his teaching job so as to focus on lobbying in behalf of the Genocide Convention. Without a permanent source of income, however, Lemkin could not sustain himself. (Lemkin kept all the notes his creditors sent him.) At that critical moment, East European émigrés came to his rescue. Occasionally, organizations like the Lithuanian American National Council and the Ukrainian Congress Committee of America provided up to two-thirds of Lemkin's annual income.[33] Thus, Pius Grigaitis, executive secretary of the American Lithuanian Council, notified Lemkin that:

> In appreciation of your increasing efforts on behalf of millions of people subjugated to the unscrupulous Soviet policy of genocide, the Council is sending you a check for $250 to help defray some of your expenses.[34]

Within a decade since Lemkin coined the word "genocide," it became a household word for various forms of communist oppression, such as forced collectivization, mass deportations, the breaking up of families, inhuman working conditions and standard of living.[35] Violations of minority rights, forced assimilation, racial discrimination, the infringement on freedom of religion—all those notions blended into an unintelligible rumbling about genocide meant to discredit political adversaries. It is hard to disagree with Peter Novick, who argued that back in the 1950s genocide became a generic category that was evoked to fit the needs of the moment.[36]

The genocide rhetoric was by no means confined to western countries. For example, Josip Broz Tito used the "G" word to counterattack Josef Stalin and his East European clients. The Yugoslav authorities condemned Czechoslovakia, Poland, and the Soviet Union for "forcibly transferring children," and Hungary and Rumania for discriminating against Slavic minorities.[37]

The stronger the effort in behalf of the Genocide Convention, the more eroded the notion of genocide became. Like King Midas, whatever Lemkin touched turned into "genocide." But when everything is genocide nothing is genocide! What started as an innocent idea to pull political strings to make an important international treaty work ended with blatant accusation of the Soviet Union of committing genocide on a global scale.[38] Lemkin explicitly stated that for him "Soviet genocide" was just an expedient: "genocide is a concept that carries the highest moral condemnation in our cold war against the Soviet Union."[39] Indeed, politically charged slogans like "genocide is the communists' favorite outdoor sport" have little value to them.[40]

Political reality pushed Lemkin into a vicious circle. He had a noble idea, which he wanted to see implemented. But he had to fight for his idea. As the fight dragged on, more and more compromises had to be made. Along the way, he had to influence a good many individuals and countries. To win the support for the Genocide Convention, Lemkin was resolved to demonstrate its contemporary relevance. He did so by drawing parallels between contemporaneous politics and examples from the recent past. However, to make that comparison, Lemkin needed to shape the notion of genocide accordingly. And that was exactly what he did. As Lemkin explained:

> I study my men and I use the approach that fits them best. I might flatter them or I might argue with them. If they like music, I talk about music, but we always get around to genocide in the end. If it will accomplish the purpose, I am even willing to bore them until they say "yes" just to get rid of me.[41]

In the end, Lemkin not only failed to make the Genocide Convention work, but also diluted the meaning of genocide beyond recognition. We now know that his tactics were bound to fail. No matter what Lemkin did, he would have been crushed by the Cold War anyway. Fortunately, the Genocide Convention outlived the postwar ideological battles. Whatever we call Soviet deportations of whole nations (which could most accurately be described as "ethnic cleansing"),[42] Lemkin forced us to think in legal terms about the Stalinist crimes. Lemkin was probably the first scholar who introduced a comparative method into the study of mass violence. That achievement alone is enough to put Raphael Lemkin on a list of the twentieth-century visionaries.

Acknowledgements

The archival research for this article was made possible through a grant from the American Jewish Archives in Cincinnati, Ohio. I am also obliged to James Fussell of *Prevent Genocide International* with whom I had stimulating conversations about the personality of Raphael Lemkin and who kindly let me use some of his materials.

Notes and References

1 Herbert Yahraes, "He gave a name to the world's most horrible crime," *Collier's*, March 3, 1951, p 56.
2 Lemkin, memo re. Genocide Convention, 1951, American Jewish Archives (hereafter: AJA), Lemkin Papers, Ms 60/Box 4/3.
3 Raphael Lemkin, *Axis Rule in Occupied Europe: Laws of Occupation. Analysis of Government: Proposals for Redress* (Washington, DC: Carnegie Endowment for International Peace, 1944), pp 79–86.

4 Vyshinsky attacked Lemkin's proposal in a Russian-language pamphlet called "Counterrevolutionary intervention through criminal law" (1935).
5 Lemkin to Cardinal Francis Spellman, September 13, 1949, AJA, Lemkin Papers, Ms 60/Box 1/14.
6 Otto Pohl and Eric Weitz committed similar fallacy in their discussion of ethnic cleansing in the Soviet Union. See: Otto Pohl, *Ethnic Cleansing in the USSR, 1937–1949* (Westport, CO and London: Greenwood Press, 1999), pp 3, 4; Eric Weitz, *A Century of Genocide: Utopias of Race and Nation* (Princeton and Oxford: Princeton University Press, 2003), p 100.
7 Interview with Lemkin, ABC Radio Network, btw June 1953 and January 1955, AJA, Lemkin Papers, Ms 60/Box 4/2.
8 Lemkin, "Genocide to be included in the message," after 1956, AJA, Lemkin Papers, Ms 60/Box 4/2.
9 Interview with Lemkin, college roundtable: UN Genocide Convention, after 1952, AJA, Lemkin Papers, Ms 60/Box 4/2.
10 Memo, the Genocide Convention: plain talk from American lawyers, 1954, AJA, Lemkin Papers, Ms 60/Box 3/4. In 1708, Peter the Great did indeed order the deportation of 800 Tartu burgers, which were exclusively German; Estonians and Latvians had not yet developed into a separate entity at that time.
11 "Soviet genocide": an interview with Lemkin and Madden, no date, AJA, Lemkin Papers, Ms 60/Box 4/2.
12 Benjamin Epstein, note re Lemkin, no date, AJA, Lemkin Papers, Ms 60/Box 3/3.
13 Interview with Lemkin, college roundtable: UN Genocide Convention, after 1952, AJA, Lemkin Papers, Ms 60/Box 4/2; Lemkin's speech at Yale University, no date, AJA, Lemkin Papers, Ms 60/Box 4/4.
14 Lemkin, draft statement on genocide, btw February 1953 and May 1954, AJA, Lemkin Papers, Ms 60/Box 4/3.
15 Lemkin's speech before the New York Chapter of the American Jewish Congress, January 18, 1951, AJA, Lemkin Papers, Ms 60/Box 4/4; Lemkin, statement, genocide and the anti-Jewish persecution behind the iron curtain, btw December 1952 and April 1953, AJA, Lemkin Papers, Ms 60/Box 4/7.
16 Joseph Rothschild and Nancy Wingfield, *Return to Diversity: A Political History of East Central Europe Since World War II* (Oxford: Oxford University Press, 2000), pp 135–136.
17 Lemkin, draft statement on genocide, btw February 1953 and May 1954, AJA, Lemkin Papers, Ms 60/Box 4/3. "Inflicting mental harm" was one of the most controversial provisions of Genocide Convention. The clause was introduced by the Chinese delegation, which argued that the Japanese intended to administer lethal doses of drugs to the Chinese people. (During WWII the Japanese built a huge opium extraction plant in Manchuria capable of producing 50 tonnes of heroin annually, about 50 times the world demand.)
18 Ibid. Lemkin did not deny the existence of anti-Semitism in western democracies. However, the differences between those countries and Russia were too substantial to call Stalin's Judeophobia "anti-Semitism." Therefore, Lemkin concluded, it was genocide.
19 Jiji Press, UN: Japan reminded on genocide convention, no date; Lemkin to Lord Robert Briscol, June 28, 1956, AJA, Lemkin Papers, Ms 60/Box 2/2; Lemkin's memo to the West German Parliament, no date, AJA, Lemkin Papers, Ms 60/Box 4/3; Lemkin to Renner, March 29, 1950, AJA, Lemkin Papers, Ms 60/Box 1/15; Lemkin, program of action on genocide (the Catholics), no date, AJA, Lemkin Papers, Ms 60/Box 4/7; Lemkin to the Assembly of the Inter-American Commission of Women, May 23, 1951, AJA, Lemkin Papers, Ms 60/Box 2/1.
20 William Korey, "America's shame: the unratified genocide treaty," in Jack Nusan Porter, ed., *Genocide and Human Rights: A Global Anthology* (New York and London: University Press of America, 1982), p 285.
21 *We Charge Genocide: The Historic Petition to the United Nations for Relief from a Crime of the United States Government Against the Negro People* (New York: Civil Rights Congress, 1951). The US was not the only western country charged with genocide. France, for example, was accused of committing genocide against the Algerian people.
22 *New York Herald Tribune*, December 30, 1951.
23 Harold Epstein to Lemkin, September 8, 1953, AJA, Lemkin Papers, Ms 60/Box 1/5.
24 Lawrence LeBlanc, *The United States and the Genocide Convention* (Durham and London: Duke University Press, 1991), pp 42, 106, 165.
25 Lemkin, memo re ratification of the Genocide Convention, no date, AJA, Lemkin Papers, Ms 60/Box 4/3; Lemkin, memo, unification of Korea and the Genocide Convention, no date, AJA, Lemkin Papers, Ms 60/Box 4/7.
26 *Genocide (The Newest Soviet Crime) as Discussed by Professor Raphael Lemkin, Author of the Genocide Pact, and Mr. Joseph P. Burns, Moderator, "WNHC-TV College Roundtable"* (WNHC-Television Program Reprint, January 30, 1953), p 7, Robert Wagner Labor Archives, JLC Collection, Anti-Discrimination Files, "Genocide Convention."
27 William Korey, *An Epitaph for Raphael Lemkin* (New York: American Jewish Committee, 2001), p 75.
28 *New York Times*, November 22 and 25, 1947.
29 Republican Congressmen, appeal to Acheson, January 1952, AJA, Lemkin Papers, Ms 60/Box 4/3.

30 Djab Namonov (Kalmyk Committee to Combat Bolshevism) to Francis Macy (American Committee for Liberation from Bolshevism), October 23, 1954, AJA, Lemkin Papers, Ms 60/Box 2/9.
31 Assembly of Captive European Nations, draft appeal, December 20, 1954, AJA, Lemkin Papers, Ms 60/Box 4/7.
32 Korey, *An Epitaph*, pp 75, 121f.
33 IRS audits of Lemkin's income tax returns for 1951 and 1952, AJA, Lemkin Papers, Ms 60/Box 2/20.
34 Grigaitis to Lemkin, November 10, 1953, AJA, Lemkin Papers, Ms 60/Box 1/7.
35 Uriel Tal, "On the study of the Holocaust and genocide," *Yad Vashem Studies*, Vol 13, 1979, p 13.
36 Peter Novick, *The Holocaust and Collective Memory* (London: Bloomsbury, 1999), p 101.
37 Yugoslav Information Center, press release, June 13, 1950, AJA, Lemkin Papers, Ms 60/Box 4/3.
38 Emilio Nunez Portuondo, "Message of faith and hope," *Christian Democratic Review*, Vol 6, No 30, 1956, AJA, Lemkin Papers, Ms 60/Box 3/4.
39 Lemkin to Frank Lausche, Governor of Ohio, after June 1951, AJA, Lemkin Papers, Ms 60/Box 2/6.
40 Editorial, "Genocide pact imperilled," *America* (Catholic weekly), Vol 84, No 2, 1950, p. 3.
41 Herbert Maza, draft article: "Raphael Lemkin," November 1950, AJA, Lemkin Papers, Ms 60/Box 5/7.
42 Norman Naimark, *Fires of Hatred: Ethnic Cleansing in Twentieth-Century Europe* (Cambridge, MA and London: Harvard University Press, 2001), pp 2–5, 85–138; Terry Martin, "The origins of Soviet ethnic cleansing," *Journal of Modern History*, Vol 70, 1998, pp 815–824.

Index

For Product Safety Concerns and Information please contact our EU representative GPSR@taylorandfrancis.com
Taylor & Francis Verlag GmbH, Kaufingerstraße 24, 80331 München, Germany

www.ingramcontent.com/pod-product-compliance
Lightning Source LLC
LaVergne TN
LVHW080658011026
849160LV00014B/1465
* 9 7 8 0 4 1 5 8 5 1 3 0 5 *

About the Authors

Robert H. Klonoff

Robert Klonoff is Dean and Professor of Law at Lewis & Clark Law School. Previously, he served as an Assistant United States Attorney, an Assistant to the Solicitor General of the United States, a partner at Jones Day in Washington, D.C., and the Douglas Stripp/Missouri Endowed Professor of Law at the University of Missouri-Kansas City School of Law. Dean Klonoff has tried dozens of cases and has argued numerous cases before the United States Supreme Court. He has also argued many cases in the U.S. courts of appeals and state appellate courts throughout the country. A graduate of Yale Law School, he belongs to the District of Columbia and Missouri Bars. He is a member of the American Law Institute and a reporter for the ALI's project, Principles of the Law of Aggregate Litigation. He has written widely in the area of class actions.

Paul L. Colby

Paul Colby is an attorney with the United State Department of Justice in Washington, D.C. He previously served as a White House Attorney-Adviser, an Assistant United States Attorney, and a Trial Judge Advocate in the United States Marine Corps. He has broad litigation and investigative experience in both civil and criminal cases, and has tried approximately 70 cases. He has also lectured in the United States and abroad on a range of legal subjects. A graduate of Columbia University School of Law, he belongs to the District of Columbia and Virginia Bars.

The views expressed in this text are solely those of the authors.

Foreword

It is very rare that a book appears that substantially reorients thinking in any area of human endeavor. It is rarer still that we come upon inspired thinking capable of rerouting pathways deeply worn by the foot traffic of long experience. Review of this book convinces me that it is such a work and that it will have that sort of effect. It is a major advance in understanding the activity of trying lawsuits and offers an analytical framework—obvious once stated, but unstated for hundreds of years—that will greatly assist lawyers in thinking more clearly about what they are doing in the courtroom.

As anyone knows who has taken a trial advocacy course or been a beginning trial lawyer lucky enough to receive the advice of more experienced hands, trial practice has long been a discipline lacking any substantial conceptual or theoretical dimension. The teaching provided in that area has been almost entirely mechanical or anecdotal. We can tell someone where to sit or stand, how close to get to the jury, and when to approach the witness. We can also offer up a blueprint for putting in real evidence of various types or getting the best out of our own experts on different subjects. We can even give some pointers on that most imponderable act of courtroom legerdemain, cross-examination. But most of all, we pass along our own war stories (and those we have heard from others), and thereby convey the messages—of strikingly limited utility—that certain techniques work sometimes and that (our own) inspiration and personal genius ultimately tell the tale.

What has hitherto been lacking is any serious effort to understand what the jury perceives to be going on in a courtroom. In our system, jurors do not simply decide what resolution of the legal dispute is appropriate, based on the law and their understanding of the facts. They are rather adjudicators of a contest in which victory for either side is governed by the application of sometimes obtuse rules. The central insight of this book is that the evidence and events occurring at trial are viewed by the jury as parts of a contest in which the participants on both sides are seeking, above all else, to prevail.

Given this concept of the lawyer's role, which is inherent in the adversary system, jurors expect and believe that an advocate will strive to put his client's case in the best possible light. The truth, the jury will assume, can be no better for a party than his advocate represents it to be, and it is a fair inference that the advocate will try to give a rosier impression than an impartial observer would draw from a full understanding of the facts. Not only can the lawyer be expected to overstate the affirmative aspects of his own case, but in fulfilling his obligation to seek victory zealously he will be expected to challenge every material aspect of the opposing case that is open to question. Thus any material assertion by the opposition that the advocate does not attack can be taken as correct.

The image of the trial as a quest for victory therefore shapes the effect that arguments and evidence will have on the jury. A lawyer's decision to present certain evidence is a statement that that evidence is important to the resolution of the dispute and, more specifically, to the acceptance of his client's own position. Thus, weak evidence offered by the prosecutor in support of criminal guilt is not simply another small plus on the prosecution side of the ledger—it is more significantly a statement of his concern about his standing in the contest. Why would a lawyer present such uncertain evidence, other than out of a belief that the outcome of the contest may ultimately turn on it? Jurors assume that everything done at trial is aimed at convincing them to return a favorable verdict. A lawyer who puts in shaky or inconsequential evidence, for reasons of candor or completeness, or simply without thinking, will likely suffer what the authors describe as the cost of overtrying.

The failure to introduce evidence may likewise take on a special significance. Sometimes omitting evidence in the course of presenting other evidence (*e.g.*, the testimony of a particular witness) may seem strained and unnatural. In that circumstance the lawyer may pay a penalty in the jury's eyes for his unusual efforts in omitting the evidence. Taking notice of that omission, and ever-conscious that the lawyer is seeking to prevail, the jurors may assume the worst about both the lawyer and the evidence.

From these and other examples the authors demonstrate that the significance and weight attached by the jurors to what they see and hear in the courtroom may vary greatly based on who presents or omits particular arguments or pieces of evidence. This book is above all else a careful and precise playing out of the implications of this thought throughout the length and breadth of the jury process. The authors work through the consequences of sponsorship on most of the types of decisions that can confront a lawyer at trial. They are never doctrinaire and do not offer the sort of cut and dried recipes that mark much existing trial practice literature. They rather consider with care and insight the components to be identified and evaluated in each case. Not surprisingly, they often find themselves convincingly at odds with the conventional wisdom.

This book thus can be expected to have a major impact on the way lawsuits are tried in this country. Its effect should be a salutary one, rendering advocacy both more streamlined and more persuasive. But the book has implications that transcend the instructional purpose for which it was written. The authors have offered a compelling and comprehensive new conceptual framework where none previously existed. Like Darwin's *Origin of the Species*, they have opened whole new areas for thought and reflection.

There is, for example, a great deal to be learned here about the role of lawyers in our society, and about the concept of truth in the adversary system of justice. Our legal system is one that defines the lawyer's role as one of zealous advocacy, presenting the position of his client in the best possible light while doing his best to diminish that of the opposition. Truth in this context is not any independently knowable reality. It is rather whatever emerges from the struggle of advocates before the jury. This notion of lawyers as ones who create rather than pursue the truth is more evidence of our society's distrust of orthodoxy and its celebration of individual autonomy. It may also, however, have something to do with the low esteem in which lawyers are held. Moreover, the penalties that await those who depart from the role of zealous advocate, that is, those who respond to concerns for candor with a full presentation of the facts to the jury, may raise even more sweeping questions in some minds.

– Donald B. Ayer
Deputy Attorney General of the United States
1990

Acknowledgments

We acknowledge several individuals who provided us with legal research and technical assistance: Rory Kramer, Andrew Lonard, Uzu Nwonwu, Valley Renshaw, and Jeremy Wikler, all of whom were then students at the University of Missouri-Kansas City; and Amie V. Colby, Esquire.

CHAPTER 1

Sponsorship Strategy

The Sponsorship Dilemma: Which Side Introduces the Evidence

The young prosecutor sat in the back of the courtroom waiting for his case to be called for trial. It was a tough case for the government. A robber had snatched a purse from an elderly and very frightened woman and was making his escape. A good samaritan, who had not seen the snatch itself, gave chase for several blocks until, in a dimly lit alleyway, the robber pulled out a knife, warded him off, and completed his escape.

The victim made clear at the outset of the police investigation that she could not identify her assailant. Thus, the entire case depended on the pursuer. Nearly a month after the robbery, at the local precinct house, an investigating detective asked the good samaritan to view a large mugbook containing randomly arranged photographs of local rogues. The witness selected the defendant as the person whom he had chased, but the significance of that selection was dubious because the defendant's photograph was the first one in the book.

The defendant was later placed in a lineup. As expected, the elderly victim was unable to identify anyone. The good samaritan again identified the defendant, but the selection—which was captured on videotape—was anything but ideal. When called forth to make his identification, the witness paused, crossed his arms, and rested his chin in his hand with apparent bewilderment as he viewed the seven men in the line. After 30 seconds, he asked, "Could I see them from the right?" After at least another minute and a half, spent getting a closer view, he stated slowly and with some hesitation: "Number...five [the defendant]." The lineup identification of the defendant was uncorroborated by any other evidence: no purse had been recovered and no confession had been made. A tough case indeed.

Nonetheless, the prosecutor was convinced that he had the right man. The good samaritan had stated at a witness conference that he had had an excellent opportunity to view the fleeing assailant and that he was "100 percent positive" of his identification. He had explained that his delay at the lineup was simply an effort to be cautious—to make sure that he selected the right man or none at all. Moreover, the witness was highly credible and had no motive to fabricate. Under the circumstances, the prosecutor believed that the witness had correctly identified the assailant and that the interests of justice demanded a trial rather than a dismissal of the case.

The young prosecutor was soon joined in the back of the courtroom by one of the senior and most experienced trial hands in the office. In hushed tones, they discussed the case. The younger one noted for his mentor that he did not intend to display the lineup videotape for the jury. The seasoned one sternly warned him that failing to present such problematic evidence to the jury would constitute a major tactical error, since the defense was certain to present it if he did not do so. Only by introducing the tape himself could the prosecutor "take the sting out of it." If the government let the *defense* introduce the tape, the learned prosecutor explained, an acquittal was a virtual certainty, since the defense could then argue that the government deliberately withheld the most important piece of evidence demonstrating reasonable doubt. The veteran prosecutor therefore recommended that the tape be introduced during the good samaritan's direct examination, and that the witness be asked to explain to the jury, as the tape was being shown, precisely what he was thinking at each moment during the selection process. While the experienced prosecutor may not have realized it, his advice was consistent with that of virtually all of the leading trial manuals and treatises: an advocate should bring out the weaknesses in his own case instead of letting his opponent do so.

Contrary to his mentor's advice, the young prosecutor never introduced the videotape in his trial of the case. He simply elicited from the pursuing witness the fact that he had identified the defendant at the lineup. The prosecutor was somewhat surprised that defense counsel, who had been present at the lineup and had reviewed the videotape during discovery, never used it in the defense case. Upon reflection, however, defense counsel's decision not to use the tape was tactically justified.

To be sure, the defendant's introduction of the tape may have cast some doubt on the identification. This is true even though the witness's explanation of his conduct at the lineup—that he was certain of his identification at the lineup and was merely being cautious—might have diluted the impact of the tape as a means of discrediting the witness. Defense counsel therefore would not have been acting unreasonably in using the tape as part of his case or during the cross-examination of the witness. By introducing the tape, the defense could have argued that the good samaritan's hesitancy at the lineup confirmed that there was a reasonable doubt with respect to the defendant's guilt.

Such a strategy, however, would have carried serious disadvantages as well. In particular, the prosecutor could have commented during summation that defense counsel had gone to all the trouble to roll in a television set and darken the room, only to have his client ultimately chosen as the robber. The prosecutor could have argued:

> You must have expected, after all this effort, that the tape would show the witness selecting someone else as the perpetrator. You must have been surprised, to say the least, when the witness in fact identified the defendant.

Even without such an argument, the jury might well have viewed the videotape as a rather odd piece of "defense" evidence.

The critical point, however, is that the prosecutor was better off not introducing the tape regardless of what the defense decided to do with that evidence. By introducing evidence damaging to his case, the prosecutor would have implicitly conceded the central significance of the tape to the verdict. Defense counsel would then have been able to argue along the following lines in his summation:

> You must have asked yourself: Why was the prosecutor so concerned that you see a tape showing a very hesitant and unconvincing witness? One thing is clear, at the very least. The prosecutor cannot deny that the tape is the most important item of evidence for you to consider in this case. Isn't that why he went

> out of his way to set up the video equipment and darken the room, only to present evidence so devastating to his case? He obviously recognizes that his duty as a prosecutor is not necessarily to get a conviction but to see that justice is done.

Such an argument would have left the prosecutor without an effective reply, since he could not credibly claim that the tape was unimportant, given his introduction of it.

To summarize, the government's strategy of not introducing the tape left the defense in a difficult dilemma. Only the *prosecutor's* introduction of the tape would have resolved that dilemma. Put another way, what the seasoned prosecutor failed to realize was that, while the introduction of the tape by the defense may have been damaging to the government's case, the prosecutor's introduction of that evidence would have been even more damaging.

The foregoing case involved an actual trial conducted by one of the authors. A second example is provided by a practitioner who applied the sponsorship technique after reading the first edition of this book. The skeptical lawyer had been a strong proponent of bringing out weaknesses. But in a criminal case in which he served as defense counsel, he decided to let the prosecutor elicit the defendant's prior criminal conviction instead of bringing it out on direct, as the conventional approach has long dictated.[1] As he recounted the experience:

> The first time I followed this philosophy [sponsorship] in court, I was terrified. It went against everything I had been taught. It worked like a charm. The jurors all stated that they thought the impeachment by the prosecutor on the prior conviction was a "cheap shot."[2]

The foregoing cases illustrate a central thesis of this book: that the impact of an item of evidence on the jury's verdict will often be decisively influenced by the identity of the party who introduces, or "sponsors," that item into evidence. Thus, in the first example, the weight that the jury would attach to the videotape could not be determined in a vacuum. Such an assessment could be made only by taking into account which side would

---

1 *See, e.g.*, H. Spellman, Direct Examination of Witnesses, § 5:5, at 85 (Prentice Hall 1968)(example of conventional commentator urging advocate to elicit prior criminal record of witness on direct).

2 Allison, *Witness Preparation from the Criminal Defense Perspective*, 30 Tex. Tech. L. Rev. 1333, 1339 (1999).

introduce it. As we have noted, the tape would have been more damaging to the government's case had it been introduced by the prosecutor rather than by the defense. Similarly, the defense attorney in the second example was better off letting the prosecutor bring out the prior conviction.

The jury's association of evidence with the party sponsoring it into evidence follows from the requirement of our judicial system that evidence be marshaled by the parties to the controversy. Under this system, each side is represented by a professionally trained advocate who is responsible for presenting his client's case in its most favorable light. So long as the attorney appears competent, the jury will assume that the case can be no better than he states it.[3]

At the same time, the advocate's favorable evidence will be viewed with skepticism, since the jury will assume that such evidence is being packaged in its best light.[4] In this manner, the weight given by a jury to a piece of evidence will depend heavily on which side introduces that evidence.

This phenomenon of "sponsorship" can be highlighted by assuming, for comparative purposes, a hypothetical system in which all evidence is presented to the jury by a disinterested source, such as the judge. Such a system is analogous to the "inquisitorial" system, a mechanism that preceded the adversary system as a way of resolving disputed issues of fact. Under that system, the judge not only decided the case but also investigated the facts and questioned the witnesses.[5] Furthermore, the decision-maker did not view the witnesses as being associated with the parties.[6] By contrast, under the adversary system, the decision-maker typically regards a witness as identified with the party who calls him.[7]

---

3 *See, e.g.*, W. LaFave, J. Israel & N. King, *Criminal Procedure* § 1.4, at 28 (Thomson West 4th ed. 2004) (noting jury's expectation that each party will present evidence in light "most favorable to its side"); L. Fuller, "The Adversary System," 31, *reprinted in* H. Berman, ed., *Talks on American Law* (Vintage Books 1961) ("[The advocate's] task is not to decide but to persuade. He is not expected to present the case in a colorless and detached manner, but in such a way that it will appear in that aspect most favorable to his client.").

4 *See, e.g.*, S. Hamlin, *What Makes Juries Listen Today* 458 (Glasser LegalWorks 1998) ("[Juries] expect you to slant questions and get answers that will only favor your witness and your case. Therefore, they're always a little suspicious of a direct examination."); *cf.* R. Carlson & E. Imwinkelried, *Dynamics of Trial Practice: Problems and Materials* § 3.3(D), at 39 (West 3d ed. 2002) (noting that because attorneys are "hired guns," the jury "tend[s] to discount what the attorneys say during trial").

5 *See generally*, S. Landsman, *The Adversary System: A Description and Defense* 49 (American Enterprise Institute 1984); Sward, *Values, Ideology, and the Evolution of the Adversary System*, 64 Ind. L.J. 301, 313–315 (1989).

6 *See, e.g.*, Ladd, *Impeachment of One's Own Witness—New Developments*, 4 U. Chi. L. Rev. 69, 79 (1936); *cf.* Fed. R. Evid. 614, Advisory Comm. Note Subdiv. (a) (noting that when the court calls a witness, "[t]he tendency of juries to associate [the] witness with the party calling him ... is avoided").

7 *See, e.g.*, Ladd, *supra* n. 6, at 79; H. Spellman, *supra* n. 1, § 4:3, at 66 (noting that under the adversary system, "there is a subconscious tendency on the part of those hearing the case to identify the witness with a party").

In the foregoing armed robbery case, if the judge had presented the jury with all of the evidence, including the videotape, the impact of that tape would not have been complicated by its association with one of the parties. Under the adversary system, however, the weight assigned to the tape depends on which side introduced it.

To demonstrate this point, assume that the strength of a piece of evidence on a disputed matter can be measured on a scale from plus ten to minus ten, with plus ten being the strongest, minus ten being the most harmful, and zero being neutral. Under the adversary system, the association of evidence with a particular party will influence the jury's determination of the weight of such evidence. As later chapters explain, if an item of evidence would be evaluated as a plus five when introduced by the judge, its value would typically be diminished, perhaps to a plus three, if introduced by the side that stands to benefit from it. On the other hand, introduction of the evidence by the party who is harmed by it will typically *enhance* its impact on the jury, perhaps to a plus seven or more.

To summarize, there is a cost associated with sponsorship that influences the weight that the jury will assign to a given item of evidence. Specifically, a party will generally be worse off if *his* attorney, rather than the opponent's attorney, introduces the evidence. This phenomenon, which we call the "cost of sponsorship," is examined in detail in Chapter Two.

Purposes of This Book

This book demonstrates the importance of sponsorship as a guide in conducting all aspects of a trial. As the following chapters will reveal, virtually no tactical decision can be fully analyzed without considering the sponsorship costs involved.

As we explain below, this book's conclusions, borne of simple logic, confirmed by longstanding evidentiary principles, and tempered by the authors' experience in conducting more than one hundred trials (primarily jury trials), contradict many of the basic teachings of the trial tactics literature. The reason for the contradiction is clear: no other book has identified sponsorship as a pervasive principle of trial strategy. Accordingly, as this book demonstrates, much of the advice given in the literature is unsound and even counterproductive. Throughout this book, we identify advice that we find to be misguided.

By the same token, however, portions of the literature are consistent with sponsorship principles. The problem is that the manuals provide no general theory to explain *why* certain advice is given. Thus, while we identify advice from other manuals with which we agree, we provide the theoretical underpinnings to demonstrate *why* such advice is sound.

Since much of our experience with juries is in the criminal area, most of our examples involve criminal cases, including many cases in which we were involved as trial lawyers. Nonetheless, the book's basic concepts—and its strategies for effective trial advocacy—operate at a level of generality that transcends the differences between criminal and civil cases. Of course, certain distinctions—involving, for example, the scope of discovery—must be taken into account when applying some of this book's recommendations. These differences are addressed where appropriate.

A major purpose of this book is to provide basic concepts and strategies that an advocate can apply almost automatically during trial, when there is no time to consult a manual. An attorney obviously cannot request a recess every time he needs to determine, for example, whether to cross-examine a witness or object to a question. The advocate who understands sponsorship can resolve such questions quickly and confidently. Contrary to a number of commentators, who assert that there is "no one 'right way'" to try a case,[8] we believe that there are a few basic rules—derived from sponsorship analysis—that can be applied to resolve most tactical issues arising at trial.[9]

Since its purpose is to provide basic concepts and strategies, this book does not catalogue every available trial technique for achieving a particular end. The literature is replete with advice of this sort.[10] Nonetheless, the principles of this book can be readily applied in evaluating the wisdom of such techniques.

Prior to recognizing and applying the sponsorship method, both authors lost several strong cases after faithfully applying conventional trial techniques. These losses occurred notwithstanding the authors' thorough familiarity with trial procedure and techniques, developed through training seminars and

8 *See, e.g.*, T. Mauet, *Trial Techniques* at xxi (Aspen Publishers 7th ed. 2007) ("In trial work, ... there is no one 'right way' to proceed .... [E]ffective [methods] are as varied as lawyers are numerous.").

9 *Cf.* II R. Jebb, *The Attic Orators from Antiphon to Isaeus* 370–371 (Russell and Russell, Inc. 1962) ("It was the essence of Greek oratory ... that its practice should be connected with a theory ... [and] from the first there was a fixed tendency to regard oratorical composition as susceptible of regular analysis ....").

10 *See, e.g.*, J. Tanford, *The Trial Process: Law, Tactics & Ethics* § 5.02, at 185 (LexisNexis 3d ed. 2002) (explaining how repeated valid objections can serve to fluster an advocate's opponent); *see generally* E. Imwinkelried, *Evidentiary Foundations* (LexisNexis 2005).

"hands on" experience in a number of jury trials. By contrast, both authors repeatedly won even their most difficult cases—many in verdicts of less than twenty minutes—once they identified and perfected the principles outlined in this book. Furthermore, as prosecutors, both authors secured convictions in retrials of cases in which other prosecutors, applying conventional techniques, had ended up with hung juries stacked heavily in favor of acquittal. These experiences convinced us that the chances for success at trial could be improved considerably by understanding and applying sponsorship principles.

We should emphasize that this is a book about jury trial advocacy. Its conclusions should not be mechanically applied elsewhere, such as in appellate briefs and oral arguments. For instance, in the appellate context, lawyers are ethically required to disclose controlling authority that is "directly adverse" to the advocate's position.[11] No similar rules exist in the trial context. Indeed, the expectations of judges and juries differ. Consistent with the ethical rules, judges *expect* lawyers to volunteer and discuss controlling adverse authority, and the failure of advocates to do so would be tactically unwise as well as unethical. But juries do not normally expect an advocate to introduce evidence damaging to his case. Because he is not ethically required to do so, the advocate should base his decisions on whether such a strategy would be tactically sound.

Of course, some of the principles of this book, such as not "overtrying" one's case, apply as well to arguments before judges. It is well known, for example, that a lawyer appealing a case should carefully limit the number of issues he raises.[12] The point is that the advocate, in assessing the applicability of sponsorship, must keep clearly in mind the precise audience and forum, and must be mindful of the extent to which sponsorship considerations may be overridden by court rules or ethical canons.

The Existing Trial Practice Literature—Inadequate and Misleading

As beginning trial lawyers, the authors searched in vain for a manual containing meaningful *tactical* guidance. More recently, in writing this book, we concluded that the existing trial manuals generally suffer from a number of major flaws.

11 *See, e.g.*, Model Code of Professional Responsibility, DR7-106(B)(1).

12 *See* page 34, n. 47 *infra*.

Most fundamentally, we found—as we had years earlier as young trial lawyers—that there is no trial book on the market containing any overarching principles. As we demonstrate throughout this book, existing manuals have for decades generally treated each phase of the trial as *sui generis*, and thus provide rules, observations, and anecdotes that apply only to the phase of the trial that is being discussed. For instance, there is no relationship between the suggested techniques for opening statement and those for cross-examination. Although some techniques set forth in this body of literature may be useful, the reader is still left in a state of confusion, having derived no theme that can be put to use in resolving the difficult—and often unique—issues that are certain to arise in his own trials. And when an issue arises that happens to be addressed in a manual, the reader is expected to accept the advice wholly on faith.

In addition, many manuals, by not recognizing the importance of sponsorship, offer advice that can harm the advocate's case. For instance, virtually all of the leading trial manuals favor the wholesale volunteering of weaknesses in the advocate's own case rather than letting the opponent present such matters.[13] As we will demonstrate, this wholesale approach is flawed.

Furthermore, many manuals focus heavily on elementary techniques, such as impeachment with prior statements and the introduction of various types of exhibits.[14] While these procedures are important and must be mastered, such procedural proficiency does not guarantee effective trial strategy. At bottom, knowledge of how to execute such techniques does not tell the advocate how to *win* trials.

Finally, many manuals devote more attention to matters of etiquette and personal style than to tactical issues. The view, apparently, is that such matters are important in persuading a jury. In our view, such advice elevates form over substance and achieves little tangible benefit. Accordingly, unlike other manuals, this book does not provide guidance on such subjects as what clothing or jewelry to wear in the courtroom,[15] how to breathe in a relaxed manner,[16] how

13 *See* page 78, n. 51, *infra.*

14 *See, e.g.*, Mauet, *supra* n. 8, § 6.3(15), at 212–14 (laying foundation for use of past-recollection-recorded exhibits); *id.*, § 6.3(3), at 185–86 (introduction of photographs and motion pictures); *id.*, § 6.3(14), at 211–12 (introduction of computer records).

15 *See, e.g.*, 1 S. Gazan, *Encyclopedia of Trial Strategy and Tactics* 1–2 (Prentice-Hall, Inc. 1962); L. Smith & L. Malandro, *Courtroom Communication Strategies* §§ 1.17–1.22 (Kluwer Law Book Publishers, Inc. 1985).

16 *See, e.g.*, F. Lane, *Goldstein Trial Technique 3d* § 1A:07–1A:09 (Thomson West supp. 2005) (describing relaxation techniques and techniques for abdominal breathing).

often to smile,[17] when to be humorous before the jury,[18] and where to sit and stand in the courtroom.[19] This book, in short, is a *tactics* manual. It begins where most other manuals leave off by providing guidance on how to *win* trials, not simply how to execute basic techniques.

Structure of the Book

The following chapters elucidate and apply the sponsorship approach. Chapter Two identifies the basic concepts. In particular, it discusses various characteristics of the jury system and identifies three separate sponsorship costs: the cost of introduction, the cost of unusual efforts, and the cost of overtrying. Chapter Three provides guidance on identifying the issues in the case. In addition, it sets forth the method for evaluating the strength of evidence bearing on those issues.

Chapters Four, Five, and Six describe the process for selecting evidence to use at trial. Specifically, Chapter Four develops and explains the fundamental rule of evidence selection for disputed issues: use only strong evidence. This simple rule, if followed, will ensure that the attorney does not "overtry" the case. It also addresses the handling of weaknesses.

Chapter Five discusses two categories of evidence selection decisions to which different rules must be applied. The first category involves evidence that an advocate must introduce in order to meet a legally imposed burden of proof. This burden applies not only to plaintiffs and prosecutors, but also to defendants presenting affirmative defenses. As we will explain, the advocate's failure to meet a legal burden of proof, even on an issue that is not disputed by the opponent, will prevent the case from even reaching a jury. The second category involves selection decisions relating to evidence that is uniquely associated with one party. The prime examples are the plaintiff (or complainant) and the defendant. Chapter Six focuses on the

17 *See, e.g.*, B. Palmer, *Courtroom Strategies* 172 (Prentice-Hall, Inc. 4th ed. 1966) (recounting the success of the "laughing defense," namely, defense counsel's use of "frequent smiles").

18 *See, e.g.*, L. Decof, *Art of Advocacy: Opening Statement* § 1.13, at 1–33 (LexisNexis 2006).

19 *See, e.g.*, Mauet, *supra* n. 8, § 4.3(7), at 72 (discussion and diagrams concerning where to stand for delivery of opening statement); *id.*, § 9.4(11), at 399 (similar diagram and discussion pertaining to where to stand in delivering a summation); R. Carlson & E. Imwinkelried, *supra* n. 4, § 10.2(J), at 261–64 (five separate courtroom diagrams relating to an attorney's positioning for the conduct of cross-examination). *See generally* S. Goldberg, *The First Trial: Where Do I Sit? What Do I Say?* at xxi (West 1982) (stating in the preface that the advice contained in the book is "so introductory that it will not be of any value after your first trial—certainly not after your third").

decisions to defend and rebut. The rules governing such decisions are based on those set forth in Chapters Four and Five.

Chapters Seven through Twelve apply the principles discussed in earlier chapters to all phases of the trial. Specifically, Chapter Seven addresses jury selection and opening statements. Chapter Eight focuses on direct examination and redirect examination. Chapter Nine discusses real evidence, demonstrative evidence, and stipulations. Chapter Ten considers issues relating to the opponent's case. In particular, Chapter Ten describes techniques for monitoring the opponent's opening statement, closing argument, and questions to witnesses. In addition, Chapter Ten discusses whether to voice objections. Chapter Eleven discusses cross-examination. Finally, Chapter Twelve provides guidance on crafting a persuasive closing argument.

CHAPTER 2

Sponsorship Principles

Overview

In the moments before opening statements begin, every trial lawyer is tempted to glance at the jurors to see what he can glean from their demeanor. Invariably, the jurors return stone-faced, impassive looks that provide little clue of what is on their minds. The lawyer will no doubt be wondering what will persuade them and how they will arrive at their verdict. In short, he will want to know what makes them "tick." This chapter addresses that question.

As will be seen, because juries are composed of ordinary citizens, they will act much like ordinary individuals act any time someone is trying to persuade them of a point. For that reason, this chapter develops the principles of sponsorship not only from trial examples but also from everyday situations arising outside of the courtroom. The chapter concludes by providing a formal statement of the three costs of sponsorship.

The Jury and the Advocate

The Jury's Assumption of Best Case with Minimum Effort

When the jurors are empanelled in a case, they face the awesome duty of deciding which party should prevail. They are told, usually at the outset of the trial, that it is their responsibility "alone [to] determine the weight, the effect, and the value of the evidence, as well as the credibility of the witnesses."[1] In discharging this duty, the jury generally cannot draw on prior courtroom experience, since the members typically consist of lay persons who are unfamiliar with how to evaluate trial evidence.[2] Moreover, the jury receives precious little assistance from the judge. Indeed, when the judge has intimated even the slightest personal opinion regarding the merits of the case, he will typically instruct the jury to disregard it.[3]

To be sure, the instructions of the court give general guidance on a number of topics, including the evaluation of evidence. Most of these instructions, however, ultimately leave discretion in the jury's hands.[4] Although judges in some jurisdictions are empowered to comment on the evidence,[5] this privilege is rarely utilized. Since the jury is unable to rely on the judge or draw on its own legal experience, it has no choice but to turn to the advocates for guidance in evaluating the weight of the evidence.[6] When it does, however, it faces a difficult dilemma.

It is basic that the jury views the advocate as the client's champion and spokesman and thus as fundamentally biased. Put another way, the jury views each attorney in the case not as a neutral arbiter, but as a "hired gun" with one task to perform: to win the case for his client.[7] Therefore, as a number of commentators have recognized, the jury assumes that everything an advocate says and does is calculated to reflect his client's case in its

---

1 *Criminal Jury Instructions, District of Columbia* § 1.03, at 8 (2002 ed.); *see also* K. O'Malley, J. Grenig & W. Lee, *Federal Jury Practice and Instructions* § 10.01, at 5 (West 5th ed. 2000)(criminal); *id.*, § 101.01, at 20 (civil).

2 *See, e.g.*, B. Kaplan, "Trial by Jury," at 49–50, *reprinted in* H. Berman, ed., *Talks on American Law* (Vintage Books 1961) (noting that juries consist of "untrained citizens ignorant of law, often of limited education, brought together to serve for a short time and unable to acquire experience in the art of judging").

3 *See, e.g.*, *Criminal Jury Instructions, District of Columbia*, *supra* n. 1, at 8 (containing model jury instructions providing that "[i]f you think that somehow I have expressed or even hinted at any opinion as to the facts in this case, you should disregard it"); O'Malley, Grenig & Lee, *supra* n.1, § 10.01, at 5.

4 *See, e.g.*, O'Malley, Grenig & Lee, *supra* n. 1, § 104.01, at 135 (sample jury instructions on burden of proof in civil cases); *id.*, § 105.01, at 161–62 (sample jury instructions providing that jurors are sole judges of credibility); *id.*, § 15.06, at 424 (sample jury instruction providing that "[i]t is the sole and exclusive right of the jury to determine the weight to be given to any prior conviction as impeachment"). Of course, the jury is occasionally given mandatory guidance on the evaluation of certain evidence or the absence of evidence. *See, e.g.*, *id.*, § 15.14, at 451–52 (sample jury instruction providing that no inference may be drawn from the failure of a criminal defendant to testify).

5 *See, e.g.*, O'Malley, Grenig & Lee, *supra* n. 1, § 7.5, at 791 (noting that "[a] federal judge ... may summarize and comment on the evidence and also express an opinion on the facts" but also noting that this practice is "not permitted in the courts of many states").

6 *Cf.* Brown, *A Juryman's View*, 2 Ga. B.J. 225, 227, 229 (1965) ("The most important persons in the courtroom to the juryman are the attorneys who participate in the trial .... [W]hat the attorneys did, said, or what they did not do or say overpowers other factors and influences the jurors' decision.").

7 *See, e.g.*, R. Carlson & E. Imwinkelried, *Dynamics of Trial Practice*, § 3.3(D), at 39 (West 3d ed. 2002) ("The jurors know that the attorneys are ... 'hired guns.'").

best possible light.[8] As Professor Lon Fuller observed, an advocate "is not expected to present his case in a colorless and detached manner." Unlike "a jeweler who slowly turns a diamond in the light so that each of its facets may in turn be revealed," the attorney "holds the jewel steady, as it were, so as to throw into bold relief a single aspect of it."[9] Stated more formally, the jury assumes that each advocate will make every contention and introduce all available evidence that he believes will materially favor his case. At the same time, it makes the corresponding assumption that each advocate will make no contention and introduce no evidence unless the advocate believes that it will materially favor his case. This follows from the jury's adoption of the fundamental principle of human behavior that individuals seek to accomplish their tasks with minimum effort.[10]

The jury's dilemma is how to evaluate an advocate's biased presentations and contentions and use them to arrive at a correct verdict. As the next section explains, the jury's basic rule is to fully accept from each advocate the bad regarding his own case but to view with great skepticism his favorable evidence. How it does this is not difficult to understand.

In essence, the jury utilizes its assumption of best case in a negative manner. Specifically, it is apt to infer that each side's case can be *no better* than that stated by the attorney. For this reason, the jury will not be inclined to identify contentions that are more favorable than those made by the advocate. Similarly, it will not be apt to speculate on the existence of favorable evidence that was not presented.

In using its assumption of best case, the jury will have little or no difficulty holding the actions of the lawyer against his client, assuming that it views the

8 *See, e.g.*, W. LaFave, J. Israel & N. King, *Criminal Procedure* § 1.4, at 28 (Thomson West 4th ed. 2004) (noting that under the adversary system, "[e]ach party is expected to present the facts and interpret the law in the light most favorable to its side, and through a searching counter-argument and cross-examination, to challenge the soundness of the presentations made by the other side"); S. Landsman, *The Adversary System: A Description and Defense* 4 (American Enterprise Institute 1984) (noting that under the adversary system, the attorneys are expected "to find and present their most persuasive evidence" and that "[a]dherence to this principle affords the decision maker the advantage of seeing what each litigant believes to be his most consequential proof"); S. Hamlin, *What Makes Juries Listen Today* 457–58 (Glasser LegalWorks 1998) (noting that the jury "expect[s] each lawyer to put the best face on his or her story" and "to slant questions and get answers that will only favor [his] witness and [his] case"); *cf.* E. Morgan, *Some Problems of Proof Under the Anglo-American System of Litigation* 3 (Columbia Univ. Press 1956) ("The theory of our adversary system of litigation is that each litigant is most interested and will be most effective in seeking, discovering, and presenting the materials which will reveal the strength of his own case and the weakness of his adversary's case. . . ."); G. Kennedy, *The Art of Persuasion in Greece* 23 (Princeton Univ. Press 1963) (terming the "right to present [one's] case in the best light possible" as "an inheritance from Greek justice imposed by the debates of the sophists").

9 L. Fuller, "The Adversary System," at 31–32, *reprinted in* H. Berman, ed., *Talks on American Law* (Vintage Books 1961).

10 *See, e.g.*, G.K. Zipf, *Human Behavior and the Principle of Minimum Effort* 6 (Addison-Wesley Press, Inc. 1949) ("[A]n individual's entire behavior is subject to the minimizing of effort.").

attorney as competent. This is because the advocate is perceived to be the client's agent or, indeed, *alter ego*. Everything the advocate says or does is treated as if the party represented had said or done it.[11] The assumption is generally a reasonable one, since the client usually sits in the courtroom during the trial listening to his lawyer's contentions, implicitly ratifying them.[12]

If the lawyer's actions, in hindsight, prove to be unwise, the jury will not assume that such actions were taken without the client's authorization. For instance, if the lawyer contends in opening statement that his client entered into a contract under duress, and if that contention is later undermined by the evidence at trial, the jury will not be likely to conclude that the duress theory was advanced against the wishes of the client and that the client had other viable defenses, such as a claim that there never was a contract.

The Jury's Negative Use of the Assumption of Best Case in Reaching a Verdict

General Principles

The recognition that the jury assumes each advocate to be presenting his best case is, by itself, of little practical use to the trial lawyer. What is of value is understanding *how* the jury utilizes this assumption in a negative manner.

In brief, because of its assumptions, the jury will accept nothing at face value that either advocate says, with one critical exception: any concession made by the advocate will be fully credited and held strictly against him. The reason for this is clear. If a competent advocate is presenting his case in its best light, then the case can be no better than he states it. No juror, after all, can be expected to espouse to his fellow jurors a position more favorable to a party than that embraced by the party's own advocate.

The jury's reasoning is quite logical. If what the jury sees and hears is the *best* the advocate has to offer, then it can conclude that there is nothing better. Moreover, because it assumes that the advocate will minimize his

11 *Cf.* McLhinney v. Lansdell Corp. of Maryland, 254 A.2d 177 (Md. App. 1969) (holding that a client is legally bound by admissions of an attorney in opening statement); Oscanyan v. Arms Co., 103 U.S. 261, 263 (1880) (noting, with reference to an admission in opening statement, that "[a]ny fact, bearing upon the issue involved, admitted by counsel, may be the ground of the Court's procedure equally as if established by the clearest proof"); United States v. Blood, 806 F.2d 1218 (4th Cir. 1986) (noting that defendant is bound by any clear and unambiguous admission of fact made by his attorney, whether the case is civil or criminal); United States v. Hurwitz, 459 F.3d 463, 481 (4th Cir. 2006)(client legally bound by attorney's admissions that are "clear and unambiguous").

12 *Cf.* 1 B. Elliott & W. Elliott, *The Law of Evidence* § 256, at 380–381 (Bobbs-Merrill Co. 1904) ("[S]tatements as to facts in controversy made by the attorney in the presence of his client may be shown as admissions, where it is also shown that the client heard them and made no objections.").

effort in seeking to present his best case,[13] the jury will view the advocate as *conceding* that every contention made and every item of evidence that he introduced is necessary and was therefore worth the effort to marshal. These implicit concessions are highly useful to the jury; they enable it to translate the advocate's words and deeds into concrete information that it can use to decide the case.

Juries have an insatiable appetite for concessions from the advocates. Concessions make a jury's task easier. They narrow the issues that it must resolve, and they remove what would otherwise be obstacles to reaching the ultimate issue, namely, which side should prevail. Accordingly, the only parts of the advocate's presentation that will be strictly relied upon in the jury room, even in the absence of any proof, are those that are *unfavorable* to his case, such as weaknesses acknowledged in opening statement, elicited in direct examination, and conceded during summation.[14] These concessions allow the jury to draw lines constituting the outer boundaries of its decision.

The jury will generally choose either one counsel's position or that of his opponent (or a compromise between the two). Rarely will it venture beyond those bounds. To be sure, on infrequent occasions, a jury will issue a note during its deliberations suggesting that it is considering a theory that neither advocate has advanced. But these rare instances do not undermine the point that the jury will seldom stray from the boundaries set by the advocates.

The jury's assumption of best case operates in evaluating what the attorney *says* and what the attorney *does* by way of introducing evidence. The following sections explain how and why this occurs.

The Advocate's Statements

It is a common observation regarding human behavior that if a person speaks falsely he is apt to do it when it benefits rather than harms him.[15]

13 *See* page 15, n.10, *supra*.

14 *Cf.* Fed. R. Evid. 801(d)(2), Advisory Comm. Note (noting the "freedom which admissions have enjoyed from technical demands [of hearsay rules] of searching for an assurance of trustworthiness in some against-interest circumstance"); Bruton v. United States, 391 U.S. 123, 139–140 (1967) (White, J., dissenting) (noting the "profound impact [of out-of-court admissions] on the jury," and stating that "an admission of guilt by the defendant ... constitutes direct evidence of the facts to which it relates. Even the testimony of an eyewitness may be less reliable than the defendant's own confession").

15 *Cf.* Jefferson, *Declarations Against Interest: An Exception to the Hearsay Rule*, 58 Harv. L. Rev. 1, 8 (1944) ("People are apt to speak freely and falsely in their own favor but are reluctant to speak falsely to their pecuniary or proprietary detriment."); Rutan, *Comment, Procuring the Right to an Unfair Trial: Federal Rule of Evidence 804(b)(6) and the Due Process Implications of the Rule's Failure to Require Standards of Reliability for Admissible Evidence*, 56 Am. U. L. Rev. 177, 198 (2006)("If a declarant utters a statement that is harmful to his own self-interest, courts can assume that the declarant thought carefully about the accuracy and reliability of the statement before making it.").

The jury views the statements of lawyers no differently: it tends to credit lawyers' negative statements about their cases but to view lawyers' favorable statements with suspicion. To illustrate the jury's perspective, assume that a teenage boy is confronted by his mother, who tells him that she waited until midnight for him to come home, at which point she went to sleep. If the teenager admits that he did not return until 2:00 a.m., the mother will assume that he was out until *at least* that time, and perhaps considerably later. She will not consider the possibility that he returned sooner, at 12:15 a.m.

It follows that if the advocate states something favorable about his client's case, the jury will be apt to view it as a concession that the matter is no better—and perhaps much worse—than stated. By the same token, if the advocate says something unfavorable about his case, the jury will be apt to view it as a concession that the matter is *at least* as bad as he has stated and is perhaps even worse.

The jury views an attorney's statements no differently than a prospective customer views statements of a salesperson. Consider, for example, a vacuum cleaner salesperson who is trying to convince a prospective customer to purchase a product. The consumer assumes that the salesperson is making the best presentation for the product. The salesperson's praise for the product—"finest on the market," "will last a lifetime," "cleans perfectly"—will thus be heavily discounted.

On the other hand, if the salesperson concedes that there is an equally good product by another company for the same price, that concession will be fully credited. The only open question is how much *better* the competitor's product may be, and the result is that the salesperson will almost certainly lose the sale unless the competing product is unavailable. No potential customer will conclude from such a presentation that the salesperson's product is *better* than the competitor's. Indeed, in the absence of independent verification, such a customer will be unlikely to conclude that the product is *as good* as the competition's. Stated more broadly, the consumer will be skeptical of any claim by the salesperson that is either favorable regarding his own product or unfavorable regarding that of his competitor. At the same time, the consumer will tend to give considerable weight to anything said by the salesperson that is either unfavorable concerning the salesperson's own product or favorable concerning the competing product.

The foregoing phenomenon is mirrored in how statements are evaluated in the political arena. For instance, prior to federal election reform legislation, it was a time-worn campaign practice to disassociate a political communication from the candidate benefiting from the communication. Thus, in President Lyndon Johnson's first campaign for a Congressional seat, his staff composed newspaper releases that were later printed as articles rather than as paid advertisements.The communications were believed to "carry more weight [that] way."[16] Significantly, current federal election law requires all paid political advertisements to identify the individual financing the communication, including his association, or lack thereof, with any candidate.[17]

In the same vein, political commentators have traced the Senate's rejection of former Senator John Tower, the elder President George Bush's first nominee for Secretary of Defense, to early revelations by presidential aides that the President himself "had his doubts" about the merits of the nomination. These revelations were termed "the first drops of poison."[18] The same concept has been described as "your-own-man-says-so."[19]

Similar thinking has been espoused in the public relations field, where it is believed that "the best way to persuade . . . is to hide the act of persuasion."[20] Consider the Easter Sunday 1929 event publicized by legendary public-relations executive Edward L. Bernays, who had ten women parade down Fifth Avenue in New York City, smoking cigarettes, in an event publicized as the "Torches of Freedom" march. Spokeswomen described the march as a blow for feminism, and the event made front page news. Bernays kept secret the fact that the event was financed by the American Tobacco Company.[21]

To illustrate the foregoing points in a setting closer to the jury trial, assume an arbitration proceeding in which the party seeking relief estimates his claim at $5,000 and the defending party acknowledges liability of only $1,000. It is highly unlikely that the arbitrator's award will fall outside of

16 R. Caro, *The Years of Lyndon Johnson: The Path to Power* 406–407 (Alfred A. Knopf 1983). *See also Philip Dormer Stanhope, Lord Chesterfield's Letters to his Son and Others* 34 (Everyman's Library 1969) ("your own excellencies, ... [i]f ... discovered without your pointing them out yourself, [gain] much more advantage").

17 *See* 2 U.S.C. § 441d(a). This statute by its terms applies regardless of whether the communication is true or false. *Cf.* United States v. Insco, 365 F. Supp. 1308, 1311 (M.D.Fla. 1973)("The statute says nothing about ... the necessity for a statement to be misleading.").

18 R. Evans and R. Novak, The Tower Scorecard, reprinted in Wash. Post, Mar. 15, 1989, at A23.

19 Jeff Greenfield, Your Own Man Says So!, Time Magazine, July 8, 1996, at 27.

20 *See* Malcolm Gladwell, The Spin Myth, printed in the New Yorker, July 6, 1998 at 66.

21 *See id.*

these boundaries. Like a jury, the arbitrator assumes that the case is no better than each advocate has stated. The $5,000 figure of the plaintiff is viewed as a concession that the case is worth no more. And the $1,000 figure of the defendant is viewed as a concession that the claim has validity *at least* in the amount of $1,000.

It should be clear from the above examples that jurors, like consumers, voters, and arbitrators, scrutinize statements of interested spokesmen for their negative content. For this reason, an advocate can harm his case by explicit concessions in opening statement and closing argument. By telling the jury that his case is somehow weak or unpersuasive, the advocate ensures that the jury will view the case in that light.

In sum, apart from the actual party, there is no better witness against a party than his own hired gun. To paraphrase a familiar admonition, the advocate should be on notice that anything he says to the jury "can and will be used against [him] in court."[22]

The Advocate's Evidence

The above discussion illustrates how the jury evaluates statements or assertions by reference to which attorney is making them. The jury's assumption of best case also colors its view of the advocate's evidence. This occurs in several ways.

First, an item of evidence introduced by an advocate will likely be viewed as the advocate's best evidence on the point. Non-courtroom examples illustrate the point. Assume that, in interviewing to hire a lawyer, an executive visits a partner at his office in a leading Wall Street law firm. During that visit, the executive notices, prominently displayed among pictures of the lawyer's family, a commendation from the City Bar Association for the lawyer's contribution to a particular Bar subcommittee. The executive will probably conclude that this commendation reflects the lawyer's most notable professional accomplishment of this kind to date. Similarly, when a restaurant posts a newspaper review of its food, the consumer will be apt to conclude that this is the *best* review and that other reviews not reproduced and posted—if any—are no better and, perhaps, are much worse. A review from several years ago (and the absence of recent reviews) will send the message that the restaurant has not received positive reviews in recent years. Here

22 Miranda v. Arizona, 384 U.S. 436, 469 (1966).

again, the customer's reaction to the posted review is no different from a juror's reaction to an advocate's presentation of evidence. Both examples illustrate the concession an individual displaying such items makes that he possesses no better items to display.

Second, the jury's assumption of best case will lead it to suspect that an advocate undertook to "package" the item of evidence so that, when viewed by the jury, it would appear in the light most favorable to his case. This suspicion will cause the jury to seek to "unpackage" the item. Again, a non-courtroom example illustrates the point.

Assume a television commercial in which the Brand A Cola Company is reporting the results of a taste test it conducted involving its own brand and that of its competitor, Brand B Cola. The viewer is apt to be highly skeptical of the results showing that Brand A Cola won. The viewer may suspect, for example, that several such tests had to be conducted before Brand A Cola prevailed in one, or that the sample of Brand A Cola used for the test was from a special stock. In short, he will have many misgivings about the validity of the test. And assertions by Brand A about the objectivity of the test will not completely eliminate the viewer's skepticism.

On the other hand, if the same television viewer opens a copy of a leading consumer magazine and reads an article about a taste test conducted under the magazine's supervision that yielded similar results, he will place far greater weight on the conclusion that Brand A was found preferable to Brand B. Finally, assume that the same television viewer goes to his accounting job and is told by a fellow accountant working on the Brand B account that everyone in Brand B's management is concerned about how to handle the results of a secret taste test conducted by Brand B in which Brand A won. In this circumstance, the viewer is apt to give the taste test the greatest weight of all. In fact, the viewer is likely to consider it settled beyond all doubt that Brand A has a better taste.

The jury is no different. It will evaluate a piece of evidence by reference to the advocate introducing it. For example, it will assume that witnesses are extensively coached and prepared so that their testimony favoring the attorney's case emerges at trial in the best light. For that reason, it will assume that the only parts of a witness's testimony that it can strictly rely upon without hesitation, even in the absence of any other proof, are those that *disfavor* the case of the advocate calling the witness. And even with respect to those unfavorable portions of the testimony, the jury will assume that the witness has presented those matters in the best light.

It follows from the foregoing that when an advocate presents evidence that is *inconclusive*, the jury will almost certainly construe such evidence in the light *least* favorable to the sponsoring advocate. To illustrate the point, assume an automobile accident case in which the issue is whether the defendant was speeding. Assume further that an expert is available to testify concerning his analysis of skid marks. If, based on the expert's analysis, the skid marks show that the defendant was traveling 60 MPH in a 30 MPH zone, then the evidence should be introduced by the plaintiff. If the expert can give only a range of between 25 MPH and 50 MPH, then such evidence is consistent with the defendant's case, and the plaintiff should *not* introduce it. The jury is apt to deem it significant that the best expert the plaintiff could find concedes that the defendant may have been driving within the speed limit. The common ground for decision is a finding that the defendant was driving 5 MPH under the speed limit, and the jury is very likely to reach that conclusion.

On the other hand, if the *defense* introduces that evidence, then the plaintiff can point out that the best expert testimony the defendant could produce is consistent with the plaintiff's contention that the defendant was speeding. This analysis reveals that *neither side* should introduce this inconclusive skid mark evidence.

The jury's assumption of best case with minimum effort colors the view of evidence in yet a third way. When the advocate introduces an item of evidence or calls a witness, he is making an implicit statement that the evidence is material and important to the case. In the worst-case scenario, the advocate's introduction of favorable evidence will be viewed as a concession that, without such evidence, he loses. The jury thus will not pause to consider whether the advocate would win without the item of evidence. The only disputed issue is whether the additional evidence is sufficiently favorable to require a verdict contrary to what it would have been without the item. In deciding that issue, the jury will preoccupy itself with considering all the reasons why the evidence is *not* sufficiently favorable. It will not dwell on the positive features of the evidence.

To use another non-courtroom example, assume that a consumer who is unfamiliar with electronics is deciding between two brands of stereo receivers carried at two competing stores. Assume further that the salesperson at one store stresses above all else that his brand delivers more watts per channel for the dollar than the competitor's brand. Finally, assume that a consumer magazine study conducted after the sales presentation found that the *competitor's* brand delivered more watts per channel for the price. The salesperson who made the erroneous statement would thereafter have great difficulty claiming that a receiver's watts per channel is irrelevant and that his product beats the competition on sound alone. The significance of a receiver's watts per channel will have been implicitly conceded.

The harm from conceding the materiality of a point is not limited to situations where the advocate cannot prove that point.[23] As the next section demonstrates, even if the advocate can prove the point, his case still might suffer if the advocate endeavors to prove more than he needs to win.

The Advocate's Use of Inferior Evidence

As noted above, the jury assumes that an attorney will *not* introduce an item of evidence unless he believes that it will materially favor his case.[24] To illustrate using a non-courtroom example, if a civil engineer's plans for boring a tunnel through a mountain call for anything other than a straight path, a person reviewing the plan is apt to assume that the engineer believed that a straight path would not have accomplished the goal.[25] Similarly, the jury will view an advocate who calls a witness as believing that the testimony was important enough to justify the effort.

Thus, where the advocate goes to the effort of introducing evidence that is inferior to other evidence that he has introduced, the jury is apt to assume that he views the inferior evidence as materially favoring his case. When the jury makes this assumption, the advocate's case is almost certain to suffer.

In the worst-case situation, the jury will assume that the advocate felt that he needed the inferior evidence to win. Put another way, the jury may conclude that the advocate has implicitly acknowledged that his other evidence is inadequate. This concession assists the jury in resolving the most fundamental

---

23 *Cf.* Letter from Abraham Lincoln to Usher F. Linder (Feb. 20, 1848), reprinted in 1 *The Collected Works of Abraham Lincoln* 453 (R. Basler ed. 1953) ("In law it is good policy to never plead what you need not, lest you oblige yourself to prove what you can not.") (emphasis omitted).

24 Juries tend to agree with Professor Wigmore's observation that "possible witnesses whose testimony would be for any reason comparatively *unimportant*, or *cumulative*, or *inferior* to what is already utilized, might well be dispensed with by a party on general grounds of expense and inconvenience." II J. Wigmore, *Evidence* § 287, at 202–203 (Little, Brown & Co. Chadbourn rev. 1979) (emphasis in original). *Cf.* Patton v. Rambo, 20 Ala. 485 (1852) (where only one of two examining physicians called, no adverse inference may be suggested to the jury as to uncalled physician without a showing that his testimony would have been *more* valuable).

25 *See, e.g.*, Zipf, *supra* n.10, at 2 (giving factually analogous example).

decision that it faces, and the one that it is least equipped to resolve: how much evidence is enough, under the applicable burden of proof (reasonable doubt, preponderance, and so forth), to sustain a given verdict.

As we will show, this concession from the use of inferior evidence alongside superior evidence is one that the advocate will have trouble overcoming. He will have difficulty convincing the jury, for example, that he presented evidence that was unnecessary or irrelevant. The jury will therefore be inclined to focus not on his superior evidence but on whether the inferior evidence is enough to put an otherwise inadequate case "over the top." The attorney is unlikely to benefit from this microscopic critique of his inferior evidence.

Accordingly, the weight given to an advocate's superior evidence will be influenced by any inferior evidence that he introduces. In general, the introduction of inferior evidence reduces the probative impact of the advocate's other, superior evidence. The reason is that the introduction of the inferior item is viewed as a statement by the advocate that the inferior item is needed in light of the inadequacy of his superior evidence. For example, when an attorney puts on a strong witness and a weak witness on the same point, the jury is likely to conclude that the attorney was not sufficiently convinced by the strong witness and felt compelled to produce additional evidence to make his case. In short, the advocate who uses inferior evidence risks that the consideration of his superior evidence will be significantly disparaged.

The Advocate's Unusual Efforts

Because of the principle of minimum effort,[26] jurors are influenced by any unusual efforts they perceive to have been required of the attorney to marshal an item of evidence. In general, the greater the perceived effort, the less favorably the jury will view evidence. This phenomenon is reflected in common experience.

For example, when a man is complimented on his sports jacket, his statement, "Oh, I was in a rush. It was the first thing I grabbed," is an attempt to enhance the viewer's impression. A contrary response—"This is my best and most expensive jacket. It took me weeks of shopping in Europe to find it."—would leave the viewer thinking, "It's not that great." [27]

---

26 *See* page15, *supra*.

27 *Cf.* E. Moers, *The Dandy* 32 (Viking Press 1960)(quoting verse of fictitious English Regency era gentleman, "My neckcloth ... costs me, each morning, some hours of flurry ... [t]o make it appear to be tied in a hurry.").

Similarly, a student's classmate will be more impressed by his high grade if he achieved the grade without studying. The student would substantially reduce the impact of the grade by stating, "I did nothing else but study for the test for two months." Fellow students will then view their classmate as compulsive and not naturally gifted, and will conclude, "Anyone could have gotten that high a grade with *that* much studying."[28]

Along the same lines, a celebrated interior designer counsels his clients, "no matter how grand the house, I like things to look easy—you don't want to show effort."[29]

The same phenomenon applies in the courtroom setting. Thus, in the trial involving the lineup tape discussed in Chapter One, the exhibit was made less desirable as a potential exhibit for either side because of the unusual efforts that would have been required to display it to the jury. Similarly, a lawyer's meager results on cross-examination will be magnified if the questioning is lengthy and labored. For example, in Robert Traver's novel, *Anatomy of a Murder*, defense counsel in summation effectively ridiculed the prosecutor for having "hammered and clawed" throughout his fruitless "terrier cross-examination."[30]

The foregoing examples illustrate the concept of the "concession of no better evidence" for a given level of effort. Specifically, the jury will assume that, for any given level of effort necessary to marshal an item of evidence favorable to the advocate's case, the advocate could not have produced evidence of equal or greater probative value by using less effort. Furthermore, whether evidence is favorable or unfavorable, successively greater levels of attorney effort to present it amplify the corresponding concession of materiality. And, where the evidence is favorable, these successively greater levels of effort increase to correspondingly greater levels the disparagement of his other favorable evidence.

---

28 *Cf.* B. Castiglione, *The Book of the Courtier* 70 (Penguin Classics 1976) (observing that a person who performs well nonchalantly convinces on-lookers that "if he took great pains and effort he would perform even better").

29 Elizabeth Lambert, *Wiltshire Perspectives, The Quiet Aesthetic of Designer Robert Kime*, Architectural Digest 150 (January 1995). *See also* J. Kronius, "Mario Buatta's Unstuffy Style," Wash. Post, Mar. 21, 2002, at H4 (leading interior designer extolling "the undecorated look," which "doesn't look like the decorator just left" but instead looks like it was simply "there for a lifetime").

30 R. Traver, *Anatomy of a Murder* 395 (St. Martin's Press 1958). *See also* S. Turow, *Presumed Innocent* 168–169 (Farrar Straus Giroux 1987) (fictional criminal defense lawyer, explaining to his client that he did not want to conduct an investigation into the accuracy of certain government records, noted, " 'I would not want to see [the government] introduce the fact that we made efforts to challenge the accuracy of these records and failed' "); C. Lesley, *Remembered Laughter: The Life of Noel Coward* 298 (Alfred Knopf 1976)(recounting theatrical play producer's dismay upon overhearing the "dire words" of an audience member, "You can see they've gone to a lot of trouble, but I don't know . . .").

The Advocate's Use of the Attack

The Importance of the Attack

Some trial manuals caution against spending much time attacking or responding to the opposition. They reason that the advocate, by so doing, is communicating that he has nothing of his own to offer and that he is forced out of desperation to attack his opponent.[31] Such advice is inconsistent with what the jury expects of an interested advocate.[32]

The jury's assumption of best case includes a mirror-image expectation as well: the jury looks to each advocate to highlight the shortcomings of the opponent's case. Thus, while the advocate must strive to demonstrate the merit in his own position, he must likewise strive to demonstrate the lack of merit in his opponent's position. As the following section explains, if the advocate succeeds in convincing the jury of the latter, then it will be largely constrained to rule in his favor. For this reason, it is normally as much to the advocate's benefit to show the flaws in his opponent's side as it is to show the strengths in his own side.

To illustrate the point in a common setting, assume that a prospective home buyer has conclusively narrowed his choice to two houses in different neighborhoods and is trying to decide between them. The real estate agent for one of the houses will, of course, attempt to influence the buyer by stressing the desirability of the house that he is selling, such as the high quality of nearby schools and easy access to public transportation. If the buyer states that he is considering another house being handled by a competing agency, the thorough agent will also stress the undesirability of the other house, such as its location in a highcrime area.

This principle was illustrated by events during the course of the 1988 presidential election.Then Republican candidate George H.W. Bush demonstrated that he could reap as great a benefit from attacking his Democratic opponent, Michael Dukakis, as he could from simply stressing

31 *See, e.g.*, J. Sonsteng, R. Haydock & J. Boyd, *The Trial Book—A Total System for the Preparation and Presentation of a Case* § 10.6 at 337 (West 1984) ("It is not wise to spend significant portions of the closing argument responding to the opponent's issues, positions, and arguments. The jury may perceive an attorney [who] does this as an advocate without any substantial positions."); 1 S. Schweitzer, *Cyclopedia of Trial Practice* § 185, at 503 (Lawyers Co-op. Pub. Co. 2d ed. 1970) ("Under no circumstances should the defendant in his opening make a direct criticism of any claim of the plaintiff.").

32 The importance of the attack has been recognized since ancient times. *See, e.g.*, G. Kennedy, *The Art of Persuasion in Greece* 131 n. 13 (Princeton Univ. Press 1963) (noting view of 19th Century scholar that the "attack on the opponent" was a "characteristic fifth-century [Greek] feature of the proof").

the merits of his own candidacy. Once he applied that strategy, he climbed dramatically in the polls and ultimately won the election.[33]

Theoretical Underpinnings for the Attack

Most experienced defense lawyers need no instruction on the value of attacking the government's or plaintiff's presentation. For them, the two methods for persuading the jury could not be more obvious: they can win both by emphasizing the strength of their own case and by contending that the prosecutor or plaintiff has not met his burden.

Nonetheless, we have found that, among many plaintiffs' lawyers and prosecutors, the requirement of a burden of proof has been an obstacle to their full appreciation of the value of attacking the defense. They reason that because *they* have the burden, their success in demonstrating the lack of merit in their opponent's defense will not make the jury more likely to find in their favor. In our view, this analysis is flawed.

To be sure, a jury is not constrained to select between the two positions urged by the parties. The jury could conceivably find for one party on a theory that was not even urged by that party. For example, if a suit filed by a plaintiff can be defended in three possible ways, the lack of merit in one of the defenses does not necessarily imply the validity of the plaintiff's claim. In logical terms, given the alternative defenses, the plaintiff's claim and the invalid defense are at best "contrary" (*i.e.*, both could be false but only one can be true) and not "contradictory" (*i.e.*, if either one is false, the other must be true).[34] If that is so, then it would seem to follow that showing that the opponent's defense lacks merit does not substantially help establish the merit in the advocate's position. The jury could still rule for the opponent on a theory that the advocate has not advanced.

Nonetheless, where defense counsel has urged only the one meritless defense, the jury will not likely seek to identify and evaluate defenses that have not been advanced. Rather, it will be apt to assume that defense counsel has selected the *best* defense and that, if that one is not enough, then the others are *a fortiori* inadequate. As a result, the plaintiff's claim and the defense urged by defense counsel assume, as a practical matter, a contradictory relationship in

33 *See, e.g.*, P.J. Buchanan, "Keep up the Pressure, George," reprinted in the San Diego Union, Aug. 30, 1988, at B7 (noting that George Bush went from an 18-point disadvantage to a 6-point lead during the month of August by going on the offensive and attacking Michael Dukakis's views).

34 *See Merriam Webster's Collegiate Dictionary* 252 (10th ed. 1997) (definitions of "contrary" and "contradictory" as used in logic).

which showing the falsity of one implies the truth of the other. Thus, the plaintiff's attorney or prosecutor who succeeds in meeting his legal burden of proof will derive as much benefit from exposing the weaknesses of the opponent's case as he will from advancing the strengths of his own case.[35]

The Costs of Sponsorship

It is useful at this point to formalize the foregoing analysis by recognizing the existence of three fundamental costs of sponsorship incurred by the advocate in making contentions and introducing evidence. Each of these costs ultimately rests on the fundamental assumption of best case with minimum efforts.

These costs bear on virtually every tactic and strategy recommended by this book. Furthermore, familiarity with them will enable an advocate to make his own tactical decisions in the heat of trial, when time does not permit the advocate to consult a manual for guidance.

The First Cost: Introduction of Evidence

When an interested advocate introduces an item of favorable evidence, the jury will conclude that the item was the best evidence on the point that could be marshaled using that degree of effort. This constitutes, as noted, a harmful "concession of no better evidence." Furthermore, the attorney's act of presenting the item of evidence is received by the jury as a "statement"—whether intended or not—that the attorney deems the item of evidence probative and material to the resolution of the case. Thus, when an advocate introduces an item of evidence favorable to his case, the advocate will, in the worst case, be viewed as making a statement that the item of evidence is *needed* to prove his case.[36] The jury will be apt to credit that concession of need but view the evidence with skepticism and discount the

35 Some commentators have suggested that a prosecutor should not adopt an aggressive trial strategy. *See, e.g.*, Alschuler, *Courtroom Misconduct by Prosecutors and Trial Judges*, 50 Tex. L. Rev. 629, 636 (1972) (arguing that a prosecutor "should avoid the 'glow and flow of the heat of forensics' and should, in fact, strive for more 'Chesterfieldian politeness'"); *cf.* Model Code of Professional Responsibility, EC 7-13 (instructing prosecutors "to seek justice, not merely to convict"). Other commentators point out, however, that while a prosecutor's goal is not simply to convict but to see that justice is done, this in no way relieves him from his duties as an advocate once he decides that there is a valid basis for bringing criminal charges. *See, e.g.*, W. Seymour, *Why Prosecutors Act Like Prosecutors*, 11 Record of NYCBA 302, 312–313 (1956) ("When we decide to prosecute, it is because we decide that this is how justice will be done .... [At trial, the prosecutor is] a full-fledged fighting advocate; and he should be .... To do otherwise would be to violate his duty in the most real sense."). We favor the latter view.

36 This phenomenon is reflected in the rhetorical principle that "the burden of proving lies always on him ... who asserts a reason as sufficient," A. Sidgwick, *Fallacies: A View of Logic from the Practical Side* (D. Appleton & Co. 1884), as well as in the legal maxim, whose attribution is unknown to us, "The law never favors the performance of an unnecessary act."

attorney's assessment of its favorable probative value.

Correspondingly, when an advocate introduces an item of evidence that is *unfavorable* to his case, the implicit "statement" or concession that the evidence is important will result in the unfavorable evidence being given enhanced weight. Put another way, the jury will view that statement as an admission that it is *the advocate's* job to show that the damaging item does not compel a verdict against him. This is far worse than the alternative of having the opponent burdened with showing that the item is important to the verdict.

Britain's experience with its former colony, Hong Kong, illustrates the point in a non-courtroom setting. The governing treaty called for Britain to relinquish control in 1997 to the People's Republic of China. News reports, however, quoted a "well placed insider" in China's diplomatic mission in Hong Kong as saying that China "had no intention of recovering Hong Kong in 1997," mindful of the fact that Portugal retained control of Macao for some 20 years after the lapse of the treaty permitting Portugal to remain in that island colony. But in 1979, Britain itself raised the issue of Hong Kong's post-1997 status with Chinese leader Deng Xiaoping. According to the Chinese government insider, had Britain not done so, transfer to Chinese rule in 1997 "could have been avoided." The suggestion, according to one news article, was that Britain's decision to raise the issue was a "blunder[]" that "sealed the colony's fate."[37]

Introduction of an item of evidence—whether favorable or unfavorable—triggers a further prejudicing of the jury's evaluation of that item. This impact stems from the jury's assumption that the advocate has packaged the item to appear in its best light. For example, when an advocate introduces a witness, the jury assumes that the advocate had one or more pretrial conferences with the witness. The jury will normally assume that such conferences afforded the advocate the opportunity to probe all dimensions of the witness's recollection and to select only those aspects that favor his client's case. It may further suspect that, if a witness at a pretrial conference initially recalled something inconsistent with the advocate's case, the advocate will have confronted the witness with the statements of other witnesses in the hope that the witness would reconsider his own recollection.[38]

---

37 *See* Washington Times, May 16, 1997, at A1.

38 *Cf.* Markus, *A Theory of Trial Advocacy*, 56 Tul. L. Rev. 95, 102–103 (1981) (noting the advocate's desire in a pretrial witness conference to "develop characteristics of the event favorable to [his] client's position," and also noting how "the witness will be encouraged to reconsider the accuracy of [his] recollection(s)" by the advocate's confronting him with the contrary recollections of other witnesses).

Similarly, with respect to items of physical evidence, the jury will be apt to assume that such evidence was packaged in its best light. For example, when it sees a photograph, the jury will assume that the picture contains the best possible angle, lighting, and distance (among available photographs) to make the advocate's point.

Given these two consequences of introduction—the attorney's statement of materiality[39] and the jury's assumption that the attorney packaged the evidence in its best light—it should be apparent that an advocate introducing evidence is generally worse off than he would have been had the evidence been introduced by the opponent. This is true regardless of whether the evidence is favorable or unfavorable. This influence can be graphically illustrated as a uniform shift to the left along a continuum, as represented in the figure below, where the numeric value after the shift occurs represents the weight assigned to the evidence by the jury.

Figure 2-1: Axis of Materiality

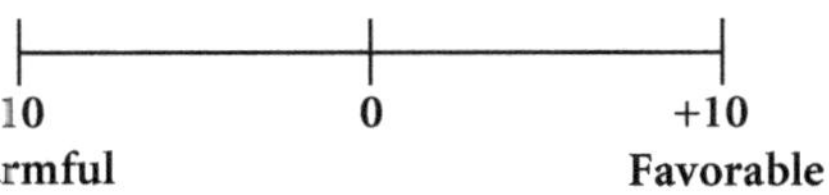

We term this uniform shift "the cost of introduction." This shift reflects the cost associated with the introduction of any item of evidence, whether favorable, neutral, or unfavorable. Put another way, other things being equal, the act of introducing an item of evidence will influence the weight that the jury gives to that item in a manner that disfavors the sponsoring advocate's case.

In general, the more an item of evidence favors the advocate's case, the lower will be the cost of introduction. This is because the concession of no better evidence is less damaging when the quality of the evidence approaches perfection. It is also because the jury expects the advocate to present all evidence that materially favors his case.

As we show in Chapter Four,[40] recognition of this cost of sponsorship leads to the rejection, as a general tactical rule, of a fundamental principle of the current trial tactics literature: that an advocate invariably gains by

39 For convenience and where appropriate, this book uses the terms "statement of materiality" and "concession of materiality" as encompassing the concession of no better evidence as well.

40 *See* page 66, *infra.*

bringing out a weakness in his case rather than leaving it to the opponent to introduce. The reason why this principle is unsound as a general rule is that when the advocate brings out the harmful evidence, *he* incurs the cost of introduction, and the item of harmful evidence is therefore given heightened weight by the jury. In addition, the opponent benefits from the cost that he would otherwise incur in having to bring out the weakness, which is favorable from his perspective.

By the same token, when the opponent brings out a weakness in the advocate's case, such as in the example discussed in Chapter One of the cross-examiner eliciting the prior conviction of one of the advocate's witnesses, the benefit to the opponent's case is reduced because he has to introduce it and incur all the sponsorship costs associated with presenting what, again, is *favorable* evidence from the opponent's perspective. For these reasons, the impact of the weakness on the advocate's case is not as great as it would have been had the advocate elicited it. Thus, while the strategy of volunteering weaknesses has applicability in certain limited circumstances (discussed in Chapter Four), it is untenable—and must be rejected—as a general principle of advocacy.

The Second Cost: Unusual Efforts

The second cost of sponsorship is based on the phenomenon discussed earlier in this chapter regarding the efforts of attorneys as perceived by the jury. Specifically, any unusual efforts perceived to have been expended by an advocate to marshal an item of evidence will influence the weight given to that item in a manner that disfavors that advocate's case. Like the cost of introduction, the impact of the cost of unusual efforts can be graphically illustrated as a uniform shift to the left along the continuum depicted in Figure 2-1 above.[41]

The cost of unusual efforts is distinct from the cost of introduction. To be sure, there is an overlap between these two costs. The act of calling a witness represents a fixed quantity of effort on the attorney's part. The attorney must go out of his way to contact and interview the witness. The attorney must also give the witness directions to the courthouse, and occasionally issue a subpoena to secure the witness's attendance at trial. It is largely the expenditure of effort in calling the witness that causes the

41 *Cf.* Castiglione, *supra* n. 28, at 67 ("facility ... excites the greatest wonder; whereas, in contrast, to labour at what one is doing and ... make bones over it ... causes everything, whatever its worth, to be discounted").

jury to conclude that the attorney deems the witness material to the case. For analytical convenience, however, this book treats the two costs separately. [42]

To illustrate the distinction between the two, assume that a witness has testimony about four facts and gives testimony concerning all four. The advocate introducing such testimony will suffer a loss in evidentiary weight as to each of these four facts by operation of the cost of introduction. If, in order to prove one of the four facts, the attorney must conduct an elaborate and lengthy examination involving multiple documents and diagrams, the jury will be apt to discount even further the weight given to that one fact.[43]

It is important to note that, on rare occasions, the jury's consideration of the efforts an attorney appears to expend may make it tactically advisable for an advocate to introduce harmful evidence himself. This will arise when the apparent effort required of the advocate to *omit* evidence from his presentation causes the jury to give that evidence *greater* weight when the opposing counsel later introduces it than it would have received had the advocate introduced it. This point is discussed in detail in Chapter Four.

The Third Cost: Overtrying

Special considerations apply when an advocate has more favorable evidence than is required to establish a *prima facie* case or disprove the opponent's case, and is therefore faced with the question of whether to use that additional evidence. As we have said, the introduction of such additional evidence can adversely impact the weight that the jury assigns to the advocate's *other* evidence. This impact is distinct from that predicted by the costs of introduction and efforts.

The jury's tendency to discount the weight it attaches to an advocate's other evidence when he introduces an item of additional evidence stems from the implicit concession that the advocate believes the evidence to be

42 For the most part, this book refers to the cost of unusual efforts as simply the "cost of efforts." This shorthand term is for convenience only. Thus, the "cost of efforts" refers solely to additional costs beyond the normal costs of introducing a witness or piece of evidence and questioning that witness.

43 The costs of introduction (excluding packaging) and unusual efforts can be considered in combination as a function of the strength of the item of evidence and the effort required to marshal it, where costs decrease with strength and increase with unusual effort.

important enough to warrant introducing it. As previously noted,[44] the jury assumes that an advocate will dispense with an item of evidence if it does not *materially* advance his case. Thus, when an advocate calls a witness who, though favorable, appears cumulative or inferior to another witness whom he has previously called, the jury is apt to view the advocate as taking a dim view of that other witness. If the advocate appears to feel this way about the other witness, the jury will tend to discount that witness's testimony.

When the advocate introduces such favorable additional evidence in his case, the jury may assume that the advocate is concerned that such evidence is *needed.* As noted above,[45] the ultimate hazard is that the jury may conclude that the advocate is worried that his other evidence, standing alone, is insufficient to win.

If this negative effect is substantial enough, a net harm can result from introducing more rather than fewer favorable witnesses or items of evidence. This phenomenon reflects the cost associated with what is commonly termed "overtrying" one's case. The critical step in understanding the cost of overtrying is to recognize the counterintuitive point that there exists *favorable* evidence that, when introduced along with other of the advocate's favorable evidence, reduces the overall persuasiveness of his presentation. Evidence causing such an effect should be omitted from the advocate's presentation.[46]

For example, assume an assault case in which the defendant is claiming misidentification and the complainant has testified unequivocally and convincingly that the defendant is the one who committed the assault. Assume further that a second witness is available to testify that he is sixty percent certain that the defendant was the assailant. In these circumstances, the advocate's calling of the second witness to corroborate the complainant is apt to diminish significantly the probative value that the jury assigns to the complainant's testimony. In our experience, the decrease in weight that the jury would give to the complainant's testimony by operation of the cost of overtrying would easily outweigh the incremental probative value of the

44 *See* page 23, n. 24, *supra.*

45 *See* page 28, *supra.*

46 For those interested in mathematics, several of sponsorship doctrine's relationships between strength and effort (and how, for example, overtrying costs are incurred) can be described using "constrained optimization" techniques familiar to students of microeconomics. The problem is formulated by positing an effort-minimizing advocate constrained to put on at least what he considers to be sufficient evidence to win. An analogous problem is set forth in A. K. Dixit, *Optimization in Economic Theory* 9 (Oxford Univ. Press 1976) (production of target output at minimum cost).

second witness (as adjusted by any costs of introduction and efforts). For this reason, the second witness should *not* be called.

In sum, an item of *favorable* evidence, when added to the other evidence in the advocate's case, can sometimes cause a net *reduction* in the overall persuasiveness of his case. Employing the graph in Figure 2-1, the effect is to *reduce* the weight placed on the other evidence, standing alone, by an amount that is *greater* than any positive increment gained from the probative value of the additional evidence.[47]

The advocate must also recognize the possibility, widely known among experienced defense attorneys, that the use of an item of favorable evidence may reduce his chances of securing a favorable verdict even when he introduces no other evidence. As explained more fully in Chapter Six, criminal defense attorneys must assess the impact of introducing *any* defense evidence on the weight given to the *opponent's* foregoing presentation. By presenting any defense evidence, defense counsel is communicating a concern that he *needs* to do so because of the persuasiveness of the opponent's case.

Specifically, the jury may view the defendant's decision to present a defense as a concession that his opponent has made out a case that, if not rebutted, would be sufficient for a verdict in the opponent's favor. In those circumstances, the impact would be to enhance the weight that the jury will give to the opponent's evidence. Employing the graph in Figure 2-1, the effect is represented by a positive or rightward shift in the weight that would otherwise be accorded to the prosecution's case. The attorney considering whether to put on a rebuttal or surrebuttal case faces similar issues.

By itself, the simple principle that overtrying a case can be harmful is not a new one. Many commentators have recognized it.[48] Nonetheless, the rationale typically given—that the jury will become bored or confused[49] —does not articulate the real danger from overtrying a case.

---

47 In Jones v. Barnes, 463 U.S. 745 (1983), the Supreme Court underscored this principle in the appellate context, stating, *id.* at 752, "[R]eceptiveness declines as the number of assigned errors increases. Multiplicity hints at lack of confidence in any one. . . . [M]ultiplying [claimed errors on appeal] will dilute and weaken a good case."; *id.*, "The effect of adding weak arguments will be to dilute the force of the stronger ones."; and *id.*, n.5, "[A] brief which treats more than three or four matters runs serious risks of . . . giving the overall impression that no one claimed error can be serious." (Quotation marks omitted.)

48 *See, e.g.*, J. Appleman, *Preparation and Trial* 211 (Coiner Pub., Ltd. 1967) ("[D]on't forget one primary rule. Never overtry a case.").

49 *See, e.g.*, *id.* at 211 ("A jury will become bored by a constant stream of witnesses upon trivial matters.").

It is important to note that the cost of overtrying incurred by the use of additional evidence is influenced by the strength of that additional evidence. Other things being equal, the stronger the additional evidence is (relative to the other evidence), the lower will be the cost of overtrying. This is because the jury expects the advocate to present all evidence that materially favors his case. To whatever extent the introduction of the additional evidence comports with this expectation, the advocate will reduce his cost of overtrying.

Likewise, the weaker the advocate's other evidence is (relative to the additional evidence), the lower will be the cost of overtrying incurred by the use of the additional evidence. In this circumstance, the advocate's acknowledgment of the weakness of his other evidence by introducing the additional evidence will be less significant because the jury will, to a great extent, already see that weakness.[50]

The advocate, of course, should not lose sight of the inherent probative value of the additional item of evidence. Net costs of overtrying from the use of evidence are incurred only where the benefit from the additional item is exceeded by the harm to the probative value of the other evidence. Where there is a net benefit, then obviously the evidence should be used. If the additional and other items are of equal probative weight, for example, other things being equal, there *will* be a net benefit.

This chapter has demonstrated how an attorney's words and deeds can influence the jury's perception of the strength of his case and that of his opponent. Most fundamentally, it has shown that the same item of evidence will be given significantly different weight depending on which side introduces it.

Some may believe that the adversarial system's requirement that the parties marshal the evidence (rather than the court or another neutral source) results in an undesirable distortion of the weight given to such evidence.[51]

50 Two further factors influence the cost of overtrying: the efforts expended in marshaling the additional evidence (which result in increased costs of overtrying) and the efforts expended in marshaling the other evidence already presented (which result in decreased costs of overtrying).

51 *See, e.g.*, Sward, *Values, Ideology, and the Evolution of the Adversary System*, 64 Ind. L.J. 301, 316 (1989) ("adversarial adjudication may overemphasize party control to the point of distortion"); *but* see S. Landsman, *The Adversary System: A Description and Defense* 4 (perceiving "advantage" in the trier's "seeing what each litigant believes to be his most consequential proof"); cf. 2 U.S.C. § 441d(a) (disclosure of candidate affiliation utilized as an *aid* to the voter in interpreting political communications). The inquisitorial system is not without its own distortions, as we explain in Chapter Eight.

Nonetheless, whether an advocate approves or disapproves of this feature of the adversary system, he must consider the costs of sponsorship in virtually every tactical decision he makes if he wishes to maximize his success at trial.

CHAPTER 3

Issue Identification and Evidence Evaluation

Overview

Any advocate facing trial must perform two critical threshold tasks before deciding upon a trial strategy. First, the advocate must identify the issues in the case and determine which ones are going to be disputed. Second, he must evaluate the strengths and weaknesses of the available evidence in light of the disputed issues. This chapter addresses those two tasks.

Identifying Issues Capable of Being Disputed

Identifying disputed issues—or, in the case of the defense, choosing which issues to dispute—is a critical task of an advocate preparing for trial. The first step in accomplishing this task is for the advocate to identify his interpretation of the available evidence—commonly known as his "theory of the case." For the plaintiff or prosecutor, this interpretation of the evidence must satisfy the requirements of the legal burden of proof applicable to the claim or offense in the case.[1] Similarly, a defendant who is disputing one or more elements of the claim or offense or who is asserting an affirmative defense must have in mind an interpretation of the evidence that defeats his opponent's claim.

1 *See* pages 94 to 96, *infra* (describing the method for ascertaining the legal elements of a claim).

The key to identifying the disputed issues in the case is for the advocate to determine, based on his knowledge of all of the evidence available to both parties, those elements of the claim or affirmative defense for which both sides have a non-frivolous position. To illustrate, assume that a defendant has been sued for breach of contract. The defendant's attorney, in planning the defense, should consider a variety of issues, such as whether there is evidence that his client even entered into a contract. The attorney may conclude that the discussions between the parties were simply preliminary negotiations that did not culminate in an offer and an acceptance.

Moreover, if the statute of frauds applies, the attorney should determine whether a sufficient writing exists to satisfy that statute. In addition, the attorney may consider whether, if a contract was formed, any affirmative defenses are available, such as undue influence or duress. After considering these and other available means of defeating the claim, defense counsel will presumably have identified those elements of the opponent's claim that he is capable of disputing.

Predicting the Issues That Will Be Disputed

In General

Where there is more than one issue for which both sides have a non-frivolous position, each advocate has an important additional determination to make. For the plaintiff's attorney or prosecutor, an educated guess should be made as to which elements of his claim the opponent will deny or which affirmative defense, if any, the opponent will advance. If the attorney anticipates an affirmative defense, the attorney must determine which element of that defense he is capable of disputing.

For defense counsel, a decision must be made as to which elements of the claim to deny or which affirmative defense, if any, to advance. If defense counsel decides to advance an affirmative defense, he must make an educated guess regarding which element his opponent is capable of disputing. The following two sections give guidance in accomplishing these tasks.

Ascertaining What the Defense Will Be

As noted, the plaintiff's lawyer or prosecutor must assess which elements or aspects of his case, if any, the defendant will deny and what affirmative defenses, if any, will be presented. In a civil suit, the rules of civil procedure facilitate this determination, and civil discovery procedures permit an in-depth exploration of a defendant's contentions.[2] By contrast, in a criminal case, the defense must normally be inferred, if possible, from defense counsel's opening statement or from such evidence as recorded statements of the defendant at the time of his arrest. Even here, however, the prosecutor may, in limited circumstances, be legally entitled to learn the nature of the defense prior to trial.[3]

Deciding Whether to Advance More Than One Defense

This section addresses the considerations pertinent to whether a defense attorney should advance more than one defense. For instance, in the foregoing contract suit example, the defendant may find that more than one defense is available under the facts of the case. The question here is whether he should assert more than one defense.

If the available defenses are inconsistent—for example, no contract negotiations ever took place, but if they did, the resulting contract was entered into under duress—only *one* defense, the stronger one, should be selected. By offering an inconsistent theory and suggesting that it could be credited, the defense would be conceding that a reasonable interpretation of the evidence exists that precludes its primary theory. Advancing both defenses would substantially reduce the weight that the jury would place on the evidence supporting the stronger defense. For this reason, we counsel against advancing inconsistent theories. This conclusion comports with the position taken by most experienced trial lawyers.[4]

The more difficult issue is whether an advocate should advance alternative theories that are not inconsistent—for example, defending a contract suit by claiming duress and also arguing that the defendant's performance did not constitute a breach of the contract. Because of the cost of overtrying, advancing the second defense may be viewed by the jury as revealing

2 *See, e.g.,* Fed. R. Civ. P. 26–37 (various discovery rules, including procedures for depositions, interrogatories, and requests for documents and admissions).

3 *See, e.g.,* Fed. R. Crim. P. 12.1 (government may request notice of defendant's intention to offer an alibi defense; such notice shall specify the defendant's whereabouts at the relevant time and list "the names and addresses of the witnesses upon whom the defendant intends to rely to establish such alibi"); Fed. R. Crim. P. 16(b)(1)(A) (requiring, upon a defense demand on the government for disclosure of documents and tangible objects, that the defendant disclose the ones that he intends to produce at trial); Fed. R. Crim. P. 16(b)(1)(B) (requiring, after the defendant requests that the government disclose the results of tests or experiments it intends to use at trial, that the defense disclose the same items to the government).

4 *See, e.g.,* R. Carlson & E. Imwinkelried, *Dynamics of Trial Practice* § 3.3(D), at 35 (West 3d ed. 2002) ("The threshold question is whether the attorney should urge all [factually inconsistent] theories at trial. Most experienced attorneys answer that question in the negative.").

the attorney's lack of confidence in his first defense. Here again, most experienced attorneys advise, as a general rule, against advancing multiple theories to the jury, even if such theories are not inconsistent.[5]

Sponsorship analysis agrees, for the most part, with the approach of not advancing alternative but consistent defenses. The agreement stems largely from the fact that in the typical case, the alternative defense is not compelling. In such a case, the cost of overtrying instructs that the jury will be apt to attribute the assertion of the weaker defense as a concession by defense counsel that his other defense is insufficient. In this respect, the jury's reasoning is similar to the reasoning it applies when assessing inconsistent defenses.

The jury will be unlikely to reach this conclusion, however, when the alternative defense is supported by equally compelling evidence. This is because, as we have stated,[6] the jury is inclined to view any advocate as committed to presenting any available evidence or argument that will *materially* advance his case. In this situation, advancing more than one defense would normally be appropriate.[7]

For example, assume an undercover narcotics distribution case in which the defendant has credible alibi evidence showing he was not the seller. Assume further that he can also call into serious question the accuracy of the government's tests showing that the substance purchased by the agent was heroin (as opposed to a harmless substance used to defraud buyers, such as baking soda). Here, the advocate may well be advised to advance both theories, assuming that he is careful in crafting his argument.[8]

Evaluating Evidence on the Disputed Issues

Once the disputed issues are discerned, the advocate can evaluate the probative value of the evidence in light of those issues.[9] It is basic that a given

5 *See, e.g.,* Carlson & Imwinkelried, *supra* n. 4, § 3.3(D), at 35-37 (citing practices of experienced lawyers); *cf.* R. Keeton, *Trial Tactics and Methods* § 10.6, at 370 (Little, Brown & Co. 2d ed. 1973) (noting dangers in asserting multiple or inconsistent defenses before the jury, but pointing out that such an approach is appropriate in drafting pleadings).

6 *See* page 15, *supra.*

7 As noted in the previous chapter, the advocate faces a similar dilemma when he has more than one item of evidence available to prove the same point. *See also* pages 151 to 152, *infra.*

8 Chapter Twelve provides guidance in making such an argument. *See* pages 208 to 209, *infra.*

9 The special considerations pertinent to evaluating the strength of evidence on undisputed issues are addressed in Chapter Five. *See* page 97, n. 14, *infra.*

item of evidence, when considered in its totality, can either help, harm, or have no influence on the strength of the advocate's case. The terms used in this book to describe these categories of evidence are "favorable," "neutral," and "harmful."

Favorable evidence is evidence that, on balance, makes the position urged by the advocate more probable in the jury's eyes than it would have been without such evidence. Harmful evidence is evidence that makes the advocate's position less probable in the jury's eyes than it would have been without such evidence.[10] Neutral evidence is evidence that, on balance, makes the advocate's position neither more nor less probable than it would have been without such evidence. In classifying evidence, the advocate must compare the persuasive impact on the jury of using the item of evidence along with his other evidence and the impact of using the other evidence alone.[11] The advocate must also recognize that, as used in this book, the terms for classifying evidence refer in the first instance to the strength of evidence as introduced by a neutral source, not to the strength of evidence as adjusted for sponsorship costs.

Evidence cannot be considered favorable, as defined in this book, merely because it seems in some respect to advance the advocate's position on a disputed issue. Before an advocate can conclude that an item of evidence is, on balance, favorable, the advocate must assess the item in its totality.

For example, in an assault case involving a claim of self-defense, the testimony of an attentive and observant passer-by witness who can give an unequivocal account of the assault that, if credited, precludes the possibility of self-defense would constitute favorable prosecution evidence. Since the passer-by is not acquainted with either of the parties, he has no motive to fabricate, and his credibility is virtually impossible to impeach. The same testimony, however, from a relative of the victim who had previously told the police that the defendant had acted in self-defense may, on balance, constitute favorable, neutral, or harmful evidence when the testimony as a whole, including impeaching materials, is considered. In making this determination, the advocate would need to consider, among other things,

---

10 *Cf.* Fed. R. Evid. 401 (defining "relevant evidence" as "evidence having any tendency to make the existence of any fact that is of consequence to the determination of the action more probable or less probable than it would be without the evidence").

11 *Cf.* 11 C. Wright & A. Miller, *Federal Practice and Procedure* § 2883, at 449 (West 1995) (in discussing, *inter alia*, whether the erroneous admission or exclusion of evidence is harmless, the probative effect of the item of evidence in question is to be determined "in light of all the evidence").

the strength of the other evidence available, the closeness of the relationship between the defendant and the victim, and the persuasiveness of the witness's explanation for the prior inconsistent statement.

The three categories—favorable, neutral, and harmful—coincide with the positive, negative, and zero portions of the materiality graph depicted in Chapter Two (figure 2-1). In addition to these three categories, this book identifies a fourth category of evidence—designated as "marginal" evidence—clustering closely around zero on the graph.[12]

The test for whether evidence is marginal is likewise a relative one. An item of evidence is marginal if, when considered in conjunction with any other evidence supporting the advocate's case, it has no *realistic* chance of causing an otherwise unconvinced trier of fact to render a verdict in the advocate's favor.

Given the foregoing test, an item of evidence may be marginal even if, as a theoretical matter, it makes the proposition that the advocate is asserting more probable than it would have been without the item. For example, where an eyewitness to a rape can state only that the rapist was white (the defendant's race), such evidence, although technically favorable to the prosecutor, is unlikely to persuade the jury to rule in the prosecutor's favor.

It is important for the advocate to be familiar with the above-mentioned categories. They are employed throughout this book as a framework for evaluating the costs of sponsorship incurred by the use of evidence.

Evaluation of Evidence Bearing on More Than One Disputed Issue

Although the basic categories of favorable, neutral, and harmful evidence carry simple titles, the determination of the appropriate category for a given piece of evidence can be a difficult one. In a case where there is more than one issue, evidence may fall into one category for purposes of one issue and another category for purposes of a second issue.

12 Courts have used the term "marginal" to describe evidence that, although erroneously admitted, was not likely to have swayed the verdict. *See, e.g.*, Lokos v. State, 434 So.2d 831, 835 (Ala. 1983) (noting that "the inflammatory aspect of [the] evidence would have been only marginal at most and certainly insufficient to establish any likelihood that the jury would have reached a different result without it").

For instance, an eyewitness to an automobile accident might have favorable testimony on behalf of the victim that the defendant was driving recklessly. That same witness, however, might testify that he observed the victim walking with a noticeable limp immediately before being struck, thereby undercutting the victim's claim for damages. Thus, while the witness may be favorable on liability, the witness's testimony might be harmful on the issue of damages. The advocate considering the use of such a witness must balance these two features of the testimony. Similarly, in a murder prosecution, graphic photographs of the victim might constitute favorable evidence on the question of premeditation but neutral evidence on the question of the perpetrator's identity.

As the above discussion has indicated, evaluating an item of evidence as favorable, neutral, or harmful is a fundamental task that the advocate must perform in deciding whether to use the item at trial. It is, however, only a preliminary step. As will be shown below, the second critical step is to evaluate the sponsorship costs in using the evidence. Only after conducting both tasks can an advocate decide whether to use it or omit it.

Categorizing Favorable Evidence as Strong

In addition to the terms harmful, neutral, marginal, and favorable, this book uses a further term—strong—to describe the strength of evidence. That term is a label that is applied to an item of evidence only *after* the circumstances of its introduction by one of the parties are taken into account. An item of favorable evidence is strong only if it is viewed by the jury as enhancing the advocate's case notwithstanding the fact of his introduction of it. To use the terminology introduced in Chapter Two, *favorable evidence is strong only if its probative value outweighs the sponsorship costs incurred by a party's introduction of it.* As a rule-of-thumb, an advocate assessing whether evidence is strong should ask whether he has a *persuasive* reply to the opponent's contention that such evidence proves *nothing* of substance. Only if the jury is apt to conclude that the evidence materially advanced the advocate's case will such evidence qualify as strong.

The advocate must consider each cost of sponsorship identified in Chapter Two in assessing whether an item of favorable evidence qualifies as strong when introduced by the advocate. Consider, for example, the decision whether to call a witness. First, the advocate must assess the cost of introduction. As explained in Chapter Two,[13] the jury assumes that witnesses are carefully prepared by the advocate who calls them. It also normally assumes that it is hearing only what the advocate wants it to hear and how he wants it heard. This makes the jury skeptical and suspicious of the testimony. Moreover, the jury will view the advocate calling the witness as making an implicit concession that the testimony is material. On this point as well, the jury will be skeptical. In the worst-case situation, the jury will ask itself, "What does that prove?"

Second, the advocate must assess the cost of any unusual efforts. For instance, any lengthy or complex testimony elicited through the use of elaborate exhibits or demonstrations would result in additional costs.

Finally, the advocate must assess the cost of overtrying. Specifically, the advocate must consider the possibility that the jury will assume that the advocate was forced to call this witness because his other evidence was insufficient. Thus, as explained in Chapter Two,[14] the advocate must consider the extent to which the jury will give less weight to his other evidence because of his own apparently dim view of it. The introduction of the additional witness may trouble the jury and prolong its deliberations. In the worst-case scenario, the additional witness could lead to an adverse verdict, as the jury concludes that the witness's testimony is not enough to put an otherwise inadequate case "over the top."

Only after this rigorous analysis will the advocate be able to evaluate the witness as the jury evaluates him. And only then will he know whether the testimony of the witness is truly favorable *as introduced by the advocate.*

The above-described analysis of how to evaluate a witness is not limited in application to testimonial evidence. Thus, the advocate must rigorously analyze the three sponsorship costs in assessing the strength of any exhibit that he is considering for use at trial. For example, a seemingly innocuous document that an advocate initially assessed, on balance, to be favorable may be viewed by the jury as harmful because of his introduction of it. The jury's critical scrutiny of the document may cause it to focus solely on those features that are damaging to the advocate's case. Most experienced trial lawyers are familiar with examples of cases where jurors got sidetracked by—and perhaps even based an adverse verdict on—some aspect of an exhibit that an advocate had carelessly introduced to support his case.

---

13 *See* pages 28 to 31, *supra.*

14 *See* pages 32 to 35, *supra.*

It is important not to be misled by the term "strong" as it is used in this book. In a weak or circumstantial case, many items of seemingly weak evidence may be categorized as strong because the sponsorship costs are so low. This is apt to be true most often where the advocate's other evidence is likewise extremely weak. In such a circumstance, the cost of overtrying is negligible. Since the advocate's other evidence is so insubstantial, the implicit concession that he needs the item in question to win will be essentially harmless. The jury will view the advocate's other evidence as weak even without regard to the additional item of evidence.

An example of this type of strong evidence would be much of the circumstantial evidence used in the 1980s to convict Wayne Williams, a serial child murderer in Atlanta. The government had no eyewitnesses to the murders. Thus, it was forced to rely on, among other things, fibers discovered on the victims' bodies that were similar to fibers recovered from Williams's home and from various automobiles he had driven.[15] Had there been eyewitnesses, much of this circumstantial evidence would have been less-than-strong.

It is critical to reiterate that the initial labeling of evidence along the continuum from favorable to harmful must be done by assuming that the evidence is not associated with either of the parties by having been introduced by one of them. The advocate's final labeling as "strong" involves adjusting for the three costs associated with having sponsored the evidence. Only after adjusting for these costs can the advocate decide whether he in fact benefits from introducing the evidence.

This chapter provided guidance in identifying the issues in the case that are likely to be disputed. It further introduced a set of definitions that an advocate should use in evaluating the strength of evidence. The following three chapters build on these principles and describe the process for selecting evidence to use at trial.

15 *See* Williams v. State, 251 Ga. 749, 312 S.E.2d 40 (1983).

CHAPTER 4

Selection of Evidence on Disputed Issues

Overview

It has long been said that a trial lawyer should not "overtry" his case.[1] Yet, while this saying is known to virtually every trial lawyer, we have found neither precise guidance on how to avoid overtrying a case nor an adequate explanation of why this rule is a sound one. Perhaps this explains why so many practitioners fail to follow this advice.

The sponsorship method provides a simple formula for not overtrying a case. Specifically, when the advocate is selecting evidence bearing on a disputed issue, he should use only strong evidence. This rule acts as a "pruning" device enabling the advocate to eliminate evidence that will detract from his presentation.

Some commentators maintain that in most cases, an advocate is compelled to introduce *all* available evidence in order to win the case.[2] We reject this position. In our view, virtually every trial involves a selection from available evidence. Even a one-witness case typically presents mul-

1 *See, e.g.,* J. Appleman, *Preparation and Trial* 211 (Coiner Pub., Ltd. 1967) ("[D]on't forget one primary rule. Never overtry a case."); *but cf. ibid.* ("All occupants of an automobile always must be called or accounted for, irrespective of the fact that they may know nothing relating to the events.").

2 *See, e.g.,* 2 F.X. Busch, *Law and Tactics in Jury Trials* § 290, at 847 (Bobbs-Merrill Co., Inc. 1959) (referring to the "situation in which there are more witnesses available than are ... necessary to establish a claim or defense," the author claims that "[m]ore often than not this situation does not exist; the advocate usually finds himself faced with the hard fact that if he is to make out a respectable case he will have to use every person who can give relevant testimony").

tiple opportunities to introduce (or refrain from introducing) exhibits or documents. And in such a case, decisions concerning the scope of direct examination require the advocate to exercise judgment in the selection of testimony to elicit. Thus, the question of what, if any, evidence to introduce on a disputed issue is one that every advocate must address, regardless of whether the case is simple or complex.

Despite the old saying, many attorneys deliberately overtry their cases. They are fearful of omitting any favorable evidence, no matter how little their cases are helped. This fear stems from a concern that the jury will speculate that the evidence not produced would have been harmful. Since such attorneys perceive no cost from introducing evidence that is at least neutral, the very idea of sifting through favorable and neutral evidence to avoid overtrying the case seems unworthy of the effort. These factors often lead attorneys to conclude that, like the "straw that broke the camel's back," *any* item of favorable evidence might be just what the jury needs to clear up a question and render a favorable verdict. By this reasoning, any item of evidence falling on the "plus" side should be introduced, even if that evidence is only slightly helpful. Ultimately, however, whether the advocate uses all available evidence out of fear of omitting anything helpful or whether he uses it all because there seems to be no harm in doing so, such a strategy is unwarranted.

This chapter establishes a framework for enabling the advocate to avoid overtrying the case. The general rule, as we have stated, is to use only strong evidence. The following three sections discuss the use of favorable, neutral, and harmful evidence at trial. The chapter concludes with a discussion of the process of selecting evidence to undermine evidence previously presented by an opponent. Chapter Five discusses two categories for which a different selection rule is required: evidence needed to satisfy a legal burden of proof and evidence that is uniquely associated with one party to the case.

Favorable Evidence

In General

This section discusses issues relating to the selection of favorable evidence for use at trial. It begins by providing the advocate with the theoretical justification for using only strong evidence. It then identifies a number of specific categories of favorable evidence that will rarely qualify as strong. The discussion then focuses on the benefits an advocate may obtain through pre-trial disclosure of certain favorable evidence. Finally, the discussion addresses considerations pertinent to the use of marginal evidence.

Theoretical Underpinnings for Using Only Strong Evidence

Because this book defines favorable evidence as evidence that, on balance, makes the advocate's position more probable in the jury's eyes than it would have been without such evidence,[3] it would seem only logical that an advocate should introduce *all* evidence categorized as favorable. Indeed, many advocates, unaware of sponsorship costs, routinely use evidence that does not materially advance their cases out of a fear that the jurors will penalize them if such evidence is omitted. A critical teaching of this book is that such a fear is unjustified as long as the item of evidence in question is equally available for use by the opponent and the jury is aware of that availability. When these conditions are met, the jury will not hold the absence of the evidence against the advocate's case.

This conclusion follows from the jury's assumption that an advocate will put on only evidence that *materially* advances his case. When an advocate fails to introduce an item of evidence, the jury is apt to assume that the evidence would *not* have significantly helped his case. And when the evidence is equally available for use by both advocates and neither advocate introduces it, the jury will assume that it would not have materially aided *either* side's case.

For instance, in a case where the jury knows that a given witness who was not called was equally available to both sides, if one juror suggests during deliberations that the witness may have seriously harmed one side's case, another juror will be apt to respond that if that witness was so harmful, the other side would have called him. As the jurors realize that *neither* attorney considered the witness's testimony material enough for the witness to be called, they will reach the same conclusion as the attorneys did. They will then move on in their deliberations.

If the advocate's fear is that his opponent will exploit in summation the non-production of the less-than-strong witness, such fear is unwarranted and should not cause the advocate to introduce the less-than-strong evi-

3 *See* page 41, *supra*.

dence. The advocate can readily rebut the point by emphasizing the equal availability of the witness. This can be easily illustrated.

Assume that a defendant struck and injured the plaintiff with his automobile and that the defendant is claiming unavoidable accident. Assume further that there were three pedestrian eyewitnesses, that the plaintiff calls only two of them, and that the testimony elicited at trial reveals that the third pedestrian was in a position to have seen the accident. Here, assuming that the defense had learned prior to trial of the identity and address of the third pedestrian, defense counsel would not benefit from highlighting the plaintiff's failure to call the witness. If he were to make such an argument, plaintiff's attorney could respond:

> Ladies and gentlemen, the whole job of a lawyer is to bring in witnesses who have testimony favoring his client's case. My opponent heard the testimony of the two pedestrians whom we called and who established overwhelmingly the elements of our case. After he heard them, you can bet that he would have had the third pedestrian up on the stand in a minute if that individual had anything helpful to say for his side.
>
> To illustrate how illogical defendant's argument is, imagine a defendant in a burglary case who had solid fingerprint evidence that the government had the wrong man. No defense lawyer would withhold such compelling evidence and base his argument solely on the fact that the government failed to introduce fingerprint evidence implicating the defendant.

This argument of equal availability should satisfy the jury that the witness can give no material testimony.[4]

In most circumstances, the jury will consider evidence to be freely available for introduction by both parties in the case. This is especially true when the evidence at trial indicated that both sides knew the identity of the particular witness or item of evidence. Occasionally, however,

4 In a criminal case, a prosecutor must exercise great care in making such an argument. He is barred from suggesting that the defendant had any obligation to put on evidence. Nonetheless, he *can* state that the defense was free to put on evidence. *See, e.g.,* United States v. Wesley, 422 F.3d 509, 516 (7th Cir. 2005) (proper for prosecutor to state in rebuttal closing argument that defendant, who did not testify, "could have subpoenaed" a witness whom the defense counsel in his own preceding closing argument had suggested was in possession of material evidence); United States v. Sblendorio, 830 F.2d 1382, 1393 (7th Cir. 1987); *see generally* Chapter Six, page 115, n. 7, *infra* (discussing restrictions on prosecutor's arguments).

this will not be the case. Some juries may erroneously believe that only one side had the ability to use certain evidence. In that situation, there is a theoretical risk that the jury will penalize one advocate for not introducing evidence that his opponent could have introduced. Nonetheless, this risk is insubstantial. As noted above, if the opposing attorney tries to exploit the absence of the witness from the advocate's case, the argument that the opponent could have called the witness should effectively neutralize the point. Where the opponent does not make the point, the jury, acting on the assumption that he is advancing his best arguments, will not be apt to make it for him.[5]

The foregoing discussion has explained how juries treat evidence that is not produced and how they react to arguments of counsel that attempt to exploit an opponent's non-production. As an aside, it should be noted that the argument of equal availability counseled by sponsorship analysis corresponds with the principles underlying the so-called missing witness doctrine. To understand why this is so, a brief explanation of that doctrine is required.

Under the missing witness rule, if a party fails to call a witness who is peculiarly within the party's knowledge and power to produce, the opponent may obtain an instruction informing the jury that the failure to produce the witness permits an inference—which the jury can accept or reject—that the witness's testimony would have been unfavorable to that party.[6] Like the sponsorship approach, the missing witness rule is premised on the fundamental assumption that an advocate will seek to put on his best evidence.[7] For present purposes, the significant point to note is that a missing witness instruction will not be given, and argument along those lines will not be permitted, unless the attorney seeking the instruction can satisfy

5 As we show in Chapter Five, there is a special category of witnesses—party-associated witnesses—for which the argument of equal availability will not be fully successful and for which one side may be penalized for not calling a witness, even if the other side does not highlight the witness's absence.

6 *See, e.g.,* K. Broun, G. Dix, E. Imwinkelried, D. Kaye & R. Mosteller, *McCormick on Evidence* § 264, at 220–21 (West 6th ed. 2006); *see generally* K. O'Malley, J. Grenig & W. Lee, *Federal Jury Practice and Instructions* § 14.15, at 338 (West 5th ed. 2000) (criminal); *id.,* § 104.25–104.26, at 149–50 (civil).

7 The rule is inapplicable, and no adverse inference may be drawn, unless the missing evidence would have been "superior" to that already produced. *See, e.g.,* II Wigmore, *Evidence* § 287, at 202–203 (Little, Brown & Co. Chadbourn rev. 1979) (terming it "plain" that "possible witnesses whose testimony would be for any reason comparatively ... *inferior* to what is already utilized, might well be dispensed with by a party ... without any apprehension as to the tenor of their testimony .... [T]here is a general limitation ... that the [adverse] inference cannot fairly be drawn except from the non-production of witnesses whose testimony would be *superior* in respect to the fact to be proved") (emphasis in the original).

the requirement that the evidence was uniquely available to his opponent.[8] This means that when a witness is equally available to both sides, neither side may argue that the missing evidence would have been unfavorable to his opponent's case.[9] This is precisely what sponsorship analysis predicts that the jury will conclude from the non-production of an equally available witness.

Generic Examples of Favorable Evidence Outweighed by Sponsorship Costs

In General

Whether favorable evidence qualifies as strong depends, among other things, on the strength of the other evidence in the case. Thus, it is not possible to identify categorically those items of favorable evidence that will be less-than-strong in every case, once sponsorship costs are assessed. Nonetheless, there are various types of evidence that usually do not qualify as strong. Some types are encountered with sufficient frequency to merit special mention.

Character Evidence

Character witness testimony often constitutes less-than-strong evidence once sponsorship costs are assessed.[10] Rarely can such a witness testify to the facts of the case. Rather, the proof of a party's good character is made in the hope that the jury will find that the conduct alleged in the suit would have been so "out of character" that the party could not have committed it.

Juries, however, normally do not view good character as precluding the commission of bad acts.[11]Moreover, they may be particularly skeptical when the character witness is a relative of the person on whose behalf he

8 *See, e.g.*, United States v. Bahna, 68 F.3d 19, 22 (2d Cir. 1995) (approving trial court's instruction that neither party may benefit from the other party's failure to call a witness whom both parties had an "equal opportunity" to present); Evans v. Multicon Const. Corp., 6 Mass. App. 291, 375 N.E.2d 338 (1978); United States v. Currier, 454 F.2d 835, 839 (1st Cir. 1972); Shurman v. United States, 233 F.2d 272, 275 (5th Cir. 1956).

9 *See, e.g.*, Pointer v. Pointer, 251 S.W.2d 334, 338 (Mo. App. 1952) ("Either party could have called [the witness] and we find no basis for an inference that [the] testimony would have been unfavorable . . . ."); II Wigmore, *supra* n. 7, § 287, at 202–204.

10 The use of character evidence is typically subject to detailed rules governing admissibility. *See, e.g.*, Fed. R. Evid. 404(a).

11 Courts have recognized that character evidence has only limited probative value. *See, e.g.*, United States v. Burke, 781 F.2d 1234, 1239 (7th Cir. 1985) ("People of impeccable reputation may commit crimes, and when they are charged with crime the question is whether they did it, not whether they enjoy a high social standing.").

is testifying or is otherwise biased in favor of that person. Even in the case of an ostensibly unbiased witness, the jury is likely to think that virtually anyone can find witnesses who will swear to a person's good character.

The message of the advocate who introduces character evidence is apt to be that the advocate lacks confidence that his other evidence, standing alone, is sufficient to prove the case. Once that message is communicated, it is extremely unlikely that the character evidence will bridge the gap in the jury's eyes. Indeed, based on the cost of overtrying alone, the character testimony may be received by the jury as harmful to the overall presentation.

To be sure, character evidence may sometimes be strong. For example, the jury might be persuaded when the character testimony comes from someone less likely to lie, such as a priest or rabbi.[12] As a general rule, however, character evidence will rarely qualify as strong and thus should seldom be used.

Corroborative Detail Evidence

Many trial advocates regularly succumb to the temptation of introducing corroborative evidence on a minor detail. The reasoning is that a case will appear stronger to the jury when various collateral details are confirmed by multiple witnesses or items of evidence.[13] For example, in a rape case where the victim has identified the defendant as her assailant, some prosecutors may be tempted to introduce test results showing that foreign pubic hair recovered from her genital area came from a person belonging to the same race as the defendant.[14] In a metropolitan area where a majority of the population belongs to this same race, however, those test results would be an example of favorable evidence that may damage the government's case in light of the cost of overtrying. If the defense is misidentification, even the defense is conceding that he is the same race as the actual assailant. Thus, at

12 Similarly, a jury may occasionally believe that someone with high standing in the community would have too much to lose to commit a crime. *See generally* United States v. Burke, *supra* n. 11, 781 F.2d at 1240.

13 *See, e.g.,* Markus, *A Theory of Trial Advocacy*, 56 Tul. L. Rev. 95, 105 (1981) ("The factfinder is more likely to accept [testimony regarding his observations] if the witness can recite [supplemental details] which confirm his ability to make those observations .... [Such] details have no significance to the [issue in dispute], but they confirm the ability of the witness to perceive and recall the recited event.") (footnote and citation omitted); 2 A. Amsterdam, B. Segal & M. Miller, *Trial Manual for the Defense of Criminal Cases* § 395, at 1-536 to 1-537 (Amer. Law Inst. 1984) ("It is vital to corroborate the [client] on every point on which corroboration is possible .... Every matter in which [he] is supported by proof that the trier of fact is likely to believe has a capacity to spread and envelop his ... testimony with an atmosphere of veracity.").

14 We assume, for purposes of this example, that DNA forensic testing techniques are not available to the prosecutor.

the very least, defense counsel will likely belittle this evidence by pointing out that it is entirely consistent with his defense.

Ultimately, the only value of the pubic hair test is in eliminating the possibility that the victim was mistaken or lying about the race of her assailant. Yet, such a theory of the case is so unlikely that, before the introduction of the test results by the prosecutor, most defense attorneys would not have thought to bring it to the attention of the jury. By introducing the test results, the prosecutor has raised theories of innocence that were not even espoused by the opponent. Because the test results are completely consistent with the defense in the case, the prosecutor has done nothing to persuade the jury on the disputed issue, namely, whether the defendant is actually the assailant. And, what is far worse, the prosecutor has enabled the defense attorney in closing argument to belittle the prosecution's case by portraying the introduction of the test results as a pathetically inadequate bid to bolster what the government must recognize is the insufficiency of the victim's identification testimony, standing alone, to merit a guilty verdict.

Informant and Accomplice Testimony

Informant and accomplice witnesses are frequently favorable to the government before sponsorship costs are taken into account. After such costs are considered, however, the testimony of such witnesses is often less-than-strong.[15] Thus, the prosecution should normally be very reluctant to call informant and accomplice witnesses, especially in the case-in-chief. The testimony of such witnesses is virtually always encumbered by one or more motives to fabricate. For instance, informants have often received payments from the government, and accomplices are often seeking to satisfy the obligations of a plea bargain or to avoid harsh punishment (if they are awaiting sentencing).

Because of the cost of introduction, some juries would evaluate such a case as if the accomplice or informant testimony did not exist at all. They might suspect that such a witness is apt to say anything to advance his own interest. Moreover, because of the cost of overtrying, some juries might go even further. Rather than simply ignoring the accomplice/informant testimony, they might actually give *less* weight to the remainder of the

15 *Cf.* O'Malley, Grenig & Lee, *supra* n. 6, § 15.02, at 364; *id.*, § 17.04, at 394 (model jury instructions that jurors should view informant and accomplice testimony with greater care than other witness testimony); *see also* United States v. Bernard, 625 F.2d 854, 857 (9th Cir. 1980) (describing accomplice testimony as "unreliable").

government's evidence in light of the prosecutor's apparent concern that he needed that testimony to win. Thus, the prosecutor is often better off omitting the accomplice or informant testimony from his case-in-chief, since this avoids the appearance of reliance.[16]

Strong Evidence the Opponent Will Introduce or Enable the Advocate to Introduce in Rebuttal

Previous portions of this chapter instruct that the advocate should use all "strong" evidence, that is, favorable evidence that outweighs sponsorship costs. This section provides a somewhat high-risk strategy that the advocate may wish to consider in the appropriate case. The strategy is for the advocate to refrain from introducing some of his strong evidence if he is virtually certain that the opponent will be introducing it.

Such a strategy may be warranted for two reasons. First, as predicted by the cost of introduction, an advocate gains more from an item of evidence if the opponent introduces it. Specifically, while the advocate avoids the jury's tendency to discount the strength of evidence that he introduces, he capitalizes on the jury's inclination to give enhanced weight to any evidence introduced by the opponent that is unfavorable to the opponent's case.[17]

Second, as we have seen, the act of introducing an item of favorable evidence is often tantamount to a concession that such evidence is essential to the advocate's case. The effect, as predicted by the cost of overtrying, may be to reduce the probative weight given to the advocate's other evidence. The advocate is therefore much better off if he can tell the jury that the evidence helps his case but that the case does not depend on it. The fact that the advocate did not introduce the evidence will lend credence to that claim. This technique only works, however, when the advocate can credibly

16 As we explain in Chapter Six, however, *see* pages 121 to 123, *infra*, the use of such testimony may be warranted as rebuttal evidence.

17 The trial tactics literature contains observations consistent with this advice. For example, one writer, in counseling against calling a witness one's adversary will be compelled to call, notes that calling such a witness "render[s] everything unfavorable said by the witness doubly operative against the party calling him, [and] also deprive[s] that party of the power of counteracting the effect of the testimony." J. Reed, *Conduct of Lawsuits* § 383, at 270–271 (Little, Brown 2d ed. 1912) (citations omitted). *Accord, e.g.*, R. Keeton, *Trial Tactics and Methods* § 2.2, at 14 (Little, Brown & Co. 1973) (urging the advocate to consider the strategy of not calling a witness with both favorable and unfavorable testimony in the hope that his opponent will call him, thus giving the advocate "the opportunity of obtaining the testimony [he] desire[s] ... without the disadvantages of calling him"). *Cf.* F. Bailey & H. Rothblatt, *Successful Techniques for Criminal Trials* § 22.3, at 498 (Lawyers Co-op. Pub. Co. 1985) ("Anything that [a] witness [called by your opponent] says for your side can be argued as beyond question."); *Trial Preparation: An Interview with Louis Nizer*, 2 Trial Dip. L.J. 6, 11 (1979) (prominent trial lawyer remarking on the value of being able to prove his case "out of the mouths of [his] very adversaries, the witnesses on the other side").

claim that he is entitled to prevail without the evidence and therefore had no need to go to the effort of marshaling it.[18]

Accordingly, a defense counsel whose strong evidence is introduced in the opponent's preceding case generally should not seek to reintroduce such evidence in his own case. Likewise, the advocate generally should not elicit points favorable to his case on cross-examination when such points have already been elicited on direct examination. The only exception is if the advocate is not sure that the jury fully comprehended the point. In that situation, the advocate should seek a clarification. For example, he might ask on cross-examination:

> Let me just get this straight, Mr. Jones. You testified on direct examination that [summarize testimony]?

Having done so, he should immediately move on to another topic. This strategy enables him to minimize his apparent reliance on those points to win the case.

This might seem to be a strategy dilemma that would almost never arise in practice. In fact, however, an advocate's introduction of evidence supporting the opponent's case is not unusual. Indeed, many trial manuals urge advocates to introduce *all* relevant evidence.[19]

Plaintiffs' attorneys and prosecutors should also consider the same strategy. Thus, if such an attorney believes that a witness with strong testimony will be called by the opponent, the attorney should consider not calling the witness. When opposing counsel calls the witness, the advocate can elicit the information in cross-examination. The opponent may even elicit the advocate's strong evidence in his direct examination of the witness, thereby relieving the advocate from the need to do so on cross-examination.

---

18 This is because jurors, like Professor Wigmore, allow for the possibility that "possible witnesses whose testimony would be for any reason comparatively . . . *inferior* to what is already utilized, might well be dispensed with by a party." II Wigmore, *Evidence, supra* n. 7, § 287, at 202–203 (emphasis in original).

19 *See, e.g.*, A.E. Morrill, *Anatomy of a Trial* 108 (C.P.I. 1968) ("[I]n the situation where the lawyer has three occurrence witnesses ... [t]he temptation is to use one good, strong witness to nail down the liability issue and avoid the risks involved in using [the others] .... Despite what he would like to do, he must use them all ...."). *See also* 1 S. Schweitzer, *Cyclopedia of Trial Practice* § 260, at 675 (Lawyers Co-op. Pub. Co. 2d ed. 1970) (recommending that plaintiff's counsel in a civil case call the defendant as a witness on the theory that "you can state on summation that you were so confident of the truth of the plaintiff's story that you took the liberty of offering the defendant as your own witness, knowing you would be bound by what he testified"); Appleman, *supra* note 1, at 215 ("I like to call, with great frequency, the opposing party as an adverse witness .... This takes a lot of sting out of the defendant appearing in his own case, at a later point in the trial."). *Cf.* H. Spellman, *Direct Examination of Witnesses* 88 (Prentice Hall 1968) ("[I]t is better to have an unfavorable matter exposed through one's own witness ...."); A.E. Morrill, *supra* at 96 (section entitled, "Bring Out The Bad Stuff In Your Own Case").

This strategy, however, is hazardous. To begin with, the judge may rule that the planned cross-examination to elicit the favorable testimony is beyond the scope of the direct examination and is thus impermissible. Moreover, the judge may bar the advocate from later introducing the evidence in rebuttal.[20] Accordingly, the advocate must evaluate the judge in the case. Pertinent considerations include whether the judge normally gives attorneys wide latitude in conducting cross-examination and whether the judge is permissive in his approach to rebuttal.

A further problem is that the advocate can never be positive that the other side will call a witness or offer a particular piece of evidence. If this happens, the jury will never hear the evidence in question unless the advocate is permitted to present it in rebuttal.

There is a further danger that stems from the jury's assumption that an advocate is committed to presenting all evidence that materially favors his case. If the other evidence in the case has pointed to that item of evidence, and the advocate withholding it is not permitted to bring it out later in the trial, the jury may assume that the item would *not* have materially advanced the advocate's case, even though it actually would have done so.

Nonetheless, in many circumstances, the advocate will have a fairly good idea whether his opponent plans to call a particular witness. One situation where a prosecutor or plaintiff's counsel can be all but certain that the opponent will call a witness is where the defense opts to make an opening statement at the outset of the trial and announces that the witness in question will definitely be called in the defense case.

A case tried by one of the authors illustrates the value in having the opponent introduce one's strong evidence. The defendant was charged with an armed assault with intent to kill. At the scene, the defendant's girlfriend, an eyewitness, told the police that the defendant had acted in self-defense, an account contradicted by other eyewitnesses. Later, however, the girlfriend testified before the grand jury that from what she had seen of the incident, the defendant had *not* acted in self-defense. She also revealed to the grand jury that the defendant had called her shortly after the incident and had confided that he had picked a fight with the victim and was disappointed that the victim had not died.

---

20 *See* pages 121 to 123, *infra* (discussing standards governing use of evidence in rebuttal).

At trial, the prosecutor decided not to call the girlfriend, even though his only other evidence of the defendant's intent to kill, namely, the gravity of the injury, was purely circumstantial. He chose to take the risk because defense counsel had revealed his plan to call her. As expected, the defense called the witness, who testified on direct examination that the defendant had acted in self-defense. On cross-examination, the prosecutor confronted the witness with her grand jury testimony. The witness ultimately admitted that her grand jury testimony had been correct. Even if the prosecutor had believed that the girlfriend, on balance, would have been a strong witness in his case because of her willingness to repeat the defendant's confession, he was almost certainly better off letting the defense call her. Because the defense called the witness, the prosecutor was able to point out that his case was bolstered by a key *defense* witness. By contrast, had the prosecutor called her, the defense could have scored points by emphasizing the witness's statements in support of the defendant at the scene of the crime.

The foregoing illustrates the benefits to the advocate from having his opponent introduce the advocate's favorable evidence. Because of these benefits, the advocate may wish to consider tendering favorable evidence to the opponent in the hope that he will use it in his case.[21]

Moreover, as suggested in Chapter Eight,[22] even if the advocate decides that it is necessary to call a witness to prove a specific point, there is still a method that can result in his opponent eliciting other points from that witness that bolster the advocate's case. That method is for the advocate to omit selected strong points and conduct a very brief direct examination of the witness after thoroughly preparing the witness for the questions anticipated on cross-examination. In criminal cases, the cross-examiner often is hearing for the first time what the witness has to say. In such cases, the cross-examiner may unwittingly elicit the advocate's strong evidence that the advocate elected not to bring out. Such evidence will be far more helpful to the advocate's case than it would have been had the advocate himself brought it out.[23] The chances of an opponent eliciting the advocate's strong evidence are even greater in a consolidated trial, where there may be several

21 A detailed discussion of the concept of tendering evidence is contained on pages 59 to 61, *infra*. It should be noted that in the criminal context, a prosecutor has a constitutional duty to tender exculpatory evidence. *See generally* Brady v. Maryland, 373 U.S. 83 (1963).

22 *See* pages 140 to 143, *infra*.

23 *See, e.g.,* Bailey & Rothblatt, *supra* n. 17, § 11.20, at 308 (acknowledging this technique as one employed by the government in criminal trials, and characterizing it as a "prosecution trap").

opponents. In that situation, one opponent may be happy to elicit points that are damaging to another.

Another circumstance in which the advocate should consider not introducing strong evidence is where he is virtually certain that the opponent will afford him the opportunity to use the evidence in his rebuttal case. As we explain in Chapter Six,[24] such an advocate is normally better off presenting a given item of evidence in rebuttal than in the case-in-chief.

In sum, the advocate should not assume, merely because he has strong evidence, that he should always introduce it. His opponent may be planning to introduce it if the advocate does not do so. In that circumstance, the advocate may want to forgo introducing it himself. Finally, if the advocate is confident that his opponent will afford him the opportunity, he should consider saving the evidence for rebuttal. For the reasons previously discussed, however, these strategies entail serious risks and should not be undertaken lightly.

The Value of Tendering Favorable Evidence to One's Opponent

Tender for the Purpose of Having the Opponent Use the Evidence

If the advocate has decided not to use an item of favorable evidence in his own case, he should consider making it available for the opponent's use at trial. By doing so, the advocate stands to gain if the opponent introduces it, since the costs of sponsorship would then be operating in the advocate's favor.

The opponent will frequently be unaware of an item of evidence that is favorable to the advocate's case. In a criminal case, a prosecutor is under no general obligation to tender inculpatory evidence to the defense. Tendering of evidence to the defense is mandatory only where the evidence is exculpatory or is otherwise subject to disclosure pursuant to an applicable rule of evidence or procedure.[25] In the typical civil case, if extensive discovery has been conducted, it is much more likely that the opponent will have learned of such evidence. Even in civil cases, however, discovery may not have uncovered everything.

---

24 *See* pages 121 to 123, *infra.*

25 *See, e.g.,* Brady v. Maryland, 373 U.S. 83 (1973); Fed. R. Crim. P. 16.

Where the opponent is not aware of an item of the advocate's favorable evidence, the question of whether to tender such evidence initially depends on whether the advocate foresees a use for it anywhere in his own case, including rebuttal.[26] This is frequently difficult to assess. If the evidence relates to a fact that at the outset seems collateral, there is always the chance that opposing counsel, unaware of the advocate's evidence, will introduce evidence that can be disproved or discredited by evidence that the advocate had previously categorized as less-than-strong. In these circumstances, if the advocate tenders such evidence, he will have unwittingly educated the opponent on the existence of such a "surprise" witness or item of evidence. Thus, while the decision to tender must be made early enough for the opponent to act on it, it should generally be postponed until the advocate fully comprehends the opponent's factual theory of the case.

Tender to Avoid the Opponent's Criticism for the Advocate's Non-Use of the Evidence

Where the evidence likely to be presented to the jury will point to the existence of evidence that is not equally available to the opponent, and the advocate has decided against using such evidence, then the advocate must tender it to the opponent or run the risk that the opponent will criticize him in summation for failing to present it at trial. A tender eliminates any argument that the advocate's failure to present the evidence indicates that it would have harmed his case. This is because the legal and practical basis for such an argument—lack of equal availability—will not be met.[27]

The advocate should be aware that, although a tender will preclude the opponent from suggesting to the jury that the missing item would have *harmed* the advocate's case, it will not prevent the opponent from noting that the advocate's case is not as strong as it would have been had that

26 This analysis assumes that the favorable evidence in question is not subject to mandatory disclosure pursuant to any court decision or rule of procedure.

27 *See* n. 9, *supra* (citing authorities). For the same reason, a tender precludes the opponent from establishing the requirements for a missing evidence jury instruction. *Cf.* O'Malley, Grenig & Lee, *supra* n. 6, § 104.26, at 150 (model jury instructions providing that if a party fails to produce evidence in his control that was not reasonably available to his opponent, then the jury "may infer that the evidence is unfavorable to the party who could have produced it and did not"). The requirements of the missing witness rule are discussed on pages 51 to 52, *supra*. It should be noted, as explained in Chapter Five, that a tender may not serve the above-mentioned purposes with respect to evidence that is uniquely associated with one party.

witness or item of evidence been favorable to his case.[28] Thus, even where opposing counsel does not establish the requirements for the missing witness instruction, he may attempt to score points by highlighting the absence of the item from the advocate's presentation. Moreover, the trial court's general instructions may lend weight to such an argument.

For example, juries are often instructed that in evaluating the testimony of a witness, they may consider whether and to what extent the witness has been "corroborated" by other evidence.[29] Thus, where the advocate has called a witness to establish a point, and where the evidence shows that there were other available witnesses with material testimony on the same point whom the advocate did not call, the opponent may be able to refer to such an instruction and ask the jury to consider that the witness was not corroborated by other evidence. Although a tender will not preclude opposing counsel from making this argument, it will at least enable the advocate to argue to the jury that the opponent could have called the witness if that witness had anything adverse to say concerning the advocate's case.

Marginal Evidence: A Shortcut to Identifying Less-Than-Strong Evidence

In a previous section,[30] we described the basic "pruning" device for the advocate to use in selecting evidence bearing on disputed issues: use only strong evidence. As we have seen, although the rule is simply stated, it involves a series of calculations, beginning with the evaluation of the evidence and ending with an assessment of the three separate costs of sponsorship. The concept of marginal evidence relieves the advocate from the need to consider the costs involved in the use of much of his evidence.

By definition, favorable evidence that is "marginal" is so weak that, when considered with the advocate's other evidence, it has no realistic chance of swaying an otherwise unpersuaded jury to vote in his favor. As a practical matter, it is neutral (or worse, harmful). Thus, given the certainty that at least some sponsorship costs will be incurred by using that evidence, such

28 *Cf.* Arnold v. United States, 511 A.2d 399, 416 (D.C. 1986) (permitting comment on absence of witness or evidence but requiring advance clearance to do so).

29 *See, e.g.*, O'Malley, Grenig & Lee, *supra* n. 6, § 15.01, at 364 (sample instruction stating, "In deciding whether you believe ... any witness, ... [a]sk yourself, ... [W]ere there things that corroborated [his] testimony ... ?"); *Criminal Jury Instructions, District of Columbia*, § 2.11, at 77 (2002 ed.).

30 *See* pages 47 to 52, *supra*.

evidence—and, *a fortiori*, neutral and harmful evidence as well—can be presumptively eliminated from the advocate's presentation.[31] The reason should be clear: if the evidence cannot sway the jury prior to adjusting for sponsorship costs—that is, even if introduced by a neutral source—then it cannot possibly help the advocate's case once such costs are taken into account. Indeed, it is generally safe to assume that such evidence will be harmful once those costs are assessed.

For example, assume that a plaintiff who is suing for injuries suffered as a result of a dog bite has two unbiased eyewitnesses who maintain that they are certain that the defendant's dog, not someone else's, attacked the plaintiff. Assume further that a third eyewitness, who was farther away from the scene than the other two witnesses, can say only that the dog "resembled" the defendant's dog. The third witness is clearly marginal. Although this witness technically supports the plaintiff, thereby making the testimony "favorable," he is substantially inferior to the other two witnesses. If the other two are not enough, then the third plainly will not make the difference. Indeed, because of the cost of overtrying alone, the third will likely reduce the weight given to the other two. The critical point to recognize for present purposes, however, is that in such a situation, the advocate can safely eliminate the third witness without even considering the costs involved. In sum, the advocate should select evidence using the rule of thumb that he will not introduce marginal evidence. This is true for both witnesses and tangible evidence.

Neutral Evidence

In General

The general rule of using only strong evidence also counsels elimination from the advocate's presentation of neutral evidence, namely, evidence that is immaterial to the jury's determination of the issues in dispute. The following sections analyze the costs that can be incurred by the use of neutral evidence and provide trial examples illustrating such costs.

31 Important exceptions to this presumptive rule of elimination are discussed below. Occasionally, for example, the influence upon the jury of the advocate's apparent efforts to *omit* less-than-strong evidence will dictate presenting it himself. This exceptional situation is addressed below (pages 68 to 71, *infra*). Also, if the less-than-strong evidence is uniquely associated with the advocate's case (*see, e.g.*, pages 103 to 105, *infra*), presenting it may be the best course.

The Sponsorship Costs of Using Neutral Evidence

As we have seen, the cost of introduction warns of the risk that the jury's scrutiny of evidence initially qualifying as neutral might result in an adverse impact on the advocate's case. Unlike favorable evidence, however, which may give rise to a cost of overtrying, the jury will not normally assume that the advocate is trying to "win" the case with that neutral item of evidence.

Nonetheless, the jury is apt to reason that the advocate himself deemed it significant that the evidence is neutral. Why else would the advocate have introduced it? The jury will thus be inclined to search for a reason motivating the advocate's desire to demonstrate that the item was neutral. As we shall show, any reason that the jury decides upon will be apt to damage the advocate's case.

Although the cost of overtrying is not strictly applicable, the jury, casting about for a reason why the evidence was presented, may conclude that the advocate did so in the hope that the jury would view it favorably. If the jury reaches this conclusion, the use of neutral evidence is apt to reduce the weight of the advocate's other evidence in a manner similar to that incurred by the cost of overtrying.

Illustrations of Dangers from Use of Neutral Evidence

As noted, because of the cost of introduction, the jury is apt to assume that the advocate introducing neutral evidence deems it important to his case. Since the evidence is not favorable, the jury will generally have no firm theory explaining why the advocate used it. The following examples illustrate some of the damaging theories upon which the jury may decide.

One type of harm from using neutral evidence is that the jury might view such evidence as "padding" by a nervous attorney seeking to bolster an otherwise shaky case. For example, eliciting excessive details concerning a lay or expert witness's biographical background—such as place of birth or education—might cause the jury to wonder why the advocate deemed such an elaborate line of questions necessary. The only rational explanation is that the advocate thought that such questions might help the jury find the witness credible. Once the jury dwells on whether it really makes the witness more credible, the advocate will be harmed if it does not.

There are other possible motivations that the jury can ascribe to an advocate's use of neutral evidence. For instance, it may assume that the advocate is concerned that, without the benefit of seeing such evidence, the jury might speculate that it would have harmed the advocate's case. This is the equivalent of communicating a concern that the jury would not find his other evidence of sufficient weight to overcome that speculative harm. In the worst-case situation, the jury will conclude that the advocate believes that his other evidence is enough to win *only* because the item is neutral. Put another way, the logical conclusion is that the advocate does not consider his other evidence very compelling.

A trial known to the authors illustrates the point. A police officer stopped a man on the street and, after briefly conversing with him, observed that he began fidgeting in an odd manner. Moments later, the officer noticed a pistol on the ground only inches from the man's feet. The man was arrested, and the pistol was recovered by the officer. The arresting officer later submitted the weapon for fingerprint tests, but no prints were obtained that could be used for purposes of comparison. The defendant was later brought to trial on charges of unlawful possession of the pistol.

During the government's case-in-chief, the arresting officer testified concerning the defendant's fidgeting and the recovery of the pistol. He further testified that he was sure that there had been no pistol anywhere near the defendant's feet before the stop. The question faced by the prosecutor was whether to elicit the absence of fingerprint evidence. His concern was that the jury might speculate about whether a fingerprint examination of the gun was conducted and, if so, what results were obtained. Fearing that such speculation could potentially harm his case, the prosecutor decided to elicit from the officer the fact that no usable fingerprints were recovered. The prosecutor, who was unaware of the principles of sponsorship, reasoned that (1) he would benefit from foreclosing any risk of jury speculation that the pistol had fingerprints belonging to someone other than the defendant, and (2) there was no cost in introducing the neutral results.

The jury ultimately acquitted the defendant. The error in the prosecutor's strategy was in assuming that his introduction of neutral evidence carried no cost and would be beneficial. First, presenting the evidence probably focused the jury on the fact that police like to get matching fingerprints in "dropsy" cases such as this one, highlighting for the jury the fact that the prosecutor's case could have been much stronger. Second, the jury may have speculated that the evidence was introduced because the prosecutor thought it important that fingerprints matching someone else were not recovered. In either case, the implicit message was that the prosecutor thought it important that no one else's fingerprints had been recovered, a message that could not have advanced his case. The prosecutor was tacitly suggesting that had the test disclosed fingerprints belonging to someone other than the defendant, the arresting officer's testimony would not have been sufficient to warrant a conviction.

Significantly, the prosecutor had tendered the inconclusive fingerprint results to the defense in discovery. Had the prosecutor opted not to raise the fingerprint issue at trial, the defense could not have persuasively accused him in summation of "hiding" potentially exculpatory fingerprint results. If he had, the prosecutor could have pointed out that all pertinent fingerprint evidence was tendered to defense counsel and that *he* could have introduced it if there had been anything exculpatory.[32]

This is not to say that a defense counsel in the foregoing situation should refrain from eliciting testimony on cross-examination regarding the failed recovery attempt. After all, police department personnel made efforts, in anticipation of litigation, to recover the fingerprints. As such, a defense counsel might benefit from making the jury aware of the government's concern—and failed attempt—to locate more favorable evidence.[33] The critical point, however, is that the prosecutor magnified the problem by eliciting the testimony himself.

As the foregoing trial example illustrates, presenting neutral evidence often serves only to highlight how much better the advocate's case could have been. This is true, for example, where the plaintiff in an automobile accident case calls a witness who was in the plaintiff's automobile at the time of the accident but who cannot offer relevant testimony because his attention was focused elsewhere or because he was asleep. Such a witness may serve to underscore to the jury that the plaintiff's case could have been stronger.

Conclusion

The central lesson regarding neutral evidence is clear: the cost of using such evidence will outweigh any risk of adverse jury speculation concerning the

32 A prosecutor making such an argument should, of course, remind the jury that the defense is not required to present any evidence. *See* n. 4, *supra*.

33 *Cf.* S. Turow, *Presumed Innocent*, at 168–169 (Farrar Straus Giroux 1987) (reflecting concern of fictitious advocate to avoid the jury learning of his failed efforts to locate evidence favoring his side).

missing evidence.[34] For that reason, the advocate should delete neutral evidence from the presentation. As we have stated, because the jury assumes that the advocate's opponent will introduce any evidence that materially advances his case, it will likely accept the advocate's argument that if the evidence was harmful to his case, the opponent would have introduced it.

Harmful Evidence

Introduction

This section discusses the use of harmful evidence. As will be seen, the general rule is that an advocate should not use such evidence because it is usually rendered considerably more damaging if he is the one who elicits it. There are, however, limited circumstances in which the advocate is harmed less by bringing out a weakness than by letting his opponent do so.

In contrast to the approach counseled by sponsorship principles, many trial manuals urge the wholesale introduction of harmful evidence, despite the abundance of authorities holding that such evidence is magnified when presented by the party whose side it harms.[35] As we will show, such advice is unsound and, if followed, can significantly harm the advocate's case.

The General Rule Against Use of Harmful Evidence

As indicated in Chapter Two, sponsorship principles dictate, as a general rule, that attorneys should *not* introduce harmful evidence. An analysis of the two sponsorship costs that are pertinent to the use of harmful evidence—introduction and efforts—demonstrates why this is so.

To begin with, the cost of introduction normally acts to magnify the harmful impact of such evidence. As explained in Chapter Two, the jury assumes that the advocate has packaged the harmful matter in the light most favorable to his case.[36] Thus, it will be inclined to believe that the matter is worse than it appears when presented by the advocate whose case is harmed by it.

---

34 Chapter Five addresses special considerations relating to less-than-strong evidence that is not available to the advocate's opponent.

35 *See* authorities cited on page 55, n. 17, *supra*.

36 The jury's assumption is confirmed by the advice of the trial literature, which counsels attorneys who introduce harmful evidence to present that evidence "in its least damaging light." T. Mauet, *Trial Techniques* § 4.3, at 70 (Aspen Publishers 7th ed. 2007).

Moreover, presenting such evidence amounts to an implicit concession that the harmful matter is material to the resolution of the case. The very fact that an interested advocate has gone out of his way to present evidence harmful to his case will ratify the significance of that evidence.[37] Given this, we find it puzzling that the very writers who instruct attorneys to volunteer their harmful evidence also urge those attorneys to tell the jury that such evidence "really has no bearing" on its decision.[38]

The commentators are correct in recognizing that the advocate will ideally want to argue that the harmful matter "really has no bearing." This being so, we fail to see why the advocate would want to be the one to highlight the matter in the first place. In our view, subject to exceptional circumstances discussed below, the better approach is for the advocate to ignore the weakness and address it only if the opponent raises it. At least under the latter strategy, when the advocate asserts that the matter "really has no bearing" on the verdict, the advocate's words will be consistent with his deeds. Finally, of course, presenting the harmful evidence relieves opposing counsel from the costs of having to introduce it.

To illustrate the foregoing, consider a case in which a plaintiff is suing his employer, claiming wrongful termination. Assume that the plaintiff's attorney has decided to volunteer the fact that his client had been fired from his previous job as well, which involved the same line of work. Assume further that the attorney did so because, in the relevant jurisdiction, such evidence is admissible and the attorney wanted to bring out the evidence first to "take the sting out of it." If the witness states that the earlier termination was simply a personality clash and, contrary to what the prior employer said, had nothing to do with job performance, the jury is apt to be highly skeptical. It will assume that it has heard only the employee's best-case scenario for the previous firing. It therefore may be apt to speculate that poor job performance was the real reason behind the firing. In addition, by eliciting such testimony, the plaintiff's lawyer will have implicitly conceded that the client's past job history bears heavily on the merits of his present claim. By contrast, if the attorney waits for the opponent to bring out the

37 *Cf.* F. Bailey & H. Rothblatt, *supra* n. 17, § 22.3, at 498 ("Anything that [a] witness says for your side can be argued as beyond question."); J. Reed, *supra* n. 17, § 383, at 270–71 (advising that calling a witness the opponent would otherwise need to call "render[s] everything unfavorable said by the witness doubly operative against the party calling him, [and] also deprive[s] that party of the power of counteracting the effect of that testimony").

38 L. Decof, *Art of Advocacy: Opening Statement* § 1.18[2], at 1–44 (LexisNexis 2006) (advising advocate to do and say this in opening statement, before opponent mentions the harmful matter).

prior firing, he will be able to argue more credibly that the prior employment incident is totally irrelevant.

It is important to recognize that when an attorney volunteers a weakness, opposing counsel can capitalize on the cost of introduction. For example, if an advocate brings out his own witness's prior criminal record, opposing counsel can argue in summation:

> The witness's prior conviction is critical to the assessment of his credibility. Even my opponent went out of his way to make sure that you knew about it.

By the same token, the attorney who brings out a weakness is robbed of the opportunity to highlight that the opponent was so lacking in meaningful grounds for impeachment that he had to rely on a collateral matter, such as a prior conviction.

In addition to the cost of introduction, if unusual efforts are required to bring out the harmful matter, even greater costs will be incurred. To be sure, as we explain below, in certain limited circumstances bringing out a weakness is warranted and advisable. In general, however, the advocate is likely to be harmed, not helped, by volunteering a weakness.

It is important to emphasize that we are not urging an advocate to ignore weaknesses once the *opponent* has put them in issue. The foregoing discussion is concerned simply with which side should introduce evidence of the weakness in the first place. Once the opponent has brought out a weakness in the advocate's case, the advocate plainly should—and must—advance any strong arguments to show why it is not material to the verdict. Since the advocate did not bring up the weakness first, these arguments will carry far more weight than they would have carried had he initially volunteered the weakness.

Exception One—When the Apparent Efforts to Omit Outweigh the Competing Considerations

Overview

This section identifies a category of harmful evidence for which the *failure* to introduce it carries even greater costs than those resulting from introducing it. In this situation, a tender of the evidence to one's opponent does nothing to alleviate the problem.

This exception comes into play only if the jury is apt to conclude that the evidence would normally have been included as part of the advocate's case, and was not presented only because the advocate, by seeming to take unusual efforts, went *out of his way* to omit it. Some authors refer to the magnified impact from the failure to volunteer such evidence as a "sting" effect.[39] Others conceive of the failure to introduce the weakness in these circumstances as rendering the advocate less credible in the jury's eyes.[40] The latter rationale, which we call the "credibility" theory, implicitly calculates the negative effect of the failure to volunteer in terms of an across-the-board percentage decrease in the persuasiveness of all the advocate's favorable evidence presented at trial. By contrast, the former rationale, which we call the "sting" theory, assesses the untoward effect simply as magnifying the negative value of the omitted evidence or testimony. It is immaterial which method is used to account for the negative effect of failing to present evidence entailing apparent efforts by the advocate to omit it from his presentation. The important point is that we agree with the conventional trial literature that there is a "cost" incurred by not volunteering this particular type of harmful evidence, and we further agree that such evidence should be volunteered. (Our disagreement with that literature, as we develop below, is that the volunteering tactic is prescribed far too broadly with regard to virtually all kinds of harmful evidence.)

For harmful evidence to qualify for introduction based on the "apparent efforts" rationale, the advocate must conclude that the jury is more apt to view the *omission* of the evidence as a concession of materiality than it is to view the *introduction* of it as such a concession.

Even if the above condition is satisfied, however, the advocate may incur costs of introduction from the tendency of the jury to assume that the advocate packaged the harmful evidence in its best possible light. Accordingly, the advocate must be satisfied that the cost that would be incurred from appearing to have undertaken efforts to omit the harmful matter is sufficient to outweigh the alternative costs stemming from the suspicion that he packaged the evidence in its best light.

39 *See, e.g.,* Mauet, *supra* n. 36, § 5.2, at 114 (noting strategy of volunteering such weaknesses to "'draw the sting' out" of them).

40 *See, e.g.,* K. Hegland, *Trial and Practice Skills,* at 116–17 (West 2d ed. 1994) (in discussing the question of whether harmful matter should be elicited on direct examination, the author states: "When should you anticipate your opponent's cross? Only [when] the failure to do so will leave the jury with the feeling that you were trying to sneak one by").

Even if both of these costs of introduction are outweighed, the advocate must consider the degree to which his use of the harmful evidence will relieve the opponent from incurring sponsorship costs. Here, the advocate must conclude that his own failure to elicit a weakness looks so bad that he is better off introducing it, even though the opponent gets the benefit of having the evidence before the jury without having to incur any costs.

Moreover, as noted, there is an additional consideration that the advocate should understand. In rare cases where the jury believes that the advocate went out of the way to hide a weakness, it may view the advocate's *entire* case with greater skepticism because it views the full presentation as untrustworthy. That is, the advocate may incur an increased cost of introduction with respect to every piece of his evidence. (This represents the previously noted "across-the-board" effect posited by the credibility theory.) As a rule, this will occur only when the costs of apparent efforts to omit are extremely high. In that situation, the advocate will have already decided to elicit the weakness. For that reason, as a general matter, the advocate need not consider the possible across-the-board increase in the costs of introduction in deciding whether to elicit a weakness. (We discuss below an important exception in the case of devastating evidence possessed by a witness whom the advocate has already decided to call.)

Given the foregoing points, the first exception to the sponsorship rule of not using harmful evidence is where the cost of apparent efforts undertaken in omitting the matter exceeds the combination of the costs that the advocate incurs in using the evidence and the costs that he saves the opponent from incurring because the opponent no longer has to introduce it.

Our experience has shown that, as a practical matter, such apparent efforts to omit will only infrequently justify the introduction of harmful evidence. For all intents and purposes, use of harmful evidence will be required only in the case of a witness whom the advocate has already decided to call to the stand in order to elicit strong evidence. The dilemma for the advocate in this situation is whether to ask questions in the direct examination to elicit a harmful point. Rarely will the advocate be warranted in calling an *additional* witness or introducing an exhibit for the sole purpose of bringing out a harmful matter. The act of calling a witness or introducing an exhibit is so significant in the jury's eyes that the cost of introduction from doing so will almost always outweigh any costs of apparent efforts involved in omitting the harmful matter.

It is important for the advocate to understand that the question of whether to elicit harmful evidence will arise only if the opponent would in all probability bring out the harmful evidence if the advocate did not do so. It would obviously be irrational for the advocate to introduce such evidence unless he believes that the opponent will introduce it if the advocate omits it. In our experience, the assumption that an opponent will introduce an advocate's harmful evidence is often unwarranted. The advocate frequently cannot be certain (or even confident) that the opponent will do so. Since the advocate's knowledge of his side of the case is generally greater than the opponent's knowledge, especially in criminal cases, it is quite possible that the opponent has not identified many of the weaknesses of the advocate's case. Moreover, in the heat of trial, the opponent may forget to bring out certain weaknesses. Finally, as the lineup videotape example in Chapter One illustrates, the opponent may decide for tactical reasons not to elicit the weakness. The opponent may, for example, conclude that the weakness is not favorable enough from his perspective to warrant its inclusion in cross-examination. In sponsorship terms, if the opponent applies the sponsorship rule of introducing evidence only if it is strong for his side, matters that are negative for the advocate's case but not strongly so will be left out of the opponent's presentation. In these situations, if the advocate whose case will be harmed by a weakness chooses not to bring it out, it will never be heard by the jury. Thus, the advocate should not assume, merely because there is a weakness in his case, that the opponent will bring it out if the advocate does not do so.

The foregoing discussion has provided guidance in determining when the introduction of harmful evidence is warranted because of the apparent efforts undertaken to omit it. It is not possible to offer a definitive list of the types of evidence falling within this category. Nonetheless, such evidence often falls into one of the three classifications described in the following sections.

Filling a Conspicuous Gap

Where items of evidence fall naturally into a series or other grouping, omitting one item from the series because it is harmful may result in very high costs of apparent efforts to omit. An illustration of this category drawn from common experience is the preparation of a resumé. In keeping with the principles of sponsorship, the job-seeker will wish to purge his resumé of all less-than-strong qualifications, neutral verbiage, and harmful information.

In some circumstances, however, the applicant will suffer more harm than good by deleting certain less-than-strong entries. Assume, for example, that the applicant is seeking a position as a Professor of Medicine at Harvard Medical School. The applicant has an undergraduate degree from Stanford, did his residency at Johns Hopkins Medical School, and did further research—for which he obtained numerous awards—at Cornell Medical School. The applicant's only weak credential is that he received his medical degree from a mediocre medical school outside the United States. The job-seeker might be tempted to omit mentioning this medical school on his resumé. The attempt to do so, however, is nearly certain to harm him. Plainly, an applicant for a faculty position at a medical school will be expected to state in his resumé where he received his medical degree.[41] In these circumstances, omission of the item from the resumé will attract greater attention to the item than it would otherwise have merited. The reader of the resumé will conclude that the applicant took pains to omit any reference to his medical school.

By the same token, if an advocate who is qualifying an expert at trial is permitted to use a resumé to summarize the expert's credentials, the advocate will want to avoid the conspicuous omission described in the foregoing example. If, instead of using a resumé, the advocate decides to elicit the expert's qualifications by questioning him, the advocate should likewise avoid the foregoing omission.

A Witness's Relationship to the Parties

When an advocate calls a witness with a significant personal relationship to one of the parties, the advocate will likely want to elicit that relationship. A defense counsel should do so, for instance, when calling a relative of the defendant as a character witness.[42] If the advocate fails to elicit such a relationship, the jury may assume that the witness was coached to conceal it. The jury's perception that the advocate took pains to conceal the fact will only highlight its significance.

In the case of a character witness, the omission of the fact might leave the

41 *Cf.* T. Jackson, *The Perfect Resume* 86 (Anchor Press Doubleday 1981) (advising that a chronological resume must be "without major gaps").

42 *Cf.* 1 Schweitzer, *supra* n. 19, § 191, at 515 (advising the direct examiner to elicit any "natural relationship between a witness and the party for whom he is testifying … [including] the relationship of a close friend of many years' standing, employee-employer, blood relationship or one created by marriage of next of kin").

jury asking itself: Who is this witness? How does he know the party? How is he qualified to offer the opinion in question? Obviously, the jury must be given such information regarding a character witness.[43]

This does not mean, of course, that an advocate should volunteer all harmful facts regarding a character witness. For instance, in the above example, the advocate should not elicit the fact that the defendant's character witness has an impeachable conviction.[44] The advocate would not appear to have gone out of his way to avoid eliciting such information.

The decision whether to elicit a personal relationship between the party and other types of witnesses requires a more difficult judgment. For example, where one of the plaintiff's witnesses to an automobile accident is acquainted with the plaintiff because they used to work together at a factory several years previously, it is not clear whether the advocate should bring out that fact. The advocate should consider, at a minimum, whether the jury would conclude that the witness was coached to avoid that fact and whether, by eliciting it, the advocate would substantially undermine his ability to claim in summation that the work relationship does not significantly bear on the witness's credibility.

The Brief Narrative

If a witness would almost certainly include a harmful fact when candidly describing an incident in everyday conversation with a close friend or relative, then the advocate should consider disclosing such a fact in direct examination under the "apparent efforts to omit" rationale. In our experience, this is a narrow category. The advocate should not allow it to swallow the general rule against introducing harmful evidence.

To illustrate the difficulty of applying this test, if a prostitute looking for customers was forced at gunpoint into a car and raped, the prosecutor may be justified in eliciting, during direct examination, the fact that the victim was "streetwalking." A prostitute who is candidly recounting the events of the rape to a relative or close friend might well include some mention of what she was doing immediately prior to the rape. If that fact is omitted and comes out only on cross-examination, the jury might conclude that the witness had to be

43 As we have noted (*see* pages 52 to 53, *supra*), character evidence will usually not constitute strong evidence. We assume here that the advocate concluded that, in the particular case, the character evidence qualified as strong.

44 *See, e.g.*, Fed. R. Evid. 609(a) (providing circumstances where a prior conviction can be used to impeach a witness).

coached to sidestep that fact in her testimony. The advocate's effort to avoid mention of that fact might highlight its significance in the jury's eyes.

Notwithstanding this, the prosecutor might choose not to bring out the fact. If the opponent brought it out, the *opponent* would have to convince the jury of its relevance. Depending on the defendant's theory, the prosecutor might be able to express outrage at the opponent's implicit suggestion that the protections of the jurisdiction's armed rape laws do not extend to victims engaged in dubious enterprises. Thus, the costs that the advocate would relieve the opponent from incurring might justify omitting a weakness even though the jury perceives that the advocate took pains to do so.

In the above example, there are arguable reasons to elicit the harmful matter. If, however, the victim had simply been a prostitute several years ago and had a prior conviction for prostitution (and assuming *arguendo* that such evidence is admissible), eliciting that conviction in direct examination would clearly *not* be warranted under the "brief narrative" test. Such a fact would not normally be included as part of a candid narrative to a relative or close friend concerning the rape, and the jury therefore would not view the advocate as having purposefully omitted it.

Exception Two—Devastating Evidence Possessed by a Witness You Have Called

As is clear, and as we develop more fully below, we believe that an advocate cannot *enhance* his credibility by exposing the weaknesses in his case. We recognize, however, that not presenting a certain kind of harmful evidence—devastating evidence possessed by a witness you have called—can *diminish* the advocate's aura of credibility with the jury, causing an across-the-board decrease in the probative weight of all his favorable evidence. This credibility-diminishing effect requires further elucidation.

In our view, each category of trial attorneys—for example, prosecutors, criminal defense counsel (both privately retained and appointed for reasons of indigency), corporate defense lawyers—starts the trial with something akin to a coefficient of credibility. Criminal prosecutors generally have the highest coefficient, say, a factor of .9.[45] The reason for this is that

45 *See, e.g.*, Cargill v. Turpin, 120 F.3d 1366, 1379 (11th Cir. 1997) ("Arguments delivered while wrapped in the cloak of state authority have a heightened impact on the jury.") (citation omitted). An advocate's credibility coefficient of .9 might be associated with a jury's tendency, because of the trial lawyer's duty to represent his client zealously, to discount 10 percent of what he says; a coefficient of .8 might mean the advocate is being discounted at a rate of 20 percent; and so forth.

jurors generally know that prosecutors can pick and choose the cases they pursue, forgoing the ones lacking prosecutive merit. By contrast, for example, jurors generally assume that attorneys for large corporations will take virtually any matter to trial on behalf of such a client, regardless of its merits, because of the large attorneys' fees corporations pay. Such advocates start the trial, therefore, with lower coefficients of credibility than prosecutors. In analyzing below the conventional wisdom's approach to harmful evidence, we argue that efforts by an advocate to *improve* his credibility by volunteering weaknesses are misplaced due to the self-serving nature of the tactic.[46] (Essentially, the coefficient of credibility the lawyer starts the trial with forms an upper limit that the tactic cannot circumvent.) As noted, however, there is a category of harmful evidence the omission of which can *decrease* the advocate's starting coefficient of credibility, so much so that the decrease can justify volunteering it. That category is *devastating evidence possessed by a witness whom the advocate has determined needs to be called in his own case.*

Before eliciting such devastating evidence from a witness he has called, the advocate must carefully calculate all the sponsorship costs incurred by doing so—as well as the sponsorship costs his opponent is relieved from incurring—to make sure they are outweighed by the across-the-board diminution in his case's persuasiveness (caused by the decrease in his coefficient of credibility) that would be suffered by not volunteering the matter. As we demonstrate below, when evidence is devastating on its face, the negative sponsorship consequences of eliciting the matter are exceedingly low.

As we recognized more than a decade ago, in the case of devastating evidence, the sponsorship costs incurred by the advocate are low when one considers each of the three sponsorship costs.[47] By definition, the cost of overtrying, a cost that is incurred only when using favorable or neutral evidence, is zero, the jury does not perceive the advocate as trying to win the case with the negative item of evidence. The cost of efforts is also not high: since the harmful matter is being elicited from a witness whom the advocate has decided to call for the positive evidence the witness possesses,

46 *See* pages 79 to 82, *infra.*

47 As we noted in an article appearing shortly after this book was first published, "[t]he more harmful the fact, the more likely it is that the attorney should elicit it." R. Klonoff and P. Colby, *A Trial Lawyer's Roadmap for Handling Bad Facts: The Role of Credibility*, 16 Trial Diplomacy Journal 139, 140 (1993).

the incremental effort in eliciting the harmful matter is low. The cost of introduction is also relatively low. As an initial matter, since the evidence is harmful, no "concession of no better evidence" is made as is the case with favorable evidence. Furthermore, while a concession of materiality undoubtedly results from using the harmful item, for truly devastating evidence, the jury will perceive its materiality no matter which advocate introduces it. The only other sponsorship cost incurred by the advocate eliciting such evidence is the cost of packaging, which is also a relatively minor cost in these circumstances.

The costs that the advocate saves the opponent from incurring because the opponent no longer has to introduce the devastating item are also very low. The opponent's cost of efforts is negligible because the opponent has presumably stood up to conduct a cross-examination of the witness anyway. There is no cost of packaging since the witness does not belong to the opponent. Most critically, there is virtually no cost of overtrying, inasmuch as the evidence is highly favorable to the opponent's case.[48]

The implication of these points is that the costs of sponsorship do not give much reason to refrain from eliciting evidence that is devastating on its face from a witness whom the advocate has already decided to call in his case. Therefore, to avoid the across-the-board effects of the decrease in the advocate's coefficient of credibility—entailed by not volunteering such devastating information possessed by a witness he has decided he must present—there will be times when the advocate should elicit such devastating evidence.

We stress that this second exception to the rule against using harmful evidence should not be allowed to swallow the general rule against eliciting harmful material even from a witness whom the advocate has called. The hallmark of the novice trial advocate is viewing all negative evidence as potentially devastating, and introducing it out of fear of the opponent's criticism for not revealing it.[49] In fact, only infrequently is evidence truly devastating to the point that the advocate who is harmed by it should himself elicit it.

If evidence is not devastating, the concession of materiality is a dispositive reason for the advocate *not* to elicit the harmful matter himself. And,

48 As noted, the more favorable the evidence is, the lower the costs of overtrying. *See* page 35, *supra*.

49 *Cf.* K. Hegland, *supra* n. 40, at 115 (urging caution in bringing out weaknesses, noting, "Overdo it ... and your case becomes one long apology").

even if evidence *is* devastating, the cost of efforts dictates that a witness should not be called solely to elicit the harmful fact.

Manner of Exposing Weaknesses

If the advocate decides that a factual weakness must be elicited, the advocate should do so in a natural and logical manner in order to minimize the emphasis given to it. For example, in the above case of a character witness who is related to the defendant, the approach *not* to take would be as follows:

> Mr. Smith, let's get something out of the way right up front.
> You're the defendant's uncle, aren't you?

This approach would send a signal to the jury that the witness's bias is critical and had to be conceded at the outset. A better line of questioning would be as follows:

> Q: Please state your name.
> A: Thomas Smith.
>
> Q: Where do you reside?
> A: 119 Est 64th Street.
>
> Q: Are you employed?
> A: Yes.
>
> Q: Where?
> A: At the local Post Office.
>
> Q: Do you know the defendant in this case?
> A: Yes, I do.
>
> Q: How?
> A: He's my nephew.

The examination would then proceed to the character issues.

As the above example shows, the advocate should not give the potentially harmful fact undue prominence. At the same time, however, the advocate must not present it in such a way as to appear that he is trying to hide it. Thus, in the above example, it would be counterproductive to try to "slip in" the relationship in the middle of the examination. Because such a fact identifies the witness, it belongs at the beginning of the testimony.

Accordingly, although it is sometimes tactically beneficial for an advocate to "bury" a weakness,[50] it is essential not to be perceived as having deliberately done so.

The Overly Broad Conventional Wisdom on Harmful Evidence

Overview

As the foregoing discussion reveals, sponsorship principles counsel that only in narrow circumstances should harmful evidence be elicited by the advocate whose side is harmed by it. In contrast to this nuanced approach, virtually every leading trial manual takes the opposite position and urges the indiscriminate presentation of harmful evidence.[51] These commentators do not base their view on any purported ethical or legal duty of an advocate to expose weaknesses to the jury.[52] To the contrary, the advice of these commentators is based solely on the premise that revealing one's weaknesses before the other side does so is tactically sound and helps win trials.[53] Since we have already

50 *See* Mauet, *supra* n. 36, § 5.2, at 114 (urging advocates to "bury [weaknesses] in the middle of the direct examination").

51 *See, e.g.,* Mauet, *supra* n. 36, § 5.2, at 114 (referring to view of the "conventional wisdom" that an advocate should "volunteer weaknesses"); D. Gianna & A. Julien, *Opening Statements 2d: Winning in the Beginning by Winning the Beginning,* §5:26, at 5–32 (Thomson West 2004)("Your opponent will race you to disclose the weaknesses in your case. Beat your opponent to the punch—every single time! ... Ignoring weaknesses is foolhardy."); M. Fontham, *Trial Technique and Evidence,* § 3-14(i), at 102 (LexisNexis 2d ed. 2002) ("If you discuss weaknesses rather than waiting for your opponent to bring them up, you usually lessen their harm."); A. Posey & L. Wrightman, *Trial Consulting* 122 (Oxford University Press 2005) ("The trustworthy attorney ... informs the jury of weaknesses in his case ...."); S. Goldberg, *The First Trial: Where Do I Sit? What Do I Say?*, at 204 (West 1982) ("Weak spots in the case are usually mentioned in opening statement. Not your opponent's weak spots, but your own."); Bailey & Rothblatt, *supra* n. 17, § 9:11, at 249; P. Bergman, *Trial Advocacy* 77 (West 1997); L. Decof, *supra* n. 38, § 1.18[2], at 1–44; 1 S. Gazan, *Encyclopedia of Trial Strategy and Tactics* 92 (Prentice-Hall, Inc. 1962); J. Sonsteng, R. Haydock & J. Boyd, *The Trial Book—A Total System for the Preparation and Presentation of a Case* § 5.5(d), at 193 (West 1984); R. Carlson & E. Imwinkelried, *Dynamics of Trial Practice* § 5.5(D), at 124 (West 3d ed. 2002); A. Julien, *Opening Statements* § 1.27, at 46 (West 2002) (referring to technique of volunteering a weakness as "[w]orkshopping" the weakness). Even the fictional literature endorses this approach. *See, e.g.,* Turow, *supra* n. 33, at 241 ("A smart prosecutor usually seeks to defuse defense evidence by mentioning it first, demonstrating from his own mouth that his case can stand the defense's strongest blows.").

52 *Cf.* Brady v. Maryland, 373 U.S. 83 (1973) (establishing a rule of *tender,* not introduction at trial, of evidence exculpating a criminal defendant); Fed. R. Crim. P. 16 (mandating discovery and inspection, but not introduction at trial); Fed. R. Civ. P. 16(b) (authorizing discovery but not requiring introduction of any specific evidence); Model Code of Professional Responsibility, DR 7-103(B) (requiring prosecutor's "disclosure," but not presentation at trial, of evidence favorable to a criminal defendant); *id.*, DR 7-106(B)(1) (requiring disclosure to court of adverse case law but not containing similar requirement of disclosure of evidence to juries at trial).

53 Although some conventional wisdom proponents are vague and could be interpreted as urging the wholesale introduction of weaknesses as a tactic to enhance credibility, most limit that strategy to situations in which the advocate believes that his opponent will elicit it if he fails to do so. *See, e.g.,* Keeton, *supra* n. 17, § 2.20, at 54–55 (urging an advocate to bring out a weakness if it "is directly related to the issues in the case and is a matter that in all probability your opponent will inquire about on cross-examination"). *See* page 71, *supra* (noting difficulty in determining whether an opponent will bring out a weakness).

explained why the wholesale use of harmful evidence is not sound in light of sponsorship analysis,[54] we now focus more closely on the reasoning underlying the conventional wisdom. In inquiring into the matter, we found it difficult to pinpoint precisely the rationale for the conventional wisdom's recommendation that an advocate should invariably volunteer harmful evidence. Although virtually every manual gives this advice, there is little detailed analysis of the underlying reasoning. Apparently, the advice is considered so obviously correct that an extended discussion of the merits of the tactic is unnecessary and can be omitted. Although we found no comprehensive explanation of the conventional wisdom's reasoning, as previously stated, the commentators have offered two general rationales, the theory of enhanced credibility and the "sting" theory.

The Theory of Enhanced Credibility

The theory of enhanced credibility holds that the advocate who discloses his weak evidence bolsters his credibility with the jury. The most extravagant proponents of this theory appear to hold that the jury will view the advocate not as a "hired gun" but as a fair and impartial arbiter striving to present a balanced and unbiased picture of the evidence—not just the client's best case but also the client's *worst* case.[55] Using the terminology of the sponsorship approach, the assumption is that the advocate's costs of introduction will be reduced across the board by volunteering weaknesses. Thus, the "packaging" component of that cost will be reduced if the jury thinks that the advocate is too impartial to prepare his witnesses to give testimony putting his client's case in the best possible light. In addition, there will be less of a concession of materiality regarding each item of his evidence if the jury—contrary to our book's assumption of best case with minimum effort—accepts the notion that the advocate will go out of his way to present the "whole picture," and not merely the evidence materially favoring his client.

In our view, this thinking is misplaced, since the jury will not embrace the proposition that an interested advocate can be relied upon to present his

---

54 *See* pages 66 to 68, *supra*.

55 *See, e.g.*, Sonsteng, Haydock & Boyd, *supra* n. 51, § 5.5, at 194 ("An open and candid disclosure of [weaknesses] will usually increase the sincerity and credibility of the attorney . . . ."). *See also* 1 Gazan, *supra* n. 51, at 92 ("Candor, absolute candor, should be the guiding consideration. Tell the jury frankly not only the strength of your case but also its weaknesses.").

case impartially.[56] The assumption that the advocate is biased will be confirmed for the jury when, in summation, he tells the jury—as the advocate inevitably must—that the weakness is not fatal to his case. Once he makes that argument, the jury will realize that the admission of weaknesses was harmless and, ultimately, self-serving. As long as the jury knows that an advocate will never confess that he should lose the case, it will be skeptical of his attempts to gain credibility by exposing weaknesses.[57]

An example from common experience illustrates the fallacy in this thinking. Assume that a diner has asked the waiter at a restaurant for recommendations concerning the entrees on the menu. Assume further that in response, the waiter admits that some customers have been complaining about the chicken curry, but that the filet mignon has garnered rave reviews. Once the diner notices that the filet mignon costs twice as much as the chicken curry, the waiter's appearance of candor will be undermined. Because the diner will suspect that the waiter's recommendations are motivated by a desire to increase the total bill, and thus the gratuity, he will not feel safe in relying on anything the waiter says about the quality of the filet mignon. (The chances are high, however, that the diner will avoid the chicken curry.)

The jury behaves no differently. Its tendency to question the reliability of statements favoring the advocate's case is reflected in evidentiary principles relating to the reliability of hearsay declarations against interest. Under the hearsay rule, such a statement is considered reliable only if, *on balance*, it is disserving.[58] Ultimately, the jury will view as *unreliable* statements that on balance are self-serving. This is contrary to the conventional view, as it is normally articulated, positing that if the advocate is willing to acknowledge the bad in his case, the jury will place greater weight on the advocate's glowing assessment of its good aspects. The flaw in this reasoning is that the jury will not view both statements—the bad and the good—*taken together*

56 *See, e.g.*, Inglett & Co. v. Everglades Fertilizer Co., 255 F.2d 342, 349 (5th Cir. 1958) (Brown, J.) ("[W]e think it an unnatural, if not virtually impossible, task for counsel, in his own case, to drop his garments of advocacy and take on the somber garb of an objective fact-stater.").

57 We agree, of course, that in some circumstances, a speaker can take steps to bolster his credibility. *See generally* Aristotle, *The Rhetoric* 1358a1, *translated in The Complete Works of Aristotle* 2155 (Barnes ed. Princeton Univ. Press 1984) (discussing the importance of a speaker's credibility). For example, politicians correctly recognize the value of obtaining endorsements from prominent and well-regarded figures, such as actors and noted scholars. Our point is simply that in the case of an *interested advocate*, such a speaker generally gains little by trying to bolster his credibility.

58 *See, e.g.*, R. Lempert & S. Saltzburg, *A Modern Approach to Evidence* 489 (West 2d ed. 1982) (noting that "[i]f [a] statement seems on balance self-serving, it will be excluded").

as a statement against interest. Because of this, it will credit the advocate's negative statements regarding his evidence but will view with suspicion his positive statements. Thus, we reject as misplaced the notion that an advocate can appreciably enhance his believability in the jury's eyes by volunteering weaknesses—a tactic based fundamentally on an effort to curry favor.[59] In our experience, unless the advocate appears to have taken pains to conceal a weakness, subject to the exception discussed above regarding devastating evidence,[60] he will not be viewed negatively for failing to volunteer it. This is because, as we suggested in Chapter Two,[61] the jury does not expect an advocate to go out of his way to present evidence harmful to his case. Put another way, the jury does not expect the advocate to portray his client's case in its worst light. For that reason, the jury will not view the advocate as unfair for failing to do so. In any event, an advocate who volunteers weaknesses in an effort to seem fair is probably defeating his purpose. As explained above,[62] the jury is apt to conclude that the advocate's case is even worse than he states and that the weak presentation is actually the advocate's *best*-case scenario.

Some advocates may take satisfaction in volunteering the weaknesses in their cases and may feel morally superior to those who practice best-case advocacy. Unless, however, such an advocate would volunteer the weakness in question even when *certain* that the opponent will not introduce it, then the advocate has no basis for any feeling of moral superiority. In this regard, while some commentators are vague on this issue,[63] we are unaware of a single trial commentator or practitioner who affirmatively and explicitly recommends volunteering weaknesses even in the absence of any expectation that the opponent will introduce the item if he does not.[64] If such an advocate did exist, we believe that he would be disserving his client, since the advocate would be presenting damaging evidence that even the opponent would not have used.

59 *Cf.* Fed. R. Evid. 804, Adv. Comm. Note (b)(3) ("a statement admitting guilt and implicating another person, made while in custody, may well be motivated by a desire to curry favor with the authorities and hence fail to qualify as against interest").

60 *See* pages 74 to 76, *supra.*

61 *See* page 15, *supra.*

62 *See* page 66, *supra.*

63 *See* page 78, n. 53, *supra.*

64 *See* page 78, n.53, *supra.*

Alternatively, an advocate may derive personal satisfaction from believing that the jury holds the advocate in high esteem for volunteering weaknesses and views the advocate as a balanced and eminently fair lawyer. In our experience, however, this high esteem rarely increases the likelihood of a favorable verdict. If such an advocate is liked by the jury, it is for acting against the client's interests by making important admissions and concessions. Not surprisingly, therefore, the trial lawyers we have known who were most determined to portray themselves as fair by parading their weaknesses had the least impressive trial records. Indeed, the authors' own early—and unsuccessful—experimentation with that strategy confirms that an advocate's image of fairness does not translate into victories.

Ultimately, the strategy of volunteering weaknesses to *enhance* one's credibility (and increase the previously discussed coefficient of credibility the advocate starts the trial with) fails because the strategy is self-serving. The jury knows that the advocate is volunteering weaknesses in an effort to *win* the case and that the advocate will never be so "fair" as to suggest that his client should *lose*.[65]

The "Sting" Theory

The second rationale for the conventional wisdom's advice in favor of wholesale volunteering of weaknesses is that the advocate who discloses his harmful evidence will take out the "sting" that would otherwise result from its introduction by the opponent.[66] Consistent with this book, this analysis posits that the impact of harmful evidence is influenced by who introduces it. The impact posited, however, is precisely the opposite of that predicted by the cost of introduction. Employing the materiality graph depicted in Chapter Two (Figure 2-1), the conventional view posits a rightward shift on the graph whenever harmful evidence is used, repre-

65 We are not rejecting the effort to appear fair as a worthwhile goal. Rather, we are simply pointing out that introducing harmful evidence in an effort to appear fair will generally be counterproductive. An advocate should by all means try to appear as fair as possible, for example, by treating the court, the witnesses, and the jurors with respect.

66 *See, e.g.*, Bergman, *supra* n. 51 ("[i]t sometimes makes sense to 'take the sting out' of an adversary's claims by first airing them yourself and showing that 'we have nothing to hide'"); Mauet, *supra* n. 36, § 5.2, at 114 (noting strategy of volunteering weaknesses to " 'draw the sting' out" of them); Bailey & Rothblatt, *supra* n. 17, § 9:11, at 249 (advising criminal defense lawyers that "[n]o matter how damaging the evidence against the accused is, expose it ... [T]he evidence sounds a lot less damaging if it comes from you"); F. Lane, *Goldstein Trial Technique 3d* § 10:49 (Thomson West supp. 2005) (advising advocates to bring out weaknesses in opening statement in order to "soften the blow"); Carlson & Imwinkelried, *supra* n. 51, § 5.5(D), at 124 ("The conventional wisdom is that the prosecutor should attempt to beat the defense to the punch and mention the weaknesses before the defense does in opening.").

senting a lessened impact on the jury. In essence, it posits a benefit, not a cost, of introduction.[67]

Two noted commentators provide a concise reason for why they believe that the harmful sting is reduced when an advocate volunteers his weaknesses: "The jury will feel that it cannot be too bad if the [party's] own attorney reveals it."[68] Similarly, another authority states:

> When you are the first to present any argument, it is important to provide an explanation of any weak points in your case before your opponent has a chance to address them. *This approach strengthens your argument because you can persuade your listener that you have considered all sides of the case and are convinced that your position is the correct one.*[69]

In our view, this reasoning is flawed. When an attorney goes out of his way to present harmful evidence, the jury is far more apt to conclude that the attorney thought it was so bad that he felt the jury would penalize him for *not* presenting it. Moreover, the "sting" is magnified because the jury thinks that it is seeing the harmful item packaged in the light most favorable to the advocate's case.[70]

By contrast, if the advocate's opponent introduces a harmful fact, the jury is apt to believe that it is seeing the same item of evidence in the light most favorable to the *opponent's* case. Furthermore, the opponent must convince the jury of its materiality—a job that the advocate relieves the opponent of by introducing it himself.

An example illustrates the point. Assume that an eyewitness to an automobile accident testifying for the plaintiff was not wearing his glasses at the time of the incident. Assume further that the witness has adequate but not perfect vision without his glasses. It is difficult to see how the plaintiff's attorney would be better off bringing out this adverse fact. If the plaintiff's attorney chose to do so, the jury would likely conclude that *he* thought it

---

67 *See, e.g.*, Mauet, *supra* n. 36, § 4.3, at 70 ("Where ... [a] weakness is apparent and known to the opponent, you should volunteer it. If you don't, your opponent will, with twice the impact.").

68 Bailey & Rothblatt, *supra* n. 17, § 9:11, at 249; *accord, e.g.*, M. Berger, J. Mitchell & R. Clark, *Trial Advocacy: Planning, Analysis, & Strategy* 206–207 (Little, Brown & Co. 1989) ("By presenting [a weakness] yourself and mentioning the problem throughout trial ... jurors may begin to think that, if you are willing to keep talking about it, it can't be that bad.").

69 R. Waicukauski, P. Sandler & J. Epps, *The Winning Argument* 161 (A.B.A. 2001) (emphasis added).

70 *See* page 66, *supra*.

significant that the witness was not wearing his glasses, and it would be skeptical of the witness's claim that his vision was adequate.

Moreover, plaintiff's attorney could not later argue with any credibility that the fact that the witness was not wearing glasses is immaterial and that the adequacy of the witness's vision should not concern the jury. If that is so, the jury will wonder, then why did the attorney elicit the testimony in the first place?

By contrast, if defense counsel brings out the fact that the witness was not wearing glasses, the plaintiff's attorney would be on solid ground in arguing the lack of materiality of that fact during summation.[71] Thus, by bringing out the harmful evidence, the plaintiff's attorney is deprived of an otherwise persuasive argument. Moreover, the plaintiff's attorney will have focused the jury's attention on an issue that cannot possibly advance his case.

As noted, this book gives some credence to the "sting" theory, but not to the extent that the conventional wisdom does. We believe a harmful item of evidence left to be introduced by one's opponent will enhance its negative impact when, as previously suggested, the attorney's costs incurred from his apparent efforts to omit the matter from his presentation outweigh the sponsorship costs he incurs by presenting the matter (costs of introduction, including packaging, and costs of efforts) plus the sponsorship costs his *opponent* would otherwise incur from having to present the matter (costs of introduction, unusual efforts, and overtrying).[72] By contrast, the precise basis for the conventional wisdom's conclusion that the impact is *always* magnified by the opponent's later introduction has, to our knowledge, never been justified by anything more than the most general anecdotal claims. It is enough to note, however, that if the conclusion was generally applicable, the asserted "benefit" of introduction would counsel an advocate's introduction of *all* evidence in the case. Thus, for example, a prosecutor in a rape case would relish the opportunity to call the defendant's alibi witnesses and character witnesses, such as a priest who has known the defendant through the defendant's charity work. By the same token, the defendant might welcome the opportunity to call as his own witnesses the victim and the doctor who examined the victim

71 Methods for handling an opponent's criticism for not introducing harmful evidence are addressed in Chapter Twelve, pages 226 to 228, *infra*.

72 *See* pages 68 to 71, *supra*.

after the attack. If there were admissible other "bad acts" committed by the defendant,[73] such as prior similar rapes committed by the defendant in the same neighborhood, the defense counsel would want to introduce these facts as well.

A review of the conventional literature reveals that, with some exceptions,[74] the manuals urging attorneys to volunteer their weaknesses recommend that approach only with respect to witnesses whom the attorneys have already decided to call.[75] They do not recommend calling a witness solely to bring out a weakness. Because of this limitation to the approach, the indiscriminate version of the "sting" rationale cannot survive scrutiny. For if the previously quoted advice of the commentators were correct that "[t]he jury will feel that it cannot be too bad if the [party's] own attorney reveals it," then there would be no principled reason to so limit the advice. For example, an advocate would presumably limit the "sting" of the opponent's calling such entirely adverse witnesses by calling them himself. The only basis for the limitation is a recognition of the prohibitively high sponsorship costs that would be incurred by calling a witness only to elicit a harmful matter. Once the proponents of the conventional wisdom concede the costs of bringing out a weakness, then the all-embracing "sting" rationale that they urge is necessarily undermined.

In sum, an advocate errs in proceeding on the assumption that he normally benefits by eliciting harmful evidence. In most situations, the advocate will be better off limiting his presentation to his strong evidence, which is what the jury expects of the advocate in the first place.[76]

The Empirical Evidence

The conventional wisdom's indiscriminate approach to volunteering harmful evidence cannot be justified based on "empirical" evidence. In 1993,

73 *See, e.g.,* Fed. R. Evid. 404(b) (permitting, *inter alia,* evidence of prior bad acts to prove identity).

74 *Cf.* Appleman, *supra* n. 1, at 215 (urging plaintiffs' attorneys to call the defendant).

75 *See, e.g.,* Mauet, supra n. 36, § 5.2, at 114.

76 Since the conventional wisdom posits a benefit of introduction of harmful evidence, it might also posit a corresponding benefit of overtrying. *Cf.* Turow, *supra* n. 33, at 241 (pertinent excerpt quoted at n. 51, *supra*). Any theoretical "benefit of overtrying," however, suffers from the same defect as the asserted "benefit of introduction": it would counsel the advocate to seek to introduce *all* evidence in the case, including his *opponent's* best evidence. Both asserted benefits fly in the face of the classic image of the advocate as someone striving to put forward *his* client's best case. *See, e.g.,* G. Kennedy, *The Art of Persuasion in Greece* 139 (Princeton Univ. Press 1963) (noting that in ancient Greek rhetoric, "[t]he necessity of fairness in presenting both sides of the case [was] forgotten and immediate persuasion [became] the sole object, divorced from all considerations of the subject which might detract from persuasion").

Douglas Rice and Ellen Leggett of the company Litigation Sciences wrote an article about a study purporting to test the validity of the sponsorship approach.[77] In the study, two control groups heard opening statements on videotape about an automobile accident in which an individual named Robert was killed. His family sued the manufacturer of the vehicle, claiming that the vehicle was prone to roll over at low speeds. The sponsorship videotape contained a plaintiff's statement that avoided any mention of the fact that Robert had been drinking at the time of the accident. On the "inoculation" videotape—Rice and Leggett's term for the conventional approach favoring the volunteering of weaknesses—the plaintiff's attorney volunteered the fact about Robert's drinking, along with an explanation that Robert was under the legal blood-alcohol limit and was not known to drink. The defense opening (which referenced Robert's drinking) was the same for both groups. According to Rice and Leggett, the inoculation control group gave the plaintiff's lawyer higher scores for honesty, organization, clarity, persuasiveness, poise, and effectiveness than the sponsorship group gave to the plaintiff's lawyer who did not inoculate.[78]

Seeing the Rice–Leggett article in 1993 and believing it to be flawed, we asked Rice and Leggett if we could review the underlying empirical data. Rice and Leggett declined our request. In our view, that was the end of the matter, since credible researchers would not refuse to disclose the backup material for their study. Because the Rice–Leggett study received virtually no publicity, we did not pursue the matter further at that time. When the study was featured in the May 2000 edition of the *Texas Bar Journal*,[79] we again tried to obtain the materials underlying it, contacting Leggett by telephone. Leggett told us, however, that, since our previous call, the files had all been lost or destroyed.

While we suspect that the backup documentation would have revealed multiple grounds for rejecting the study, several features of the study—apparent from Rice's and Leggett's write-up itself—demonstrate that it was no test of sponsorship at all. As an initial matter, from the authors' description of the sponsorship videotape, it appears that the mock jury

---

77 Rice & Leggett, "Insight: Empirical Study Results Contradict Sponsorship Theory," 7 *Inside Litigation* 20 (1993). The two authors thereafter posted the article on the Web site of a consulting entity named the Jury Research Institute.

78 *Id.*

79 *See* Brogdon, *Inoculating Against Bad Facts: Brilliant Trial Strategy or Misguided Dogma?*, 63 Tex. B.J. 443 (May 2000). We responded, 63 Tex. B.J. 754 (Sept. 2000), and Mr. Brogdon replied, *id.* at 756.

either never learned—or learned only in the most indirect way from the defense attorney—that Robert's blood alcohol level was below the legal limit and that he did not have a reputation for drinking. But if the inoculating plaintiff's attorney was able to give better facts for his side, then the study is obviously meaningless.[80]

Worse still, the inoculating plaintiff's attorney was given other critical advantages over the sponsorship attorney. According to Rice and Leggett's write-up, in both cases, the defense attorney made an argument "mak[ing] full use of the negative case fact." However, the sponsorship plaintiff's attorney was forced to let go *unrebutted* the defense attorney's characterization of the fact as material—maybe case dispositive. At a minimum, the sponsorship lawyer should have been allowed to reply, as he would be allowed to do in a real trial, with arguments that the fact was not material, such as by pointing out that the small amount of alcohol that Robert consumed could not have resulted in his arrest even for a traffic violation, much less have caused his vehicle to roll over at a low speed. By contrast, the inoculating plaintiff's attorney was unfairly permitted in argument to make comments that attempted to, in Rice and Leggett's words, "control the damage."

The sponsorship attorney's hands were tied in another critical way. As we have explained throughout this book, an important advantage of our technique is in capitalizing, especially in closing argument, on the inoculating attorney's concession that the bad fact was so damaging as to demand acknowledgment up front. But the way the study was designed, the defense attorney was silent on the point and thus could not capitalize on plaintiff's concession of materiality. Therefore, not only did the study give the inoculating advocate major advantages over the supposed "sponsorship" advocate; it shielded the inoculator from the vulnerabilities of the tactic. As such, the study did not test sponsorship but instead tested an easily toppled straw man.

Selecting Evidence to Undermine Evidence Previously Presented by the Opponent

The foregoing sections of this chapter have addressed the topic of selecting evidence to put forth one's best case. By contrast, this section addresses

80 During our telephone conversation, Leggett stated that she did not remember whether the sponsorship group heard these mitigating facts.

the topic of selecting evidence to undermine evidence previously presented by one's opponent. Here, the advocate is not seeking to use the evidence to bolster his own case. Rather, the advocate is seeking to demonstrate that the evidence presented by the opponent fails to advance the opponent's case.[81] In these circumstances, the advocate's selection of evidence focuses primarily on the harm to his opponent's case rather than on the benefit to his own case. Specifically, the rule for selecting evidence to undermine the opponent's evidence is simply the mirror image of the rule of using only strong evidence: *an advocate should use evidence to undermine his opponent's evidence only where the amount by which he can reduce the probative value of the opponent's evidence outweighs the sponsorship costs incurred by the advocate in doing so.* In applying this test, the advocate should recognize that reducing the probative value of an item of the opponent's evidence will tax the opponent with costs of overtrying. This reduction in the probative value of the opponent's *other* evidence must be taken into account when deciding whether the advocate's own sponsorship costs are outweighed.

Under the foregoing rule, the advocate will occasionally be warranted in using evidence that, when analyzed without regard to the opponent's evidence, is *unfavorable* to the advocate's case. This will be true so long as the reduction in the probative value of the opponent's evidence outweighs the advocate's costs in using it. In this situation, the jury will understand that the advocate is using such evidence solely to reduce the value of the opponent's evidence, not to bolster his own case.[82]

For example, assume an accident involving two eyewitnesses. The first is called by the plaintiff in the case-in-chief and gives testimony favorable to that side. The witness acknowledges that he cannot see well without glasses but maintains that he was wearing his glasses at the time of the accident. The second witness, who has favorable substantive testimony for the defense, is called by the defense not only to provide that testimony but also to testify that the first witness, who was standing next to him, was

---

81 As previously noted, the jury looks to each advocate not only to present his own best case but also to undermine his opponent's best case. *See* page 26, *supra*.

82 Strictly speaking, such evidence is "favorable" as that term is defined in this book. *See* page 41, *supra*. When viewed together with the opponent's evidence, the item of evidence increases the likelihood of the advocate's position in the jury's eyes. *See* pages 27 to 28, *supra* (benefit of the attack). Given this, the rule of using only strong evidence would be sufficient, as a formal matter, to guide the selection of such discrediting evidence. This book employs the mirror image rule for the selection of such evidence, however, because that rule does not require the advocate to characterize evidence as "favorable" or "strong" when that evidence, standing alone, would in fact be *unfavorable*.

not wearing glasses at the time of the incident. The latter testimony is not "favorable" to the defense in a substantive sense, since the first witness's testimony, however much undermined, can still serve only to support the plaintiff's version of the events. Nonetheless, defense counsel's decision to elicit such testimony will be warranted as long as the reduction in the probative value of the opponent's witness's evidence exceeds the defense's sponsorship costs in eliciting the testimony.

A common situation in which the mirror image test will apply is in the decision whether to ask questions on cross-examination in order to discredit a witness. The advocate's purpose in doing so is not to present affirmative substantive proof, but rather to impeach or otherwise undermine the probative value of the opponent's evidence.[83] For example, consider again the automobile accident case in Chapter Two in which the plaintiff's expert testified, based on skid marks, to the speed that the defendant was driving. Assume that the expert testified that the defendant was traveling 40 MPH in a 30 MPH zone. Assume further, however, that the figure was in fact based on a mathematical error and should have been 31 MPH. The defense counsel who has detected that error would almost certainly be warranted in forcing the expert to admit that his own figures revealed a speed of only 31 MPH. This is so even though testimony that the defendant's speed was 31 MPH is not, standing alone, "favorable" to the defendant.

Similarly, it is common for prosecutors to impeach defendants with inconsistent exculpatory statements. For example, if a defendant testifies at trial that he was with his girlfriend at the time of the crime, his testimony will be substantially discredited if he is shown to have made a prior statement to the police that he was at home alone and asleep at the time of the crime. Obviously, the prosecutor, in bringing out the prior statement during cross-examination or rebuttal, is not asking the jury to accept the statement as true. Rather, the prosecutor is using it to show that the defendant must be guilty since he cannot keep his alibi straight.

For the same reason, an advocate will be justified in bringing out a neutral fact where it substantially undercuts the testimony of an opponent's witness. For instance, if a nurse in a medical malpractice case testifies for the plaintiff that the treating physician appeared tired on the morning of

83 *Cf.* O'Malley, Grenig & Lee, *supra* n. 6, § 15.06, at 415 (sample jury instruction providing that prior inconsistent statements "are admissible only to discredit or impeach the credibility of the witness and not to establish the truth of these earlier statements made somewhere other than here at trial").

surgery, the defense obviously should elicit the fact that the nurse did not even work on the day in question and therefore had the wrong day in mind. The defense is not using the nurse to provide evidence favoring his own case. Nonetheless, he will have succeeded in substantially reducing the probative value of the nurse's testimony for the plaintiff, while incurring only minimal costs.

The critical condition permitting an advocate to gain by using evidence that does not favor his own case is that the opponent, by calling a witness or introducing an item of evidence, has conceded the materiality of that evidence to his case. The advocate would not benefit by delving into these points without his opponent's first having put them in issue. Thus, in the above automobile accident example, had the plaintiff not called the witness, the defense would have severely damaged his case by calling that witness to testify that the defendant was driving 31 MPH, a speed exceeding the speed limit. Similarly, in the malpractice example, had the plaintiff not called the nurse, there would have been no reason for the defendant to have called the nurse to elicit that the nurse was not working on the day the allegedly negligent medical procedure occurred.

This chapter has introduced the sponsorship method's general rule of evidence selection on disputed issues: use only strong evidence. This rule enables an advocate to avoid overtrying his case by eliminating favorable evidence that is outweighed by sponsorship costs. This chapter has also explained why an advocate should avoid burdening his case with weaknesses unless such a strategy is warranted by the cost of apparent efforts to omit the weakness or by the rule pertaining to devastating information possessed by a witness the advocate has decided to call. Finally, this chapter has introduced a mirror image rule to the rule of using only strong evidence. The mirror image rule applies when an advocate is attempting to undermine evidence previously presented by the opponent.

The rule of using only strong evidence, while fundamental, must occasionally yield to other considerations. The following chapter describes two categories of evidence to which the rule does not apply.

CHAPTER 5

Selection of Evidence: Undisputed Issues and Party-Associated Evidence

Overview

As Chapter Four demonstrated, the sponsorship approach prescribes a general rule, applicable to disputed issues, of using only strong evidence. There are, however, two special categories of evidence selection decisions to which different rules apply.

The first category is limited to certain selection decisions faced by advocates who must sustain a legal burden of proof, namely, plaintiffs' attorneys, prosecutors, and defense attorneys asserting affirmative defenses. Here, the task for the advocate is to determine the quantity of evidence that he must introduce on those elements of his claim (or affirmative defense) that are undisputed by the opponent. The second category relates to the use of what we term "party-associated evidence." Briefly stated, party-associated evidence is evidence that the jury preconceives to be uniquely associated with one of the parties to the case—the plaintiff, the complainant in a criminal case, or the defendant. This chapter sets forth and applies the rules of evidence selection for undisputed issues and for party-associated evidence.

Undisputed Issues

In General

In any lawsuit, civil or criminal, the party suing for relief must satisfy a legal burden of proof. Thus, plaintiffs' attorneys and prosecutors will always be faced with having to satisfy such a burden. By contrast, the party sued—the defendant—will have *no* legal burden of proof except in cases where he presents an affirmative defense.

Any legal burden of proof consists of one or more elements, each of which must be satisfied by the party required to meet such a burden. In any trial, the party's opponent will be disputing one or more of those elements. At the same time, the opponent will typically be conceding the merits of the party's position on other elements, rendering them undisputed.

The focus of this section is on the evidence that an advocate facing a legal burden of proof must introduce to sustain his burden on undisputed elements. As this section will demonstrate, the jury does not expect an advocate to be concerned with introducing evidence on those elements of his claim that the opponent does not dispute. For those elements, the jury will fully credit the opponent's concession. Notwithstanding this, the advocate must still introduce at least a minimum amount of evidence to satisfy the judge that the legal burden has been met.

The first section that follows elaborates on the need for a separate rule of evidence selection on undisputed issues. The second section provides guidance in identifying the legal elements applicable to the claim or defense at issue. The third section addresses the quantity of evidence necessary to establish those elements. Finally, the fourth section specifies the general rule dictated by sponsorship analysis for the selection of evidence on undisputed issues: use only that amount of evidence required to satisfy the applicable legal burden. The remainder of the chapter is devoted to discussing the special rule of evidence selection applying to party-associated evidence.

Need for a Separate Evidence Selection Rule on Undisputed Issues

As we explained in Chapter Four, when the advocate's position on an issue is *disputed* by the opponent, the jury expects the advocate to put on his best case on that issue. That task is accomplished by adhering to the rule of using only strong evidence.

By contrast, where the advocate's position on an issue is *not* disputed, the jury does not expect the advocate to put on his best case on that issue. Here, the jury will not be apt to detain itself on the sufficiency of the evidence introduced with respect to that issue. To be sure, the jury is instructed by the court that it must find that the advocate has satisfied every element of the claim or defense before it can rule in the advocate's favor.[1] Since the opponent does not contend that the evidence is inadequate, however, the jury will not be apt to reach such a conclusion. This follows from the jury's assumption of best case. As a general rule, the jury will rely more heavily on the failure of the opponent's lawyer to dispute a point than it will on any evidence that the advocate can introduce. To persuade the jury on the undisputed issue, the advocate need only point out in summation the opponent's lack of disagreement. For example, in an assault prosecution in which the defense is asserting self-defense, the prosecutor's concession that the complaining witness punched the defendant before the defendant fired his gun at the witness will be taken as true, without any need for the defense to offer corroborating evidence.

Even though the jury does not expect an advocate carrying a legal burden of proof to put his focus on presenting evidence on undisputed issues, such an advocate is nonetheless required by law to introduce evidence on each such issue, unless the opponent's decision not to dispute the issue is formalized in a stipulation. Because, as will be seen, the standard for satisfying the legal burden of proof on undisputed issues differs from the standard for persuading the jury on disputed issues, the advocate must apply two different evidence selection rules.

The advocate must recognize that satisfying the legal burden of proof on undisputed issues has nothing to do with persuading the jury to render a verdict in his favor.[2] Satisfaction of such burdens is purely a legal requirement that must be met before the jury is even allowed to deliberate on the merits of the advocate's case. The purpose of the requirement is merely to ensure that the advocate's case is substantial enough to warrant submission to the jury for a decision.[3] Accordingly, as a practical matter, the judge is the

1 *See, e.g.*, *Criminal Jury Instructions, District of Columbia* § 2.08, at 70 (2002 ed.).

2 Where the opponent *disputes* the element in question, the legal burden of proof is likewise irrelevant to the selection of evidence to persuade the jury. The advocate obviously cannot assume, merely because his evidence is sufficient to satisfy his legal burden of proof, that this evidence will be sufficient for the jury.

3 *See, e.g.*, 26 *Moore's Federal Practice 3d* § 629.02[3], at 629-8 (LexisNexis 2006) (noting that the reason for a legal standard "is that a defendant is entitled to protection against an improper or irrational verdict of the jury").

only person in the courtroom who must be satisfied that these minimum legal requirements are met.

Identifying the Requirements for Satisfying the Legal Burden of Proof

The requirements for satisfying a legal burden of proof are determined solely by reference to law. In identifying the essential elements of his case, the advocate can consult a variety of sources for guidance. For instance, the advocate can examine the jury instructions applicable to a particular claim or offense.[4] He can also examine the statute governing the claim at issue as well as the cases construing that statute. In addition, the advocate can consult various secondary sources, such as treatises on the proof required in various kinds of cases.[5]

Quantity of Evidence Necessary to Satisfy the Legal Burden

The term often used to describe the quantity of evidence sufficient to meet a legal burden of proof is the "*prima facie* case." The advocate's task in introducing evidence sufficient to establish a *prima facie* case is generally not a substantial one. In a federal civil case, for example, a motion for a directed verdict against the plaintiff will be denied so long as reasonable minds could reach different conclusions based on the evidence introduced.[6] In a federal criminal case, a motion for judgment of acquittal will be granted only if there is no evidence upon which a reasonable mind might fairly conclude guilt beyond a reasonable doubt.[7]

If the advocate's legal burden of proof has already been satisfied during the opponent's preceding presentation, the advocate is relieved from

4 *See generally* K. O'Malley, J. Grenig & W. Lee, *Federal Jury Practice and Instructions* (West 5th ed. 2000) (containing model jury instructions for numerous civil and criminal actions).

5 *See, e.g.*, D. Drussel & J. Wade, *Plaintiff's Proof of a Prima Facie Case* (Callaghan & Co. 1982 & 2005 Supp.).

6 *See, e.g.*, Mid America Title Co. v. Kirk, 867 F. Supp. 673, 679 (N.D. Ill. 1994)(directed verdict warranted only if "reasonable persons could [not] differ as to the evidence"), *aff'd*, 59 F.3d 719 (7th Cir. 1995); Onufer v. Seven Springs Farm, Inc., 636 F.2d 46, 48 (3d Cir. 1980) (citation omitted); Edward J. Sweeney & Sons, Inc. v. Texaco, Inc., 478 F. Supp. 243, 254 (E.D. Pa. 1979), *aff'd*, 637 F.2d 105 (3d Cir. 1980); *compare* J. Nolan, *Trial Practice: Cases and Materials* 133 (West 1981)("[P]laintiff ... must 'get across the rail' by producing a prima facie case. This attainment consists of producing some evidence beyond a mere scintilla in support of every element in the case.").

7 *See, e.g.*, Curley v. United States, 160 F.2d 229, 232–233 (D.C. Cir.), *cert. denied*, 331 U.S. 837 (1947); United States v. Lumpkin, 448 F.2d 1085, 1093 (D.C. Cir. 1971); Austin v. United States, 382 F.2d 129, 138 (D.C. Cir. 1967); *compare* Nolan, *supra* n. 6, at 134 ("A prima facie case [in a criminal matter] is one in which the government has introduced *some* evidence on every required element of the crimes for which the defendant is being tried ....") (emphasis in original).

satisfying that burden in his own case. This can occur, for instance, where defense counsel in a contract case establishes his affirmative defense of duress during cross-examination of the opponent's witnesses.

Similarly, one or more elements of the advocate's legal burden of proof will frequently be stipulated to by the opponent. In such a circumstance, as long as the record for appeal is clear, there is no need to introduce evidence to satisfy the uncontested element.

Often, the opponent who opts not to dispute an element of the advocate's burden of proof will nonetheless refuse to formalize his decision in a stipulation. In these circumstances, the advocate is required to introduce evidence to satisfy the undisputed element. For instance, in a prosecution for distribution of heroin, the government must offer evidence that the substance in question is in fact heroin even if the defendant does not dispute the chemical analysis of the substance showing that it is heroin, but claims instead that he is not the person who sold the drugs. Likewise, in a federal prosecution for extortion under the Hobbs Act,[8] the prosecutor must demonstrate that the alleged extortion affected interstate commerce even if the defense does not contest that aspect of the case. Similarly, in a breach of contract suit, the plaintiff must show that a contract was formed even if the defense is asserting accord and satisfaction and does not dispute the formation of the original agreement.

Satisfying an undisputed element will not help an advocate persuade the jury. As noted, the only purpose is to prevent the court from summarily rejecting the claim or defense without letting it reach the jury. This point can be illustrated in the context of an appellate brief. The body of the brief is designed to convince the judges to rule in the advocate's favor. Other technical portions of the brief, however, while necessary under court rules, are not concerned with persuading the court. For instance, in the federal system, even if the appellee does not dispute the appellate court's jurisdiction, the appellant's brief must nonetheless contain a statement of the course of proceedings and the disposition in the lower court.[9] Such a statement will not help the advocate win the case except in the narrow sense that a failure to submit such a statement will cause the court of appeals to reject the brief for violation of the applicable rule.

8 18 U.S.C. § 1951(a).

9 *See* Fed. R. App. P. 28(a)(3).

One final comment is in order on the mandatory nature of the legal burden of proof. Chapter Four, in setting forth the pertinent evidence selection rule where the element of the claim or defense is *disputed*, demonstrated that persuading the jury requires an advocate to balance the sponsorship costs of introducing an item of evidence against its inherent probative value. Under the principles set forth in that chapter, the advocate may conclude, for instance, that a piece of favorable evidence should not be introduced because the costs are too high.

When evidence is necessary to sustain a legal burden of proof, however, the advocate does not have the luxury of omitting the item from his presentation. The failure to introduce evidence on every element of the claim or affirmative defense will result in a summary rejection of that claim or defense.[10]

The Rule for Selecting Evidence on Undisputed Issues

Chapter Four provided the rule, applicable to disputed issues, of using only strong evidence. Since the quantity of evidence required to satisfy a legal *prima facie* burden is a minimal one, it should be clear that as a practical matter, applying the "use-your-strong-evidence"rule will invariably satisfy any legal *prima facie* burden applicable to a disputed issue (assuming, of course, the burden can be met at all). The only real question facing the advocate concerns the appropriate rule of evidence selection to apply at trial on *undisputed* issues. This section sets forth that rule and the reasons underlying it.

It should be clear that presenting even the minimum amount of evidence necessary to satisfy the legal burden on an undisputed issue may entail sponsorship costs. Most significantly, the jury might view the advocate as putting on undisputed evidence in an effort to bolster his weak evidence on the disputed issues.[11] Any such costs, however, are unavoidable since the advocate must satisfy the legal burden just to get his case to the jury. Thus, the advocate need not even consider the sponsorship costs incurred by presenting such minimum evidence.

10 *See, e.g.*, Fed. R. Crim. P. 29(a) (court "shall order the entry of judgment of acquittal ... if the evidence is insufficient to sustain a conviction"); Fed. R. Civ. P. 50(a) (motion for directed verdict in civil case).

11 Of course, if the opponent directly criticizes the advocate for presenting evidence bearing on undisputed issues, the advocate can simply respond that he is required to present minimal evidence on all elements of the claim or charge, including undisputed ones. Because presenting such evidence is mandatory, the advocate's costs of overtrying will be low or non-existent.

By contrast, once the advocate's legal burden has been satisfied, the advocate is free to evaluate whether to introduce *additional* evidence on the undisputed issue. Such an approach is warranted only if the benefits exceed the costs incurred. With respect to undisputed issues, there is generally no reason to risk incurring the costs of putting on more than the minimum amount of evidence. As we explained,[12] the jury will tend to fully credit an opponent's failure to dispute an issue. Accordingly, the advocate, in not introducing more than the minimum amount of evidence on an undisputed issue, runs no significant risk that the jury will rule against him on that issue.[13]

While there is no real value in presenting more than the minimum amount of evidence on undisputed issues, there is a serious disadvantage in doing so. The jury is likely to speculate that the advocate focused so heavily on the undisputed facts because he had very little to offer on the matters in dispute. For this reason, the rule for selection of evidence on undisputed issues is that *the advocate should introduce no more than is necessary to satisfy the legal burden.*[14]

Any additional evidence will not benefit the advocate and might result in considerable sponsorship costs. To illustrate, consider a murder case in which defense counsel delivers his opening statement immediately after the prosecutor's opening statement and announces unequivocally that, while his client concedes that the crime occurred, the client maintains that someone else committed it and that he was erroneously identified as the perpetrator. Although the prosecutor in such a case has the legal burden of proving that the murder actually took place, he should not concern himself with that issue, since his opponent has conceded that there was a murder.

Thus, although the prosecutor must tender at least minimal evidence showing that the crime occurred in order to establish the *prima facie* case,

---

12 *See* page 92, *supra*.

13 As we show in the next section, however, this conclusion does not apply where the evidence bearing on the undisputed issue is "party-associated."

14 In evaluating evidence as it bears on *undisputed* issues, there is no need for the advocate to consider whether an item is "strong." That consideration relates only to persuading the jury on disputed issues. In addition, in assessing whether an item of evidence is "favorable" on an undisputed issue for purposes of satisfying his legal burden, the advocate need not consider whether it is "favorable" in the jury's eyes as that term was defined in Chapter Three. This follows from the fact that the legal burden of proof is not, as a practical matter, an issue for the jury. The advocate need only do two things. He must, of course, ensure that the evidence meets the test for admissibility which, in federal court, requires the evidence to have a "tendency to make the existence of [the] fact [to be proved] more probable ... than it would be without the evidence." Fed. R. Evid. 401. Second, he must ensure that it has sufficient probative content to meet the previously noted minimal legal standard of a "prima facie" case that the element is satisfied.

the prosecutor should not introduce multiple grisly photographs of the slain victim. Highlighting the seriousness of the offense will do nothing to help the jury resolve any doubts it might otherwise have about whether the defendant is the murderer. To the contrary, it will only provide the defense counsel with a basis to disparage the prosecutor's evidence on the disputed element.[15] Furthermore, the very seriousness of the offense may provoke the opposite reaction. The jury, knowing that a harsh penalty is certain upon conviction, may be even more reluctant to convict what may be the wrong man. Indeed, such reluctance could be magnified when the jurors realize that an erroneous conviction would not only punish the wrong man, it would close the case as well, leaving the real perpetrator free to commit similar ghastly crimes.[16]

In contrast to the rule governing undisputed issues, if the element in question is *disputed*, the advocate will not want to use simply the minimum amount of evidence necessary to satisfy the *prima facie* burden. For disputed issues, the advocate must *persuade* the jury of the merit of his position. Thus, the same grisly photographs of the murder victim that should not be presented where the defendant is claiming misidentification may be relevant in defeating a claim of self-defense. In that situation, a photograph showing multiple stab wounds would be highly probative on a *disputed* issue.

Party-Associated Evidence

In General

As we have previously demonstrated, an advocate's usual insurance policy in refraining from introducing evidence is the argument that the *opponent* could have introduced the evidence. As will be seen, for evidence that is party-associated, such an argument will not be apt to satisfy the jury. The reason is that the jury preconceives party-associated evidence to be unavailable to the opponent and thus does not expect him to use it. Accordingly,

15 *See, e.g.*, R. Traver, *Anatomy of a Murder* 397 (St. Martin's Press 1958)(closing argument by fictional defense attorney criticizing the prosecutor in a murder trial for "spen[ding] hour after hour and witness after witness—and incidentally dollar after public dollar" on the "gory details" of the murder at issue even though the defendant, who was claiming temporary insanity, had "never denied" the shooting).

16 *Cf.* Manson v. Brathwaite, 432 U.S. 98, 127 (1977) (Marshall, J., dissenting) ("[I]f the police and the public erroneously conclude … that the right man has been caught and convicted, the real outlaw must still remain at large. Law enforcement has failed in its primary function and has left society unprotected from the depredations of an active criminal.").

a different rule of evidence selection is necessary where the evidence is party-associated.

Identifying Party-Associated Evidence

Overview

This section provides guidance on identifying party-associated evidence. It first describes common characteristics of witnesses and tangible evidence falling within that category. It then provides a basic test—grounded in the fundamental concept of unique availability—that an advocate can employ with respect to any piece of evidence that he believes may be party-associated to aid him in making a reliable determination.

Practical Unavailability as the Key Characteristic

Party-Associated Witnesses

The key characteristic of party-associated evidence is the jury's preconception that it is not fully available to the opponent despite the opponent's physical access to it. For witnesses, the jury preconceives such witnesses to be in the advocate's "camp" or to be known prior to trial only to the advocate's side.

A typical characteristic of a party-associated witness is that he is likely to be heavily biased in favor of one side and would, in the jury's mind, be likely to go out of his way to help that side. The jury is apt to assume that such a witness is not likely to have submitted to pretrial interviews with the opponent's investigators. It is further apt to believe that, even if the witness were to have granted such an interview, the witness probably would have been uncooperative. For these reasons, the jury's assumption that the opponent will present all of his best evidence is suspended. The jury does not expect him to make efforts to overcome these obstacles and subpoena such a witness for trial without knowing what his testimony will be, even if the opponent has reason to suspect that the witness could have materially advanced his case.[17]

On occasion, even a completely unbiased witness may qualify as party-associated. This will be true where the jury thinks that information concerning the witness is in one party's exclusive custody. An example is when events at trial reveal that someone known only to that party witnessed the

17 This is especially so in a criminal trial, where compulsory pre-trial discovery regarding the other side's witnesses is limited.

incident in question and could corroborate his version of it. Such a witness is considered uniquely available to that party unless the jury is informed that the witness's name and address were disclosed to the opponent prior to trial.

Party-Associated Tangible Evidence

For items of tangible evidence to qualify as party-associated, the jury must ordinarily preconceive the item to be in the possession, custody, or control of one of the parties or in some other manner uniquely available to that party.[18] When this is so, the jury will assume that the opponent would have been impeded in his inspection of the item as a potential exhibit. The jury will thus tend to excuse the opponent for not introducing it. Here, too, the jury's assumption of best case is suspended.

Even where the jury learns that the opponent had the opportunity to inspect the item, its preconception of unique availability may sometimes not be eliminated. This comports with actual conditions that often hamper an attorney's inspection of the opponent's physical evidence. For example, in civil discovery, where opposing counsel is permitted to inspect voluminous business records at the company's offices, the corporation's custodian and attorney will often be hovering close by and noting those documents that opposing counsel finds significant. Similarly, when a criminal defense lawyer seeks to examine the government's photographic evidence, his consideration of that evidence will sometimes be hindered by the impatience of the watchful police custodian. Despite the foregoing phenomena, however, it will be rare for a jury to continue to preconceive of an item of tangible evidence as uniquely available to an advocate when he affords the opponent a formal opportunity to inspect it.

The Basic Test

The test for identifying party-associated evidence consists of determining whether the tender argument set out in Chapter Four will be fully persuasive.[19] Specifically, the advocate should assume that neither side has introduced an item of evidence at trial. The advocate should further assume that the opponent does not raise the issue of non-production in his summation,

18 *Cf.* O'Malley, Grenig & Lee, *supra* n. 4, § 104.25, at 150 (missing evidence instruction is limited to being given regarding evidence "under [a] party's control").

19 *See* pages 60 to 61, *supra*.

but that a juror raises the issue during deliberations and suggests that an adverse inference should be drawn against the advocate's case because he failed to produce the evidence. The test is whether the members of the jury would be satisfied with the observation of another juror that the *opponent* could have introduced the evidence and that *no* adverse inference should be made in either direction.

It should be clear that the pivotal factor for the deliberating jury in resolving this issue will be whether the other evidence at trial has revealed that both sides had access to the missing item or that the missing item was available only to the advocate. If the other evidence has given no clue concerning the availability of the missing item, then the jury will almost certainly apply its default preconception that the evidence was available to both sides.

Analogy to the Missing Witness and Missing Evidence Doctrine

The task of identifying party-associated evidence is similar to a court's task in deciding whether to permit an advocate to urge the jury to draw an adverse inference from his opponent's failure to introduce evidence, even where it is physically available for the advocate's use. Under basic missing witness principles, an advocate is permitted to urge such an adverse inference from the non-production of evidence that is uniquely available to the opponent.[20] Moreover, the doctrine also allows an advocate to urge an adverse inference from missing evidence *notwithstanding* the advocate's ability to secure the evidence himself by subpoena, so long as there is a legally sufficient relationship between the missing evidence and the non-producing opponent.[21] A court's decision as to what constitutes such a legally sufficient relationship is analogous to the trial lawyer's determination of whether the relationship between an item of evidence and the opponent's side is sufficiently exclusive as a practical matter to constitute party-associated evidence. Typically, a court making such a determination

20 *See, e.g.*, II J. Wigmore, *Evidence* § 285, at 192 (Little, Brown & Co. Chadbourn rev. 1979).

21 *See, e.g.*, Kean v. Comm'r of Internal Revenue, 469 F.2d 1183, 1188 (9th Cir. 1972) ("The determination of the question of equal availability depends upon all the facts and circumstances bearing upon the witness's relationship to the parties and not merely upon his physical presence at trial or accessibility for service of a subpoena."); Pointer v. Pointer, 251 S.W.2d 334, 338 (Mo. App. 1952) (noting that "if the relationship of the witness to a party is such that the witness would reasonably be expected to testify in favor of that party and against the other, such a witness is not equally available"). *See generally* Annotation, 5 A.L.R. 2d 893 (1949) (collecting cases under the topic of "Relationship between party and witness as giving rise to or affecting presumption or inference from failure to produce or examine witness"); II Wigmore, *supra* n. 20, §§ 285–291, at 192–229 (detailed discussion of missing witness and missing evidence rules).

for purposes of the missing witness doctrine—like the trial lawyer—will find the relationship to be sufficiently exclusive where the advocate's claim of lack of practical availability is a reasonable one.

For this reason, much of the case law under this aspect of the missing witness doctrine can be consulted for general guidance on the question of whether a given item of evidence is party-associated. This should not be surprising: under both sponsorship principles and the missing witness doctrine, the assumption that the advocate will use all of his best evidence is suspended where the evidence is not fully available to the advocate because of party association.

The trial advocate, however, should exercise caution in seeking guidance from this body of case law. We have found that this book's category of party-associated evidence is generally a narrower one than the corresponding category under the missing witness doctrine. For example, many courts apply a general rule that an employee is not available to the employer's opponent, notwithstanding the opponent's knowledge of and physical access to the witness.[22] A trial attorney would be remiss, however, in mechanically treating an employee as party-associated with his employer based solely on the fact of that relationship. Ultimately, in determining whether a particular employee is a party-associated witness, the advocate should apply the test set out earlier in this chapter turning on the jury's preconceptions of the witness's availability to opposing counsel.[23]

The Rule for Selecting Party-Associated Evidence for Use at Trial

In Chapter Four, we discussed a risk that may arise when an advocate omits evidence from his presentation.[24] The risk is that the jury, not having seen the evidence, will speculate that such evidence would have harmed the advocate's case. This risk does not arise, we stated, when the evidence is also available for the opponent's use. When evidence available to both sides is introduced by neither, the jury will be apt to assume that such evidence

22 *See, e.g.*, Kean v. Comm'r of Internal Revenue, supra n. 21, 469 F.2d at 1187–1188; Illinois Central Railroad Co. v. Staples, 272 F.2d 829, 834 (8th Cir. 1959) ("[W]here witnesses are employees of one of the parties, they are not equally available to the other party . . . ."); *see generally* Annotation, 5 A.L.R.2d 893, supra n. 21, at 897–913 (collecting cases); Note, *Drawing an Inference From the Failure to Produce a Knowledgeable Witness: Evidentiary and Constitutional Considerations*, 61 Cal. L. Rev. 1422, 1424 (1973).

23 *See* pages 100 to 101, *supra*.

24 *See* pages 49 to 50 & 60 to 61, *supra*.

would not have materially advanced or harmed *either* side's case. In sum, given equal availability, the advocate need not be concerned with any risk of adverse jury speculation from his omission of evidence.

This is not true in the case of party-associated evidence. Here, the jury has no logical basis for inferring from the opponent's omission of the evidence that it would have failed to benefit his case. Accordingly, because the jury preconceives that party-associated evidence is not equally available, the rule of evidence selection must take into account the risk of adverse jury speculation that arises when an advocate omits such evidence.

On the other hand, any rule for party-associated evidence must also assess the harm from the alternative of *using* it. Specifically, when the evidence bears on a disputed issue and is not strong, the advocate must evaluate the sponsorship costs incurred by using it. When it bears on an undisputed issue, as we also explain below, the advocate must likewise evaluate whether he incurs any costs by using it. Given these competing concerns, the rule of evidence selection for party-associated evidence is as follows: *use only that party-associated evidence for which the risk of adverse jury speculation from omitting it outweighs the harm from introducing it (with sponsorship costs considered)*. It should be clear that this rule involves a comparison of alternative adverse consequences.

As we explain below, the application of this rule will vary depending on whether the issue upon which the evidence bears is disputed or undisputed. The following sections focus separately on the alternative adverse consequences of omitting the evidence and using the evidence in these two contexts.

Disputed Issues

The Risk from Non-Use of Less-Than-Strong Party-Associated Evidence on Disputed Issues

As a preliminary matter, it should be clear that no issue arises with respect to whether *strong* party-associated evidence should be used. Since the need for a special rule of evidence selection arises only from the *omission* of party-associated evidence, and since the use of any strong evidence will, by definition, benefit the advocate's case, the advocate should plainly use all strong party-associated evidence.

When the evidence is less than strong, however, the advocate must consider whether its use is nonetheless warranted. He cannot rely on the general rule to the contrary, which depends on equal availability of the evidence in question, a condition that is not satisfied in the case of party-associated evidence. When evidence is party-associated, the advocate must understand that, even though the evidence "harms" the advocate's case because of the sponsorship costs incurred by presenting it, that harm may be outweighed by the risk that the jury will speculate that the omitted evidence is *more* harmful than it really is. Specifically, if the opponent criticizes the advocate for not producing such evidence, the advocate cannot persuasively respond that the opponent could have introduced it. Thus, the jury may speculate that it could have helped the opponent's case, perhaps significantly.

Assume, for example, a lawsuit arising out of an automobile accident in which the plaintiff's brother, a passenger in his car, was asleep and thus could not testify for his brother. Defense counsel may decide to argue:

> You heard, ladies and gentlemen, that the plaintiff's brother was in the car at the time of the accident. But did you hear him come in here to lend any support to the complainant's unusual account of how this accident occurred? No, you didn't. And I suggest that you recall that fact in your deliberations when you consider, as the judge will instruct you to do,[25] the extent to which the plaintiff's version is supported by other evidence in the case.[26]

As suggested in Chapter Four,[27] the danger to the plaintiff from such an argument is that the jury, not having heard the witness, may speculate that the brother's testimony would have *harmed* the plaintiff's case. The advocate must assess the likelihood of such speculation and the extent to which it could be reduced by reminding the jury that his opponent was free to call the brother.

The failure to introduce less-than-strong party-associated evidence on a

---

25 *See, e.g.,* O'Malley, Grenig & Lee, *supra* n. 4, § 15.01, at 364 (sample instruction stating, "In deciding whether you believe ... any witness, ... [a]sk yourself, ... were there things that corroborated [his] testimony ... ?").

26 If the court finds that the close family relationship rendered the brother not equally available to the defendant, then it might permit the defendant to urge an even stronger point: that the jury should draw an adverse inference from the plaintiff's failure to produce the brother. *See generally* Annotation, 5 A.L.R.2d 893, *supra* n. 21, at 928–937 (collecting pertinent authorities).

27 *See* pages 60 to 61, *supra*.

disputed issue will not always risk such consequences. The risk arises only when such evidence, in the jury's eyes, would materially bear on a disputed issue.[28] Whether it does will depend on the other evidence presented. Only where the other evidence indicates that the less-than-strong party-associated evidence might materially bear on the issue will there be a risk of adverse speculation. Returning to the above example, if the evidence conclusively revealed that the brother was asleep, the risk of adverse jury speculation would be non-existent.[29]

Occasionally, even the testimony of the party-in-interest will not materially bear on the disputed facts. For example, where a homeowner who loses his home in a fire sues an insurance company to recover on his policy, and the only disputed issue is whether he deliberately set the fire to defraud the company, it is unlikely that a company representative can say anything that will bear on the issue.

The Harm from Use of Less-Than-Strong Party-Associated Evidence on Disputed Issues

The harm from using less-than-strong party-associated evidence should by now be obvious. By definition, evidence is less than strong because the three sponsorship costs of using it outweigh its favorable value. When the evidence is favorable, the most significant cost will generally be the cost of overtrying, since the jury is apt to assume that the advocate introduced the party-associated evidence because he viewed his other evidence on the disputed issues as insufficient.

For example, assume a rape prosecution in which the victim's twelve-year-old daughter was a witness. Assume further that the defense is misidentification. If the daughter can testify only that defendant was about the same height as the rapist, the jury might conclude that the prosecutor thought he needed such testimony to win. A defense suggestion that proof of defendant's guilt hinged on that testimony would be hard to rebut.

When the evidence is neutral or unfavorable, the most significant cost

28 The analogous missing witness rule requirement is that the witness must "elucidate[]" the transaction. II Wigmore, *supra* n. 20, § 285, at 192. As defined in cases interpreting the requirement, the phrase "elucidate the transaction" means that the evidence is material to a *disputed* issue in the case. *See, e.g.,* Thomas v. United States, 447 A.2d 52, 57 (D.C. 1982); United States v. Young, 463 F.2d 934, 940 (D.C. Cir. 1972); Cooper v. United States, 415 A.2d 528, 533 (D.C. 1980); Dent v. United States, 404 A.2d 165, 170 (D.C. 1979).

29 In addition, the judge would not permit the opponent to urge the adverse inference because, as a legal matter, such an inference can only be based on the nonproduction of a witness who can materially "elucidate[]" the event at issue. II Wigmore, *supra* n. 20, § 285, at 192.

to consider will generally be that of introduction. The jury will give the equivocal or harmful evidence enhanced and unwelcome weight because of the prosecutor's concession of materiality and because the jury will seek to "unpackage" the evidence.

In the first edition of this book, we gave an example wherein the rapist in the foregoing case left his belt behind at the victim's house. We assumed further that, prior to trial, the prosecutor had advised defense counsel of the existence of the belt and allowed it to be inspected pursuant to an applicable criminal discovery rule;[30] that defense counsel opted against its use as an exhibit at trial; and that the prosecutor likewise opted against using it, since the prosecutor could not be certain it would fit the defendant. Finally, we assumed that during the cross-examination of the complainant, defense counsel inadvertently elicited testimony about the belt having been left behind and recovered by the police. With such testimony now before the jury, the prosecutor was faced with the decision of whether to use the exhibit to foreclose adverse jury speculation. We noted that if the belt, when introduced, fit the defendant but only tightly, the prosecutor would incur costs of overtrying, signaling to the jury that he thought it important for the jury to see it. The prosecutors in the *O.J. Simpson* murder trial, occurring after we published this "belt" example, faced a remarkably similar situation involving a glove that apparently belonged to the assailant. The prosecutors did not follow our book's advice and presented a glove that fit Simpson, but only tightly. In closing argument, the defense counsel exacted these costs from the prosecution, stating triumphantly (and to devastating effect), "If [the glove] doesn't fit, you must acquit!"[31]

The Presumption Against Use

An advocate concluding that an item of his less-than-strong evidence bearing on a disputed issue is party-associated should not assume that he will necessarily be better off introducing it than not doing so. In our experience, it will be exceedingly rare for the risk of adverse jury speculation resulting from the omission of the evidence to outweigh the harm from using it.

For example, in a criminal prosecution following an arrest on a busy

30 *See, e.g.*, Fed. R. Crim. P. 16(a)(1)(C) (requiring, upon defense request, that the government permit inspection of, *inter alia*, objects "belong[ing] to the defendant").

31 Simpson's attorney would not have been able to argue this as convincingly, of course, had the defense offered the equivocal glove into evidence.

street corner, the jury's common experience may tell it that the responding police officers usually obtain the names and addresses of witnesses at the scene. And the jury might not assume that such names and addresses are made available to the defendant.[32] Thus, there is at least a theoretical risk of the jury's speculating that the eyewitnesses not called by the government would have harmed its case.[33] We have found, however, that the harm from use in such a case will almost invariably outweigh the risk of omission. Most significantly, the jury will be apt to think that the attorney calling these witnesses deemed them important to his presentation on the disputed issue. The attorney will normally have no means of dispelling the opponent's criticism for calling such witnesses. Accordingly, the advocate considering the use of less-than-strong party-associated evidence should adopt a general presumption against use when applying the rules for selecting such evidence.

Before an advocate decides to use such evidence to foreclose adverse jury speculation, he should consider his alternatives. Above all, the advocate should consider what steps he can take to dispel the jury's preconception of unique availability short of presenting the evidence himself. Presenting such evidence should be viewed as a last resort.

Undisputed Issues

The Risk from Non-Use of Party-Associated Evidence on Undisputed Issues

Earlier in this chapter, we explained why an advocate seeking to satisfy a legal burden on an undisputed issue should use no more than the minimum amount of evidence necessary to satisfy that burden.[34] When evidence bearing on an undisputed issue is not equally available to the opponent, however, the jury may not be satisfied that the opponent had the information necessary to make a reliable determination of whether the issue was capable of dispute. Moreover, in these circumstances, the jury will not be apt to expect the opponent to go out

32 Indeed, the law often permits prosecutors to deny defense requests for the identities of their witnesses unless the witnesses are exculpatory. *See, e.g.*, United States v. Dreitzler, 577 F.2d 539, 553 (9th Cir. 1978) (noting that Fed. R. Crim. P. 16 does not require government to disclose witnesses), *cert. denied*, 440 U.S. 921 (1979); *see generally* Brady v. Maryland, 373 U.S. 83 (1963) (discussing government's constitutional duty to disclose exculpatory evidence).

33 Presumably, this is the rationale behind the advice of those commentators who suggest that a prosecutor must call *all* available eyewitnesses or suffer adverse tactical consequences. *See, e.g.*, A.E. Morrill, *Anatomy of a Trial* 107–108 (C.P.I. 1968).

34 *See* pages 96 to 98, *supra*.

on a limb by making an issue of the matter where he is handicapped by a lack of information. When this is true, the advocate's failure to introduce evidence on an undisputed issue that was not fully available to his opponent might cause the jury to penalize the advocate.

Here, as with party-associated evidence relating to a disputed issue, the advocate should be aware that the failure to introduce party-associated evidence on an undisputed issue will not always give rise to a risk of adverse jury speculation. Indeed, the risk from non-production is apt to be non-existent unless the testimony relates to a factual matter at the very foundation of an element of the claim or defense. The reason is that the jury will not bother to second-guess the opponent's failure to dispute an issue unless it believes that the evidence that was unavailable to him could have been verdict-determinative. For this reason, the risk of adverse jury speculation on undisputed issues is limited to evidence that goes to the foundation of an element of the claim or defense.

The two sections that follow set forth the considerations pertinent to the use of party-associated witnesses and tangible evidence going to the foundation of an element of the claim or defense. As will be seen, even though such evidence does not bear on disputed issues, the advocate's failure to consider the use of such evidence can lead to grave consequences.

Party-Associated Witnesses on Undisputed Issues

The above discussion made clear that the advocate should not call a party-associated witness to provide testimony on an undisputed issue unless the testimony bears on a factual matter going to the foundation of the claim or defense. The need to call such a witness can be illustrated by using a paradigm party-associated witness—the injured complainant.

In both criminal and civil cases, where an injured victim's attorney does not call him to testify about his injury, a matter which obviously goes to the foundation of his claim, the victim incurs a risk even where the defense does not dispute the fact of the injury. Clearly, the jury will not be convinced by the argument that the defendant could have called the victim since it views the victim, as a practical matter, to be unavailable to the defense. Consequently, the non-production of the victim will encourage the jury to speculate about the fact of the injury, and such speculation may result in an adverse verdict.[35]

The armed robbery trial recounted in the first chapter, with one factual change, illustrates the foregoing point. Assume that the good samaritan actually had witnessed the holdup of the elderly woman and had seen the perpetrator take the purse. As a technical matter, the victim's testimony would be unnecessary to establish the prosecutor's legal burden. The eyewitness could establish both the fact that the robbery occurred and the identification of the assailant.

Nonetheless, a prosecutor who failed to bring on the complainant to testify that she was robbed would be taking an unwarranted risk. In the worst-case scenario, the jury might conclude that the complainant would have testified that the defendant was *not* the assailant. Alternatively, it might conclude that the whole case was a setup and that the government could not find an elderly woman willing to fabricate the role of victim. The prosecutor would score no points by observing that the defendant could have called the complainant. Because the jury preconceives the complainant as not being fully available to the defense, it will not assume that defense counsel is able to present his best case regarding the victim's testimony. As a result, the jury might decide that the absence of the complainant makes an acquittal the only fair verdict. In this limited circumstance, it might render its verdict based on grounds not even urged by the defense counsel. Accordingly, under such circumstances, the prosecutor should call the victim and elicit brief testimony concerning the fact of the injury.

Of course, the mere fact that the advocate has decided to call a party-associated witness to testify on an undisputed issue does not mean that he should elicit whatever testimony the witness has to say on the *disputed* issues. Each point elicited must be independently justified under the rule applicable to the selection of party-associated evidence.

Moreover, it is important not to overdo the examination of the witness on an undisputed issue. This can only incur sponsorship costs. Returning again to the armed robbery case recounted in Chapter One, it will be recalled that the defendant did not deny the occurrence of an armed robbery, but claimed instead that someone else committed the crime. At the actual trial, the prosecutor elicited testimony of the elderly victim for

35 The failure to produce the defendant, which raises similar issues, is treated in Chapter Six.

the purpose of covering the undisputed elements of the armed robbery. Nonetheless, knowing that the victim was never able to make an identification, the prosecutor did not elicit the fact that the victim could not identify the defendant. Such a question would have amounted to eliciting evidence that was at best neutral on the disputed issue, thereby highlighting how much stronger the case could have been.

Party-Associated Tangible Evidence on Undisputed Issues

As with party-associated witnesses bearing on undisputed issues, the only occasion in which the advocate will need to consider introducing party-associated tangible evidence bearing on such issues is when the evidence goes to the foundation of an element of his case. When the party that the jury preconceives as having custody of such evidence does not introduce it at trial, the jury will not attach significance to the opponent's failure to do so. Specifically, because of its preconception of unequal access to the evidence, the jury will not be apt to rely on the opponent's failure to dispute the issue. For this reason, it may conclude that the advocate did not satisfy his burden, even on an issue that the opponent did not dispute.

Some examples will illustrate the point. In a counterfeiting prosecution, the jury preconceives the counterfeit money seized to be maintained in the custody of the government. Thus, unless there is something troublesome about the exhibit[36]—or the advocate otherwise has reason to believe that he will incur high sponsorship costs by using it—the government should normally produce it *in specie*, rather than through testimony, unless its absence is somehow explained. In such a case, even if the defense asserts a claim of misidentification and does not dispute that *someone* used counterfeit money, and even if introduction of the counterfeit bills is not legally required, the jury may indulge in adverse speculation if the prosecutor omits the evidence.

Similarly, in a bank robbery prosecution, the government should normally introduce the note that the robber passed to the teller. If the robber retrieved the note and it was never recovered, the fact of the robber's retrieval should be brought out through testimony. Likewise, in a prosecution for receiving stolen property, the prosecutor should normally introduce the stolen goods or account for his failure to do so.

36 *See* pages 165 to 166, *infra* (discussing occasional need to use substitutes for tangible evidence).

The jury's unfavorable response to the omission of such evidence is not based on any legal obligation that certain physical evidence be produced. As we have noted, the standards for a legal burden of proof differ from what should be presented to persuade the jury. For example, in a bank robbery case, the production of the note is not legally required for the government to prove its case. The jury may conclude, however, that the absence of such basic evidence uniquely possessed by the government masks a fatal defect in the evidence. For instance, it might speculate that the handwriting on the note did not match the defendant's handwriting. It might even conclude that there was no note at all and that the government's whole case is fabricated. Obviously, it is important for the advocate to avoid such speculation.

The Harm from Use of Party-Associated Evidence on Undisputed Issues

An advocate considering the use of party-associated evidence bearing on undisputed issues must evaluate the potential harm from such use. Specifically, the advocate must assess the possibility that the jury will view his use of that evidence to prove an undisputed issue as an attempt to conceal the inadequacy of his evidence on *disputed* issues.

As the foregoing sections revealed, the only party-associated evidence that the advocate should consider using on undisputed issues is evidence going to the foundation of an element of the claim or defense. Where the evidence is so fundamental to the case, the cost of overtrying incurred by its use is generally negligible. The jury will not be apt to view the use of such evidence as an effort to mask the inadequacy of evidence on the disputed issues. If the advocate is criticized for using such evidence, the jury will be apt to accept the advocate's response that it is his job to prove all elements, even undisputed ones. In sum, the harm from the use of such fundamental evidence on undisputed issues will normally be insubstantial.

The Presumption in Favor of Use

In general, there is a considerable risk of adverse jury speculation from the failure to introduce party-associated evidence bearing on an undisputed issue where that evidence goes to the foundation of the claim or defense. At the same time, the sponsorship costs of using such evidence are apt to be very low. Accordingly, although he should not overdo it,[37] an advocate should generally follow a presumption in favor of using such evidence.

The following chapter focuses on whether to present a defense case and whether to present rebuttal evidence. As will be seen, the decision whether to defend is complicated considerably by the fact that the defendant is a party-associated witness.

---

37 *See, e.g.*, pages 97 to 98, *supra* (discussing excessive use of evidence bearing on an undisputed issue).

CHAPTER 6

Selection of Evidence: Defense and Rebuttal

Overview

The defendant is being tried for murder, and the prosecutor has just rested after presenting a compelling case. Defense counsel must now decide whether to present a defense case. His client denies any involvement in the murder and has two witnesses who say he was elsewhere when the crime occurred. The problem is, however, that the defendant has a prior armed robbery conviction, and the two alibi witnesses are not very credible. Does the advocate call the defendant to the stand to deny the charges? Should the alibi witnesses be used? How will the jury react if the advocate decides not to put on any evidence? These are difficult tactical decisions.

This chapter explains how the sponsorship approach helps to resolve such questions. More generally, the chapter focuses on the evidence selection decisions involved when the opponent has already presented his case. For defense attorneys, the question is whether to put on a defense; for plaintiffs' attorneys and prosecutors, the question is whether to follow a defense case with a rebuttal case. Both contexts are addressed below.

The Decision to Defend

In General

Several factors bear on whether to put on a defense.[1] In large part, the decision will be governed by the rule of using only strong evidence, set forth in Chapter Four, along with its mirror image rule of using only strong discrediting points. (The latter rule is discussed below.) As will be seen, however, the decision to defend is greatly complicated by special considerations involving whether the defendant—a party-associated witness—should be called as a witness.

A critical cost to consider in putting on a defense is the cost of overtrying. Specifically, the advocate may be viewed as acknowledging that the opponent's preceding case is substantial. The lower the probative value of the evidence presented by the defense, the more likely it is that defense counsel's decision to defend will signal the jury that, in his view, the opponent established a sufficient case that must be rebutted.

There is a further dimension to presenting a defense case stemming from the jury's assumption of best case. Because of this assumption, the jury will view any presentation as the defendant's best case. It will not be inclined to explore alternative theories that defense counsel did not view as worthy of advancing. If the jury finds the defense case to be unpersuasive, it may settle on the plaintiff's/prosecutor's presentation for the sole reason that it presents the only viable alternative. In this worst-case scenario, the plaintiff's or prosecutor's burden of persuasion is essentially lifted.

This burden lifting is not a legal one, but a practical one.[2] Simply put, the jury's focus is no longer on whether the plaintiff or prosecutor has met his legal burden. Instead, the jury's focus is on comparing the *relative* strengths of the two cases. The risk is that the contest will collapse into a "battle of competing theories." Other things being equal, this shift from the legal burden of proof harms the defense. Before the defendant presents any evidence of his own, the plaintiff's attorney or prosecutor is more obliged to impress the jury with the merits of his own case.[3] Once the defendant

1 This section addresses only the threshold decision whether to defend. Once that decision is made, the question of what evidence to use should be resolved based on the guidance previously provided in Chapters Four and Five.

2 We are not discussing here instances when defense counsel mounts an affirmative defense (for example, statute of limitations, accord and satisfaction), which entails a *legal* burden of proof.

3 As we note below, however, the advocate is not prevented from attacking defense counsel's *theory* of the government's or plaintiff's evidence. *See* page 222, *infra*.

presents evidence, however, the plaintiff's lawyer or prosecutor can attack the defense case.[4]

The practical consequence of lifting the plaintiff's/prosecutor's burden by presenting a defense ultimately reflects the cost of overtrying. Specifically, by presenting a defense, defense counsel enhances the weight that the jury will be apt to attach to his opponent's evidence.

Not presenting a defense, however, also carries considerable disadvantages. Because the jury assumes that defense counsel will put forward his client's best case, it might infer from the lack of a defense case that the client has no respectable case whatsoever. Furthermore, as we explain below,[5] even when a defense is presented, the decision not to call the defendant as a witness in his own case may severely prejudice the defendant's chance of victory.

The impact of resting without calling the defendant or otherwise presenting a defense is, other things being equal, greater in a civil case than in a criminal case. The first reason stems from a criminal defendant's Fifth Amendment right not to testify or otherwise present a case. In civil cases, an attorney is free to comment on the significance of the defendant's failure to testify or present a defense case.[6] In the criminal context, however, such comments are largely prohibited.[7] The second reason is due to the lower burden of proof for the plaintiff in a civil suit (preponderance or clear and convincing) compared with that of a criminal prosecutor (beyond a reasonable

---

4 Experienced defense attorneys recognize that presenting defense evidence incurs serious burden-shifting costs. *See, e.g.,* J. Nelson, *Her Life is Her Job*, Wash. Post, June 12, 1988 (Magazine) 35 ("[P]utting on defenses ... ultimately shifts the burden .... I'd much rather have the prosecutor try to explain away the weaknesses in his case than have him point out the weaknesses in ours.") (quoting prominent former District of Columbia Public Defender).

5 *See* pages 117 to 119, *infra*.

6 *See, e.g.,* F. Lane, *Goldstein Trial Technique 3d*, § 23:10 (Thomson West 2005 supp.) (comment permitted on civil defendant's failure to testify).

7 Comment on a criminal defendant's failure to testify is generally prohibited. *See generally* United States v. Robinson, 485 U.S. 25 (1988); Griffin v. California, 380 U.S. 609 (1965); *but cf.* Robinson, 485 U.S. at 32 (comment on defendant's silence permissible when it is "a fair response to a claim made by defendant or his counsel," such as a claim that the government prevented the defendant from telling his side of the story). Indeed, the defendant is entitled to an instruction, upon request, that his silence may not be used against him. *See* Carter v. Kentucky, 450 U.S. 288 (1981); K. O'Malley, J. Grenig & W. Lee, *Federal Jury Practice and Instructions* § 15.14, at 451-52 (West 5th ed. 2000) (model instruction). However, comment on the lack of defense *evidence* has been held permissible so long as no adverse inference regarding the *defendant's* silence can be drawn. *See, e.g.,* United States v. Wesley, 422 F.3d 509, 516 (7th Cir. 2005); United States v. Sblendorio, 830 F.2d 1382, 1392 (7th Cir. 1987); F. Bailey & H. Rothblatt, *Successful Techniques for Criminal Trials* § 25.24, at 580-581 (Lawyers Co-op. Pub. Co. 1985) (noting, based on case law, that it is generally permissible for the prosecutor to state that his evidence is uncontradicted, unless such statement can be construed as comment on defendant's failure to testify). *Cf.* Lockett v. Ohio, 438 U.S. 586, 594–595 (1978) (prosecutor's reference to government's case as "unrefuted" and "uncontradicted" not reversible error where defense counsel had outlined defense case in opening statement but then offered no evidence to rebut government's case).

doubt). Since the latter's evidence needs to be stronger to win, it is less likely in the criminal context that defense evidence of a given probative value is needed to overcome the opponent's preceding presentation. A defense decision to rest in a criminal case without presenting any evidence accordingly sends less of a signal to the jury that the evidence the defense is not presenting is weak.

The following sections discuss the considerations pertinent to whether to defend (and whether to call the defendant) in two situations: (1) when favorable defense evidence is available and (2) when it is not.

The Decision to Defend When Favorable Defense Evidence Is Available

This section assumes that the defendant has favorable evidence available. The initial question here, as elsewhere, is whether the favorable aspects of the evidence outweigh the three sponsorship costs. Although determining this requires the advocate to perform the analysis outlined in Chapters Three and Four, further discussion is needed to explain the assessment of the cost of overtrying.

Two variables will bear on the cost of overtrying incurred by the use of an item of favorable defense evidence: the strength of that defense evidence and the strength of the opponent's preceding case. In general, as common sense would indicate, the more compelling the defense evidence, the lower will be the cost of overtrying. Because the jury expects an attorney to put on all evidence that materially favors his case, the attorney will lessen costs of overtrying when his evidence comports with that expectation. Similarly, the stronger the *opponent's* case, the more apt the defense counsel should be to use a given item of favorable defense evidence. This is because the acknowledgment of the strength of the opponent's preceding case resulting from presenting defense evidence will not be as likely to "shore up"the opponent's case when that case is already strong. If, on the other hand, the opponent's case is weak, presenting a defense may significantly enhance the opponent's evidence. In this latter circumstance, therefore, the advocate should be less inclined to put on a defense, other things being equal.

Returning to the murder case example at the beginning of this chapter, assume that the government has rested. If the government's case is compelling, a favorable alibi witness will be more apt to qualify as strong, since the costs of overtrying will be minimal. By contrast, where the government's case is weak, the likelihood that the same witness should be called is lower, since those costs will be greater. Of course, even where the government's case is weak, calling an extremely favorable alibi witness may be warranted, because presenting such highly probative evidence incurs minimal overtrying costs.[8]

It should be apparent that before defense counsel presents a case, he must assess not only the cost of overtrying but also the costs of introduction and efforts. Setting aside party-associated evidence, defense counsel should present evidence on a disputed issue only if the evidence is still favorable after applying all three costs.

The status of the defendant as a party-associated witness complicates the foregoing analysis. If the defendant provides favorable evidence outweighing sponsorship costs, then he plainly should be called for the reasons stated above. Obviously, the defendant should also be called even if he is the *only* strong witness. By contrast, if the defendant's testimony, standing alone, would be considered less-than-strong after applying sponsorship costs, and if there is other defense evidence available that qualifies as strong, defense counsel must consider whether to put on such other evidence without calling the less-than-strong defendant.[9]

As we stated in Chapter Five, the defendant is a party-associated witness. Where, as is virtually always the case, the evidence indicates that the defendant would have something material to say, defense counsel who is considering not calling his client must account for the risk of adverse jury speculation about what the defendant would have said had he been called. This is because the jury does not expect the defendant to be called by the plaintiff or prosecutor even if his testimony would have advanced the plaintiff's or prosecutor's case. Indeed, in a criminal case, the jury is normally instructed that the defendant cannot be compelled to testify against his will under any circumstances.[10] Given these factors, where defense

8 Some commentators recommend that a criminal defendant present no evidence after a weak government case, apparently without regard to the strength of the defense evidence available. *See, e.g.*, Bailey & Rothblatt, *supra* n. 7, § 15.1, at 392 ("If the prosecution has put in a poor case and there is an excellent chance that the jury may completely ignore and disregard the flimsy evidence presented, you should rest and rely upon this lack of evidence."). In our view, such advice goes too far. If the defense has compelling evidence available to it, the benefit of putting on a defense may outweigh the sponsorship costs, even when the government has put on a weak case. Analogous is the benefit to a plaintiff of calling two witnesses in his case-in-chief where both are highly favorable and equally probative.

9 The same consideration must be made with any party-associated evidence, not just the defendant. For simplicity, we address only the problem posed by the less-than-strong defendant.

10 *See* n. 7, *supra* (citing authorities); O'Malley, Grenig & Lee, *supra* n. 7, § 15.14, at 451-52 (model instruction stating that the defendant has "an absolute right" not to testify).

counsel decides to present other evidence but not to call the defendant, the risk of adverse speculation will be at a maximum, since the absence of the defendant's testimony will be magnified. The jury will recognize that calling the defendant would have required little effort, since the defendant is sitting in the courtroom, only feet from the witness stand. For example, if the defense calls an alibi witness who testifies that he and the defendant were out of town together at the time of the murder, the jury is likely to notice the defendant's failure to take the stand more keenly than it would have if the alibi witness had not been called.[11] This problem is more significant in a civil case, where the opponent is permitted to comment on the defendant's failure to testify.[12]

Thus, for the foregoing reasons, as well as for the reasons set forth more generally in Chapter Five, other things being equal, calling a defendant with less-than-strong testimony to the stand will more likely be justified when other defense evidence is being presented than when no such defense evidence is being offered.

Nonetheless, the advocate obviously should not conclude from the above analysis that the defendant should *always* be called when a defense case is being presented. In some circumstances, the harm from calling the defendant will outweigh its value in foreclosing adverse jury speculation concerning his testimony. Thus, in the foregoing murder example, if the defense is presenting strong alibi witnesses, defense counsel would normally be justified in *not* calling the defendant when he would have to admit to a prior murder conviction. As with any party-associated evidence, defense counsel must balance the risks incurred by not calling the defendant against the harm from the jury's actually hearing his less-than-strong testimony.

There is a final consideration stemming from the unique challenges posed by the conspicuousness of omitting the defendant—a party—when other defense evidence is being presented.[13] The omission might render the risk of adverse jury speculation so high that the defense counsel should decide not to present the other defense evidence notwithstanding his determination that the other evidence, standing alone, qualifies as "strong" after

11 This example recognizes the inclination of some juries in criminal cases to give weight to a defendant's failure to testify, notwithstanding instructions to the contrary. *Cf.* Lakeside v. Oregon, 435 U.S. 333, 340 n. 10 (1978).

12 *See, e.g.,* Lane, *supra* n. 6, § 23:10 ("In a civil case, counsel may comment on a party's failure to testify.").

13 We are, of course, addressing here the case of a defendant who appears from the other evidence presented to be able to provide relevant testimony on the disputed issue.

assessing the sponsorship costs incurred by its use. Specifically, defense counsel must consider whether this other evidence still results in a net benefit to his case given the enhanced risk of adverse jury speculation incurred by the defendant's conspicuous absence from the presentation. Defense counsel must satisfy himself that there is such a net benefit before opting in favor of presenting a defense that does not include his client.

The Decision to Defend When No Strong Evidence Is Available

If defense counsel finds himself without any strong evidence-in-chief, he should not automatically decide against presenting a defense case. The advocate should first consider whether he is warranted in presenting evidence solely for the purpose of undermining evidence presented by the opponent.[14] For example, in the videotape case in Chapter One, it was shown that defense counsel might have been warranted in introducing the videotape to demonstrate the hesitancy of the government's star witness in identifying the defendant. This is true even though the videotape could not possibly have been considered beneficial to the defense, had the government not called the witness appearing in the videotape.[15]

Even if no such discrediting evidence is available, defense counsel should consider whether a less-than-strong defendant should testify where no other defense evidence is being presented.[16] When the defense does not present other evidence, the defendant's absence is not highlighted to the same degree as it is when other defense evidence is presented. Thus, the risk of adverse jury speculation from not calling the defendant is apt to be less when no other evidence is being presented. Nonetheless, the need to consider the risk of not calling the defendant obviously cannot be overlooked. The rule for whether the defendant should be called, as with any party-associated witness, is whether the risk of adverse jury speculation from non-use outweighs the harm from use.

To illustrate, assume that in the foregoing murder example, the defense has no available evidence except the defendant's own uncorroborated—and not very credible—alibi. Employing the above test, if the defendant has a

14 *See* pages 87 to 90, *supra*.

15 This might have been the case, for example, had the government been able to locate another eyewitness.

16 We note that the use of other party-associated defense evidence raises equivalent considerations (though the defendant's status as a party makes these considerations far more important). As in the foregoing section, however, the presentation in this section is simplified by limiting the discussion to the case of the defendant.

prior narcotics conviction, the defense may be justified in calling him. On the other hand, if the defendant has a prior conviction for murder, calling the defendant would likely be unjustified. In the latter situation, calling the defendant would probably be at least as damaging as the adverse speculation from not calling him.

If the use of less-than-strong evidence cannot be justified under either rationale discussed above, and the advocate has no strong evidence available, then he should not present a defense case. By doing so, the advocate would be incurring costs of overtrying by signaling a concern about the strength of the opponent's case. When the defense evidence is not strong, the advocate, by definition, would reap no counterbalancing benefits.

General Observations on the Decision to Defend

Because the jury could view a defendant's failure to present any evidence as reflecting that he has *no* defense, it might appear logical to conclude that there should be a strong presumption in favor of putting on a defense. We believe that any such presumption is unwarranted. Each case must be analyzed on its own merit, based on the above considerations, with no presumption either way. As former prosecutors, the authors recall many cases that were lost by defense lawyers who, instead of resting without presenting a case, followed a thin government case with a weak defense case.

A case tried by one of the authors illustrates this danger. Two police officers observed packets of narcotics being thrown out of the windows of an automobile containing five occupants. The officers retrieved the narcotics and then stopped the vehicle. A search of the vehicle uncovered no more drugs, but the police did recover various items of drug paraphernalia. Although the officers could not specifically link any one individual to the packets or paraphernalia, a heavy aroma of phencyclidine-laced marijuana permeated the automobile. Accordingly, the officers arrested all five occupants. At trial, after the government rested, the prosecutor was concerned that the defense would present no evidence and that the jury, after hearing arguments and instructions, would quickly return from its deliberations with five not guilty verdicts. To his surprise, however, each of the five defendants opted to testify. Each stated he was certain that no one had tossed drugs from the vehicle. Some of the defendants had prior convictions, and their testimony, viewed jointly, was very unpersuasive. The jury rapidly returned guilty verdicts against all five defendants. The consensus of those viewing the trial was that the defendants all would have been acquitted had they not presented any evidence.[17]

The Decision Whether to Rebut

The purpose of rebuttal is to refute evidence previously presented by an opponent.[18] Specifically, rebuttal evidence may serve to "explain, repel, counteract, or disprove evidence of the adverse party."[19] When the advocate is considering use of rebuttal evidence, he should employ the rule urging the use of discrediting evidence that outweighs sponsorship costs.[20]

In assessing his costs of overtrying, the advocate should analyze all of the evidence previously presented in the case—his own as well as his opponent's—to determine the impact of his rebuttal evidence. This requires two principal inquiries. The first involves the strength of the defense case in light of his own preceding case. If the defense case was comparatively weak, a given item of discrediting rebuttal evidence is less apt to qualify for use. The jury will wonder why the advocate went to the effort to rebut a seemingly weak case and will be apt to find it significant that he felt a need to do so. Moreover, the advocate may lose the ability to assert with credibility that the defense case was so weak that no rebuttal evidence was necessary.

The second inquiry involves the strength of the rebuttal evidence. The greater its impact in undermining the defendant's evidence, the less likely the advocate will suffer costs of overtrying. As previously indicated,[21] an advocate is *expected* to marshal evidence that significantly undermines the opponent's case.

Where the rebuttal evidence substantively *favors* the advocate's *own* case and does not simply undermine an item of the opponent's previously presented evidence, the advocate saving it for rebuttal benefits from its favorable value without incurring the higher sponsorship costs of using it in his case-in-chief (assuming, as discussed below, that the court would

17 *Cf.* T. Twiss, Life of Lord Eldon (1844)(quoting English jurist Edward Thurlow, "I was with you, Mr. Scott — until I heard your argument."), *reprinted in* E. Frost-Knappman and D. Schrager, The Quotable Lawyer 14 (Facts on File, Inc. rev. 1998)

18 *See, e.g.*, VI J. Wigmore, *Evidence* § 1873, at 678 (Little, Brown & Co. Chadbourn rev. 1979).

19 United States v. Allard, 464 F.3d 529, 535 (5th Cir. 2006)(quotation marks omitted); United States v. Mallis, 467 F.2d 567, 569 (3d Cir. 1972), *quoting* Luttrell v. United States, 320 F.2d 462, 464 (5th Cir. 1963).

20 *See* pages 87 to 90, *supra*.

21 *See* page 26, *supra*.

accept the evidence on rebuttal). A case tried by one of the authors illustrates the point.

An accomplice to a bank holdup who plea-bargained for lenient treatment identified the defendant as the "wheelman" or getaway-car driver in the incident. At trial, the prosecutor called the accomplice in his case-in-chief. The case ended in a hung jury.

On retrial, a different prosecutor (the author) tried the case. The new prosecutor decided not to call the accomplice in his case-in-chief. After the defendant testified and denied any role in the holdup, the prosecutor determined that the ability of the accomplice's testimony to undermine the defendant's version outweighed the cost of using him and thus called him as a rebuttal witness.

In summation, defense counsel, who had vigorously cross-examined the accomplice, argued at length that the accomplice's testimony could not be trusted. The prosecutor responded in his rebuttal argument that his case did not depend on the accomplice, but only on the evidence in the case-in-chief, and that the accomplice was called only because he so effectively undercut the defendant's testimony.

The jury returned a guilty verdict in under an hour. Defense counsel, in discussion with the prosecutor, attributed the verdict to the fact that the previous prosecutor, by calling the accomplice in the case-in-chief, had made his whole case depend on whether the jury credited that witness. Thus, while defense counsel's focus on the accomplice in his summation was effective in the first trial, he believed it was much less effective in the second trial.

This case illustrates that an advocate who calls a witness in his case-in-chief is apt to incur higher costs of overtrying than when the advocate calls that same witness in rebuttal. In the above case, although the second prosecutor incurred sponsorship costs, those costs were lower than those incurred by the first prosecutor. Specifically, when the second prosecutor called the accomplice in rebuttal, the jury might have given less weight to the prosecutor's case-in-chief, reasoning that the prosecutor was concerned that the defendant's testimony had rendered his evidence-in-chief inadequate. Nonetheless, this was a lesser cost than the first prosecutor's implicit concern, reflected in his decision to call the accomplice in his case-in-chief, that his other evidence was insufficient to convict even *prior to* the negative impact of the defendant's testimony. The second prosecutor, by saving the accomplice for rebuttal, was still able to argue with some credibility that the evidence presented in his case-in-chief, standing alone, was sufficient to convict.

In Chapter Four, we set forth a high-risk strategy of withholding strong evidence in the expectation that the advocate will be able to present it in rebuttal.[22] While the benefits of such a strategy may be substantial, the advocate must realistically assess the likelihood that the court will rule that the evidence in question does not qualify as rebuttal evidence. Some courts are reluctant to permit the use of evidence in rebuttal that would have qualified for admission in the case-in-chief.[23] Thus, the advocate who withholds evidence for use in rebuttal should assure himself that he will have a supportable rationale for how such evidence will qualify as rebuttal evidence. Furthermore, the advocate must recognize that in saving a witness for rebuttal, he risks not being able to use the witness at all if his opponent decides not to present a case.

The Five Steps of Sponsorship Analysis for Evidence Selection

This chapter and the three preceding it have discussed the issues involved in evaluating evidence and in selecting what, if any, evidence to introduce. The following chapters apply the sponsorship approach to each phase of the trial, from jury selection and opening statement to closing argument. Before doing so, however, it is useful to summarize the process of evidence selection. The various decisions that must be made can be summarized in five steps:

1. Identify the disputed and the undisputed issues.
2. For undisputed issues, use only the minimum evidence necessary to satisfy *prima facie* legal burdens, if any, unless the evidence bearing on the undisputed issue is party-associated with your side, goes to the foundation of the case, and the risk of adverse jury speculation from omitting the evidence outweighs the harm in using it (with sponsorship costs considered).

22 *See* pages 55 to 59, *supra*.

23 *See, e.g.*, *Jones on Evidence*, § 24:1, at 74 (Lawyers Co-op Pub. Co. 6th ed. 1972)(citing authorities for "[t]he rule ... that a party may not withhold part of his proof and introduce it as rebuttal instead of offering it as part of his case in chief").

3. Evaluate the strength of available evidence on the disputed issues to identify your strong evidence, namely, your favorable evidence that outweighs the costs of introduction, efforts, and overtrying.
4. Use all strong evidence on disputed issues.
5. Use no less-than-strong evidence on disputed issues unless:
    a. the evidence is party-associated with your side, would be viewed by the jury as materially bearing on the disputed issue if omitted, and the risk of adverse jury speculation from omitting the evidence outweighs the harm in using it (with sponsorship costs considered).

    or

    b. The apparent efforts in omitting the evidence would outweigh the sponsorship costs of its use plus your opponent's resulting saved sponsorship costs.

    or

    c. The evidence is devastating information possessed by a witness you have decided you must call, and not eliciting the information yourself would damage your credibility so severely that the resulting across-the-board decrease in the persuasiveness of your favorable evidence would be greater than the sponsorship costs of eliciting it yourself plus your opponent's resulting saved sponsorship costs.

Utilizing the foregoing five steps enables the advocate to avoid a common fault of many trial lawyers, especially beginning ones: presenting too much evidence. In our experience, many practitioners select evidence using a different set of assumptions. Those assumptions are (1) there are no costs associated with the use of evidence, or at least none significant enough to affect the decision whether to present it; (2) the jury might rule against the advocate if the evidence is not used, even where such evidence does not relate to any disputed issue; (3) an argument that the opponent could have used the evidence will not relieve the advocate from the need to introduce it; and (4) given the foregoing, there is no need for a precise evaluation of the strength of available evidence bearing on the disputed issues. This strategy results in an approach to evidence selection that is far more inclusive than the above rules counseled by the sponsorship approach. As a result, cases are overtried and unnecessary burdens are assumed. The five steps described above will help to avoid that pitfall.

CHAPTER 7

Jury Selection and Opening Statement

Overview

This chapter addresses the sponsorship method's bearing on two phases of the trial: jury selection, commonly known as voir dire, and opening statements. These portions of the trial are the first exposure that an advocate will have to the jurors in the case. As the foregoing chapters have made clear, the jurors will be monitoring the advocate's every word and deed from the moment he files into the courtroom for jury selection. This chapter provides guidance on how, during these early parts of the trial, the advocate can advance his chances for a favorable verdict. It also emphasizes how the advocate can harm those prospects by ill-considered and careless actions.

Voir Dire

During voir dire, the jury is selected from a panel of prospective jurors drawn from the local community. From the public's perspective, the purpose of voir dire is to ensure, to the extent possible, that the jurors selected will render a fair and impartial verdict. The mechanism for accomplishing this goal is to place all of the prospective jurors under oath and examine them on matters bearing on their ability to be impartial. Classic examples of such examination are questions designed to identify those individuals who are personally acquainted with one of the parties to the case or who have knowledge of the dispute and have formed preconceptions concerning it.

The advocate's perspective is different. His job is *not* to ensure that the opponent's side of the dispute is sympathetically heard; that is the opponent's job. The advocate's responsibility is to ensure that *his* client's side of the dispute is given fair consideration. Thus, the advocate's goal in voir dire is to eliminate from the panel those individuals who are apt to be unsympathetic to his client's contentions. To illustrate the foregoing, assume that an advocate represents a discharged employee claiming wrongful termination. The advocate might conclude, for example, that his client will receive a less sympathetic hearing from a juror who is an employer rather than an employee. Having reached this conclusion, the advocate should seek to identify and eliminate from the array potential jurors who are employers.

To accomplish this screening task, the advocate must gather whatever information is available about the prospective jurors, such as a potential juror's age, location of residence, and occupation. In some jurisdictions, the attorneys receive basic biographical data concerning the jurors in written form at the outset of the jury selection process. More often than not, however, the advocate must rely on answers to specific questions posed to the entire panel and to questions posed to individual jurors. Questions of this nature may include, in the appropriate case, such things as whether the prospective juror was ever a party to a civil suit (and, if so, the circumstances of the case), whether he has any close relatives in the law enforcement field, and whether he has ever been a victim of or witness to a crime.

In sum, it is important for an advocate to screen jurors for basic sympathies regarding the nature of the dispute, such as whether a prospective juror is likely to be "pro-defense." Beyond this, the advocate concerned about a specific weakness in his case may want to eliminate jurors based on how they are apt to react to that weakness once it is brought out at trial. The trial tactics literature generally encourages the advocate to question jurors about the weaknesses of his case.[1] The advocate, however, should recognize the dangers involved in such a strategy. It is obviously in the advocate's interest to eliminate prospective jurors who would be inclined

1 *See, e.g.*, J. Tanford, *The Trial Process: Law, Tactics & Ethics* 216, 227–230 (LexisNexis 3d ed. 2002)(quoting authorities on the benefits of bringing out in voir dire, *inter alia*, a client's criminal record, the accident record of a plaintiff in a negligence case, and various other unfavorable matters); M. Berger, J. Mitchell & R. Clark, *Trial Advocacy: Planning, Analysis & Strategy*, 206–207 (Little, Brown & Co. 1989)(noting the importance of screening jurors by exposing them to weaknesses in the advocate's case).

to give a weakness in his case undue weight. The tactical dilemma faced by the advocate is whether his case will be harmed if the weakness is raised during voir dire. The risk is that the weakness will be given such prominence that the advocate will later have difficulty arguing at trial that it is not significant and does not bear on the verdict.

The resolution of this dilemma involves a difficult weighing process. On the one hand, the advocate must consider the benefit derived from identifying and eliminating potential jurors who will be more apt to hold the weakness against his case. On the other hand, he must consider the detriment to his case from parading his weakness before the potential jurors.

With respect to the potential benefit of disclosing a weakness, the advocate must be realistic about his prospects for identifying potential jurors who are most apt to hold the weakness against his case. In our experience, the effectiveness of voir dire as a mechanism for detecting such predispositions is questionable. It is certainly the case that direct and pointed questions about a person's ability to render a fair verdict are unlikely to identify potentially biased jurors. Unless they are deliberately trying to be excused from jury service, most people will not admit in front of a large group of strangers that they hold biases or prejudices or that they could not decide a case fairly. Occasionally, however, an advocate can craft a question in a more subtle way, to identify individuals who are likely to be unsympathetic to his case.

To illustrate the foregoing, assume a criminal prosecution in which the victim was shot while trying to collect on a debt owed by the alleged assailant's thirteen-year-old younger brother. Assume further that the reason for the debt was that the victim had supplied narcotics to the brother. Finally, assume that the victim has a long record of drug arrests and convictions. The prosecutor must decide whether he will benefit from having the prospective jurors examined regarding their attitudes about convicted drug dealers. Plainly, many of the potential jurors are apt to be sympathetic to the defendant for his understandable anger at the victim's having supplied the defendant's younger brother with narcotics. Nonetheless, few potential jurors will be apt to come forward when asked in voir dire whether they would be unable to render a fair verdict given the circumstances surrounding the shooting.

It is unclear whether a more indirect question would achieve better results. For example, the potential jurors could be asked simply whether they have very strong feelings against narcotics dealers. The advocate can make note of those with affirmative responses. Of course, with a question that broad, the advocate might elicit an affirmative response from the majority of the panel members. A follow-up question of whether those holding such strong feelings would be unable to render a fair verdict in a case involving a drug dealer might yield few or no affirmative responses. As this example illustrates, it is unclear whether voir dire concerning the unsympathetic victim will yield useful information.

In various circumstances, it may be possible for an advocate to make some headway in identifying persons on the jury panel who are predisposed to hold a weakness against his case. The task is a difficult one, however, and will depend on the nature of the weakness and on the advocate's ability to craft a question that will yield useful information. In our own cases, we have generally avoided raising any such negative matters in voir dire.

Even if an advocate believes that he might be able to identify some potentially biased jurors by highlighting a weakness, this does not necessarily mean that such a strategy should be followed. The advocate must be alert to the fact that whether he or the judge asks the questions implicating the weakness, that weakness will have been given prominence at a very early stage of the proceedings. The advocate's later attempts to downplay the significance of that weakness will be hampered by this fact.

If the advocate conducts the voir dire examination concerning the weakness, he makes the implicit concession that the weakness is a matter of such importance that it must be addressed even before the opponent has raised it.[2] This is the same dilemma faced by an advocate who volunteers a weakness during the trial itself. In the above drug case, for example, a prosecutor who highlights the victim's criminal background and his involvement in a drug transaction with the defendant's brother conveys at the very least a concern that the jurors will consider those facts to bear on the defendant's guilt or innocence. Since the prosecutor himself singled out those facts as early as voir dire, he will have difficulty arguing later that such facts are irrelevant and have nothing to do with the case.

Furthermore, even if the judge conducts the examination raising the weakness, the advocate suffers from the fact that the opponent is thereby

2 Jurisdictions vary in their approaches to whether the judge or the attorney is responsible for conducting voir dire examination. In some jurisdictions, the attorneys have control over the questioning. In others, including many federal courts, the judge conducts the entire voir dire, although he will consider asking written questions submitted by the attorneys. Still other jurisdictions have a practice in which the judge conducts general interrogation and then turns the questioning over to the attorneys. *See generally* Tanford, *supra* n. 1, at 110–12 (discussing the various voir dire practices); T. Mauet, *Trial Techniques* § 3.3, at 33-34 (Aspen Publishers 7th ed. 2007) (same).

relieved from raising it for the first time. As noted in Chapter Two,[3] an attorney, by introducing evidence that is favorable to his case, makes an implicit statement that he is relying on that evidence to win. Thus, in the foregoing murder example, if defense counsel is the first to raise the weakness, such as during the cross-examination of the victim, *he* will have to convince the jury that the fact is somehow relevant. Put another way, *he* will suffer the sponsorship costs. If the *judge* highlights the weakness during voir dire, the opponent will be relieved of some of the burden of showing that the weakness bears on the verdict.

To summarize, there may be a considerable cost in bringing out one's own weakness during voir dire. Unless the advocate foresees a substantial likelihood that he will be able to eliminate jurors likely to be predisposed against his case, the advocate should avoid highlighting a weakness during voir dire. Instead, the advocate should let the opponent bring out the weakness during the trial.

Opening Statement

In General

Opening statement represents the advocate's first chance to give the jury a detailed overview of his case. From the jury's perspective, it provides the opportunity to hear a summary of the *best* case supporting the advocate's position. As will be seen, sponsorship principles are fully applicable to opening statements, and the content of the remarks must be planned with the utmost care. The first part of this section provides guidance in crafting an effective opening statement.

Although plaintiffs' attorneys and prosecutors have no choice over *whether* to give an opening statement (they must), or *when* to do so (it must be at the outset of the trial), defense attorneys are not subject to the same restrictions. The final part of this section addresses the questions of whether, and when, defense counsel should give an opening statement.

Content of the Opening Statement

Importance of Content of Opening Statement

The content of an opening statement is significant for several reasons. To

3 *See* pages 32 to 35, *supra*.

begin with, apart from what the jury can glean through voir dire, this is the jury's first introduction to the advocate's case, and it will be listening carefully to hear his best-case scenario. It will assume that the case is no better—and perhaps much worse—than stated. Moreover, opening statement provides the advocate with the opportunity to identify his theory of the case. This will assist the jury in following the evidence that the advocate later introduces.

The jurors may not be the only ones listening carefully to the advocate's opening statement. If the opponent is savvy, he will be listening for any alternative or inconsistent theories advanced by the advocate. He will also be listening to the advocate's promises on what his evidence will show, and will later take the advocate to task for any shortcomings in the evidence the advocate ultimately presents.

The following sections provide guidance in crafting an opening statement. The principles follow directly from sponsorship principles.

Organization Based on the Case Theory

An advocate should organize his opening statement around his interpretation of the facts, namely, his theory of the case. This theory should be highlighted early in the presentation, and the advocate should attempt to show how each witness and each piece of evidence advances that theory.[4] For example, defense counsel in a contract case should know at an early time—well before his opening statement—whether his theory is mistake, duress, accord and satisfaction, incapacity, failure of consideration, or some other defense. The advocate's opening statement should link each key piece of evidence to that defense.

Discussion of the Evidence

The plaintiff's attorney or prosecutor who has learned the opponent's defense should not identify it for him in opening statement. Rather, he should simply highlight the *facts* weighing in his own favor on the disputed issues. The advocate should also provide at least some discussion of evidence on each element of his *prima facie* legal burdens, even if the opponent is not likely to dispute a particular element. The jury, which is unfamiliar with the

4 *Accord, e.g.*, R. Carlson & E. Imwinkelried, *Dynamics of Trial Practice* § 5.5(C), at 114-15 (West 3d ed. 2002). As we explained in Chapter Three (pages 39 to 40, *supra*), an advocate should not present inconsistent theories, and he frequently invites trouble advancing alternative theories, even if they are not inconsistent.

case, expects to hear from the plaintiff's attorney or prosecutor about the entire incident, not just about the parts in dispute. The plaintiff's attorney or prosecutor who focuses selectively on the issues likely to be disputed will inevitably deliver a disjointed presentation. Indeed, in some jurisdictions, the court will enter a directed verdict against an advocate who has a burden of proof if his opening statement does not include a discussion of the evidence supporting each element of the claim or defense, whether disputed or not.[5] By contrast, defense counsel should forcefully highlight only those facts that advance his specific defense.

When discussing evidence bearing on disputed issues, the advocate must be attentive to the need to describe all of the strong evidence he plans to introduce. This is important because the jury expects to hear a summary of his case in its best light.[6]

At the same time, the advocate should not identify any testimony or piece of evidence unless he is certain that he *can* and *will* introduce it. Indeed, it is improper for an advocate to refer in opening statement to evidence that he does not intend to introduce or that he knows will be ruled inadmissible.[7] From a tactical viewpoint, the advocate's later failure to introduce such evidence will almost certainly be highlighted during the opponent's summation.[8]

With regard to less-than-strong evidence, since the sponsorship approach holds that the advocate generally should not introduce such evidence during his own case, he obviously should not discuss such evidence in his opening statement.[9] An opening statement is designed to outline evidence that the advocate plans to introduce, not evidence that he has decided to omit. Even if the advo-

---

5 *See generally* Tanford, *supra* n. 1, at 152 (citing authorities).

6 *Accord, e.g.,* R. Aron, J. Fast & R. Klein, *Trial Communication Skills* § 21.04, at 243 (Shephard's/McGraw-Hill, Inc. 1986) (discussing importance of stressing strengths in opening statement).

7 *See, e.g.,* 1 *American Bar Association, Standards Relating to the Prosecution Function and the Defense Function* (1971), § 5.5, at 119 (prohibiting reference to evidence in opening statement "unless [the advocate has] a good faith and reasonable basis for believing that such evidence will be tendered and admitted in evidence"); *see also id.,* § 7.4, at 165-166.

8 Techniques for highlighting an opponent's failure to keep his promises in opening statement are discussed in Chapter Twelve, page 218, *infra.*

9 Most commentators take the opposite approach and urge advocates to identify their weaknesses in opening statements. *See, e.g.,* S. Goldberg, *The First Trial: Where Do I Sit? What Do I Say?* at 204 (West 1982) (pertinent excerpt set forth in Chapter Four, page 78, n. 51, *supra*); Mauet, *supra* n. 2, § 4.3 at 70 (urging advocates to volunteer weaknesses in opening statement if such weaknesses are known to the opponent); S. Schweitzer, *Cyclopedia of Trial Practice* § 181, at 493 (Lawyers Co-op. Pub. Co. 2d ed. 1970) (providing sample opening statement showing how to bring out weaknesses); 1 S. Gazan, *Encyclopedia of Trial Strategy and Tactics* 93 (Prentice-Hall, Inc. 1962) (advising the advocate to "take the jury into your confidence by telling them that the proof will show that your client is a gambler or a bartender or a race track tout [or any other occupation against which a juror may have a prejudice]"); Aron, Fast & Klein, *supra* n. 6, § 21.04, at 243; *id.,* § 21.10, at 248; J. Eannace, *An Art— Not a Science: A Criminal Lawyer's Perspective on Opening Statements,* 11-DEC NBA Nat'l B. Ass'n Mag. 41-42 (1997)("Find a way to address any weakness in your case in opening statement.").

cate decides, however, that he must introduce less-than-strong evidence, the advocate should avoid highlighting such evidence in opening statement. The jury will tend to place exaggerated weight on such evidence and will, as a result, pay insufficient attention to his discussion of the strong evidence.

Highlighting any harmful matter is destructive to the advocate's presentation. To illustrate the point, picture twelve newly empanelled jurors in a stabbing case involving a claim of self-defense. Assume that the prosecutor, during his opening statement, tells them: "You will hear evidence that the defendant stabbed the victim with all his might," and "you will hear as well that the victim was a pretty mean guy." At the outset of the presentation of evidence, the jury will not have made up its mind about whether the defendant used all his might to stab the victim. One fact, however, will already have been established beyond all doubt: the victim was "pretty mean" and probably more vicious than suggested by the prosecutor, a person bound to portray matters in his side's best light.[10] We reject the conventional trial literature's view that this technique will enhance the advocate's aura of credibility with the jury.[11] As noted in Chapter Four, the jury will view the two statements together as, on balance, self-serving and give the prosecutor no special credit.[12]

The sponsorship approach also counsels the advocate to eliminate all neutral matter from his opening statement. Many advocates take the opposite approach and devote considerable attention, for example, to discussions of neutral legal principles involving subjects such as the purposes of an opening statement and the lack of evidentiary value in the advocates' remarks. Thus, one leading commentator provides the following sample of how to begin an opening statement:

> As the court has told you, this part of the trial is called the opening statements. Often the evidence in a case is presented in little bits and pieces and it's sometimes difficult to understand how each piece fits into the case. For that reason we are permitted to

10 Likewise, contrary to the suggestion of one commentator, Schweitzer, *supra* n. 9, § 181, at 493, if the advocate is concerned, for example, about the fact that his witness's ability to observe was affected by his having had three drinks, it is counterproductive to disclose the drinking and then assert that the witness was *not* intoxicated. The jury will fully credit the fact that the witness had at least three drinks, but it will be highly skeptical of the advocate's claim that the witness was sober.

11 *See, e.g.*, J. Sonsteng, R. Haydock & J. Boyd, *The Trial Book—A Total System for the Preparation and Presentation of a Case* § 5.5, at 193-194 (West 1984) ("An open and candid disclosure of [weaknesses during opening statement] will usually increase the sincerity and credibility of the attorney and will often reduce the impact of the opposition's tactics.").

12 *See* pages 79 to 80, *supra*.

> tell you what the overall picture will be now, so that each piece of evidence you hear will make sense when you hear it.[13]

Contrary to the numerous trial manuals urging such an approach,[14] our view is that such discussions generally serve no useful purpose and should ordinarily be avoided. Remarks of this sort do not explain why a verdict should be rendered in the advocate's favor. In fact, there is at least a theoretical risk that the jury will view such discussion as "filler" to disguise the lack of evidence supporting the advocate's position. It follows *a fortiori* that an advocate should never undermine his opening statement by self-effacing statements concerning his own bias or lack of personal knowledge.[15] The jury already views the advocate as a "hired gun," and such statements only heighten the problem.

In sum, the advocate should avoid *all* remarks that do not bear directly on why the evidence supports his version of the facts. The focus of the opening statement should be on the strong evidence that the advocate plans to introduce at trial. Introductory and generalized remarks should be avoided. Similarly, the advocate should not understate his case or highlight his bias as an advocate. Finally, while the opening statement must not be argumentative,[16] the advocate should nonetheless strive to show the jury why his side plainly deserves to win the case.

The Importance of Enthusiasm

Opening statement is no time for modesty or understatement.[17] The advocate's delivery must be enthusiastic and confident.[18] Although the jury will

---

13 Mauet, *Fundamentals of Trial Techniques* § 3.5, at 65 (Little, Brown & Co. 2d ed. 1988).

14 *See, e.g.,* F. Lane, *Goldstein Trial Technique 3d,* § 10.11 (Thomson West 2005 supp.) (urging extensive introductory remarks and providing examples); *See generally* Tanford, *supra* n. 1, at 154 (citing authorities).

15 *Accord,* A. Julien, *Opening Statements* §§ 1.12, 1.13, at 1-16, 1-18 (Callaghan & Co. 1980) (calling the advocate who uses self-effacing statements "Mr. Fairness" and noting that such an advocate "is fair to everybody except his own client"). *Contra, e.g.,* J. Appleman, *Preparation and Trial* 190 (Coiner Pub., Ltd. 1967) ("It must be explained to the jury that you were not present at the scene, and your understanding of some of the facts may prove to be in error . . . ."); *id.* at 792 ("It is often well . . . to admit candidly to the jury that your views are probably biased."); *id.* (urging that the jury be told that the advocate, "through [his] intense study of the case, may have gotten too close to it and may be mistaken").

16 *See, e.g.,* Y. Kamisar, W. LaFave & J. Israel, *Modern Criminal Procedure* 1472 (West 11th ed. 2005); Lane, *supra* n. 14, § 10.11 (reference to "inference, conclusion, or opinion . . . should be reserved for closing argument").

17 *Contra,* Schweitzer, *supra* n. 9, § 176, at 483, 506 ("[U]nderstate your case. It is proof of your sincerity and integrity."); Sonsteng, Haydock & Boyd, *supra* n. 11, at 195 ("Understatement can be a useful credibility-building device for an opening statement presentation.").

18 *Cf.* G. Kennedy, *The Art of Persuasion in Greece* 144 (Princeton Univ. Press 1963) (stating that a speaker's "intense earnestness . . . is the most effective way to carry off sophistic arguments").

not fully credit the advocate's characterization of his evidence, that characterization is nonetheless the starting point for the jury's discounting process. Thus, the jury's skepticism should not lead the advocate to abandon his efforts to persuade; it should lead him to redouble those efforts. If the advocate ranks his case as a ten out of ten, the jury may decide that it is a seven, but if, in a deliberate effort to understate his case (as some commentators urge),[19] he describes it as a seven, the jury will surely rank it a four or less.[20] For this reason, we find no merit in the advice of some authorities that jurors should be told to "keep their minds open" and "not to reach a decision until the court has instructed them on the law."[21] The advocate should, however, keep his zeal within limits. *Gross* inflation or overstatement of the strength of one's case is, we believe, another way in which the advocate can jeopardize his built-in credibility level with the jury and cause an across-the-board decrease in the persuasiveness of his evidence.[22]

The Beginning and Ending of the Opening Statement

It is critical for the advocate to begin and end his opening statement on a strong note. The advocate should start with a brief summary of what his evidence will show. For instance, in a medical malpractice case, plaintiff's attorney may begin his opening statement as follows:

> The evidence in this case will show that on January 10, 1987, Mr. Jones suffered permanent brain damage as a result of the defendant's carelessness and negligence in failing to detect Mr. Jones's brain tumor.

At the end of the opening statement, after summarizing the evidence, the advocate should return to this theme along the following lines:

> After you have heard all the evidence, you will see that it points to only one conclusion: that the defendant is liable for his negligence in failing to detect Mr. Jones's brain tumor.

---

19 *See* page 135, n. 17, *supra*.

20 *See, e.g.*, Carlson & Imwinkelried, *supra* n. 4, § 3.3(D), at 39 (noting that "jurors tend to discount what the attorneys say during trial").

21 Schweitzer, *supra* n. 9, § 187, at 506.

22 *See* page 74, *supra* (discussing the adverse across-the-board decrease in the persuasiveness of an advocate's case as a result of failing to elicit a devastating weakness from a witness whom the advocate has called).

In sum, the advocate must portray throughout opening statement—and particularly at the beginning and the end—an aura of complete confidence in the strength of his case. As we have noted,[23] the advocate is viewed as a "hired gun" who is expected to present his case in its best light. If the advocate appears ambivalent about his position, he cannot expect the jury to be enthusiastic. [24]

Timing Of the Defense Opening Statement

A threshold issue for a defense attorney is whether to make an opening statement or to waive it altogether. We agree with those commentators who note that there is virtually never any reason for a defense counsel to waive his opening statement.[25] At a minimum, an opening statement enables the defense to emphasize that the evidence warrants a verdict in its favor. This opportunity should not be forfeited unless there are compelling reasons to do so in a particular case.

The more difficult issue—in jurisdictions that give attorneys the choice —involves the *timing* of the defense opening statement. In a number of jurisdictions, a defense counsel must present his opening statement directly after the prosecutor's or plaintiff's opening statement unless the court, in its discretion, permits defense counsel to reserve opening statements until after the opponent has rested.[26] Other jurisdictions, however, leave the decision to the advocate. Some trial manuals, citing the "primacy" and "recency" theory—namely, that individuals remember best what they hear first and last—advise the defense attorney to give his opening statement immediately after the government's (or plaintiff's) opening statement.[27] Most defense lawyers in fact follow this advice.[28]

Whatever the merit in the primacy/recency theory, there are several advan-

23 *See* page 14, *supra*.

24 *Cf.* I *Corinthians* 14:8 ("If the trumpet give an uncertain sound, who shall prepare himself to the battle?").

25 *See, e.g.*, Lane, *supra* n. 14, § 10:10; Mauet [2007 ed.], *supra* n. 2, § 4.3 at 71; Tanford, *supra* n. 1, at 170.

26 *See, e.g.*, W. LaFave, J. Israel & N. King, *Criminal Procedure* § 24.7, at 1143 (Thomson West 4th ed. 2004); *cf.* Lane, *supra* n. 14, § 10.09 (discussing legal requirements regarding timing of defense opening).

27 *See, e.g.*, K. Hegland, *Trial and Practice Skills* 193-94 (West 1994) ("psychologists tell us the importance of primacy and it's almost impossible to overcome first impressions"); P. Bergman, *Trial Advocacy* 250 (West 1979) (urging such a strategy); F. Bailey & H. Rothblatt, *Successful Techniques for Criminal Trials* § 9:2, at 242 (Lawyers Co-op. Pub. Co. 1985) ("In some jurisdictions, defense counsel is permitted to reserve his opening statement until the conclusion of the prosecution's case. This is not usually the best policy. As a general rule you will do best to take the sting out of the prosecutor's opening at once.") (citations omitted). *Cf.* Tanford, *supra* n. 1, at 171 (noting that in most cases, the defense opening should immediately follow the opponent's opening, but giving arguments for deferring the defense opening); Mauet [2007 ed.], *supra* n. 2, § 4.3, at 71–72 (noting occasions where deferring opening statement benefits the defense).

28 *See, e.g.*, Mauet [2007 ed.], *supra* n. 2, § 4.3, at 71 (noting common practice of defense attorneys).

tages to giving an opening statement immediately after the plaintiff's or prosecutor's statement. To begin with, the defense avoids giving the jury the impression that he waited to hear the opponent's evidence before deciding on a defense.[29] Moreover, this approach allows the jury to think about the defense as it listens critically to the prosecutor's or plaintiff's presentation.

There are, however, strong reasons for deferring the opening statement until after the opponent has rested. Only then will the defense fully know what the plaintiff's (or government's) case is about and what the best defense strategy will be. At the same time, such an approach avoids giving the opponent insight into the defense theory, thus preventing him from organizing a presentation and selecting evidence with that information in mind. Of course, if defense counsel is sure that he is not going to present a defense, then defense counsel must give his opening statement immediately after the opponent's statement or else lose the opportunity altogether.

The worst strategy, in our view, is for a defense counsel who plans to present a case to stand up, right after the prosecutor's or plaintiff's opening statement, and say basically nothing of substance. We have heard the following type of argument made by numerous criminal defense lawyers who are uncertain at the outset of the trial what evidence they will be introducing:

> Although the defendant is not required to present a defense, we plan to do so. We will show you that the government's case has numerous gaps and does not establish proof beyond a reasonable doubt. We therefore ask you to keep an open mind during the government's presentation. Thank you.

This type of opening statement accomplishes nothing. Even assuming that the primacy/recency theory is valid, the only point that the jury will remember is that the defense plans to present a case. Had defense counsel waited, he would have been able to fill in the details and show just how he planned to attack the government's case.

In sum, defense counsel's decision whether to postpone his opening statement until after the opponent has rested entails a variety of considerations. While the common practice is *not* to reserve the opening statement, there may sometimes be compelling reasons to do so.

29 *Cf.* D. Alexander, *Preparing for More Effective Closing Argument,* 17 Me. Bar J. 194 (2002)(jurist author states, "if a defendant is present and testifies, the prosecutor may comment on the defendant's presence and the opportunity that presence provides to tailor the defendant's testimony to the testimony of preceding witnesses"), *citing* Portuondo v. Agard, 529 U.S 61 (2000).

CHAPTER 8

Direct Examination

Overview

It is difficult to overstate the importance of direct examination. Many commentators view it as the most consequential part of the trial.[1] This chapter demonstrates how sponsorship principles can bolster the effectiveness of direct examination. Specifically, it provides guidance on seven topics: (1) the importance of anticipating the cross-examination of the witness; (2) planning the content of the direct examination; (3) the manner of conducting direct examination; (4) preparing witnesses for direct examination and cross-examination; (5) tactical considerations faced by an advocate who has more than one witness with testimony on a given point; (6) deciding whether—and how—to conduct redirect examination; and (7) examination of witnesses by the court.

The Need to Anticipate Cross-Examination

The rule of using only strong evidence dictates that an advocate should not call a witness unless the value of the witness's favorable testimony outweighs the sponsorship costs of calling him. In assessing the proba-

1 *See, e.g.*, J. Tanford, *The Trial Process: Law, Tactics & Ethics* 201 (LexisNexis 3d ed. 2002) ("Direct examination is the most important part of the trial."); T. Mauet, *Trial Techniques* § 5.1, at 97 (Aspen Publishers 7th ed. 2007) ("Experienced trial lawyers recognize that most trials are won on the strengths of their case in chief . . . ."); R. Keeton, *Trial Tactics and Methods* § 2.1, at 10 (Little, Brown & Co. 2d ed. 1973) ("[M]ore cases are won by evidence on direct than by that on cross-examination.").

tive value of a witness, the advocate must anticipate the degree to which the opponent's cross-examination may ultimately reduce that probative value. Only if the witness can be viewed as strong *after* taking into account the likely cross-examination will the advocate be justified in calling him.[2]

Content of the Direct Examination

In General

Planning the content of direct examination involves applying the same considerations implicated in any other evidence selection decision. Here, however, instead of selecting among various witnesses and items of tangible evidence, the advocate will be selecting among subject-matter areas. Ultimately, the task is to decide which questions to ask and which to leave unasked.

This section provides guidance on the content of the direct examination. It begins by discussing what favorable evidence should be elicited. It then discusses whether—and when—to elicit neutral and harmful testimony.

Elicit Only Favorable Points Qualifying as Strong

The advocate who has decided to call a witness and is considering what questions to ask should apply the same rule that applies to evidence selection generally: elicit only strong points. Given the sponsorship costs associated with introducing evidence or asking questions of witnesses, the sponsorship method counsels brevity as the guiding principle.[3] Accordingly, a witness should not be taken through a laborious analysis of every detail relating to the events in question.

For example, assume that a witness to an automobile accident testifies that the defendant hit the plaintiff's car after running a red light. If, upon being asked to describe his opportunity to view the incident, he responds, "Excellent; I was very close and my vision was unimpeded," there is no need to inquire much further, if at all. If the cross-examiner chooses not to inquire, then the answer will stand unchallenged. Frequently, however,

2 One method for anticipating an opponent's cross-examination is set forth on page 149, *infra*.

3 A number of commentators agree that brevity should be a guiding rule. *See, e.g.*, K. Hegland, *Trial & Practice Skills* 118-19 (West 1994); F. Wellman, *Day In Court* 146 (MacMillan Co. 1926) ("I am inclined to put clearness, simplicity, and brevity before everything else in the conduct of a case in court, including the examinations of witnesses and the attempt to keep salient facts ever prominent before the jury.").

the cross-examiner will probe, hoping to establish something helpful. If he does, each answer that bolsters the plaintiff's case will have far more impact than if the plaintiff had elicited it.[4]

Consider, for example, in the above-mentioned automobile accident case the costs a cross-examiner would incur by making the following effort to discredit an eyewitness:

> Q: Your vision is rather poor, isn't it?
> A: Not with my glasses on, and I was definitely wearing my glasses at the time of the accident.
>
> Q: But you weren't really concentrating on the intersection, were you?
> A: In fact, I was. I was looking at the plaintiff's Cadillac and thinking to myself how beautiful the car looked. That's when your client's car crashed into it.

These answers are far more powerful for the plaintiff when elicited during cross-examination because the cross-examiner has raised the stakes by asking the questions.

A brief direct examination creates a dilemma for the cross-examiner. If he decides not to cross-examine on a point made on direct examination, the jury may treat that testimony as uncontested. On the other hand, if the cross-examiner elicits testimony that does not substantially undercut the direct testimony, he will incur the costs of having gone to the effort of conducting an unproductive examination.

Consider, for instance, the foregoing automobile accident example in which the plaintiff's eyewitness, on direct examination, gives only a skeletal description of his opportunity to observe. Assume further that the cross-examiner is equipped with information on the surrounding circumstances, such as the precise distance of the witness from the accident. In this circumstance, the cross-examiner must make the difficult decision whether to elicit such details.

---

4 *Accord, e.g.*, F. Bailey & H. Rothblatt, *Successful Techniques for Criminal Trials* § 11:20, at 308 (Lawyers Co-op. Pub. Co. 1985) ("It is far more effective from [the prosecutor's] standpoint for [the cross-examining defense counsel] to get hit with unfavorable testimony than for him to introduce it on direct."); J. Appleman, *Successful Jury Trials* 181 (Coiner Pub., Ltd. 1952) (noting benefit of holding back favorable facts on direct examination so that they will be brought out on cross-examination, "thus having a much more dramatic effect than if elicited upon direct testimony").

If the cross-examiner asks no questions, the direct examiner can argue in summation that the excellence of the witness's opportunity to observe is established as an uncontested, unrebutted fact. If the defense attorney decides to ask questions, each fact elicited that favors the plaintiff will be given greater weight than if the plaintiff's attorney had elicited it.[5] Similarly, where the points elicited on cross-examination are neutral, such cross-examination will appear unproductive. Thus, if the cross-examiner elicits that the eyewitness was standing 20 feet from the accident, such evidence will have the jury thinking: "How does that help the defense?" The plaintiff enjoys the benefit of having the jury's skepticism about the significance of that fact directed at his opponent's case rather than at his own.

This tactical dilemma facing the cross-examiner is even greater when he is equipped with little or no information about the surrounding circumstances. This is often true in the criminal context, where discovery is very limited.[6] Here, the technique of the brief direct examination places the cross-examiner deciding what questions to ask in even greater jeopardy than his civil counterpart.

In planning the content of the direct examination, the direct examiner should be careful to avoid not only costs of introduction but also costs of overtrying. Each additional question asked risks sending a message to the jury that the additional point was needed to make the witness credible or to bolster the direct examiner's case. If the additional point is not very probative, the point should be eliminated from the examination.

The direct examiner should also avoid the appearance of any unusual efforts to elicit a point, such as where the point requires a lengthy process to refresh the witness's recollection by showing him a series of documents or transcript pages. If such an undertaking is required, the direct examiner must ensure that the jury will conclude, based on the strength of the point elicited, that it was truly "worth the effort." Moreover, because the jury normally assumes that the direct examination was preceded by extensive pre-trial preparation, it may conclude that a need to refresh the witness's recollection reflects that *no* amount of preparation could ensure that the witness would testify as the direct examiner wanted.

5 *See* n. 4, *supra*.

6 *See* page 59, *supra*.

In sum, the direct examiner must apply all three costs of sponsorship in considering the use of favorable testimony. This process will ensure that his presentation is limited to favorable testimony outweighing the sponsorship costs of its use.

The rule of eliciting only strong testimony applies to all witnesses—occurrence witnesses (including those that are hostile), records witnesses, other custodial witnesses, character witnesses, and expert witnesses.

The case of the expert witness illustrates the point. When the decision is made to present expert testimony, the advocate must confront the initial question of how much of the expert's qualifications to elicit.[7] Under sponsorship principles, only the highlights should be emphasized. For instance, when an expert witness is a member of more than twenty professional organizations, nothing is gained by having the witness recite a long list of organizations that will be unfamiliar to the jury. It is more powerful for the witness simply to state that he belongs to more than twenty organizations, listing perhaps one or two of the most impressive ones. If the other side asks the witness to identify some of the other organizations, the credibility of the witness will be enhanced more than it would have been had the direct examiner brought out that same information.

As to the length of the expert's testimony, again, the testimony should be kept as brief as possible. Assuming, as is usually the case, that the expert is more knowledgeable in the subject matter than opposing counsel, the additional questions asked by the cross-examiner in the areas omitted on direct will likely work to the direct examiner's benefit. Often, the expert will be able to show that the cross-examiner's labored efforts stem not from a flaw in the witness's testimony but from the lawyer's inadequate understanding of the expert's field.

Of course, before calling an expert witness, the advocate must have addressed the more fundamental question of whether his case is enhanced by calling the witness at all. As with other witnesses, the decision to call an expert should be made only after a careful determination that his testimony as a whole is strong. The aura established for an expert witness when his list of impressive credentials is paraded before the jury is wholly undercut when the substance of his testimony is not compelling.

7 Evidentiary rules require that the expertise of such a witness be established. *See, e.g.,* Fed. R. Evid. 702; *see generally* Tanford, *supra* n. 1, at 337-38.

Omit Neutral Points

Because of the sponsorship rule limiting the direct examination to strong points, it follows that neutral details should not be elicited during direct examination.[8] For instance, there is generally little reason to conduct a lengthy inquiry concerning a lay witness's educational background, employment history, or other biographical facts. Such neutral evidence generally adds little or nothing to the presentation.[9]

The use of neutral evidence has been justified on the ground that such questioning gives the witness a chance to "relax and get used to testifying in the courtroom environment."[10] In fact, however, this device of asking "warm-up" questions may be hazardous.

To begin with, such questions may open the door for damaging cross-examination that the direct examiner has not thoroughly anticipated. Moreover, a seemingly innocuous question may provide the opponent with ammunition to make an effective argument in summation.[11] Accordingly, the time to get the witness ready for the rigors of trial is *not* in front of the jury but in pre-trial practice examinations, preferably in an actual courtroom setting.

The General Rule Against Impeaching One's Own Witness

Under the common law, an attorney was generally *prohibited* from impeaching his own witness.[12] Although this prohibition has been abandoned in most jurisdictions,[13] this trend does not mean that impeaching one's own witness is sound trial strategy. To the contrary, the earlier approach is largely consistent with what the sponsorship approach counsels as tactically sound. Specifically, an advocate normally should not elicit testimony on direct examination that is harmful to his case or the witness's

---

8 *Cf.* H. Spellman, *Direct Examination of Witnesses*, § 4:7, at 76 (Prentice Hall 1968)("As a general rule, ... defendant's counsel should develop uncontroverted facts only when it is necessary to reaffirm these facts as a framework for the full understanding of the testimony of a defendant's witness."); *id.* § 5:8, at 94 ("Counsel ... should avoid the injection of details that may ... divert the attention of the fact-finder from the question to be decided.").

9 *Accord, e.g.,* Spellman, *supra* n. 8, at 85 (noting that "the introduction [of a lay witness] should be very brief" and that questions relating to his general background should be "few").

10 Mauet, *Fundamentals of Trial Techniques* 90 (Little, Brown & Co. 1988).

11 *See* Chapter Twelve, pages 215 to 217, *infra* (techniques for criticizing the opponent for eliciting neutral evidence).

12 *See, e.g.,* P. Robinson, *Rough Edges in the Alignment of Legal Systems at the ICTY,* 3 J. Int'l Crim. Just. 1037, 1056-57 (2005)(referring to the "quintessentially common-law" rule of "non-impeachment by a party of its own witness"); Thomas, *The Rule Against Impeaching One's Own Witness: A Reconsideration,* 31 Mo. L. Rev. 364 (1966).

13 *See, e.g.,* Fed. R. Evid. 607 & Adv. Comm. Notes.

credibility and probative force. Instead, the advocate generally should leave that task to the opponent.[14]

Evidentiary rules often set forth specific categories of permissible impeachment of a witness. The Federal Rules of Evidence, for example, permit impeachment by use of prior convictions.[15] We can recall no trial, however, in which a direct examiner was (or would have been) better off eliciting prior convictions instead of letting the opponent do so. Thus, in our view, the advocate will be safe in assuming, absent extraordinary circumstances, that he should *never* elicit such matters in direct examination. For such matters, sponsorship analysis counsels that the same fact, when elicited on cross-examination, is ordinarily much less damaging than when it is brought out on direct examination. Under sponsorship principles, where the advocate impeaches his own witness, the weight given to that impeachment will be maximized. Moreover, by not eliciting the matter himself, the advocate preserves his ability to argue with credibility in summation that the matter has no significant bearing on the assessment of the witness's testimony. The trial recounted in Chapter One fittingly illustrates this point as it relates to prior convictions.[16]

After publication of the first edition of our book, one criminal defense attorney, agreeing with our teaching that the defendant's prior convictions should be left to the prosecution to elicit, offered posing something along the following lines to the defendant-client as the last question on direct examination:

> That is all the questions I have, your honor, except one. Mr. Jones, it is now the prosecutor's turn to examine you. Are you willing to answer each and every one of his questions fully and

14 The commentators are virtually unanimous in urging just the opposite. *See, e.g., Dombroff on Direct and Cross Examination* § 2.2, at 7 (Wiley Law Pub. 1985) ("The obvious advantage ... is that new matters are not raised out of the mouths of your witnesses under questioning by your opponent."); Keeton, *supra* n. 1, § 2.20, at 54–55 ("Ordinarily if the harmful evidence is directly related to the issues in the case and is a matter that in all probability your opponent will inquire about on cross-examination, it is preferable to produce it on direct examination."); *but cf.* J. Sonsteng, R. Haydock & J. Boyd, *The Trial Book—A Total System for the Preparation and Presentation of a Case* § 6.3, at 219 (West 1984) (noting that a weakness that will come out on cross-examination should generally be elicited on direct examination, although "[i]t may be left for re-direct if the witness has an effective response for cross-examination inquiries").

15 *See* Fed. R. Evid. 609(a) (impeachment permissible based on prior felony convictions and other convictions involving crimes of dishonesty). The commentators are also nearly unanimous in urging that a witness's prior convictions should be elicited in the direct examination. *See, e.g.,* Spellman, *supra* n. 8, § 5:5, at 85 (noting the advantage in eliciting unfavorable facts, such as the witness's prior criminal record, on direct examination because such a strategy "deprive[s] the opposition of the opportunity to bring out [such] unfavorable facts on cross-examination")

16 *See* page 4, *supra.*

> to the best of your ability, no matter how irrelevant you consider them?

The client, of course, will answer "yes." We endorse this stratagem.

One explanation for eliciting weaknesses is that the attorney doing so will enhance his credibility with the jury.[17] We previously explained why this is not so.[18] The jurors will view the direct examiner's acknowledgment of the harmful matter as, on balance, self-serving, and therefore they will not view him as credible. Moreover, an attorney who elicits harmful items on direct examination in an effort to enhance his own credibility with the jury does so at the expense of the *witness's* credibility. The direct examiner cannot make much use of the witness's honest answer, since the jury will assume that the attorney would not have asked the question without the assurance that an honest reply would be forthcoming.

It should be emphasized, however, that while sponsorship principles generally counsel against eliciting weaknesses on direct examination, the witness must be instructed to disclose such matters *without hesitation* when asked about them during cross-examination. As indicated below, it is critical for an advocate to tell his witness to be forthcoming and truthful at all times. Evasive answers, and those brought out only after repeated prodding, serve to undermine the witness's credibility.

The foregoing having been said, the direct examiner must be mindful of the two instances discussed in Chapter Four calling for impeachment of one's own witness. The first instance is when the advocate's apparent efforts to omit the impeaching material warrant the tactic.[19] Reiterating, this routinely occurs when eliciting the impeaching material serves to fill a conspicuous gap; reveals a close personal relationship of the witness to a party in the case; or would be included in the witness's recounting of the matter at issue to a close friend or relative.[20] The second instance is when the evidence is so devastating that omitting it from the direct examination would injure the attorney's credibility and decrease the overall persuasiveness of his case.[21]

---

17 *See* pages 79 to 82, *supra.*

18 *See* pages 79 to 82, *supra.*

19 *See* pages 68 to 71, *supra.*

20 *See* pages 71 to 74, *supra.*

21 *See* pages 74 to 77, *supra.*

Manner of Conducting Direct Examination

This section discusses the bearing of sponsorship principles on the manner in which direct examination should be conducted. As will be seen, the approach confirms the value of a number of well-accepted techniques.

The most fundamental technique for direct examination is that an attorney should normally avoid asking leading questions on direct examination. Indeed, evidentiary rules generally prohibit an attorney from doing so.[22] A tactical rationale frequently advanced for not using leading questions is that the weight given to the testimony will be reduced if the jury views the direct examiner rather than the witness as the source of the testimony.[23]

This reasoning comports with sponsorship analysis, which also predicts a reduction in the weight given to direct testimony elicited through leading questions. The amount of the reduction will depend on the degree to which the witness is associated with the party conducting the direct examination. Thus, the reduction will be small when the witness is the advocate's own client, because the advocate is viewed essentially as the client's *alter ego*.[24] It will also be small when the witness, although not the client, is party-associated. The reduction will be greater when a neutral witness is involved. It will be at its maximum when a hostile or adverse witness is being examined. This last point reveals that, unless the direct examiner is forced to ask leading questions of a hostile witness in order to control the witness,[25] he should avoid doing so whenever possible.[26]

To illustrate the difference in impact between leading and nonleading questions, assume that a government investigator, who had been dispatched to an oil tanker after a spill, is called to testify concerning his encounter with the tanker's allegedly intoxicated captain. The use of leading questions, if permitted, might proceed as follows:

---

22 *See, e.g.*, Fed. R. Evid. 611(c) (barring leading questions on direct examination "except as may be necessary to develop the witness' testimony"); S. Goldberg, *The First Trial: Where Do I Sit? What Do I Say?* 213–225 (West 1982); Sonsteng, Haydock & Boyd, *supra* n. 14, § 6.3, at 218 (noting general prohibition but listing numerous exceptions, such as the use of leading questions on preliminary matters, to identify a topic, to refresh the recollection of a witness, and to lay the foundation for exhibits).

23 *See, e.g.*, Goldberg, *supra* n. 22, at 213–215. The rule against leading questions is also supported by the concern that, in using leading questions, the direct examiner is suggesting the answers to the witness. *See, e.g.*, Fed. R. Evid. 611(c), Adv. Comm. Note; Tanford, *supra* n.1, at 244–45.

24 *See* pages 15 to 16, *supra*.

25 The law permits a direct examiner to ask leading questions of a hostile witness. *See, e.g.*, Sonsteng, Haydock & Boyd, *supra* n. 14, § 6.3, at 218.

26 The same point applies to cross-examination. *See* pages 191 to 192, *infra*.

Q: When you reached the bridge of the ship and found the captain, there was an odor of alcohol, wasn't there?
A: Yes.

Q: And the odor was overpowering, wasn't it?
A: Yes.

The same information could be elicited through non-leading questions in the following manner:

Q: What happened when you reached the bridge of the ship?
A: Well, first, I have to say that when I entered the pilot house and ran into the captain, I was immediately struck by an overpowering odor of alcohol.

The latter presentation is obviously more forceful than the former one.

As a related matter, the direct examiner should strive to elicit testimony by asking as few questions as possible. The more the jury hears from the witness, the less it will be preoccupied by the notion that the witness's testimony has been packaged by the attorney.

A well-known means of avoiding leading questions is to begin as many questions as possible with one of the following five words beginning with the letter "W": who, what, when, where, and why. The simple question "What happened next?" is illustrative.

A note of caution is in order, however. While use of leading questions on direct examination is objectionable, questions that are designed to elicit a long narrative response may also be objectionable.[27] Thus, the direct examiner seeking to avoid the use of leading questions must also avoid asking questions that call for a lengthy narrative.

While conducting direct examination, the advocate should use notes or a checklist. This serves to ensure that nothing important is omitted. The alternative—being forced to recall the witness to elicit a fact that the attorney neglected to ask—entails considerable sponsorship costs because of the unusual efforts required. Other things being equal, the jury will view

27 *See, e.g.,* K. Broun, G. Dix, E. Imwinkelried, D. Kaye & R. Mosteller, *McCormick on Evidence* § 5, at 19 (West 6th ed. 2006)("some trial judges enforce a general prohibition of questions calling for a narrative"). The main problem with a narrative is that it impedes an opponent's opportunity to object before the witness provides inadmissible testimony.

the points less favorably if elicited during the second examination than if brought out during the first one.

Finally, while the direct examiner should ensure that the testimony is understandable, he should avoid unnecessary repetition. The more often a point is repeated, the more likely the jury is to view the advocate as relying on that point to win the case. Similarly, the direct examiner should maintain a "poker face" during the examination, and should avoid nodding or other reactions. Any facial expressions will be interpreted as revealing a reliance on the testimony (if his expressions are approving) or a concern with it (if his gestures are disapproving).

Preparation of the Advocate's Witnesses

It is elementary that thorough witness preparation is essential to effective trial advocacy.[28] Accordingly, once the advocate has determined the content of a witness's direct examination, he should prepare a detailed outline of the questions that he intends to ask and should use the outline to conduct pretrial practice examinations. The advocate's goal is to avoid surprises at trial, since there is nothing more damaging to the advocate's case than a harmful "surprise" out of the mouth of his own witness. Any minor loss in spontaneity as a result of pretrial rehearsals will be amply justified by the reduced risk of surprise. It goes without saying, however, that witnesses should not be rehearsed to the point of memorization.[29]

Furthermore, no witness should be presented at trial without first undergoing one or more thorough mock cross-examinations. Such a session enables the advocate to learn the true value of the witness's testimony. It can also identify exaggeration, ill-considered misstatement, and deliberate falsehood, thus enabling the advocate to delete such testimony from his presentation. Only after completing this task will the advocate have an informed basis to decide whether a non-essential witness should even be called. The advocate may decide that the probable testimony on cross-examination would be so damaging that the witness's testimony would, on balance, be less than strong, neutral, or harmful.

28 Most leading trial manuals emphasize this point. *See, e.g.*, Mauet [2007 ed.], *supra* n. 1, § 5.2, at 117-18.

29 *Cf.* I. Younger, *The Art of Cross-Examination* 26–28 (A.B.A. Monograph Series 1976) (recounting case in which cross-examination revealed that witness had memorized her direct examination).

In addition, only when the advocate has a clear understanding of the content of the witness's testimony can he decide which questions to pose on direct examination and which areas to leave to the cross-examiner. Of course, he cannot be certain of what questions the opponent will ask on cross-examination. Nonetheless, the process of developing and executing the mock cross-examination will facilitate the advocate's ability to predict what the opponent will ask during the actual cross-examination.

In rehearsing the cross-examination, no difficult question should be overlooked. Moreover, the witness should be exposed to any tangible, documentary, or testimonial evidence with which he is likely to be confronted at trial. Indeed, the mock examination might itself result in the identification of additional evidence to which he should be exposed prior to trial.

As we have stated,[30] the witness must understand the critical need to answer *all* questions forthrightly and without hesitation, even those dealing with the most difficult matters. The witness should also be informed, however, that he should *not* gratuitously offer any information. Such conduct might underscore whatever interest he has in the outcome of the case. Moreover, the witness might bring up harmful evidence that the cross-examiner would not have elicited.

The witness should further be advised that the cross-examiner need not be permitted to control the witness's answer—for example, by cutting off the witness in the middle of a sentence—so as to present it out of context. Under sponsorship principles, the direct examiner is better off when the cross-examiner is forced to elicit any explanation that may exist for a harmful point.

For instance, if an eyewitness was not wearing his glasses at the time of the incident in question but was wearing contact lenses, the witness need not simply answer "No" to the question of whether he was wearing glasses. He can say, "No, but I was wearing contact lenses."[31] If the cross-examiner tries to cut the witness off after the word "No," the advocate can object and ask the court to let him finish the answer. If the court does not grant that request, the advocate can still elicit the fact during his redirect examination.[32]

One rough gauge of the adequacy of witness preparation will be the extent of redirect examination that is required. Ideally, the witness's

30 *See* page 146, *supra.*

31 As noted above, however, the witness should be cautioned against appearing overly eager to supply information gratuitously. Being gratuitous risks the trial judge rebuking the witness for nonresponsiveness.

32 *See* pages 157 to 159, *infra* (discussing techniques for redirect examination).

answers on cross-examination will be so effective and well-considered that no redirect examination will be necessary.[33] Perhaps an even more important gauge, however, is whether the cross-examiner succeeds in broaching matters that the advocate and his witness had not explored during the mock sessions. In the best of all worlds, the cross-examiner will touch upon only those areas that had been covered in pretrial preparation. A witness is much more apt to make inadvertent errors when confronted unexpectedly on something without time to think through his answer.

Multiple Witnesses

In General

When multiple witnesses are available to testify regarding the same area, some commentators urge a mandatory rule that all of them should be called to testify.[34] Sponsorship analysis reveals the dangers of such an approach. The following sections address such dangers in a variety of contexts.

Multiple Favorable Witnesses on the Same Point

Where the testimony of each of several witnesses on the same disputed point, if introduced alone, could be characterized as strong, an attorney might be tempted to call all of them. Under sponsorship analysis, such a strategy would not necessarily be sound. At some point, the calling of additional witnesses would become counterproductive. For example, calling multiple witnesses to prove a discrete point, such as whether a traffic light was green or red, is apt to strike the jury as a concession that the advocate deems each witness's testimony as essential. The cost of overtrying in calling an additional witness will at some point exceed the witness's incremental probative value. Once this threshold of diminishing returns is reached, the overall presentation will, on balance, be harmed by calling so many additional witnesses.[35]

---

33 Of course, even where the witness has provided careful testimony on cross-examination, some redirect examination may be necessary where the cross-examiner has successfully restricted the witness's ability to explain an answer.

34 *See, e.g.*, A.E. Morrill, *Anatomy of a Trial* 108 (C.P.I. 1968). *Cf.* J. Appleman, *Preparation and Trial* 211 (Coiner Pub., Ltd. 1967)("All occupants of an automobile always must be called or accounted for, irrespective of the fact that they may know nothing relating to the events.").

35 Astute opposing counsel will capitalize on the overtrying in closing argument. *See, e.g.*, Silkwood v. Kerr-McGee Corp., Civ. No. 76-0888 (W.D. Okla. May 14, 1979), *reprinted in* R. Cover, O. Fiss & J. Resnik, *Procedure* 990 (Foundation Press, Inc. 1988) (closing argument by celebrated plaintiff's attorney Gerald Spence emphasizing that his opponent "kept calling witnesses and calling witnesses, [and] I sort of got the impression that he's fallen in love with us over here and just didn't want to quit calling witnesses").

One Strong Witness and One or More Less-Than-Strong Witnesses on the Same Point

As noted, some manuals advise calling multiple witnesses to testify on the same factual area, irrespective of the strength of each witness.[36] Sponsorship analysis rejects this advice. Regardless of how much the opponent may criticize the advocate for presenting a "one-witness case," the problem is magnified when the advocate presents a second less-than-strong witness, because the jury may view the weak witness as a concession that the strong one is insufficient. Given this cost of overtrying, where the advocate has one strong witness and one or more less-than-strong witnesses on the same issue, sponsorship analysis unequivocally counsels use of only the strong witness.

A case that we recall illustrates the importance of not calling less-than-strong witnesses. The defendant was charged with a late-night burglary of a record store. Two eyewitnesses viewed the burglary from their apartment windows. Based on descriptions given by the witnesses, the police stopped a suspect and later brought the witnesses to look at him. One witness positively identified the suspect. The other said that, while it "looked like" him, there were differences in clothing and appearance, although the similarities probably outweighed the differences.

The prosecutor opted to introduce both witnesses, a strategy he soon regretted when defense counsel, during closing argument, focused most of his attention on the less-than-strong witness. The jury ultimately acquitted the defendant. The error in the prosecutor's strategy was that, by introducing a less-than-strong witness, he was implicitly conceding that the strong witness was not sufficient to convict. The jury was thereby likely to concentrate on whether the additional witness was enough to put the government's case "over the top," a shift in focus that was enhanced by defense counsel's focus in summation on the less-than-strong witness. By introducing both witnesses, the prosecutor undermined his ability to make a credible argument that the first witness was sufficient to convict.

Notably, defense counsel had told the court that if the prosecutor did not put on the second witness, he intended to do so. This would have been a far better situation for the prosecutor. He could then have attacked the strength of this "defense" evidence—a witness testifying that the defendant resembled the suspect and that the similarities probably outweighed the

36 *See* page 151, n. 34, *supra*.

differences. The prosecutor could have noted that the defendant's own witness "ruled him in, not out." In any event, even if the defense had not presented the witness, the government's case still would have been more compelling with only the strong eyewitness.

Multiple Witnesses Who Agree on Collateral Details

The basic rule advising brevity in direct examination—including not eliciting unnecessary detail—was already discussed earlier in this chapter. Even if an advocate who has decided to call multiple witnesses generally embraces this rule, however, he may be tempted to stray from it when those witnesses agree on matters of collateral detail. The reasoning would be that this agreement on collateral detail will bolster the witnesses' credibility concerning the more important matters.[37] As noted in Chapter Four,[38] however, this strategy is generally unsound because corroborative detail evidence is normally less-than-strong. Moreover, no amount of pretrial preparation can ensure against some shade of inconsistency resulting from such a direct examination. Thus, the decision to undertake this type of bolstering should be approached with great caution.

Even assuming that the advocate is justified in believing that the witnesses' consistency on collateral detail is strong evidence, he might still be better off not eliciting the detail himself. This would be true if he has reason to believe that the cross-examiner will elicit such detail in an uninformed attempt to develop an inconsistency between the witnesses. In these circumstances, the direct examiner may want to consider the strategy, described in Chapter Four,[39] of refraining from using strong evidence in the expectation that his opponent will elicit it.

In the civil context, an opponent is most likely to fall into that trap when there has been insufficient discovery. In the criminal context, in which discovery is limited, it will be quite common because there is no general requirement that an advocate disclose the names of witnesses or the substance of their testimony.[40]

37 *See, e.g.*, A. Amsterdam, B. Segal & M. Miller, *Trial Manual for the Defense of Criminal Cases* § 395, at 1-537 (Amer. Law Inst. 1984).

38 *See* pages 53 to 54, *supra*.

39 *See* pages 55 to 59, *supra*.

40 *See, e.g.*, United States v. White, 116 F.3d 903, 918 (D.C. Cir. 1997)(governing constitutional case law "creates no government duty to disclose names of witnesses" prior to trial)(quotation marks omitted); *see generally* 33 F.R.D. 53, 53–128 (1963) (comprehensive discussion concerning discovery in criminal cases). *Cf.* page 58, n. 21, *supra* (noting prosecutor's duty to disclose exculpatory evidence).

For example, in a case in which the defendant is charged with negligently striking the plaintiff-pedestrian with his vehicle, and where the disputed issue is whether the plaintiff ran into the street against the traffic signal, the observations of plaintiff's eyewitnesses will be critical. If all of them recall the make and model of the defendant's car, plaintiff's lawyer might be tempted to elicit this fact from each of them in the belief that this attention to detail, although collateral, could enhance their credibility.[41]

Nonetheless, even if the plaintiff's attorney determines that this factual detail is strong, he may be better off not eliciting it. If defense counsel does not know about the witnesses' agreement concerning that detail and is the type of attorney who likes to "fish" for inconsistencies, the plaintiff's lawyer might be advised to let defense counsel do so. As previously noted, the impact on the jury is greatly enhanced when the cross-examiner, whom the jury assumes is striving to put on his best case, raises the stakes by attempting to demonstrate *inconsistencies* between the witnesses, and succeeds only in eliciting the consistencies on even the most collateral details. By contrast, the jury is considerably less impressed when those details are brought out on direct examination. The advocate is implicitly telling the jury that it is important to his case that these details match. The jury then expects them to match, is not impressed when they do, and is highly unforgiving if they do not.

Multiple Witnesses Who Disagree on Matters of Detail

The preceding section touched upon the problems that arise when witnesses disagree on various details and the advocate, unaware of such disagreement, unwittingly elicits the discrepancies during direct examination.[42] When an advocate is *aware* of such discrepancies prior to trial, however, he is in a position to decide on the best strategy for dealing with the problem.

The threshold question, of course, is whether to call witnesses who will offer conflicting testimony. For example, assume that an advocate has two witnesses, each of whom, if called alone, could be characterized as strong. Assume further that the two witnesses disagree on a particular detail. In these circumstances, the direct examiner must decide whether the benefit from calling both witnesses would outweigh any costs incurred by the

41 The hypothetical assumes that this was not a hit-and-run incident, where make and model might be needed to identify the automobile.

42 *See* page 153, *supra*.

revelation of the inconsistency. To make this calculation, he must consider whether *he* would be the one to elicit the discrepancy. The sponsorship method counsels that, as a general rule, he should not do so. Doing so would be tantamount to conceding that it is material to the case. Instead, if the advocate decides to call both witnesses, he should let the opponent bring out the discrepancy.

A case tried by a former colleague illustrates why eliciting discrepancies can be harmful. The case involved an armed robbery in which both the victim and an eyewitness identified the perpetrator. The only discrepancy between the witnesses—which the prosecutor himself elicited—was that one witness recalled the gun being in the suspect's right hand while the other recalled that it was in his left hand. The jury ultimately acquitted the defendant. In later discussions with the prosecutor, the jury revealed that, in its view, the discrepancy alone had created a reasonable doubt.

The prosecutor might have been better off calling only the victim. The prosecutor would then have had one solid identification and no contradictions. If the *defense* had taken the unusual step of calling the eyewitness, the discrepancy would have appeared trivial to the jury, since the defense would have been sponsoring a witness identifying his client as the armed robber. Moreover, the prosecutor could have mockingly emphasized in summation the "odd" defense strategy of calling a witness who positively identified the defendant as the robber. Defense counsel's pathetic reliance on the discrepancy to make his case would be hard for him to dispel.

Assuming in the above case that the prosecutor had a valid reason to use both witnesses, such as a concern that the victim was not entirely convincing, he should nonetheless have let the *defense* elicit the inconsistency. That way, the prosecutor would have been able to argue with credibility that the discrepancy was totally irrelevant. As a practical matter, the burden would have been on defense counsel to show why this disagreement on a small detail during a terrifying incident should negate two strong, positive identifications of the defendant.

Redirect Examination

Deciding Whether to Conduct Redirect Examination

After cross-examination is completed, the advocate will be afforded an opportunity to conduct redirect examination. As an initial matter, it should be noted that the scope of redirect examination is normally limited by law to matters raised in the cross-examination.[43] Although it is usually within the discretion of the trial court to allow redirect examination on new topics,[44] courts generally do not allow such examination.[45] Thus, if an advocate neglected to elicit an important matter on direct examination, he may not be permitted to raise it on redirect examination. For that reason, he should not consciously withhold truly essential testimony during direct examination on the assumption that he will be able to inquire about it later.

From the standpoint of sponsorship, there is an important distinction between direct and redirect examination. With respect to the former, the jury tends to assume that the advocate is relying on the information elicited in order to win his case, since he took the effort to call the witness solely to elicit that information. By contrast, the advocate conducting redirect examination is merely trying to undo the opponent's gains on cross-examination. Furthermore, there is little additional effort expended in conducting redirect examination because the advocate is merely asking additional questions of a witness who is already on the stand. Thus, the costs incurred in asking a question on redirect examination are apt to be less than those incurred by asking the same question on direct.

The decision whether to conduct redirect examination depends upon the purpose of the opponent's cross-examination and the extent to which that purpose was accomplished. If the cross-examiner exceeded the scope of the direct examination and used the witness to establish points favorable to the cross-examiner's case, the mirror-image rule for selection of discrediting evidence should be used. Specifically, the direct examiner should conduct redirect examination only if the reduction in the benefit to the cross-examiner's case outweighs the sponsorship costs of the redirect examination. On the other hand, if the cross-examination was aimed at discrediting the witness, the advocate should employ the rule of using only strong evidence. In particular, redirect examination in that case should be

43 *See, e.g.*, United States v. Terry, 187 F.3d 650 (9th Cir. 1999)(Table)("As a general rule, the scope of redirect examination is 'limited to the scope of cross-examination.'"), *quoting* United States v. Lopez, 575 F.2d 681, 686 (9th Cir. 1978); United States v. Riggi, 951 F.2d 1368, 1375 (3d Cir. 1991)("[t]he tradition in the federal courts has been to limit the scope of redirect examination to the subject matter brought out on cross-examination"). *See generally* Broun, Dix, Imwinkelried, Kaye & Mosteller, *supra* n. 27, § 32, at 141-42.

44 *See, e.g.*, United States v. Riggi, supra n. 43, 951 F.2d at 1375; *cf.* Fed. R. Evid. 611(a) (giving trial court "reasonable control over the mode and order of interrogating witnesses").

45 See, e.g., J. Nolan, Trial Practice: Cases and Materials 81–82 (West 1981).

conducted only if the recoupment in benefit to the direct examiner's case outweighs the costs of conducting the redirect.

In both situations, the sponsorship approach comports with the commonsense conclusion that if an advocate has not been harmed by cross-examination, he should not undertake redirect examination.[46] By rising to conduct redirect, the advocate is communicating a concern about the significance of the points elicited on cross-examination. This concern is heightened with each additional question asked.

For instance, assume that a plaintiff driver is suing an automobile manufacturer for injuries resulting from "sudden acceleration" (acceleration without depression of the gas pedal). Assume further that during the cross-examination of the plaintiff, defense counsel elicits the inconsequential fact that the plaintiff had never had the wheels of his one-year-old vehicle aligned. At most, the fact that plaintiff's maintenance of his vehicle was not perfect is only slightly harmful to his case, since the defense could not show that sudden acceleration had anything to do with wheel alignment. In considering whether to rehabilitate the plaintiff by eliciting testimony regarding his otherwise impeccable maintenance record, the plaintiff's attorney should probably decide against doing so. The plaintiff's attorney certainly should avoid redirect examination requiring, for instance, refreshing plaintiff's recollection through the use of multiple service records. The jury may view such unusual effort as reflecting a serious concern on the part of the plaintiff's attorney, thus suggesting that the points scored by defense counsel were significant. On the other hand, if the advocate can show that the plaintiff *had* aligned the wheels by means of an easily obtainable document, the advocate would be warranted in doing so, assuming that the document could be authenticated by the plaintiff during the redirect examination.

Manner of Redirect Examination

Evidentiary rules normally require the advocate conducting redirect examination to employ non-leading questions.[47] An exception applies where leading questions are necessary to focus the attention of the witness to the

46 *See, e.g.,* Tanford, *supra* n.1, at 275 ("If cross-examination has not weakened the direct, then you would be wise to forgo redirect examination.").

47 *See, e.g.,* 3 F.X. Busch, *Law and Tactics in Jury Trials* § 445, at 951 & n. 50 (Bobbs-Merrill Co., Inc. 1959) (citing authorities).

specific area of inquiry.[48] The ability to use using leading questions on redirect for this limited purpose will often afford the redirect examiner with an important tactical opportunity.

Many trial manuals stress the cross-examination technique of cutting off the witness when he seeks to provide an explanation for a damaging fact.[49] The ability to use leading questions on redirect examination in such circumstances permits the redirect examiner, in eliciting the explanation, to enhance the apparent efforts to omit that the cross-examiner incurred by cutting off the witness. To illustrate this point, assume that a cross-examiner in a murder case has elicited the following testimony:

> Q: Officer, isn't it a fact that you waited an hour before tranporting the gun to the property office of the police station?
>
> A: Yes, but ...
>
> Q: Thank you. And isn't that a violation of police department procedures that require officers to turn in seized weapons *immediately*?
>
> A: Well, technically, but ...
>
> Q: Just a yes or no answer is fine, Officer. Now let me ask you this [the defense attorney then brusquely moves onto another subject].

On redirect examination, the prosecutor can proceed as follows:

> Q: My opponent asked whether you took the gun directly to the property office. What were you trying to say when he cut you off?
>
> A: I wanted to say that I was on my way to the property office when I saw a severely injured pedestrian on the side of the road. I stopped to administer first aid and call an amblance. Once the ambulance arrived, I drove directly to the property office and turned the gun over to the property clerk.

48 *See, e.g.*, Broun, Dix, Imwinkelried, Kaye & Mosteller, *supra* n. 27, § 6, at 26 ("[Leading questions] may be employed to suggest a subject or topic, as distinguished from an answer.")(discussing direct examination); M. Graham, *Federal Rules of Evidence* § 611.8, at 524 (West 1986) (noting that the use of leading questions is permissible on redirect examination to focus the witness's attention to the subject matter).

49 *See, e.g.*, Younger, *supra* n. 29, at 28 ("A trial lawyer must *never* permit the witness to explain anything on cross-examination.") (emphasis added). *See* page 191, *infra* (rejecting such unqualified advice).

The use of leading questions for this purpose on redirect examination, if successful, will tax the cross-examiner with substantial costs of apparent efforts to omit the rehabilitative testimony. The advocate should keep in mind, however, not to use leading questions for the purpose of suggesting an answer to the witness. As explained above,[50] such a technique is not only impermissible but tactically unwise as well, since the witness's testimony will be given less weight if the jury feels that the testimony was suggested by the direct examiner.

Examination by the Court

Once a witness has been examined by all parties, the judge may be inclined to ask questions of his own, as he is permitted to do in most jurisdictions.[51] Examination of witnesses by the court raises various sponsorship-related issues.

As an initial matter, it should be clear that an item of favorable evidence is given more weight when it is introduced by the judge rather than by the advocate who stands to benefit from it.[52] The judge, as a disinterested participant, is not apt to be viewed with suspicion except in the unusual case where he has shown himself to be biased in favor of one side. Accordingly, the jury will not suspect that the judge "packaged" the witness's testimony. Moreover, his implicit statement that the matter is material will not tend to be discounted as it is when the interested advocate sponsors a matter favoring his case. To the contrary, because it represents the view of a jurist, it will be received as an indication of the materiality of the matter.[53]

An advocate can reap practical benefits by being aware of the foregoing point. To begin with, an advocate, after getting permission to approach the bench, should consider objecting when a judge pursues a line of questioning that favors his opponent. One legal argument in support of such an

---

50 *See* pages 147 to 148, *supra*.

51 *See, e.g.,* Fed. R. Evid. 614(a), (b); 3 C. Mueller & L. Kirkpatrick, *Federal Evidence*, § 334, at 540-41 nn. 5-6 (Lawyer's Co-op. Pub. Co. 1994) (citing numerous state statutes).

52 Most authorities are in accord. *See, e.g.,* Mueller & Kirkpatrick, *supra* n. 51, § 336, at 548 ("[t]he stature and assumed impartiality of the judge are likely to lend weight to his questions that does not come with similar questions from litigating attorneys"); *cf.* United States v. Karnes, 531 F.2d 214, 217 (4th Cir. 1976) (noting that the jury in the case may have afforded witnesses called by the court "greater credibility" than if they had been called by the party who benefited by the testimony).

53 As the example of the judge makes clear, the rhetoric of the *disinterested* speaker, under the teaching of sponsorship, will involve certain *benefits* of sponsorship rather than costs. Moreover, these benefits generally increase with the prestige and credibility of the speaker. The fundamental flaw of the conventional wisdom, which implicitly posits such benefits from the advocate's presentation of favorable evidence, is its failure to take into account the jury's view of the advocate as an *interested* speaker.

objection would be that the questions jeopardize the judge's aura of impartiality,[54] and that his opponent is free to pursue the inquiry.

In addition, the case law reflects that courts have occasionally agreed to call witnesses considered unsavory, where the party seeking the testimony did not want to vouch for the witness.[55] The advocate should obviously object if an opponent attempts to have the court call such a witness with testimony supporting the opponent's case.[56]

Finally, whenever the judge elicits a fact favoring the advocate's case, the advocate should emphasize to the jury that the *judge* was the one who asked the question and elicited the favorable matter. This will enable the advocate to reap the benefit from the fact that the judge, rather than an interested advocate, introduced the evidence.

This chapter has addressed issues involving the direct examination of witnesses. It has emphasized the importance of following the rule of eliciting only strong points.

The advocate must frequently decide not only whether to call certain witnesses or elicit certain testimony but also whether to use documents or other exhibits. Moreover, the advocate will often be presented with the opportunity of stipulating to certain facts as a substitute for presenting evidence. The next chapter addresses the principles that should guide the advocate's consideration of such matters.

---

54 *Cf.* page 14, n. 3, *supra.*

55 *See, e.g.*, United States v. Leslie, 542 F.2d 285, 288–289 (5th Cir. 1976); Mueller & Kirkpatrick, *supra* n. 51, § 335, at 542.

56 *See, e.g.*, Estrella-Ortega v. United States, 423 F.2d 509, 510 (9th Cir. 1970) (upholding trial court's refusal of a criminal defendant's request that court call as witness a government informer that the government chose not to call; court rejected defendant's claim that such a step was necessary "[to] prevent [the informer's] unattractive gloss from reflecting on [the defense] case").

CHAPTER 9

Non-Testimonial Evidence

Overview

This chapter addresses tangible evidence and evidence in the form of stipulations. As will be seen, sponsorship analysis provides important guidance on the use of such evidence. As with testimonial evidence, the advocate cannot make an intelligent decision on whether—or how—to use such evidence until the benefits of the evidence have been balanced against the sponsorship costs.

Tangible Evidence

The Probative Value and Sponsorship Costs of Exhibits

As many commentators have recognized, exhibits can be very powerful. Exhibits can dramatize concepts or establish points where testimony alone may be inadequate.[1] For example, where a defendant is charged with possession of a large quantity of drugs for distribution and claims that the drugs were for personal use, the prosecutor should introduce the actual drugs seized from the defendant rather than simply offer testimony concerning the amount.

1 *See, e.g.*, J. Tanford, *The Trial Process: Law, Tactics & Ethics* 255 (LexisNexis 3d ed. 2002) (asserting that exhibits "can convey information that may be impossible to communicate in words"); S. Schweitzer, *Cyclopedia of Trial Practice* § 204, at 542–543 (Lawyers Co-op. Pub. Co. 2d ed. 1970); T. Mauet, *Trial Techniques* § 6.1, at 169-70 (Aspen Publishers 7th ed. 2007) (contending that exhibits have more impact than testimony because they are "more interesting" and "more reliable").

Another legitimate rationale for introducing an item of real or demonstrative evidence is that it serves as a substantial aid in the presentation of the case. For example, a diagram of a scene at issue—such as the scene of an automobile accident—may be necessary for the jury to follow the testimony. Likewise, an X-ray may be necessary or useful to enable the jury to understand complicated medical testimony. Similarly, in a case involving large numbers of documents or numerical compilations, a diagram summarizing these materials may be important to enable the jury to follow the testimony.

A case tried by one of the authors illustrates the probative value of an exhibit. The defendant was charged with shooting the victim in the mouth. The victim claimed he was shot from a distance of about 10 feet. Defense counsel delivered his opening statement immediately after the prosecutor's statement, representing that the evidence would show that the victim was the one with the gun, and that the gun went off accidentally during a struggle, with the barrel of the gun only about an inch from the victim's face.

In his case-in-chief, the prosecutor called the physician who had treated the victim. The physician testified that the hole in the victim's face where the bullet had entered was approximately the diameter of a pencil. He also testified that there were no burn marks or visible gunpowder residue on the victim's face. The prosecutor also called a firearms expert, who had test-fired the weapon used in the incident (which had been seized by the police) into a cardboard diagram from various distances. The cardboard diagram was displayed to the jury. The bullet hole caused by a shot fired at a range of 10 feet was about the size of a pencil, and there were no burn marks or gunpowder residue. The bullet hole caused by a shot fired at the 1-inch range, however, was about 3 inches in diameter, and the boundary of the hole showed visible burn marks and gunpowder residue. The defense had no answer to this compelling exhibit, and the jury promptly convicted the defendant.

Notwithstanding the immense probative value of some exhibits, there can also be great danger in using exhibits, as commentators have correctly recognized.[2] These dangers correspond with the three costs of sponsorship.

First, the advocate's use of virtually any exhibit will entail costs of introduction. To begin with, the jury is apt to view an advocate's use of

2 *See, e.g.*, Tanford, *supra* n. 1, at 266-67; Mauet, *supra* n. 1, § 6.4, at 219-22.

an exhibit as an implicit claim that it is material and probative, and it will tend to discount that claim. Moreover, the jury is likely to view the exhibit as being packaged in its best possible light. Accordingly, the jury will be apt to study the exhibit carefully to see if it contains some latent support for the opponent's case. Similarly, opposing counsel will likely scrutinize the exhibit for features that corroborate his case, and he will almost certainly bring such features to the jury's attention.

Thus, before an advocate decides to introduce an exhibit, such as a photograph of the scene at issue, he must scrutinize it for harmful features.[3] For example, in a malpractice action in which the principal issue involves damages, the plaintiff should introduce photographs of the victim when they are gruesome or powerful, and the defense should consider introducing the photographs when the injuries are difficult to observe or appear trivial. In a landlord–tenant dispute involving claims of poor living conditions, the tenant should introduce photographs of the apartment only if such photographs reveal terrible conditions. If the jury's likely reaction to the photographs is, "this place isn't so bad," then the tenant should not introduce such pictures.[4]

Second, the advocate using an exhibit may incur costs of overtrying. Consider an exhibit designed as an aid to the presentation. To assess the costs of overtrying incurred by the use of such an exhibit, the advocate should ask himself whether, in response to his opponent's claim in summation that the exhibit did not advance the advocate's case, he can credibly respond that it facilitated the jury's understanding of the case.[5]

Third, the advocate must consider whether the use of an exhibit would result in costs of unusual efforts. The more elaborate the exhibit, the greater the opponent's ability to attack and criticize it. These costs of efforts must be assessed in deciding whether (and in what form) to introduce an exhibit and whether to conduct a view or demonstration.

For example, an advocate should not take a jury to view the scene of a crime or accident—a step the jury is likely to consider (correctly) quite un-

3 *Accord, e.g.*, Mauet, *Fundamentals of Trial Techniques* § 5.4, at 200 (Little, Brown & Co. 1988) ("review the exhibit[] to determine if there is anything, directly or inferentially, that your opponent can use to support his positions").

4 While this point may seem obvious, it runs counter to the suggestion that photographs depicting the scene at issue should virtually *always* be introduced. *See, e.g.*, D. McCarty, *Psychology and the Law* 411 (Prentice-Hall 1960).

5 *Cf.* K. Hegland, *Trial and Practice Skills* 110 (West 1994)("Courtroom demonstrations can … increase the jury's understanding.").

usual—unless something substantial can be accomplished. Similarly, a normal 3-inch by 5-inch photograph will incur less costs of efforts than a blown-up version. If enlarging the photograph fails to serve any legitimate purpose, the enhanced size will, in the jury's eyes, serve only to emphasize the advocate's reliance (often misplaced) on that photograph to sway the jury.[6]

An advocate should also exercise caution regarding the manner in which he establishes a foundation for an exhibit—that is, how the advocate demonstrates that the exhibit is "what its proponent claims."[7] The more lengthy and involved the process is, the more the advocate is apt to incur sponsorship costs. In some circumstances, the advocate must also establish a proper chain of custody in order to demonstrate that the item has not been tampered with. The advocate must recognize that if the custodial chain is a lengthy and elaborate one, considerable sponsorship costs may be incurred. For this reason, the advocate should attempt, whenever possible, to obtain a stipulation from his opponent that the exhibit is authentic.[8] By the same token, the advocate should recognize that if he agrees to stipulate to the authenticity of one of the opponent's exhibits, the advocate enables the opponent to *save* sponsorship costs.

Even if the advocate cannot obtain such a stipulation, other techniques can streamline the process of authenticating an exhibit. For instance, the advocate should have the foundational questions for his exhibits thought out—and perhaps written out—well in advance, and he should rehearse the questions with the authenticating witness prior to trial.

Moreover, the advocate should reflect at length before requesting that an exhibit be "published" to the jury during trial. Typically, the trial must stop for several moments as each juror looks at the exhibit, one juror at a time. The advocate's apparent reliance on the exhibit will be at its maximum in such a circumstance.

Furthermore, an advocate should avoid the costs incurred by over-emphasizing his reliance on exhibits in argument. Devoting substantial

6 *Contra, e.g.*, M. Dombroff, *Unfair Tactics* § 14.12, at 482 (Wiley Law Pub. 2d ed. 1988) ("A rule of thumb whenever you deal with demonstrative evidence is that you should make the particular piece of evidence, whether a chart, graph, diagram, model, or any other technique available to you, as large as possible. Indeed, the limiting factor should not be what you think is too large, but rather how large an exhibit the courthouse doors and elevators permit you to bring into the courtroom.").

7 Fed. R. Evid. 901(a). *See generally* E. Imwinkelried, *Evidentiary Foundations*, §§ 4.04-4.10, at 4-1 to 4-137 (LexisNexis 2002)(sample foundations for authenticating evidence); Mauet [2007 ed.], *supra* n. 1, § 6.3, at 177-219 (same).

8 The topic of stipulations is treated more fully in a later section of this chapter.

time in summation to parading exhibits before the jury may well be counterproductive.

In contrast to the approach dictated by the sponsorship approach, many advocates feel compelled to buttress their cases with less-than-strong physical evidence.[9] For instance, advocates frequently introduce photographs or diagrams that merely depict the scene at issue but do nothing to advance the advocate's relative position vis-a-vis the opponent. Advocates must avoid any inclination that they may have to adorn their cases with irrelevant exhibits. This approach not only fails to *advance* the advocate's case, it actually *harms* it.

One final point merits emphasis. The advocate deciding whether to introduce a party-associated exhibit must, as we explained in Chapter Five, consider its use on disputed issues even if it is less-than-strong, and must consider its use on undisputed issues even if it is not necessary to establish his legal burden of proof. To illustrate the latter, the prosecutor should normally introduce or account for the murder weapon in a murder case. Similarly, the plaintiff's attorney in a products liability case should normally produce or account for the defective product if possible. Because of its preconceptions about custody of such exhibits, the jury will not normally be persuaded by the argument that the opposing counsel could have introduced them. As stated in Chapter Five, the advocate incurs no substantial costs of overtrying by introducing such basic evidence going to the foundation of the disputed issue in the case.

Substitutes for Exhibits

In certain circumstances, the advocate may wish to use a substitute for an exhibit instead of introducing the item *in specie*. The reason is that occasionally, because of an irrelevant flaw in the actual exhibit, a substitute is more effective in making the advocate's point. An armed robbery case tried by one of the authors after a prior trial had produced a hung jury illustrates the point. In that case, the weapon used to commit the crime was a toy pistol and the defense was misidentification.[10] The first prosecutor who tried

9 *Cf.* McCarty, *supra* n. 4, at 411 ("Photographs of the scenes and persons are a 'must' in most cases . . . ."); P. Bergman, *Trial Advocacy* 119 (West 1979) ("[A]dvocates should search for potential uses of real evidence during trials.").

10 A toy pistol is sufficient in various jurisdictions to establish the "armed" element of armed robbery. *See, e.g.*, State v. Kemp, 896 So.2d 349, 357 (La. App. 2d Cir. 2005)(toy gun was "dangerous weapon" for purposes of attempted armed robbery offense); Boyles v. State, 175 N.W.2d 277 (Wisc. 1970)(unnecessary for prosecution to show that gun used to commit attempted armed robbery was lethal weapon).

the case had introduced the toy gun *in specie*, and the jury was unable to reach a verdict. Although the precise reasons why the first jury could not reach a verdict were not known to the second prosecutor, he was nonetheless concerned about the potentially adverse influence of the toy pistol. At the first trial, the victim had described her terror upon seeing the weapon, which glistened under a streetlight that was located near the crime scene. The toy pistol, however, looked harmless under ordinary lighting conditions, such as those in the jury room.

Upon review of the physical evidence, the second prosecutor located a photograph of the toy pistol that the first prosecutor had opted not to use. That photograph depicted the pistol on the street where the defendant had dropped it after the crime. In that photograph, the pistol appeared more like the victim described it: glistening under the streetlight. Opting to present the government's case in its "best light," the second prosecutor introduced only the photograph. Although the actual exhibit had been tendered to defense counsel prior to trial, he chose not to use it as part of his case. Such a decision was understandable. Since the toy was legally sufficient,[11] defense counsel's reliance on the appearance of the gun—and his indirect concession that his client was the assailant—would have struck the jury as a weak defense. The jury returned a guilty verdict in less than 30 minutes. As this example illustrates, notwithstanding the jury's preference to see the best evidence of a tangible item, namely, the item itself, using a substitute (or relying solely on testimony concerning the item) will occasionally be to the advocate's advantage.[12]

Stipulations

Because an opponent's admission on a given point is normally *at least* as probative as evidence on that point from an impartial source, such as the

11 See n. 10, *supra*.

12 The jury's expectation to see the *best* evidence reflects suppositions about the fact finder's preferences similar to those underlying the best evidence and hearsay rules. Under the best evidence rule, the original of a writing must be produced if its terms are material, unless the writing is unavailable through no fault of the proponent. *See generally* K. Broun, E. Imwinkelried, D. Kaye & R. Mosteller, *McCormick on Evidence*, §§ 230-243.1, at 85-121 (West 6th ed. 2006). *Cf.* Freeman v. Commercial Union Assurance Co., 317 S.W.2d 563, 568 (Tex. Civ. App. 1958) (requiring under the "best evidence rule" for writings that the document "relat[e] to a matter which ... form[s] the foundation of a cause, or the defense thereto"); Doman v. Baltimore & O.R. Co., 22 S.E.2d 703 (W.Va. 1942) (same). *See also* Fed. R. Evid. 801–806 *et seq.* (rules governing hearsay which, absent circumstances of reliability, restrict evidence of out-of-court declarations offered for the truth of the matter asserted and require the testimony of the declarant himself).

judge, it follows that an advocate should normally prefer a stipulation on a point favorable to his case over the alternative of having to prove the point himself.[13] A formal stipulation serves to highlight the opponent's concession, and it enables advocates to capitalize on that concession by emphasizing that the fact was so clear that the opponent did not even put him to his proof. These advantages are lost if the advocate must introduce testimony to prove the fact. Use of the testimony is apt to be discounted by the jury, as predicted by the cost of introduction.

The approach of many trial lawyers is to *refuse* to stipulate to facts favorable to their cases. The reasoning is that the advocate shortchanges his case unless the favorable evidence comes in through the testimony of live witnesses and tangible exhibits. We have found from our experience, however, that the value of the opponent's stipulated concession usually exceeds the power of the witness's live testimony, as adjusted by sponsorship costs.

In our view, the only disadvantage in obtaining a stipulation of an advocate's favorable facts is when such facts are not fully communicated to the jury in the stipulation. Consider, for example, the decision of whether an advocate should seek to obtain a stipulation from the opponent concerning the qualifications of the advocate's expert witness. Such a stipulation is often preferable to the introduction of evidence concerning the expert's credentials. This is particularly true when the expert's qualifications, while substantial, are not likely to impress the jury. When that is so, a stipulation enables the advocate to argue that his expert's qualifications are so strong that the opponent consented to relieve him from proving them.[14] On the other hand, if the expert's credentials are unusually impressive and the opponent, in agreeing to stipulate, will not allow mention of specific accomplishments, then the advocate would be better off not stipulating and instead presenting evidence relating to the expert's credentials.

For the same reasons, an advocate should be reluctant to stipulate to evidence that is favorable to the opponent's case. The opponent can use the stipulation to bolster the strength of that evidence in the jury's eyes. Moreover, the opponent avoids the sponsorship costs incurred by presenting the evidence himself. Of course, countervailing considerations, such

13 *Cf.* 2 F.X. Busch, *Law and Tactics in Jury Trials* § 219, at 443 (Bobbs-Merrill Co., Inc. 1959) ("The party having the burden of proof usually gains more by a formal stipulation than his opponent . . . .").

14 *Contra, e.g.*, J. Frederick, *The Psychology of the American Jury*, § 6-202, at 225 (The Michie Co. 1988) ("Do not stipulate to the credentials of your witness. Let the jury be impressed with the witness's qualifications.").

as pressures from the court, or the desire for a reciprocal stipulation, may cause an advocate to temper this strategy. Although, strictly speaking, a court cannot normally *force* an advocate to accept a stipulation,[15] it may be unwise for an attorney to be stubborn on minor matters if the court is likely to become irritated. If the advocate has no practical choice but to agree to a stipulation favorable to the opponent, he should attempt to keep the terms of such a stipulation to a bare minimum.

Having discussed the advocate's own case, we now turn to a discussion of what the advocate should be doing during the opponent's presentation.

15 *See, e.g.*, People v. Cajina, 26 Cal. Rptr.3d 171, (Cal. App. 4th 2005)(noting "strong policy against ... forcing the prosecutor to accept stipulations that soften the impact of the evidence"), *citing* People v. McClellan, 457 P.2d 871, 877 (Cal. 1969).

CHAPTER 10

The Opponent's Presentation

Introduction

This chapter addresses the tasks that an advocate must undertake during his opponent's opening statement, examination of witnesses, and closing argument. The tasks are divided into two areas: the need to monitor the opponent's conduct at trial and the need to make appropriate objections.

Monitoring the Opponent's Presentation

The advocate takes his seat at counsel table after completing the direct examination of his star witness. He pulls out a fresh note pad and listens with rapt attention as his opponent's cross-examination begins. His main concern is in identifying any damaging points that his opponent will succeed in eliciting during the cross-examination. He resolves to note these points on his pad so that his redirect examination can neutralize them. With pen in hand, he listens intently to avoid missing any such point.

As the cross-examination proceeds, however, it begins to meander. Many of the cross-examiner's questions simply enable the witness to reiterate his testimony on direct examination in even stronger terms. Other questions appear to reflect shifting points of attack and inconsistent theories of his case, none of which makes any headway. After a few minutes of this, the advocate puts down his pen altogether, having made only a few notes of instances in which his witness was caught in a seeming inconsistency.

By taking this familiar approach, the advocate has performed only half of his job and has missed a golden opportunity to gather concessions from his opponent. Although noting damaging points is a critical task, sponsorship analysis reveals that it is also critical for the advocate to note the cross-examiner's unproductive questions as well as the answers that the cross-examiner receives.

One of the key teachings of sponsorship analysis is that everything an opponent says or does can potentially be used against him. It is surprising how often a remark by opposing counsel, especially when it is ill-conceived or careless, can provide the advocate with ammunition to resolve a disputed point in the advocate's favor. For that reason, an advocate must make note of every assertion the opponent makes, every question he asks, and every piece of evidence that he introduces. Each represents a potential concession that something is material to the advocate's case, and this record will enable the advocate to evaluate, at the end of each day of trial, how these actions of opposing counsel can be used against him.

The importance of focusing on the opponent's own words cannot be overstated. An argument that would otherwise appear to erect a straw man can be very powerful when the opponent has, by his own remarks, conceded the materiality of a point. The Vice-Presidential debate in the 1988 Presidential election provides a classic illustration. The following remarks were made in response to the moderator's question concerning Senator Dan Quayle's qualifications to assume the Vice Presidency:

> Quayle: I have far more experience than many others that have sought the office of Vice President [of] the country. I have as much experience in the Congress as Jack Kennedy did when he sought the Presidency.
>
> Senator Lloyd Bentsen: Senator, I served with Jack Kennedy. I knew Jack Kennedy. Jack Kennedy was a friend of mine. Senator, you're no Jack Kennedy.
>
> Quayle: That was really uncalled for, Senator.
>
> Bentsen: You're the one that was making the comparison, Senator ....[1]

1 N.Y. Times, Oct. 6, 1988, at 322 (transcript of debate).

Had Senator Quayle not brought up the comparison with President Kennedy, Senator Bentsen's remarks would have appeared unfair and "uncalled for." Because Senator Quayle did so, however, Senator Bentsen's remarks were viewed as very powerful and were considered decisive in the general public impression that Senator Bentsen had won the debate.

For some unknown reason, the trial tactics literature virtually ignores the importance of monitoring the opponent's conduct. Indeed, when the subject is alluded to at all, it is often for the purpose of advising the attorney *not* to do so. For example, one commentator advises defense attorneys to do the following during the prosecutor's opening statement:

> With every faculty you have, you listen and watch the effect the prosecutor's opening is having on the jury, and as an experienced trial counsel, you will not spend much time in taking notes; a date, a fact, a name, a phrase perhaps, but little more.
>
> Sir Charles Russell, one of England's greatest advocates, one day glanced around at his junior and said, "What are you doing?" "Taking a note," was the answer. Russell looked at him and said: "What the devil do you mean by saying you are taking a note? Why don't you watch the case?" Watch the case! I agree with Judge Parry who, in recounting Russell's observation, declared it to be "the golden rule."[2]

Sponsorship analysis unequivocally endorses the approach of the young English lawyer, not that of his distinguished mentor, Sir Charles Russell. The benefits of carefully recording the opposing counsel's remarks for possible use as concessions far outweigh the missed opportunity to monitor the jury. In our experience, an advocate has no reason to be concerned that he will miss a chance to assess the jurors' expressions as they listen to his opponent. Little, if any, relevant information can be gleaned from monitoring the jury; the jurors are normally expressionless during opening statements. If the advocate had nothing else to do, and wouldn't be noticed by the jurors as he was looking at them, we might recommend it. But it is *far* more important for the advocate to ensure that he has fully comprehended—and recorded—his opponent's remarks.

---

2 L. Stryker, *The Art of Advocacy* 45–46 (Zenger Pub. Co., Inc. 1979).

In sum, the advocate should endeavor to record the substance of virtually everything the opponent says—his opening statement, his closing argument, and the questions he poses to witnesses. The advocate should also record the substance of the witnesses' responses to the opponent's questions. What may seem innocuous or irrelevant at the time may turn out to be critical in light of later events at trial. Furthermore, the advocate cannot simply rely on expedited transcripts to preserve his opposing counsel's remarks and questions. Aside from the considerable expense of such transcripts, even an overnight service temporarily deprives him of the information at a time when he may need it most, such as to follow up on cross or redirect examination of a witness.

Monitoring the opponent's conduct is important not only for defense lawyers but also for plaintiffs' attorneys and prosecutors. This is because, as we have previously noted,[3] *any* advocate who has met his applicable legal burdens (if any) will derive an equal benefit from exposing the weaknesses of the opponent's case as he will from advancing the strengths of his own case.

At first blush, this tactic would seem to be available to prosecutors and plaintiffs' attorneys only when the defense has opted to present a case and put on evidence. In fact, however, it can also be used when the defense has put on *no* evidence. Even in this circumstance, defense counsel will almost invariably be advancing a theory of the case that supports a verdict in his client's favor. The defendant's position will be reflected either explicitly in defense counsel's opening statement or closing argument or implicitly in the questions posed during his cross-examination.

The plaintiff's attorney or prosecutor must pay careful attention to defense counsel's remarks and questions to identify the opponent's theory of the case. In his own closing argument, the plaintiff's attorney or prosecutor must identify the defendant's theory and demonstrate, based on the evidence, the lack of merit in that theory.[4]

The principle that an advocate should strive to demonstrate the lack of merit in the opponent's position applies *a fortiori* to defense lawyers, who may find themselves without much defense evidence. For reasons we

3 *See* pages 27 to 28, *supra.*

4 In a criminal case, the prosecutor must be careful not to suggest that the defense has any duty to support his contentions by presenting evidence. Any such suggestion may constitute grounds for reversal. *See* page 115, n. 7, *supra.*

have previously explained[5] and as virtually all experienced defense counsel know, a defense attorney will score as many points by identifying the flaws in the plaintiff's or prosecutor's case as he will from persuading the jury that he has a valid defense. Thus, the defense attorney should adopt an aggressive trial strategy in which his opponent's case is thoroughly dissected and criticized.

Objections

Danger of Overuse

One of the most over-utilized devices at trial is the objection. Perhaps this reflects the influence of Hollywood, where vigorous objections make for good drama. The overuse of objections is certainly not the fault of the existing trial literature. The leading commentators leave no ambiguity about the need to exercise great caution in making objections, stressing that, as a general rule, advocates should object only where they are likely to be harmed by the evidence.[6] However, some law school and continuing legal education courses on trial advocacy are so preoccupied with teaching advocates how to *identify* an objectionable question that they devote little or no attention to the difficult issue of whether an objection would be tactically wise.

Recognizing an improper question or an objectionable piece of evidence, while important, is only the first step in deciding whether to voice an objection. An advocate must understand the considerable costs involved in objecting in front of a jury. This portion of the chapter provides guidance on the decision whether to object. As will be seen, some of the recommendations dictated by sponsorship analysis conform to the existing trial tactics literature, but many do not.[7]

---

5 *See* pages 27 to 28, *supra*.

6 *See, e.g.,* T. Mauet, *Trial Techniques* § 10.3, at 450 (Aspen Publishers 7th ed. 2007) ("Unless you are reasonably sure that the answer to a question will hurt your case, it is usually better not to object."); J. Tanford, *The Trial Process: Law, Tactics & Ethics* 184-89 (LexisNexis 3d ed. 2002)(listing factors to be considered before objecting); R. Keeton, *Trial Tactics and Methods* § 4.2, at 167 (Little, Brown & Co. 2d ed. 1973) (noting that an objection can emphasize the evidence objected to); J. Nolan, *Trial Practice: Cases and Materials* 129 (West 1981) (noting that frequent objections may lead the jury to sympathize with the opposing attorney and his client); 5 F.X. Busch, *Law and Tactics in Jury Trials* § 604, at 298–299 (Bobbs-Merrill Co., Inc. 1959) (noting that jurors become angry at an attorney's frequent objections).

7 This discussion assumes that an objection is not required to preserve an error for appeal. Depending on the likelihood of reversal on appeal as a result of preserving an error, an objection that is otherwise not tactically warranted may be sound. *See generally* Keeton, *supra* n. 6, § 4.12, at 190–195 (discussing objections to preserve errors for purposes of appeal).

The Decision Whether to Object

The sections that follow set forth the considerations pertinent to the decision whether to object. The first section provides the applicable rule for the advocate who can object outside the jury's presence. The second section provides the rule when the advocate must object in the jury's presence. As will be seen, when the advocate must voice an objection before the jury, analyzing the merits of objecting is more complicated. Invariably, the advocate who must object in the jury's presence suffers in ways that are avoided when he is able to object outside the jury's presence.

Objections Outside the Presence of the Jury

There is an easily stated rule for an advocate who is deciding whether to object outside the jury's presence to the opponent's introduction of evidence: he should do so if and only if the evidence is strong evidence from the opponent's perspective. The first implication of this rule—counseling the advocate to object when the evidence is strong—should be obvious. The objection, if sustained, will prevent the jury from hearing evidence that is sufficiently favorable to the opponent's case to outweigh his sponsorship costs of using it.

The second implication of the rule—advising the advocate *not* to object when the evidence is less-than-strong—is less obvious and unappreciated by the existing trial advocacy literature. Here, the advocate should refrain from objecting not only to evidence that is favorable to the *advocate* but also to certain evidence that, if introduced by a neutral source, would be considered by the jury to favor the *opponent's* case. Because the opponent's sponsorship costs of using any less-than-strong evidence will by definition outweigh its probative value, allowing the jury to consider such evidence, *as introduced by the opponent*, would serve to *reduce* the persuasiveness of the opponent's case, principally due to his costs of overtrying. Accordingly, the advocate should *welcome* the opponent's use of such less-than-strong evidence.

An advocate who must object in front of the jury incurs risks that are not incurred by an advocate who can object outside the jury's presence. For this reason, the advocate who has decided to object should do so outside the jury's presence whenever possible. Thus, where an advocate is aware of objectionable evidence prior to trial, he should consider filing a motion *in limine* in order to obtain a ruling in advance of trial.[8] The advantage of this

8 *See, e.g.*, Tanford, *supra* n. 6, at 75 (discussing use of motions *in limine* to keep out inadmissible evidence); R. Carlson & E. Imwinkelried, *Dynamics of Trial Practice* § 6.2, at 135-37 (West 3d ed. 2002) (same).

approach, of course, is that the advocate avoids the risk of adverse speculation incurred by objecting in front of the jury.

Frequently, however, the advocate will have no warning prior to trial that the opponent plans to ask a particular objectionable question. In that situation, he should consider voicing the objection at side-bar, or "at the bench." In that way, he can argue against the admission of the evidence without the jury hearing his objection. Of course, even when this device is used, the jury will likely figure out that the advocate's repeated requests for bench conferences are an effort to keep out evidence. Thus, this approach will not necessarily eliminate the risks of objecting before the jury. The advocate also cannot apply this approach too frequently because the trial judge, who wants to move the proceeding along quickly, is apt to become irritated. If the advocate finds that he cannot object outside the jury's presence, then he must consider the factors described below.

Objections in the Presence of the Jury

In General

In deciding whether to make an objection that can only be made before the jury, the advocate must assess the harm to his case from the admission of the evidence against the risk of adverse jury speculation if the objection is sustained. If the objection is overruled, the jury will hear the evidence and know that the advocate tried to keep it out. When this is so, the advocate making the unsuccessful objection will incur costs of perceived efforts to omit. Specifically, the jury will be heavily inclined to interpret the advocate's efforts as concern that the evidence will hurt his case. For that reason, the jury will tend to give it greater weight. The advocate is thus worse off when evidence is admitted over an objection than when it comes in without objection.[9]

On the other hand, if the objection is sustained and the evidence never comes in, the jury will be apt to speculate that the evidence would have materially advanced the opponent's case. This follows from the jury's assumption that opposing counsel will seek to present only evidence that materially favors his case. Although the jury is typically admonished not to speculate what the witness would have said had an objection not been

9 *Accord*, Keeton, *supra* n. 6, § 4.2, at 167–168 (noting that "the added emphasis given to [an opponent's item of evidence] by your unsuccessful effort to keep [the jurors] from considering it may cause it to be more damaging than if you had permitted it to come in without objection").

sustained,[10] human nature suggests that jurors will have great difficulty controlling their urge to engage in such speculation. Where the evidence is less-than-strong for the opponent, the advocate, by successfully objecting, will achieve only a Pyrrhic victory. The opponent, in addition to not suffering the consequences of offering less-than-strong evidence, may actually *benefit* from the jury's assumption that the excluded evidence would have materially advanced his case.

Accordingly, as with objections made outside the presence of the jury, the advocate should not even consider objecting to the evidence unless it is strong for his opponent. Assuming for purposes of this analysis that the opponent's evidence is strong for his case, the rule on whether to object in the presence of the jury will depend on the advocate's degree of certainty that the objection will be sustained.

Where the Objection Is Virtually Certain to be Sustained

The rule in this instance is straightforward. If the objection in the jury's presence is virtually certain to be sustained, the advocate should object only where the harm from the item coming into evidence, as reduced by the sponsorship costs that the opponent incurs in presenting it, would outweigh the risk of adverse speculation if the jury is prevented from considering the evidence. As noted above, where the jury is not permitted to consider evidence because an objection is sustained, it normally will assume that the omitted evidence would have materially favored the opponent's case. Unless the actual evidence would be even more damaging to the advocate's case than the risk of this possible adverse speculation, the advocate is better off allowing the jury to hear the evidence. In light of these points, and as noted above, *an advocate should forgo objecting to marginally harmful material—the opponent's marginally favorable evidence—even when the objection is certain to be sustained.*[11]

Where the Advocate Is Uncertain Whether the Objection Would be Sustained

When the advocate's grounds for objecting are of questionable legal merit, he obviously cannot be certain that the objection will be sustained. As noted

10 *See, e.g.,* K. O'Malley, J. Grenig & W. Lee, *Federal Jury Practice and Instructions* § 10.01, at 6 (West 5th ed. 2000).

11 *See* page 42, *supra* (defining marginally favorable evidence).

above, if he objects in these circumstances and the objection is overruled, that objection will increase the weight given by the jury to the evidence once it is admitted. Specifically, the objecting advocate will incur costs of apparent efforts to omit by trying to keep evidence from the jury.

Thus, even when the opponent's evidence is strong for his case, if the advocate must take the chance that an objection will be overruled in the presence of the jury, he may not be justified in objecting. Put another way, the less certain that the advocate is regarding the merit of a potential objection, the more powerful the opponent's evidence must be before he should object.

One additional problem bears discussion. On occasion, the advocate required to make the foregoing cost/benefit calculations will not have information concerning the substance—and, thus, the strength—of the opponent's objectionable evidence. For instance, the opponent might ask a witness, "And what did you hear that individual say to the neighbor?" In such a case, the question appears to call for inadmissible hearsay but the advocate may have no idea what the witness's answer would be. In that circumstance, the advocate may wish to request permission to approach the bench in order to get a proffer from the opponent concerning the expected response from the witness. Most judges will grant such a request, given that the question asks for hearsay. If that approach does not work, however, then the advocate must attempt to ascertain from the context of the question and the other evidence being elicited from the witness whether the testimony would likely be strong for the opponent. Ultimately, before deciding whether to object, the advocate must make his best guess concerning the strength of the potentially inadmissible evidence that the opponent is attempting to elicit.

Assuming that the advocate decides to object in front of the jury, it is important for him to use the proper technique. Most significantly, regardless of the importance of the evidence that he is trying to keep from the jury, he must remain calm and unexcited. Apparent efforts to omit—or, alternatively, risks of adverse jury speculation regarding excluded evidence —are increased considerably when an advocate jumps to his feet suddenly and shouts "objection" in a loud and nervous voice as if something devastating is about to happen.[12]

12 *Accord, e.g.,* Carlson & Imwinkelried, *supra* n. 8, § 6.3(E), at 143 ("In almost all cases, you should remain low-key and business-like when you object.").

Considerations Involving Specific Objections

This section addresses the merits of making various specific types of objections. After first discussing a number of generic categories of objections, it focuses in detail on one specific objection: cross-examination exceeding the scope of the direct examination.

As a preliminary matter, we note that it is not possible to draw any sweeping conclusions with respect to the types of objections that should always be made or that should never be made. Nonetheless, there are certain types of objections that, if meritorious, should often be made because of the potential harm to the advocate's case from the admission of the evidence. Examples include objections to evidence of subsequent remedial measures, compromise and offers to compromise; payment of medical expenses or other similar expenses; pleas and plea discussions; liability insurance; and a rape victim's past behavior.[13] Of course, if the witness's answer in any of these circumstances would not materially advance the opponent's case, then the advocate should not object.

For example, a prosecutor should ordinarily object if a defense attorney in a rape case seeks to question the victim about her active sexual past. The prosecutor, however, would obviously be unwise to object if the victim had no sexual experience before the incident. By allowing the evidence to come in, he could capitalize in summation upon defense counsel's unproductive cross-examination.[14] By keeping the evidence out, the prosecutor may cause the jury to speculate—erroneously—that the victim was sexually active.

The foregoing sections have assumed that the objections, if successful, would keep out evidence. There are, however, certain types of objections that are largely formal in nature in the sense that they generally do not result in the exclusion of evidence. Examples include objections to questions that are leading; were previously asked and answered; call for a narrative response; and are ambiguous, compound, or indefinite as to place or time.[15] The value of making such objections may be minimal, and the attorney risks appearing overly concerned with trivial matters. Thus, an attor-

13 *See, e.g.*, Fed. R. Evid. 407–412.

14 Techniques for capitalizing on an opponent's unproductive cross-examination are contained at pages 206 to 207, *infra*.

15 *See generally* R. Carlson, *Successful Techniques for Civil Trials*, §§ 2:1-2:24, at 120-51 (Lawyers Co-op. Pub. Co. 1992).

ney might well decide not to object to such questions or to do so only after a series of similar improper questions.

One such formal objection warranting special treatment is the objection challenging cross-examination exceeding the scope of direct examination.[16] An advocate not attuned to sponsorship considerations might conclude that this is a futile objection, even when the cross-examiner is eliciting strong evidence for his case, since the cross-examiner often can simply recall the witness in the cross-examiner's own case-in-chief. In fact, however, as noted earlier, sponsorship analysis counsels that it is to the cross-examiner's advantage to present his case through the advocate's witnesses if he can do so.[17] Moreover, if the opponent is forced to recall the witness, *he* will incur all of those costs. For that reason, other considerations aside, the advocate should seek to limit the scope of such cross-examination when evidence harmful to his case is being elicited.[18]

To illustrate the point, assume that a witness can testify to facts A, B, and C, all of which are favorable to the direct examiner, but that he can also testify to fact D, which involves a different subject and a fact *unfavorable* to the direct examiner. A seasoned cross-examiner will try to bring out fact D on cross-examination if it was not brought out on direct. This tactic can be quite harmful, since the cross-examiner is making his case through the direct examiner's witness, expending no substantial attorney effort in doing so, with the result that the jury is apt to credit fact D more heavily than facts A, B, and C.[19]

16 The permissibility of conducting cross-examination outside the scope of direct examination depends upon the rules of evidence in the particular jurisdiction. Although many jurisdictions limit cross-examination to matters covered on direct, others permit essentially unlimited cross-examination. *Cf.* Fed. R. Evid. 611(b) (cross-examination limited to scope of direct except when court in its discretion rules otherwise); *see generally* K. Broun, G. Dix, E. Imwinkelried, D. Kaye & R. Mosteller, *McCormick on Evidence* §§ 21-27, at 115-28 (West 6th ed. 2006)(discussing alternative approaches). Of course, regardless of the rule, some cross-examiners will either purposefully or unknowingly exceed the scope of direct examination.

17 *Cf.* F. Bailey & H. Rothblatt, *Successful Techniques for Criminal Trials* § 22.3, at 498 (Lawyers Co-op. Pub. Co. 1985) ("Favorable evidence obtained on cross-examination is probably more valuable than the testimony of your own witnesses .... Anything that [an opponent's] witness says for your side can be argued as beyond question."). *See generally* page 184, *infra* (encouraging technique where permissible).

18 In jurisdictions limiting cross-examination to the scope of the direct examination (*see* n. 16, *supra*), an advocate is entitled to require the cross-examiner to recall the witness if he wants to inquire beyond the scope of the direct. *See, e.g.,* 4 *Jones on Evidence* § 25:2, at 111 (Lawyers Co-op. Pub. Co. 6th ed. 1972) ("[I]f a party wishes to examine a witness as to matters other than those covered by direct examination, he must do so by calling the witness in his own behalf, and not by cross-examining him."); *cf.* Resurrection Gold Mining Co. v. Fortune Gold Mining Co., 129 F. 668, 675 (8th Cir. 1904) ("If the cross-examiner would investigate [subjects beyond the scope of direct examination] ... he may and he must make him his own witness, and *stand sponsor* for the truth of [the] testimony.") (emphasis added).

19 Under the sponsorship method, unless it falls within one of the exceptional categories discussed in Chapter Four, *supra*, harmful fact D would be credited even more fully if it had been elicited during direct examination. Thus, the direct examiner does not solve the problem by eliciting fact D himself.

Furthermore, if the objection is sustained, the advocate is better off regardless of what strategy the cross-examiner adopts in the face of such a ruling. To begin with, unless fact D is critical to the cross-examiner, he will probably be reluctant to take the step of recalling the witness, a step that juries normally view as extraordinary.[20] Indeed, unless fact D constitutes strong evidence for the cross-examiner's case, the whole strategy of recalling a witness in his own case would be counterproductive. If fact D is less-than-strong for the cross-examiner, the direct examiner can comment in summation along the following lines:

> You must have thought, when my opponent went to the effort of recalling [the witness], that you were going to hear something extraordinary, perhaps even a recantation of his earlier testimony. You must have been surprised when [the witness] merely testified to [fact D].

In any event, even if the cross-examiner finds it beneficial to recall the witness, the direct examiner is still better off than if the cross-examiner had elicited the information on cross-examination. Since the cross-examiner is now unquestionably burdening his case by offering the witness with respect to fact D, the jury will give it less weight than it would have received had it been elicited during cross-examination.

In short, the "beyond the scope" objection—while considered merely formal in nature—often results in the evidence *never* being introduced because the cross-examiner normally decides not to recall the witness. Even if the cross-examiner does recall the witness, his sponsorship of that witness will reduce the harmful impact of the evidence.[21]

---

20 *Cf.* H. Wouk, *The Caine Mutiny* 389 (Doubleday 1952) (eyebrows of fictional foreman of jury "signaled astonishment" when defense counsel announced his intention to have a witness whom he had just finished cross-examining recalled as his own witness).

21 Similar reasoning applies to the objection that an opponent has unfairly introduced only part of a writing or recorded statement and should be required to introduce additional portions as well. *See, e.g.,* Fed. R. Evid. 106. Since the advocate entitled to make this objection can simply introduce the remainder of the item himself, most advocates unschooled in the sponsorship method consider it pointless to do so. However, setting aside the special considerations posed by "devastating" and other harmful matters uniquely calling for impeachment of one's own witness or case (discussed in Chapter Four), sponsorship analysis reveals that the advocate is better off when the opponent is forced to introduce all relevant portions of the material in question.

CHAPTER 11

Cross-Examination of the Opponent's Witnesses

Purpose and Appropriateness

Experienced trial lawyers know that, unlike on television, witnesses almost never "crack" under cross-examination. Indeed, cross-examination normally fails to achieve truly major inroads. Nonetheless, many attorneys feel that, regardless of what they will accomplish, they will be harmed more by not asking questions than by asking them. For some, cross-examination is a time to "take a stand" before the jury by communicating, through the tenor of the questioning, a lack of belief in the witness's testimony. For others, it is a time for "fishing" in the hope that something favorable to the cross-examiner will be elicited. Still others conduct cross-examination out of a fear that the client will not believe that his cause is being effectively advanced without at least an attempt to discredit the opponent's witnesses.

If advocates consult the trial literature for guidance, they will find conflicting advice. Many commentators urge a restrictive approach and advise that cross-examination to discredit a witness should not be undertaken unless the cross-examiner's case has been significantly harmed.[1] Others,

1 *See, e.g.*, J. Nolan, *Trial Practice: Cases and Materials* 104 (West 1981); J. Tanford, *The Trial Process: Law, Tactics & Ethics* 296 (LexisNexis 3d ed. 2002); R. Carlson & E. Imwinkelried, *Dynamics of Trial Practice* § 10.2(D), at 251-53 (West 3d ed. 2002); C. Fricke, *Planning and Trying Cases* 373 (West rev. ed. 1957).

however, suggest that it is rarely wise to forgo cross-examination.[2] As we shall show, cross-examination is virtually never appropriate except in two circumstances: (1) where the cross-examiner can elicit a strong point for his own case, or (2) where he can elicit a point sufficiently harmful to the opponent's case to outweigh the sponsorship costs of asking the question.

The first section discusses general issues relating to cross-examination and explains why sponsorship costs are generally lower on cross-examination than on direct examination. The second section addresses the considerations that are relevant when a cross-examiner is inquiring for the purpose of building up his own case. The third section focuses on cross-examining for the purpose of discrediting a witness. Finally, the fourth section discusses techniques for conducting cross-examination.

The Lower Sponsorship Costs of Cross-Examination

The sponsorship costs incurred by cross-examination are generally lower than those incurred by direct examination. To begin with, the costs of introduction are normally reduced. As noted in Chapter Two,[3] when an advocate calls a witness, the jury tends to assume that he took pains to package the witness's testimony, organizing and perhaps even sculpting it to reflect his best case. This attitude is one of the two major sources for the discounting phenomenon reflected by the cost of introduction. By contrast, little, if any, of this skepticism is directed towards the cross-examiner. To a great extent, the jury's skepticism is still directed toward the direct examiner who, the jury assumes, prepared the witness for the cross-examination as well as the direct. Accordingly, an advocate will generally incur lower costs of introduction by eliciting a point on cross-examination than he would have incurred had *he* called the witness and elicited the same point on direct.[4]

2 *See, e.g.,* A.E. Morrill, *Trial Diplomacy* 59 (C.P.I. 1971); L.W. Lake, *How to Cross-Examine Witnesses Successfully* 93 (Prentice-Hall 10th ed. 1970) (section entitled "Only Lawyers Without Trial Experience Fail to Find Sensible Questions to Ask [on Cross-Examination]").

3 *See* page 21, *supra*.

4 To the extent that the cross-examiner strays beyond the scope of the "packaged" direct examination, the difference in the cost of introduction incurred by direct examination and cross-examination will diminish somewhat.

There is a second reason why the cost of introduction is generally lower on cross-examination. As we have explained,[5] when an advocate asks a question on direct examination, he is implicitly conceding the materiality of the testimony. Specifically, the jury tends to assume that the questions posed on direct examination were the reason the direct examiner called the witness at trial. By contrast, the jury assumes that a cross-examiner has decided merely that his cross-examination is worth standing up to ask questions of a witness who is already on the stand. Thus, the concession of materiality resulting from eliciting a given point in a direct examination will, other things being equal, be much greater than that involved in eliciting the same point during cross-examination.

The cross-examiner will also normally incur lower costs of overtrying. Specifically, the jury is far less apt to conclude that the cross-examiner is relying on a given response to win the case than it is with respect to the lawyer who took the greater step of calling the witness himself. Thus, the cross-examiner's implicit concessions regarding the strength of his evidence and of the opponent's evidence are not as great.

The foregoing discussion should not be read to suggest that the cross-examiner suffers *no* costs of introduction and overtrying. Whenever a cross-examiner asks a question, he signals the jury that the subject matter of the question is material and that the witness's answer is important. For instance, when the cross-examiner attempts to discredit a witness and fails, he may suffer considerable harm. Each question posed by the cross-examiner raises the stakes for his case with respect to what the answer will be, since the cross-examiner is suggesting to the jury, with every line of questions he pursues, that he expects to expose a flaw or weakness. When the witness simply reaffirms or bolsters what he said on direct, the cross-examiner looks worse than if the question had not been asked at all.

Unlike the costs of introduction and overtrying, the cost of unusual efforts will not depend as much on whether such efforts are undertaken by the direct examiner or the cross-examiner. A cross-examiner who takes unusual steps to prove a point—such as impeaching a witness through the use of a large number of documents—will incur substantial costs of efforts even though he did not call the witness.[6]

---

5 *See* page 28, *supra*.

6 Of course, because of the direct examiner's opportunity to prepare the witness before trial, it is worse when he experiences the same difficulties in getting the witness to say what he wants him to say.

In sum, while the cost of unusual efforts does not depend as much on the distinction between direct and cross-examination, the costs of introduction and overtrying *do* depend heavily on that distinction. These two costs are apt to be considerably lower on cross-examination than on direct. Notwithstanding these points, however, an attorney errs in believing that he suffers no costs by conducting unproductive cross-examination. The cross-examiner must recognize that in cross-examination, as in direct and redirect examination, there is no such thing as a "free" question.

Cross-Examining for Purposes of Advancing One's Case

We have already remarked on the tactical advantages that an advocate reaps by presenting his own case through the opponent's witnesses.[7] Even though the advocate's questions raise the stakes of the witness's response and result in some sponsorship costs, such costs are greatly reduced by the fact that the witness was called by the opponent.

Thus, where local practice permits,[8] one worthwhile goal of cross-examination if the opportunity arises is to establish one's case to the maximum extent possible through the opponent's witnesses. Each witness whom the advocate is relieved from calling, and each question that he no longer needs to ask in his own presentation, benefits the advocate by minimizing sponsorship costs.

Here, as with direct examination, the advocate should not elicit a point unless it qualifies as strong. Eliciting less-than-strong evidence is, by definition, an unproductive strategy that results in a net harm to the cross-examiner's overall presentation. In evaluating whether a given point qualifies as strong, the advocate should keep in mind, as explained above, that the sponsorship costs incurred by cross-examination are much lower than those incurred by direct examination. The advocate should also recognize, however, that the extent of the difference is not quite as great when the cross-examination exceeds the scope of direct examination. This is because the jury, as noted, is less apt to assume that the witness's cross-examination testimony was packaged as carefully as the direct examination.

---

7 *See* page 179, *supra.*

8 *See* page 179, n.16, *supra.*

A cross-examiner who is considering the use of an opponent's witness to advance his own case must recognize that he may face the difficult tactical posture of asking the jury to credit the witness's testimony on some matters yet reject it on others. For instance, if an eyewitness to an armed bank robbery identifies the defendant as the robber but states on cross-examination, contrary to the government's theory, that the assailant did not brandish a weapon, defense counsel will have great difficulty relying on the latter testimony while at the same time challenging the identification. Although this can be achieved in the proper case,[9] it complicates the cross-examiner's presentation and may make the tactic ill-advised.

Undercutting the Testimony of an Opponent's Witness

Introduction

The following discussion addresses the considerations pertinent to cross-examining an opponent's witness for the purpose of discrediting him. The first section focuses on identifying a theory for such cross-examination. The second section sets forth the rule for selecting questions to advance that theory.

Developing a Theory for Discrediting the Witness

Before the cross-examiner can decide whether to conduct cross-examination in order to undercut the testimony of an opponent's witness, he must first identify the possible theories for doing so. The potential theories will normally fall into one or more of the following: (1) the witness fabricated the testimony or shaded it in the opponent's favor; (2) the witness, while attempting to be truthful, was mistaken; and (3) even if the testimony is correct, it does not materially advance the opponent's case.

Evidence supporting the first theory will often include, for example, prior convictions or bad acts, indications of bias or interest in the outcome, opinion and reputation evidence showing lack of veracity, and indications that the testimony was memorized. Evidence supporting the second theory would include the inadequacy of the witness's memory or his lack of ability to perceive due to such factors as poor hearing or vision. Evidence sup-

9 *Cf.* 6 J. Bentham, *Rationale of Judicial Evidence* 401 (Bowring ed. 1827) ("No man is so habitually mendacious as not to speak [falsely] a hundred times for once that he speaks [the truth]").

porting either the first or second theory would include such matters as internal inconsistencies in the witness's testimony, the inconsistency of the testimony with that of other witnesses, and the fact that the testimony is illogical or does not comport with human experience.

The third theory—that the witness's testimony does not materially favor the opponent's case—can be advanced by questions that define and limit the witness's testimony. Here, a successful cross-examination will serve to demonstrate that the testimony, even if true, is essentially irrelevant. For example, in a drug distribution case tried by one of the authors, three men testified that they were in the same area as the defendant on the day in question and did not see him selling any narcotics. Each witness conceded under questioning, however, that he was paying no particular attention to the defendant and was definitely not watching the defendant's every move. The prosecutor was able to argue with credibility that the witnesses' testimony, while true as far as it went, proved nothing.

In selecting a theory for discrediting the witness, the cross-examiner must recognize the potential dangers of advancing more than one theory simultaneously.[10] Most significantly, he should understand that costs of overtrying may be incurred by advancing alternative theories. For example, if the cross-examiner expends unusual efforts in attempting to show that the witness's testimony was fabricated, it will be more difficult to argue that the testimony, even if true, does not materially bear on the verdict. Of course, as in corresponding situations (witnesses, case theories), if two theories for discrediting the witness are equally strong, and not inconsistent, then, other things being equal, both should be pursued.

The Rule for Selecting Questions to Undercut the Testimony of an Opponent's Witness

As should be clear from the discussion in Chapter Four,[11] the rule for selecting questions to undercut the testimony of an opponent's witness mirrors the rule of using only strong evidence in the advocate's own case. That rule is that *an advocate should cross-examine to discredit only where the amount by which he can reduce the probative value of the testimony outweighs the sponsorship costs incurred in doing so*. In applying this rule, the cross-

10 *See* pages 39 to 40, *supra* (discussing risks in advancing alternative theories).

11 *See* pages 87 to 90, *supra*.

examiner should take into account the fact that the probative value of the evidence introduced by the opponent will be reduced not only in the objective sense, as an item of evidence standing alone, but also by his opponent's increased costs of overtrying if he has introduced other evidence.[12]

In applying this rule, the advocate should recognize that as long as he can elicit testimony sufficiently harmful to the opponent's case to outweigh the sponsorship costs, he should do so. The advocate should not set any artificial limit on how long he spends on cross-examination or on how many questions he asks.

In contrast to this view, one noted commentator advises an inflexible rule of *never* eliciting more than three points on cross-examination.[13] In our experience, such a rule can result in the loss of valuable cross-examination. There are often more than three points available that qualify as sufficiently harmful to the opponent, and in such circumstances, all of the points should be elicited. One needs only to picture an inexperienced trial lawyer following the commentator's advice who has four powerful ways to undercut the witness, hopelessly unable to decide which of the four to omit. Sponsorship analysis suggests that so long as sponsorship costs are outweighed by the benefits, the more points that an advocate can make, the better off he is. Of course, as should be clear,[14] at some point the sponsorship costs of eliciting an additional harmful point may outweigh its value. This will occur when the jury concludes that the question reflects the advocate's belief that his prior points are insufficient to discredit the witness. Questions on very minor points fall into this category and should normally not be asked.

Conversely, just as the advocate should not feel compelled to limit his cross-examination to three points, he should not normally feel that a witness must be cross-examined. Specifically, the advocate should not ask a single question to discredit unless he determines that the harm to the opponent's case will outweigh his own sponsorship costs. For instance, where the advocate must make substantial efforts to elicit only a minor point, he is far better off not asking any questions. In this circumstance, the advocate should state confidently: "I have no questions of the witness."[15]

---

12 *See* pages 87 to 88, *supra* (describing this phenomenon).

13 *Trial Techniques with Irving Younger* 51 (R. Oliphant ed. 1978).

14 *Cf.* page 151, *supra.*

15 Followers of the classic 1950s television series "Perry Mason" will recall that this fictional giant of the law regularly employed this tactic. *Cf.* T. Mauet, *Trial Techniques* § 7.2, at 252 (Aspen Publishers 7th ed. 2007) (advising that cross-examination is not "essential" where you have not been harmed).

In short, an advocate should not rise to conduct cross-examination without a careful cost/benefit analysis. This is so even though the sponsorship costs of cross-examination are generally much lower than those on direct. Indeed, notwithstanding the lower sponsorship costs of cross-examination, we believe that the main problem in cross-examination—for inexperienced and experienced lawyers alike—is conducting too *much* cross-examination, not too little. We have seen case after case in which the points elicited are minor or trivial and thus harmful to the cross-examiner's case, once his sponsorship costs are considered.[16] Accordingly, as with any other evidence selection decision, the cross-examiner should proceed with caution in deciding whether to ask a particular question on cross-examination. His general approach should be one of reluctance to ask additional questions rather than one of reluctance to stop.

Notwithstanding the foregoing, there is one situation in which the advocate should be extremely hesitant simply to announce "no questions." That is where the witness at issue is the opponent's central witness. In the jury's eyes, cross-examination of the opponent's central witness is a critical point in the trial. A complete failure to cross-examine might be viewed as an admission by silence.[17] Because of the great harm in letting a crucial witness leave the stand without any cross-examination, the advocate should make a thorough search of all potential avenues of impeachment to find something to use against the witness. If the cross-examiner has conducted such a search, he will usually find at least one or two points that he can make to cast doubt on some aspect of the witness's testimony or otherwise render it less probative.

It is extremely rare that the testimony of a central witness cannot be undermined by some cross-examination. In the first place, because of the lower sponsorship costs incurred by cross-examination generally, the advocate has somewhat more flexibility in eliciting matters on cross than on direct. Moreover, if the witness's testimony was strong for the

16 *Accord, e.g.*, J. Clark, *Preparation of Cross-Examination* 3 (P.L.I. 1946) (noting that cross-examination of a "witness who testifies as to a purely formal matter or as to incidental facts which are not in dispute or as to matters which are not damaging" is "purposeless," can be "harmful," and "creates an atmosphere of needless contentiousness").

17 *Qui tacet consentire videtur* (he who is silent appears to consent). *Cf.* R. Keeton, *Trial Tactics and Methods* § 3.3, at 98 (Little, Brown & Co. 2d ed. 1973) (an attorney should generally conduct some cross-examination unless he is "willing to adopt the witness' testimony"); Mauet, *supra* n. 15, § 7.8, at 305-06 (suggesting that in some instances cross-examination is necessary even though "you have nothing that has a chance of succeeding, [because] the jury will expect some kind of cross-examination").

opponent's case, as the testimony of the central witness is likely to be, the costs of overtrying incurred by cross-examination are generally lower than otherwise. This is because the damage from the implicit concession that the witness's direct examination was strong enough to warrant cross-examination will be at a minimum, since the jury will most likely see that damage regardless of whether the advocate decides to cross-examine.

Finally, the opponent's central witness will often be heavily interested in the outcome of the case. This will obviously be true in the case of the defendant and the plaintiff (or complainant). The jury assumes, for example, that such a witness would have declined to cooperate with the opposing lawyer prior to trial and that the witness's testimony thus could not have been packaged by that lawyer. With such witnesses, cross-examination emphasizing bias will normally be appropriate.

In the many trials in which we have personally been involved as trial counsel, we can recall only one trial where the attorney might have been better off conducting little or even no cross-examination of his opponent's central witness. This was an assault case where a neutral and attentive eyewitness, just a few feet from the assault, gave testimony totally precluding the defendant's claim of self-defense. Defense counsel conducted some cross-examination but only made matters worse for his case, since the witness merely reiterated his testimony on direct. In that case, as damaging as it would have been, the defense might have been better off asking no questions. Even here, however, defense counsel might have benefited by showing that the witness was thoroughly prepared by the prosecutor. For example, the defense could have elicited that the witness had attended several witness conferences with the prosecutor and had carefully reviewed his prior statements and grand jury testimony.[18]

Cross-Examination Techniques

This section collects some basic techniques for conducting effective cross-examination once the threshold decision to cross-examine has been made. Sponsorship principles reveal why these techniques are effective.

First, a cross-examiner should never ask a witness to repeat a point favoring the opponent unless the cross-examiner has a specific tactical reason for

18 One commentator refers to this type of cross-examination as "apparent" cross-examination. Mauet, *supra* n. 15, § 7.8, at 305.

doing so. For example, it is perfectly appropriate to ask a witness to repeat a seemingly damaging fact when the cross-examiner's next step is to impeach the witness with a contradictory statement. Absent such a situation, however, there is usually no reason for a cross-examiner to compound the damage from direct examination by eliciting a witness's repetition of a harmful piece of testimony. In our experience, much of the cross-examination elicited in actual trials produces a great deal of repetition of a witness's main points on direct, sometimes in even stronger terms.[19] As should be clear, the answers will normally have more impact upon repetition during cross-examination than they did on direct examination.

Second, the cross-examiner should generally not ask a question unless he knows in advance what the witness's answer will be. This point is well known and should be obvious, since the evaluation of the probative value of the expected answer is basic to deciding whether to incur the costs of asking the question. It is important to emphasize, however, that the rule is not an inflexible one.[20] There may be times—especially in criminal cases, where discovery is limited—when the cross-examiner has little choice but to probe in the dark.[21] For instance, where a witness has given harmful testimony on direct that could not get much worse, the cross-examiner may sometimes be justified in searching for weaknesses, particularly where the witness's story seems implausible and there is a good chance that the cross-examiner can cast some doubt on it.

Third, in establishing a point that damages the witness, the cross-examiner should avoid permitting the witness to offer an explanation. Instead, only the point that disfavors the opponent's case should be elicited, thereby forcing the opponent to supply the mitigating context on redirect. This tends to make the opponent, not the cross-examiner, the sponsor of the explanation.[22]

The best means of accomplishing this purpose is to use leading ques-

19 *See, e.g.*, Washington Post, Feb. 23, 1989, at A1, col. 3 (reporting that at the criminal trial of former White House aide Oliver North, the defense lawyer's "day long" cross-examination of a prosecution witness resulted in the witness "[making] points on cross-examination in even stronger language than he had on direct questioning by [the] prosecutor").

20 *Contra*, I. Younger, *The Art of Cross-Examination* 23 (A.B.A. Monograph Series 1976) ("[Y]ou should *never* ask a question to which you do not already know the answer.") (emphasis in original).

21 *Accord, e.g.*, F. Bailey & H. Rothblatt, *Successful Techniques for Criminal Trials* § 11.20, at 307 (Lawyers Co-op. Pub. Co. 1985).

22 *But see* pages 158 to 159, *supra* (discussing methods of redirect examination for making the cross-examiner largely responsible for the witness's explanation).

tions. This puts the advocate who initially called the witness in the position of being held accountable for any imperfections in the explanation. Even if the explanation is a plausible one, the cross-examiner is better off letting the opponent elicit it, since the jury is likely to give it less weight.[23]

Some commentators suggest strict rules of *never* permitting a witness to explain an answer and *never* using non-leading questions on cross-examination.[24] While these rules are generally sound, we believe that there are times when both of them must be violated.

For instance, it will frequently be counterproductive for an advocate to attempt to cut off a witness's answer. An advocate who makes substantial efforts to do so may suggest to the jury that he has something to hide. As a result, the jury may give the testimony heightened weight when the witness ultimately gives a complete explanation.[25] Thus, a cross-examiner will only harm his case by taking pains to hide a witness's explanation, such as by interrupting the witness and shouting, "I just asked for a 'yes' or 'no' answer."

The rule of using only leading questions on cross-examination is likewise not an inflexible one. To begin with, when the cross-examiner concludes that he must probe even though he does not know the precise answer,[26] he obviously cannot ask leading questions. More fundamentally, the technique of using leading questions is generally beneficial only when the cross-examiner knows or suspects that a complete explanation will put the witness's answer in a perspective that is more favorable to the opponent's case. When the cross-examiner is virtually certain that the witness's answer *and* explanation will benefit the cross-examiner's case, it will normally be in the interest of the cross-examiner to ask *nonleading* questions. As we explained in Chapter Eight with reference to direct examination,[27] an advocate can reduce sponsorship costs by using nonleading questions. This applies *a*

---

23 Many commentators recommend using leading questions on cross-examination. *See, e.g.,* K. Hegland, *Trial and Practice Skills* 158-59 (West 1994)(reciting benefits of leading questions); R. Carlson, *Successful Techniques for Civil Trials* § 4:10, at 276 (Lawyers Co-op. Pub. Co. 1992) (identifying the use of leading questions as a "principle[ ]" of cross-examination).

24 *See, e.g.,* Younger, *supra* n. 20, at 23 ("[Y]ou should *never* ask anything but leading questions on cross-examination.") (emphasis added); *id.* at 28 ("A trial lawyer must *never* permit the witness to explain anything on cross-examination.") (emphasis added); *cf.*; Mauet, *supra* n. 15, § 7.4, at 257 (noting that "[o]pen-ended questions are inappropriate on cross-examinations" and that "[q]uestions that ask 'how' or 'why' or elicit explanations of any kind invite disaster ... [and] are best avoided altogether").

25 *See* pages 158 to 159, *supra.*

26 *See* page 190, *supra.*

27 *See* page 147, *supra.*

fortiori to cross-examination of an opponent's witnesses, since the jury has no reason to suspect that the witness's responses were verified in advance in a pre-trial witness conference.

Fourth, as in most trial situations, the cross-examiner must maintain a "poker face," regardless of how harmful he views the witness's response. The cross-examiner does not want to signal the jury that his case was harmed by testimony that he has elicited.[28]

Fifth, the manner in which cross-examination is conducted bears critically on the sponsorship costs that are incurred. To minimize the cost of efforts, the cross-examiner must not appear to be expecting to accomplish very much, if anything, as a result of questioning. The only message communicated by a lengthy and acrimonious cross-examination is that the advocate *needs* to make inroads to win the case.

For example, in impeaching a witness with a prior conviction, the cross-examiner should not approach the witness waving a certified copy of the conviction, booming loudly, "Isn't it a fact, sir, that you were convicted of second degree burglary in 2006?", and then return to counsel table with a triumphant smirk after receiving the witness's affirmative response. The jury will only conclude that the advocate deemed it significant to his case to establish the point. Instead, the advocate should casually ask the witness during the course of examination: "Are you the same John Jones who was convicted of second-degree burglary in 2006?" After receiving an affirmative response, the advocate should then move immediately to his next point.

In short, the cross-examination should appear effortless. If great efforts—such as a lengthy impeachment involving numerous documents—are necessary to elicit a point, then the cross-examination will be less effective and may not be appropriate.[29]

Finally, the cross-examiner should keep in mind, in crafting a cross-examination, that an alert opponent will be monitoring his every move. The cross-examiner should thus avoid asking questions that supply the opponent with ammunition for closing argument. Most importantly, as Chapter Twelve will demonstrate, the questions should not suggest inconsistent theories (and usually should not suggest alternative theories).

28 *Accord, e.g.*, J. Kestler, *Questioning Techniques and Tactics* § 1.23, at 23 (Shepard's/McGraw Hill, Inc. 1982).

29 An effort-minimizing "best case" advocate will, as we have stated, use that evidence which gives him the greatest value for the quantum of effort expended. Thus, labored efforts on cross-examination to elicit minor points will underscore the limited amount of superior evidence available to the advocate.

To summarize, an advocate faces difficult issues in deciding whether to cross-examine and, if so, what questions to ask. While the sponsorship costs are low, thus permitting more leeway in examination, a labored examination dwelling on minor points will be counterproductive. In addition, the cross-examiner must keep in mind that even one ill-considered question can seriously damage his case.

CHAPTER 12

Closing Argument

Overview

When the time has come for closing argument, the jurors will have heard all of the evidence and perhaps will have arrived at some initial conclusions. Because of their inexperience, however, they will understandably lack confidence in these initial assessments and will have many questions on their minds. They will be waiting anxiously for the lawyers' remarks.

In a rape case, for example, they will look to the lawyers for guidance in assessing the victim's testimony. Have they been too gullible regarding certain aspects of his testimony? They will be waiting to see if defense counsel raises that issue. Did defense counsel go "too far"—that is, was he too abusive—in cross-examining the victim on her previous intimacies? The jurors will be looking to see if the prosecutor makes an issue out of this. They will be relying on each trained advocate to explain the defects and inadequacies of the opponent's presentation, as well as the merits of his own case. Each advocate's view of the evidence will come to represent the best-case scenario for his side and the worst-case scenario for the opponent's side. Criticisms not made—as well as strengths not identified—may be lost forever.

This chapter instructs how to craft a persuasive closing argument. The first section discusses various threshold considerations. The second section offers a detailed framework for structuring the argument. In particular, it emphasizes the critical need for the advocate to present his own evidence in its best light and his opponent's evidence in its worst light. It also stresses the value of highlighting the opponent's concessions. The third section focuses on arguments to rebut the opponent's remarks.

A note of caution is in order. The rules on proper argument vary widely from jurisdiction to jurisdiction. Accordingly, the advocate must satisfy himself, through legal research or otherwise, as to the propriety of any argument he makes as a result of the recommendations in this book.

Threshold Considerations

Comment on the Advocate's and Opponent's Respective Strengths and Weaknesses

If the advocate has adhered to the guidance set forth in this book, his case will be concise and easily analyzed for the jury. If the opponent has failed to adhere to the sponsorship method, then his presentation will be overloaded with extraneous evidence, comments, and questions asked of the witnesses that did not advance his theory of the case. Moreover, there will normally be many concessions by opposing counsel upon which the advocate can capitalize. For these reasons, the advocate's discussion of the flaws in the opponent's case may consume even more time than discussion of his own evidence.

The techniques an advocate should employ in discussing the strengths and weaknesses of his own case and that of the opponent can be easily derived from the principles outlined in Chapters Two and Four. As explained in Chapter Two, no juror during deliberations should be expected to espouse a favorable argument or perception concerning the advocate's case that the advocate himself fails to make.[1] This means that arguments not made in summation will probably not be made for the advocate in the jury room. To be sure, a juror will occasionally make such an argument. For instance, in a criminal case, there will sometimes be a member of the jury who delights in making himself appear astute by espousing theories of innocence not even urged by defense counsel. The advocate is obviously unwise, however, in deliberately omitting a favorable argument and relying on such an argument to be made for him by a juror. For this reason, when the advocate has put on evidence, he must discuss that evidence in its

1 *See* page 15, *supra.*

best light. The advocate likewise must discuss the opponent's evidence and contentions in their worst light.

The sponsorship approach counsels that arguments by an advocate designed to accomplish this task must never be delivered half-heartedly.[2] As with opening statements, this is no time for understatement,[3] since anything the advocate says that favors his case or criticizes the opponent's case will be heavily discounted by the jury.[4] Although an advocate is not permitted to state his personal belief or opinion on disputed matters of fact,[5] he plainly wants to avoid communicating a *lack* of belief in matters material to his case. The only means of ensuring against this is to maintain an enthusiastic demeanor regarding both the strength of his case and the weakness of the opponent's case. Where possible, the advocate's goal should be to have the jury wondering why the opponent even filed the case (if the opponent is the plaintiff or prosecutor) or why, if the opponent is the defendant, he did not settle it or plead guilty.[6]

A useful way to illustrate the goal of dwelling on one's own strengths and the opponent's weaknesses is to consider two glasses of water, the first representing the advocate's theory of the case and the second his opponent's theory. No matter how much water is in the two glasses, the advocate's strategy for summation must be to emphasize the full part of his glass and the empty part of the opponent's glass.[7]

---

2 *Cf.* A. Kruger, *Modern Debate: Its Logic and Strategy* 193 (McGraw-Hill 1960) ("Since most people are disturbed when they experience feelings of doubt, [the] appeal [by the confident manner] attempts to allay their doubts and help make up their minds. Debaters often use this technique by introducing such terms as 'certainly,' 'obviously,' 'perfectly clear' and 'surely.'").

3 *Contra, e.g.*, T. Mauet, *Fundamentals of Trial Techniques* § 7.2, at 276 (Little, Brown & Co. 2d ed. 1988) (describing understatement as a potentially "powerful argumentative tool").

4 *Cf.* L. Pearson, *The Art of Demosthenes* 9 (Scholars Press 1981) ("Demosthenes ... often overstate[d] his case ... [with the] object ... [of] forc[ing] his opponents to suggest to the jury the kind of judgment that they will be willing to pass.").

5 *See, e.g.*, Model Code of Professional Responsibility, DR 7-106(C)(4) (forbidding attorneys from expressing personal opinion); 1 *American Bar Association, Standards for Criminal Justice* (2d ed. 1980), Standard 3-5.8(b), at 3-87 (prosecutor); *id.*, Standard 4-7.8(b), at 4-96 (defense counsel in criminal case); *cf.* Model Code of Professional Responsibility, EC 7-24.

6 Of course, the advocate must avoid stating that his opponent should have given up his right to a trial.

7 As to the shortcomings in an opponent's case, consider an example from the oratory of Demosthenes' teacher, Isaeus:

> [My opponent] ought to have given us figures and brought witnesses: he ought to have gone through each ... item in the account .... He ought to have examined the decrees, the amounts imposed, the amounts paid, the persons who collected them, and then, if all was satisfactory, he ought to have accepted my statement; or, if it was not, he ought *now* to have brought witnesses regarding any false item in the outlay which I charged ....

II R. Jebb, *The Attic Orators from Antiphon to Isaeus* 305 (Russell and Russell, Inc. 1962) (quoting from an oration of Isaeus). *Cf.* Aristotle, *Rhetoric*, 1392a1, *translated in* II *The Complete Works of Aristotle* 2217 (Princeton Univ. Press, Barnes ed. 6th printing 1995) ("[T]he topic of size is common to all oratory; all of us have to argue that things are bigger or smaller than they seem ....").

As set forth more fully below, an important technique is for an advocate to compare his case with a hypothetically weak case in the same subject area. This technique facilitates the jury's appreciation of the evidence that the advocate presented to support his case. Similarly, it is useful to compare the opponent's case with a hypothetically strong case in the same subject area, thus facilitating the jury's appreciation of how much better the opponent's case could have been. By the same token, the advocate should avoid discussing the degree to which his glass is empty and the opponent's glass is full. That is the opponent's job.

The Advocate's Goal of Minimizing His Burden of Proof

An overriding goal of any trial attorney should be to minimize the degree to which the jury views him as having the burden of persuasion.[8] For the plaintiff's attorney or prosecutor, there is, of course, an initial burden of proof that must be satisfied as a matter of law. The first task of such an advocate will be to impress upon the jury that the evidence that he has presented satisfies this burden. If the defense has opted to present a defense case, the advocate should frame the issue for the jury as one of determining whether the opponent's evidence is sufficient to overcome the advocate's otherwise sufficient case.[9]

If the defense has not presented a case, then the plaintiff's attorney or prosecutor should frame the issue as one of whether the defense's *contentions* are sufficient to overcome the advocate's otherwise sufficient case. As suggested in Chapter Ten,[10] in this latter case, before closing arguments begin, the prosecutor or plaintiff's lawyer must define the defendant's version of the facts using defense counsel's opening statement and the questions that defense counsel asked on cross-examination. In his closing argument, the prosecutor or plaintiff's lawyer should identify for the jury the defendant's competing version of the facts, capitalizing on the relevant portions of his lawyer's opening statement and questions he posed to the witnesses. The

8 An example can be found in the oratory of Antiphon, the so-called father of Sophist rhetoric. In *On the Murder of Herodes*, a closing argument for a defendant charged with murder, the argument avoided offering explanations of how some other individual could have committed the crime, stressing that the defendant did not need to show who else could have committed the murder. The main focus of the argument was on the unreliability of a key prosecution witness. The defendant did not focus at length upon his alibi, or attempt to prove it, but mentioned it only incidentally. Finally, the defendant made no bid for sympathy. *See* R. Jebb, *The Attic Orators from Antiphon to Isaeus* 55–61 (MacMillan and Co. 1893).

9 A prosecutor, of course, must be careful not to suggest that a criminal defendant has any burden or was required to put on a case. *See* page 50, n. 4, *supra*.

10 *See* page 172, *supra*.

prosecutor or plaintiff's lawyer should then expose the weaknesses in that defense version, just as he would have done had the defense chosen to support its competing theory by presenting a defense case-in-chief.

The perspective of the defense lawyer is different from that of the plaintiff's lawyer or prosecutor. Since the defense has no burden of proof except with respect to affirmative defenses, any talk of the merits of the "defense case" plays into the hands of the opponent. It tends to shift the burden—and thus the jury's tendencies to discount and scrutinize—to the defense.

The best of all worlds for defense counsel is where he is not forced into the position of having to discuss his evidence at length. This will be true when the opponent has called all available witnesses and introduced all pertinent exhibits, including those favoring the defense theory of the case. In such a case, all of the jury's tendencies to discount and scrutinize will be directed at the opponent. This will be even more true where defense counsel's opponent took the additional step of volunteering all matters favorable to the defense as part of the direct examination of those witnesses.

Even where defense counsel has opted to present his own case or conduct extensive cross-examination of the opponent's witnesses, his primary attention usually should be focused on scrutinizing and attacking the opponent's case. The advocate should suggest, where appropriate, that the evidence that he introduced is really part and parcel of evidence that the opponent introduced and is best viewed that way.[11] Of course, defense counsel should recognize the importance of stressing the probative value of evidence that he chooses to introduce. The advocate does not want to open himself to attack for abandoning his own evidence.

The Rule of Using Only Strong Contentions

In crafting a closing argument, the advocate must recognize that any comment or contention an advocate considers making must be subjected to the same cost/benefit analysis that applies to evidence. A comment about an item of evidence, for example, may be discounted by the jury because of the costs of introduction. Specifically, the jury may assume that the advocate carefully chose (or packaged) his words and phrasing to make the point in the most persuasive manner possible. This cost of packaging can be countered, at least in part, by using the technique of deprecating one's

11 *Cf.* pages 157 to 159, *supra* (discussing analogous technique for redirect examination).

own oratorical skills while complimenting those of the opponent.[12] This technique may also serve to undermine the jury's assumption that it has seen the advocate's best case, while fortifying its assumption that it has seen the *opponent's* best case.[13] In recognition of the jury's suspicion that the summation is packaged, the advocate should carefully prepare his remarks to achieve at least the corresponding benefit of packaging.[14] At the same time, the advocate should avoid the impression that he carefully prepared and packaged every phrase.

In addition to the packaging component, there is the concession of materiality component: the advocate will be viewed as conceding the materiality of any point that he makes.[15] And, because of the cost of overtrying, the comment might cause the jury to give less weight to the advocate's other comments.

In addition, the advocate must be mindful of the costs of unusual efforts. Consider, for example, defense counsel's decision whether to raise his voice and denounce as an "outrage" the government's prosecution in the face of "such flimsy evidence!" The situation is similar to the decision of whether to introduce an enlargement of a photograph. In both situations, the advocate must decide whether the benefits are worth the costs of unusual efforts. Just as he should not introduce an enormous blow-up of a photograph that does not advance his case, the advocate obviously should not scream a trivial argument at the top of his lungs. By the same token, if an advocate spends excessive time making a given comment or contention, he will incur costs of unusual efforts. Those efforts must be justified by the favorable value of the comment or contention.

---

12 George W. Bush used this technique in the 2000 presidential campaign, warning the public prior to the presidential debates that his opponent, Al Gore, was the more experienced debater. The Bush team repeated this technique in 2004, "manag[ing] expectations" by "talk[ing] up [his opponent Senator John] Kerry's experience as a debater, citing [Kerry's] 20 years in the Senate and his participation on his prep school's debate team." Kerry Rips Bush on "Mission Accomplished" Remark, CommonDreams.org News Center, http://www.commondreams.org/headlines04/0927-24.htm, visited on January 13, 2007.

13 *Cf.* B. Castiglione, *The Book of the Courtier* 67 (Penguin Classics 1976)(referring to "outstanding orators of the ancient world who ... tried hard to make everyone believe that they were ignorant of letters; and, dissembling their knowledge, they made their speeches appear to have been composed very simply and according to the promptings of ... truth rather than effort and artifice").

14 *Cf.* Jebb [1893], *supra* n. 8, at lxxi (noting that "Demosthenes would never speak [without preparing his remarks] when he could help it").

15 Superior advocates will be alert to capitalize on an opponent's concessions of materiality. *See, e.g.*, W. Wyse, *The Speeches of Isaeus* 217 (Cambridge Univ. Press 1904) (containing following excerpt: "You will learn best the justice of our cause from our opponents .... [T]hey rest their claim to inherit [the decedent's] estate [on the contentions] that they are somehow related to him and that for a time he was friendly with them. Will not this answer be in favor of us rather than of them? We are nearer relations, we, as all the world knows, were on more friendly terms with him").

Finally, as should be apparent from the foregoing chapters, juries view concessions of counsel as very significant and place heavy reliance on them. Thus, closing argument should be used not just to summarize the evidence in the case but also to summarize and exploit any concessions—explicit as well as implicit—made by opposing counsel during the trial. If the opponent's conduct at trial strayed from principles of sponsorship, the advocate will have collected many concessions to stress to the jury. At the same time, the advocate who has adhered to the sponsorship method in his conduct of the trial will have minimized the risk of exposure to such criticism during the opponent's summation. The advocate, of course, should not reflexively highlight every concession made by the opponent. As with any other comment, the value of the opponent's concessions must outweigh the sponsorship costs of bringing them to the jury's attention.

In sum, in crafting the closing argument, the advocate must adhere to the general sponsorship rule of using only strong contentions and comments. Less compelling arguments should be omitted.[16]

Framework for Argument

In our experience, the optimum organization for a closing argument—for plaintiffs' attorneys, prosecutors, and defense attorneys alike—consists of five parts: initial remarks; comment on the evidence introduced by the advocate carrying the initial burden of proof; transitional remarks; comments on the evidence and contentions of the advocate not carrying the initial burden; and concluding remarks. The following sections give guidance on crafting each of these portions of the summation.

The sections are set forth in the order that they should be delivered by the plaintiff's attorney or prosecutor. The defense attorney should transpose the section entitled "Comment on the Opponent's Case" with the section entitled "Comment on the Advocate's Case." In this way, he can dwell first on how his opponent failed to sustain his burden of proof before turning to how his own evidence confirms that the defense should prevail.[17]

16 This sponsorship rule is consistent with the practice of the orator Antiphon, who is said to have "tend[ed] to pick out one argument and ... not systematically exhaust all possible arguments." G. Kennedy, *The Art of Persuasion in Greece* 131 (Princeton Univ. Press 1963).

17 *Accord*, Aristotle, *supra* n. 7, at 1418b1 (translated in *Complete Works of Aristotle*, at 2266) ("Both in political speaking and when pleading in court, if you are the first speaker you should put your own arguments forward first, and then meet the arguments on the other side by refuting them and pulling them to pieces beforehand .... If you speak later, you must ... attempt some answer to your opponent's speech ... [by] attack[ing] that first ....").

Initial Remarks

The advocate's initial remarks should focus solely on the issues in dispute and how the evidence requires a verdict in the advocate's favor. For example, in a negligence case involving a defense of unavoidable accident, defense counsel should begin the argument along the following lines:

> Ladies and gentlemen of the jury: At the beginning of the trial, I told you that the evidence would show that the accident in this case was unavoidable. You have now heard all of the evidence and I submit to you that it clearly leads to only one conclusion: the defendant is not liable for plaintiff's injuries.

The advocate should then proceed directly into the second part of his argument (an attack on his opponent's evidence and contentions).

In contrast to this approach, many trial attorneys believe that a closing argument should begin with a discussion of neutral legal principles or remarks about the jury system, such as noting that what the lawyers say is not evidence. In our view, nothing is gained by such remarks.[18] The advocate is not advancing his case in the least by highlighting points of law that do not lead the jury to rule in his favor. In addition, while there may be times that the advocate will want to deprecate his own skills or praise his opponent's skills,[19] it is unwise to tell the jury that his memory is not as good as the jury's and that the jury's recollection should control.

One leading commentator provides the following passages as the ideal way to begin a closing argument:

> This is my final opportunity to talk to you about this case. At the outset let me say that if my recollection of any of the facts or testimony given in this trial is at variance with your own, accept your own recollection. It is as good or better than my own.
>
> I have lived with this case for some time, and there is always the possibility that during the excitement of a trial, I will not have had the full opportunity to observe all the facts in their

18 Some commentators recognize this point. *See, e.g.*, S. Goldberg, *The First Trial: Where Do I Sit? What Do I Say?* 206 (West 1982); J. Jeans, *Trial Advocacy* § 10.12, at 314-15 (West 1993). Others, however, have argued that such discussion is useful. *See, e.g.* Mauet[1988 ed.], *supra* n. 3, § 7.5, at 297, 311.

19 *See* pages 199 to 200, *supra*.

> true light. If my recollection of any matter is erroneous, I assure you it is not intentional.
>
> It is my purpose in this final argument to sum up the facts and the facts alone. I will try to add up the testimony and evidence presented in this trial, and see if we can arrive at a total that will do justice to the plaintiff, to the defendant, and to your own consciences as jurors.
>
> It is also my purpose to state the facts fairly and frankly, and to make my comment as honest and sincere as it is in my power to make. Please bear in mind that my comment, like that of my opponent, is naturally biased.
>
> Remember further that neither my opponent nor myself saw this accident, [and] our powers of deduction and inference are no better than your own. You know now as much about this case as the lawyers or the judge. And I ask that you remember that fact when you begin your deliberations upon the issues.[20]

In our view, this presentation serves no useful purpose. The advocate will probably have lost the jury's attention before he even begins to discuss the evidence. At a minimum, such initial remarks represent a lost opportunity. At worst, they might actually damage the advocate's case.

First, the advocate has given the jury reason to doubt the accuracy of his recollection, and the jury may therefore be less inclined to focus on what he says during the rest of his argument. Second, the advocate has underscored that his view of the case is biased. While the jury no doubt assumes this, there is no reason to highlight the point. Third, the advocate has undermined the force of his presentation by pointing out that an attorney's power of deduction and inference is no better than that of the jury. A jury looks to the advocate, a trained professional, for guidance in identifying the merits of his case and the weaknesses of his opponent's case. If the jury concludes that the advocate has no special skills in assessing the evidence, then it will be less inclined to credit his arguments.

In short, the above-quoted introduction to a closing argument accomplishes nothing with respect to the advocate's goal of obtaining a verdict in his favor. At best, such remarks are neutral principles that will benefit both

20 1 S. Schweitzer, *Cyclopedia of Trial Practice* § 273, at 701–702 (Lawyers Co-op. Pub. Co. 2d ed. 1970).

sides equally. At worst, such statements will cause the jury to lack confidence in the advocate when he begins to focus on the evidence. In addition, while it is important to be courteous and well-mannered, we caution against the use of kind words for the jury, such as praise for its patience and attention. Remarks of this type have no realistic chance of swaying the jury to render a verdict in the advocate's favor.[21]

Furthermore, contrary to the view of the above-quoted commentator, juries are not so naïve as to accept an advocate's claim that his purpose in delivering his closing comments is "[to] do justice to the plaintiff [and] . . . the defendant"; "to state the facts fairly and frankly"; and "to make [his] comment as honest and sincere as it is in [his] power to make." As misplaced as this commentator's approach may appear, it is not an aberration. Rather, it reflects the consistent tenor and focus of the advice offered by most of the existing conventional trial advocacy literature—that the advocate should devote valuable court time attempting to enhance his credibility with the jury, all on the assumption that such credibility gains are the key to winning jury trials. While our book recognizes certain narrow instances in which an advocate must be mindful not to *injure* his standing with the jury (by omitting devastating information from direct examinations and by gross overstatement), we consider such elaborate and patronizing gambits designed to enhance credibility as this pointless and, as we have demonstrated throughout this book, often tactically damaging.[22] Accordingly, in light of all the foregoing points, we believe that the above-quoted passage should be viewed as a model of how *not* to begin a closing argument.

Comment on the Advocate's Case

Highlighting Strengths

The first task for an advocate in summarizing the merits of his case is to highlight its strengths. If the advocate has followed the principles of sponsorship in the presentation of his case, this task will involve a brief recount-

21 *Cf.* G.W. Keeton, *Harris's Hints on Advocacy* 35 (Stevens & Sons, Ltd. 18th ed. 1943) ("Nothing makes a jury more keenly sensitive of your contempt for their mental capacity than flattering them.").

22 The disagreement of sponsorship analysis with today's conventional treatise writers on this and other points addressed in this book mirrors the disagreement of the "[ancient] Greek orator, who tend[ed] to argue his audience into believing something," with the "Roman [orator, who] by his authority convince[d] the audience that something should be believed because he says so." G. Kennedy, *The Art of Rhetoric in the Roman World* 42 (Princeton University Press 1972). Regardless of the latter tactic's merit in some contexts, it is of virtually no utility in the courtroom, where jurors know that lawyers are bound to advocate zealously on their clients' behalf.

ing of the testimony of each witness that he has called, each major point elicited therefrom, and each exhibit introduced. If any of the advocate's witnesses or exhibits do not bear mention at this point, he probably should not have introduced such evidence in the first place.[23] Giving due emphasis to the strengths of one's case reflects the more general rule that the time and emphasis an advocate devotes to any particular point he makes in closing argument should be kept in proportion to the probative weight of that point relative to all the other points he is making.[24]

With regard to the structure of the argument, we believe that a presentation in a story or chronological form is more effective than a straight witness-by-witness approach. The latter approach tends to bore and confuse the jury.

Minimizing Reliance on Any One Item of Evidence

When the advocate has introduced multiple items of strong evidence, he will often be in a position to argue that certain items, standing alone, warrant a verdict in his favor. The approach when he has introduced such evidence is to isolate and identify for the jury each such item. This approach will minimize the cost of overtrying by communicating that he is not relying on any particular piece of evidence to win.[25]

An example will illustrate the point. Assume that the defendant in a civil automobile accident case is alleged to have been driving while intoxicated. Assume further that the arresting police officer can testify that the defendant's breath had a strong odor of alcohol, that the defendant could not maintain his balance, and that his speech was slurred. Finally, assume that the breathalyzer test revealed a blood alcohol level consistent with intoxication. Plaintiff's attorney could argue along the following lines:

> The testimony of the arresting officer concerning the defendant's intoxicated state at the scene of the accident is, by itself, easily sufficient to find by a preponderance of the evidence that the defendant was intoxicated. Without any other evidence,

23 An exception is any less-then-strong evidence that the advocate was required to present in accordance with the rules set forth in Chapters Four and Five.

24 Analogous principles guide the appellate advocate. *See, e.g.,* Kozinski, *Humor: How You Too...Can Lose Your Appeal,* 23 Montana Lawyer 5, 22 (Oct. 1997)(arguing that one way to lose an appeal is by "bury[ing] your winning argument in the midst of nine or ten losers").

25 *Cf.* Jebb [1893], *supra* n.8, at 55-61 (citing example of Antiphon stressing in argument the independent sufficiency of two separate grounds for a verdict in his favor).

> that testimony is far more than the plaintiff needs. However, we also have scientific evidence showing the defendant's high blood-alcohol level. That scientific evidence, without more, also easily proves defendant's intoxication. Taken together, the evidence is overwhelming and establishes beyond all doubt that the defendant was under the influence.

This argument is important in keeping the jury from concluding that the advocate felt that he needed *all* of his evidence to prove the point.

Comparison of the Advocate's Case to a Hypothetically Weak Case

Where appropriate, the advocate should compare the degree of evidence supporting his case to a hypothetically weak case of a similar type. This directs the jury's attention to the "full part of the glass," as it were, and maximizes its appreciation of the advocate's evidence. It further serves to bolster a contention, in cases where it is warranted, that the advocate's evidence is "strong" or "overwhelming."

For example, continuing for simplicity with the negligence case involving an automobile accident, assume the plaintiff's case is supported by two strong eyewitnesses and by a sobriety test revealing the defendant's intoxication. In such a case, the plaintiff should point out that the jury is not being asked to find liability based on a single witness of doubtful strength. Rather, the plaintiff has offered *two strong* witnesses, as well as strong scientific evidence.

Highlighting the Opponent's Unproductive Cross-Examination

Juries invariably perceive cross-examination as a time for testing. They tend to believe that the major reason for asking questions on cross-examination is to challenge the witness's version of the facts. If the advocate's witness gives satisfactory answers to the opponent's questions, the advocate should note for the jury that cross-examination is the greatest engine ever developed for determining truth and that the opponent's efforts to test the witness only served to underscore the accuracy of the testimony. The opponent will have no credible means of disputing the advocate's characterization of his reason for examining the advocate's witness. The jury will be apt to conclude that the witness's answers were verified.

Even if the matters elicited are slightly harmful to his case, the advocate can belittle them by mockingly characterizing them as "awful revelation[s]."[26] Furthermore, the greater the effort expended by the opponent in his failed attempt, the more powerful the argument will be. Where appropriate, a compliment regarding the opponent's skills and high proficiency as an attorney will emphasize the meagerness of the results of his cross-examination.

Finally, when opposing counsel asked no questions of one of the advocate's witnesses, the advocate should argue that the witness's testimony was undisputed and conceded by the opponent. The opponent will have great difficulty countering such an argument.

Highlighting Jury Instructions That Support the Advocate's Case

As we explained in Chapter Eight,[27] because of the costs involved when an advocate introduces any item of evidence, regardless of its strength, he is normally better off if his evidence is introduced by his opponent or by the court. This phenomenon of reduced sponsorship costs applies as well to statements concerning the law. If the advocate summarizes the applicable law favoring his side in his closing argument, the jury will tend to view the summary with skepticism. The advocate can reduce that skepticism, however, by prefacing discussions of legal points, where applicable, with the phrase, "As the Judge will tell you . . . ."[28] The jury will be impressed when the judge later confirms what the advocate has said.

Thus, for example, if the advocate represents a defendant in a case in which the government's chief witness was a paid informant, the advocate should emphasize that the *judge* will instruct the jury that the testimony of the witness "must be examined and weighed . . . with greater care than the testimony of a witness who is not so motivated."[29]

---

26 R. Traver, *Anatomy of a Murder* 395 (St. Martin's Press 1958) (phrase used in fictional summation).

27 *See* pages 140 to 141 and page 159, *supra*.

28 Numerous commentators have recognized the value of this technique. *See, e.g.,* F. Bailey & H. Rothblatt, *Successful Techniques for Criminal Trials* § 21:10, at 482 (Lawyers Co-op. Pub. Co. 1985) (counseling defense reference to the court's instruction regarding high burden of proof in a criminal prosecution).

29 K. O'Malley, J. Grenig & W. Lee, *Federal Jury Practice and Instructions* § 15.02, at 364 (West 5th ed. 2000) (sample jury instructions).

Discussing the Purpose of the Advocate's Introduction of Evidence Bearing on Undisputed Issues

As explained in Chapter Three, the advocate with the burden of proof must introduce evidence to satisfy his legal burden even on elements of his claim that are not disputed by the opponent. In summation, such an advocate should, of course, stress the opponent's failure to dispute the element. In addition, however, the advocate will want to refer to the evidence that he introduced to satisfy the undisputed elements and tell the jury that the introduction was merely designed to meet technical legal requirements. This will serve to ensure that the advocate suffers no costs of overtrying from the use of such evidence.

Techniques for Arguing Alternative Theories

As we explained in Chapter Three,[30] although an advocate should never advance inconsistent theories, there are apt to be occasions in which it is useful to advance alternative consistent theories. In Chapter Three, we gave the example of a defendant charged with heroin distribution who had an alibi defense but who could also cast doubt on the accuracy of tests showing that the substance was heroin.[31] As we indicated, the defense attorney might find it beneficial to argue that his client was not the one who sold the substance and that, in any event, the substance was not heroin.

The important point for an advocate to keep in mind in arguing alternative theories is that he must not suggest that he is conceding the inadequacy of evidence supporting either theory. In the heroin case, for example, the advocate should *not* argue: "Even if you believe that my client was the one selling the substance, there is insufficient evidence to show that it was heroin." Such an argument might be read by the jury as an implicit concession that the evidence linking his client to the sales activity was compelling and that the advocate felt that, in order to win, he needed to convince the jury that the substance sold was not heroin.

Instead, the advocate should underscore that each theory is independently strong. In the above heroin case, for example, the advocate may wish to suggest that the case before the jury is one of those rare cases where the government's evidence is so weak that the jury can in essence return two not guilty verdicts

30 *See* pages 39 to 40, *supra.*

31 *See* page 40, *supra.*

rather than just one: one for the defendant and one for the real seller, who got away but who was also innocent of any criminal activity (except taking money under false pretenses). The advocate making such an argument must, however, avoid imparting the impression of relying on the inadequacy of the chemical tests to win. In that regard, the advocate must be careful to focus his indignation on the insufficiency of the evidence bearing on identification.[32]

Transitional Remarks

After completing his discussion of the burdened party's evidence, the advocate should make some transitional remarks before addressing the evidence and contentions of the non-burdened party.[33] For the plaintiff's attorney or prosecutor, the transition should set forth a brief recapitulation—no more than several sentences—of his own evidence, along with the submission that the burden of proof is easily met by that evidence. Such an advocate should then turn the jury's attention to the defense presentation. Thus, immediately after his recapitulation, the advocate should say something like:

> That, ladies and gentlemen, is the plaintiff's case—a strong case for liability. Now, what is the defense theory of the case?

The burdened advocate should then proceed directly into a discussion of the defense evidence and contentions, employing the guidance contained in the following section.

In substance, the defense attorney will want to do precisely the mirror image of what we recommend for his burdened opponent. Thus, after discussing the opponent's evidence at length in accordance with the guidance set forth in the following section, the defense counsel should briefly recapitulate the failings in the opponent's case and evidence, and conclude that the opponent's evidence totally fails to meet his burden of proof. Assuming that the defense counsel has presented evidence of his own beyond evidence designed

---

32 No matter how the second theory is argued, alert opposing counsel will attempt to tax the advocate with overtrying costs for having advanced it. *See, e.g.*, Wyse, *supra* n. 15, at 661 (containing following excerpt from speech of Isaeus: "My opponents ... [n]ot content with arguing [their first contention] ... shelter themselves behind a second plea ....").

33 As we noted above, both sides will discuss the burdened party's evidence first. For plaintiffs' lawyers and prosecutors, this will be a discussion of their own evidence using the techniques in the preceding section entitled, "Comment on the Advocate's Case." For defense counsel, this will mean attacking the evidence presented by the plaintiff's lawyer or prosecutor, using the techniques in the next section, "Comment on the Opponent's Case."

merely to rebut, he should then turn the jury's attention to his own proof. The following provides an illustration of defense counsel's transition:

> That, ladies and gentlemen, is the plaintiff's evidence. Standing alone, it fails utterly to make his case. But it is even worse for the plaintiff, since the *defense* has compelling evidence affirmatively showing the defendant's lack of liability. Now, what was the defense evidence?

The defense attorney would then discuss his own evidence in accordance with the principles contained in the foregoing section.

If the defense evidence was not substantial and consisted only of limited testimony or exhibits addressing discrete factual aspects of the burdened party's preceding case, discussion of that evidence should be integrated into the defense counsel's preceding "Comment on the Opponent's Case." In this situation, and also when the defense presents no evidence at all, the defense attorney will not devote separate arguments to either "Transitional Remarks" or "Comments on the Advocate's Case." He should proceed instead directly to delivering his "Concluding Remarks."

Comment on the Opponent's Case

As we have noted throughout this book, the jury expects the advocate to expose the shortcomings of his opponent's case. In mounting the attack, however, the advocate must avoid the appearance of creating a "straw man." To accomplish this, the advocate must limit criticism of the opponent's case to matters that the opponent has put into issue.

This book has demonstrated that virtually any action of opposing counsel—even a solitary question posed on cross-examination—may qualify as a subject matter for attack. Thus, before developing a plan for criticizing the opponent's case, the advocate should carefully review notes containing his record of opposing counsel's statements, questions to witnesses, and evidence introduced. So long as opposing counsel put a matter in issue by one of these three means, the advocate should consider it a candidate for use in his attack, regardless of—indeed, as we show, often because of—how little the matter bears on the dispute.

The rule here, which mirrors the rule of using only strong evidence, is to inflict all rhetorical blows that outweigh the sponsorship costs of doing so. In this regard, the advocate need not be concerned that his rhetorical attack on the opponent's case will alienate the jury. As we have stated, the jury expects it.[34]

One final preliminary point should be made. As previously noted,[35] the advocate should strive to minimize reliance on any one item of his own evidence. By contrast, the advocate will want to argue to the maximum extent possible that the opponent *needed* each item of evidence to have any chance of winning.

The advocate, however, should be especially mindful not to attribute the opponent's actions to opposing counsel's *beliefs* about the quality of the evidence presented at trial. Thus, if the opponent has called a strong witness and a weak one, the advocate cannot state:

> Mr. Smith called that second witness [the weak one] because he obviously believed that the first one was not sufficient.[36]

Rather, assuming no governing authorities to the contrary, the advocate should argue along the following lines:

> My opponent had no choice but to call that second witness: the first was not sufficient.

The Opponent's Evidence

Minimizing the Significance of the Opponent's Strong Evidence

The advocate must at some point in his argument address the question of what weight the jury should give to the opponent's strong evidence. The advocate cannot simply ignore that evidence, since the jury will be waiting to hear his views on the matter. If the advocate is silent on the issue, they will be apt, in the worst-case scenario, to take his silence as a concession that he has no explanation and that the evidence can properly be given great weight.[37]

---

34 As previously noted, such pointed advocacy has ancient antecedents. Scholars have suggested, for example, that Demosthenes' speech *On the Crown* is "the masterpiece … of the spoken word" notwithstanding his devastating charges against his opponent. Kennedy [*Greece*], *supra* n. 16, at 229. *See also* II Jebb [1962], *supra* n. 7, at 304 (describing Demosthenes's approach of not arguing in a "stately manner" but rather "at close quarters, with the grip as of wrestlers").

35 *See* pages 205 to 206, *supra*.

36 The personal opinions and beliefs of counsel may not be shared with the jury. *See generally* Model Code of Professional Responsibility, DR 7-106(C)(4) (providing that an attorney must not "[a]ssert his personal opinion as to the justness of a cause, as to the credibility of a witness, … or as to the guilt or innocence of an accused; but he may argue, on his analysis of the evidence, for any position or conclusion with respect to the matters stated herein.").

37 *See* page 188, n. 17, *supra*.

Thus, the advocate must state his client's best case position regarding the opponent's strong evidence. Above all, he must exploit whatever shortcomings there are in the evidence. Specifically, he should emphasize any concession or admission suggested by the evidence.

If the evidence is testimonial in nature, the summation must exploit and emphasize whatever theory the advocate used on cross-examination to show that the witness did not harm his case.[38] After showing that the witness does not warrant a verdict in the opponent's favor, the advocate should, where appropriate, emphasize the opponent's heavy reliance on the witness. When that witness is the only witness whom the opponent called to establish the point on which he testified, the advocate should emphasize the absence of corroboration. If the facts permit, the advocate should argue that the opponent's proof boils down to a "one-witness" case. And where the opponent has introduced multiple items of evidence, the advocate should point out that the opponent needs every single item to win, and that even the totality of that evidence falls far short.

Although the advocate must address the opponent's strongest evidence and contentions, he should minimize efforts in refuting them. Too much effort expended in discussing the opponent's strongest evidence can overly emphasize it and result in a harmful concession of the materiality of the advocate's weak counterpoints. He should also avoid dealing with it at either the outset of his address or at the end of the argument. The jury typically assumes that the advocate devotes the greatest attention to preparing his first and last remarks on any topic. The jury is also normally at its most attentive at the beginning of the advocate's address. Thus, the optimal point to mention the opponent's strong evidence or contentions is somewhere in the middle of the argument.[39]

---

38 The method for determining the theory for undercutting a witness was described in Chapter Eleven, pages 185 to 186, *supra*.

39 Demosthenes followed the same practice. In *On the Crown*, a proceeding on whether to award Demosthenes a golden crown for his service to the state, his opponent, who argued first, called on Demosthenes to deal in his own argument first with the opponent's strongest contentions—two points about the legality of the prospective award. *See Orations of Demosthenes* 373–375 (Colonial Press 1900). At the outset of his argument Demosthenes refused, calling it "but just, that [he] first speak a few words" about other less powerful contentions his opponent had advanced, "most of them the grossest falsehoods, ... [so] that none of [the audience] be influenced by matters foreign to the cause." *Id.* at 405. Demosthenes then dealt with these weaker contentions of his opponent at length, returning later to dispute only briefly the opponent's stronger contentions, after which he turned immediately to other matters. *See generally Demosthenes' Public Orations* 314–316 (Everyman's Library 1966) (providing paragraph-by-paragraph synopsis of *On the Crown*).

Criticizing the Opponent's Introduction of Less-Than-Strong Evidence

One of the most important portions of an advocate's closing argument will be the discussion of the opponent's less-than-strong evidence. If the opponent is unacquainted with sponsorship considerations, he probably will have marshaled less-than-strong exhibits and elicited less-than-strong testimony. As the next several sections reveal, the advocate can benefit enormously by highlighting this less-than-strong evidence.[40] (While the following sections discuss highlighting such less-than-strong evidence, the advocate also should not overlook opportunities, as we have suggested at various points in this book, to tax his opponent with overtrying costs for pursuing inconsistent or less-than-strong alternative *theories.*[41])

Less-Than-Strong Favorable Evidence

If the opponent has introduced any favorable evidence that is less-than-strong, the advocate should challenge him in summation to explain how such evidence materially advances his case and, if it fails to do so, why he introduced it at all. The advocate should consider suggesting to the jury the "obvious reason" such meager evidence was introduced: the weakness of the opponent's other evidence. The advocate can then note that the additional evidence obviously does not "shore up" the opponent's case.[42]

Less-Than-Strong Elaborate Exhibits

Where opposing counsel has introduced an elaborate exhibit, the advocate should first determine whether the effort undertaken to prepare the exhibit was warranted by some legitimate need, such as to aid in the jury's understanding of the case. If so, the advocate should not criticize it merely because it is elaborate. If, however, no such justification for the exhibit exists, the advocate should note opposing counsel's efforts in having prepared it, pointing out that it did nothing to advance the opponent's case and certainly did not justify the effort spent in putting it together.

---

40 *Cf.* II Jebb [1962], *supra* n. 7, at 286 (noting that Isaeus customarily placed "the stress of the assault precisely on the enemy's weakest point and assail[ed] it with blow upon blow").

41 *See, e.g.*, pages 39 to 40, *supra*.

42 Again, prior to making any such argument, the advocate must ensure that no rule prohibits it. Moreover, the prosecutor must be especially mindful not to violate the rule prohibiting suggestions that a criminal defendant has a burden of proof to meet.

Less-Than-Strong Scientific Evidence or Expert Testimony

Where the opponent has introduced less-than-strong scientific evidence or expert testimony, the advocate should stress to the jury that the opponent's other evidence alone fell short and that the opponent therefore needed corroborative scientific evidence or expert testimony. The advocate should consider challenging the opponent to demonstrate how the opponent's scientific evidence or expert testimony provided the necessary corroboration.

The Witness Who Fails to Deliver

The opportunity to attack an opponent for producing a witness who performs poorly on direct examination will not arise frequently, since the opponent and his witness will have presumably taken great care to rehearse the examination prior to trial. Occasionally, however, a witness testifies without proper preparation. Moreover, even the most well-rehearsed witness can occasionally disappoint the attorney who called him. This is particularly likely on cross-examination, where the witness may not have anticipated or thought about a particular line of questioning. Whenever an opponent's witness does not perform well, the advocate can profit by highlighting that fact in summation.

For instance, assume that an accomplice agrees to provide testimony favorable to the government as part of a plea bargain. If he is called by the prosecutor in the expectation—perhaps announced to the jury—that he will "finger" the defendant, and if he fails to do so in whole or in part, defense counsel should stress to the jury that the evidence the prosecutor needed to win was not forthcoming. Defense counsel should also point out that, however distasteful the use of the accomplice might have been to the prosecutor, the government had no choice but to rely on him in light of the weakness of its other evidence. The defense should consider further noting that such reliance was ultimately misplaced, since the accomplice did not salvage what was otherwise an inadequate case.

When an opponent's witness fails to deliver, the advocate should emphasize, if he can, that the witness's testimony was consistent with the advocate's case. In these circumstances, if the advocate was able to elicit anything favorable on cross-examination, he should state that, had the jurors not known otherwise, they would have concluded that the witness was called by the advocate.

If the damaged witness was central to the opponent's case, the tactic of dramatizing the witness's failure to perform will be even more powerful. Perhaps because of television dramas, certain colloquialisms can serve to exploit the opponent's sponsorship costs. An example is the term "star witness." This term, conjuring up the notion of a "top billing," connotes a witness who is called to provide critical support to the case. If the opponent called such a witness and the witness was severely damaged by the advocate's cross-examination, the advocate should consider referring to him in summation as the opponent's "star witness." This term not only emphasizes the opponent's reliance on the witness but also enhances the impact of the witness's lackluster performance on cross-examination.

The advocate, of course, will want to highlight any gains he made in cross-examining the witness. This is true whether his gain was in eliciting evidence helpful to his own case or simply in eliciting testimony that undermined the witness's direct examination.

Exploiting the Opponent's Use of Neutral Evidence

The advocate should be alert to any opportunity to make an effective argument based on the opponent's use of neutral evidence. As we have noted,[43] when the opponent introduces evidence that is neutral, the jury will be puzzled as to why he did so. It may view the opponent as implicitly telling it that the item of neutral evidence is important to his case. Yet, this message will confuse the jury, since the evidence will not appear to advance the opponent's case. It is critical for the advocate to use his summation to exploit the jury's bewilderment over the opponent's use of such evidence.

The trial recounted in Chapter Four involving the pistol found near the defendant's feet illustrates the point.[44] In that case, the prosecutor introduced testimony regarding the arresting officer's submission of the pistol for fingerprint analysis because the test turned up no fingerprints adequate for comparison purposes. The message unwittingly communicated to the jury was that if the pistol had turned up fingerprints matching anyone but the defendant, his other proof would have been called into doubt. Specifically, if the *absence* of the fingerprints of a third person was important for the jury to know, then the *presence* of such fingerprints might have meant that the

43 *See* pages 63 to 65, *supra*.

44 *See* pages 64 to 65, *supra*.

government would not even have brought the case. The message was, in other words, that the police officer was a weak witness.

To maximize the prospects that the jury in such a case will reach this conclusion, the advocate may wish to argue along the following lines:

> When the prosecutor made a point out of questioning the arresting officer about his having submitted the pistol for fingerprint analysis, you must have asked yourselves: why is that fact significant? And that's a critical question, ladies and gentlemen. The answer is that, under the most charitable view of the evidence, the prosecutor's case is hanging by a thread. If the fact that no one else's fingerprints were recovered is so important to his case, isn't that because his case would have collapsed had such fingerprints been discovered? And if that is so, it can only mean that the evidence linking the defendant to the gun is extremely weak. Had the gun been in the defendant's pocket, he wouldn't have *cared* whose prints were on it.

It is difficult to conceive of any persuasive rebuttal to the foregoing argument. The prosecutor would score no points by suggesting that the officer, in attempting to locate fingerprints, was just trying to develop more evidence against the defendant. Even the argument that he was just following police procedures is problematic. Logically, this could only mean that the importance of matching fingerprints has been institutionally recognized by the government. The only means of foreclosing this kind of criticism is by carefully avoiding any endorsement of the significance of neutral evidence.

One technique for enhancing the damage to the opponent when he introduces neutral evidence is to highlight the anticipation when the opponent's witness took the stand and then to note the surprise the jury must have felt when it heard the neutral testimony. Assume, for example, that a defendant charged with causing an accident by running a stop sign calls as a witness a hitchhiker who was a passenger at the time of the accident. Assume further that the hitchhiker testifies that he fell asleep in the car and therefore could not comment on whether the defendant ran the stop sign. Plaintiff's lawyer could argue as follows:

> When the hitchhiker took the stand, you must have thought, "Here it comes, the bombshell, the witness who will corrobo-

> rate the defendant's claim that he came to a full stop at the stop sign." You must have been shocked when the hitchhiker said that he was asleep and therefore didn't see anything.

Even if defense counsel warned the jury in opening statement that the hitchhiker would not provide useful testimony, plaintiff's lawyer can still employ a variant of the above argument:

> You must have thought, when you heard the defense attorney say in opening statement that one of his witnesses was asleep at the time, that you had misunderstood his statement. And when the hitchhiker took the stand, you must have thought, "Now I'll be able to see if I heard correctly." And you must have been relieved but puzzled to learn that there was nothing wrong with your hearing, only with the defendant's case.

Under either scenario, the advocate may also wish to challenge defense counsel to explain in his summation why he called a witness who had nothing helpful to say. As we previously indicated,[45] the defense attorney will rarely have a convincing reply.

Highlighting the Opponent's Harmful Evidence

A witness or item of evidence presented by the opponent will sometimes constitute evidence that is unfavorable to the opponent's case. Indeed, if the opponent adheres to the conventional wisdom of volunteering his own weaknesses,[46] his case is likely to contain an assortment of weaknesses that he deliberately volunteered. The opponent's case may also contain unanticipated weaknesses. In either case, the advocate should exploit such weaknesses to his full advantage in the manner recommended in earlier chapters.[47]

Highlighting the Implausibility of the Opponent's Version of the Facts

If the opponent's case is based on a series of implausible events, the advocate should point out the "amazing coincidences" that must have occurred under that version of events. This would be true, for example, where the

45 *See* pages 216 to 217, *supra.*

46 *See* pages 78 to 85, *supra.*

47 *See, e.g.*, pages 3 to 4, *supra.*

defendant is claiming misidentification in a robbery case, even though he was apprehended near the scene of the crime dressed in clothing identical to that of the assailant (as described by the victim). The prosecutor can point out that, for the defendant to be the wrong person, all of the following must be true: (1) the defendant had a look-alike in town, (2) the two people had identical clothing, (3) the two people were on the same block at the same time dressed in that identical clothing, and (4) the look-alike (that is, the assailant) must have left the area just before the police arrived, since the police, having thoroughly canvassed the area, saw only one person—the defendant—who matched the description.

Evidence That the Opponent Failed to Produce: Unfulfilled Promises in Opening Statement

A widely used tactic to discredit an opponent is to show that he overstated his case in his opening statement.[48] The sponsorship method endorses that tactic. By discussing particular evidence and making specific contentions in his opening statement, an opponent will normally have conceded the materiality of that evidence and those contentions to the verdict. Thus, if opposing counsel did not fulfill a promise regarding what his evidence would show, the advocate can use the opponent's own words to impress upon the jury how much stronger the opponent's case could have been.

The opponent obviously will not concede that his failure to marshal the evidence is fatal to his case. Yet, if opposing counsel contends that his remaining evidence is sufficient, the jury will wonder why he made such a point of promising to produce the other evidence. And if the opponent goes further and claims that the evidence that he failed to produce is irrelevant, the jury will wonder why the opponent bothered to mention it at all. Accordingly, where appropriate, the advocate should seize upon his opponent's unproven assertions and argue that the opponent's actual evidence is insufficient.

Comparing the Opponent's Case to a Hypothetically Strong One

In order to emphasize the lack of strength of the opponent's case, the advocate should compare it, if possible, with a hypothetically strong one. This will focus the

48 *See, e.g.,* T. Mauet *Trial Techniques*, § 4.3, at 69 (Aspen Publishers 7th ed. 2007)("Your opponent during closing arguments will in all likelihood point out each [representation in opening statement] that you failed to deliver on.").

jury's attention on evidence the opponent was unable to produce. For example, in a case involving a burglary of a store, where the defendant was apprehended by police a block away with a television set taken from the store, defense counsel should stress, among other things, the lack of fingerprints lifted from the scene and the absence of eyewitnesses placing his client at the scene of the burglary itself.

A note of caution is in order, however. Where the difference in strength between the opponent's case and a hypothetically strong case is insubstantial, the advocate's representation of the latter as strong may serve to ratify the strength of the former. Thus, this strategy will not work when the opponent has a very strong case.

Arguments Based on Missing Evidence

The foregoing section emphasized the need to discuss hypothetically how much stronger the opponent's case could have been if other evidence, such as a corroborative witness, had been available. This section, by contrast, focuses on the value of commenting on an opponent's failure to use evidence that was *in fact* available to him.

There are two fundamental ways to criticize the opponent's failure to use available evidence. The first is merely to note that the opponent's presentation did not include the particular item of evidence.[49] The message the jury will get is that the opponent's case could have been stronger than it is.

The second type of comment is to urge the jury to infer that the omitted evidence is *adverse* to the opponent's case. This argument, as we have noted,[50] will not be persuasive where the advocate could have used the evidence himself. Indeed, missing evidence case law prohibits the advocate from urging an adverse inference from an opponent's non-production of evidence absent a demonstration that the evidence was uniquely available to the opponent.[51] Accordingly, the advocate should always consider whether he can productively—and lawfully—urge such an adverse inference when the opponent has failed to introduce certain evidence. To determine whether the argument is permissible, the advocate must consult his jurisdiction's applicable missing evidence case law.

49 Juries are often explicitly instructed that the absence of corroboration is a factor bearing on the assessment of credibility. *See generally* O'Malley, Grenig & Lee, *supra* n. 29, § 15.01, at 364. A sample argument of this type is set forth in Chapter Five, page 104, *supra*.

50 *See* pages 49 to 50, *supra*.

51 *See* page 101, n. 21, *supra* (setting forth requirements of missing evidence doctrine).

Finally, assuming that the requirements for urging an adverse inference are met, the advocate should seek to have the court give a missing evidence instruction.[52] If the court agrees to do so, the advocate should emphasize *the court's* recognition that the jury may draw an adverse inference from the opponent's failure to call the witness in question.

The Opponent's Statements

Overview

This section describes how an advocate can use his opponent's remarks as potential concessions. Such remarks include not only opening statement and closing argument but questions of counsel as well.

Opening Statement and Closing Argument

As noted above,[53] the advocate can use his opponent's promises in opening statement whenever the evidence fails to comport with those promises. Other benefits can also be obtained from carefully monitoring the opponent's opening and closing remarks.

To begin with, any explicit concession made by the opponent about a weakness in his case—such as a credibility problem with one of his witnesses—should be highlighted in the advocate's summation. By the same token, any admission by the opponent about the strength of the advocate's case should be stressed. Furthermore, indications that the opponent is advancing alternative theories or has abandoned a theory may be worth emphasizing.[54] For example, if the opponent advances a particular theory in opening statement and then advances a totally different theory in closing argument, this substitution of theories should be highlighted.

The advocate should also pay careful attention to what the opponent does *not* say in closing argument. For instance, if the opponent offered lengthy testimony from a witness and then failed to mention that witness in his summation, the advocate can point out that the opponent is apparently no longer relying on the witness. Where the advocate discredited the witness during cross-examination, he can give the "obvious" reason why the opponent did not mention him: because the witness was rendered totally useless in light of the cross-examination.

52 *See* pages 51 to 52, *supra*.

53 *See* page 218, *supra*.

54 *See* page 172, *supra* (discussing how to identify and exploit the opponent's theory of the case).

Questions of Counsel

While an opponent's opening statement occasionally provides good grist for attacking his case, the opponent's questions to witnesses during direct examination and cross-examination frequently provide an even stronger basis for attack. This is because the opponent, perhaps mindful of the dangers of overstatement in opening statements, normally takes much greater care in crafting his opening statement to avoid overextending himself. While he may also take pains in planning direct examination, many of his questions on cross-examination are likely to be spontaneous and ill-considered. Thus, questions that the opponent asks on cross-examination often provide an even more fertile ground for criticism than those posed on direct examination.

An advocate should recognize that even one ill-considered question by the opponent can provide the basis for highlighting the opponent's inconsistent theories. For instance, in an assault case tried by one of the authors, defense counsel acknowledged in opening statement that his client had injured the complainant, but claimed that it was in self-defense. Defense counsel later cross-examined an eyewitness who was only a short distance from the incident and asked questions suggesting that the assailant was someone other than the defendant. For instance, he sought to get the witness to concede that the assailant was considerably taller than the defendant. The prosecutor highlighted these inconsistent theories in summation, asking rhetorically why defense counsel would pose such questions if, as he conceded in opening, it was his client—not another, taller person—who injured the complainant. He then suggested that perhaps the defense was forced to abandon the self-defense theory in favor of a misidentification theory because the evidence of self-defense turned out to be so weak.[55]

An attorney attempting to explain questions raising an inconsistent theory will not want to argue that he merely asked those questions without thinking or that he was wasting the jury's time on an irrelevant matter. Yet, the attorney also will not want to concede that he is advancing inconsistent theories. Such careless questions place the examiner in a dilemma and serve only to suggest that he really has no legitimate theory.

---

55 A prosecutor who is considering such an argument must exercise caution. If, because of unusual facts in a case, the change from one theory to another is consistent with innocence, a court may question the propriety of such an argument. *See, e.g.*, United States v. Sblendorio, 830 F.2d 1382, 1394–1395 (7th Cir. 1987).

Using the opponent's questions to demonstrate that he is espousing inconsistent or alternative theories is but one benefit of the device. In some circumstances, an opponent's questions can also be used to demonstrate that the opponent is relying on a highly improbable explanation of the evidence. For example, in a case tried by one of the authors, the police arrested several joyriding teenagers in a vehicle after discovering narcotics in plain view. At trial, one of the defense attorneys indignantly asked the arresting officer whether he knew that the vehicle belonged to the *mother* of one of the defendants. The prosecutor used this question in summation to argue that the only defense theory for how the drugs got into the car was the absurd one that the mother had left them there in plain view when she loaned the car to her son.

Where the opponent's questions seek to establish less-than-strong points, the advocate should remind the jury of that unproductive examination. For example, when appropriate, the advocate can point out that the opponent vigorously cross-examined the witness on minor points but carefully avoided any question going to the heart of the dispute. The advocate can assert that the witness's testimony remains unchallenged on the crucial issues. The advocate should not allow the opponent's persistence in attempting to establish a minor point—whether successful or not—to escape the notice of the jury.

Considerations When the Defense Puts on No Evidence

As noted in Chapter Ten,[56] an advocate can criticize the opponent's theory even when the opponent has not put on any evidence.[57] The problem is in identifying that theory when the opponent does not articulate any theory in his opening statement. Related to the prior section, one way to do so is through the opponent's questions to witnesses. A case tried by one of the authors illustrates the point.

The defendant was charged with possessing several tin-foil-wrapped packets of an illegal narcotic substance. According to the government's evidence—which consisted of the observations of a single police officer at 3 a.m. on a dark night in a high-drug area—the defendant threw down a bag of tin foil objects and ran off when he saw the police. At the out-

56 *See* page 172, *supra*.

57 As noted (*see* page 172, n. 4, *supra*), the prosecutor in a criminal case must not state or in any way suggest that the defense has any obligation to put on evidence.

set of the trial, the most probable defense theory appeared to be that the officer did not see the defendant throw down anything, and that the drugs must have already been on the ground (or, worse, planted by the police). Defense counsel, however, had not identified any theory in his opening statement.

During his cross-examination of the police officer, defense counsel asked the officer whether he was aware that a local fast food restaurant sold small, foil-wrapped corn on the cob. The prosecutor used this question as a theme in his closing argument. He pointed out that defense counsel's question could advance only one conceivable defense theory: that the defendant threw down corn on the cob late at night, in a high-narcotics area. This theory was extremely favorable to the prosecution. Assuming no police fabrication, the jury could find for the defendant only if it concluded that (1) a bag of valuable drugs just happened to be on the ground right where the tin-foil-wrapped corn was supposedly dropped; (2) the officer saw *only* the drugs on the ground, not a bag of corn on the cob as well; (3) the defendant was present in a high-drug area late at night solely to buy corn on the cob; and (4) the defendant felt compelled to "ditch" the corn on the cob and flee when he saw the police.

Having posed such an ill-advised question, defense counsel could not challenge the prosecutor's characterization of the defense theory without admitting that he was simply "fishing" and had no firm theory. Moreover, by carelessly posing the question, defense counsel had undermined his chances for advancing a more credible theory: that the officer, eager to make a case, was mistaken or lying in asserting that the defendant had thrown down *any* object. The fact that something had been thrown down was implicitly conceded in the defense counsel's question. His careless and damaging question illustrates the principle that there is no such thing as a "free" question.

Concluding Remarks

The advocate's summation should end on a note of strength and confidence. The advocate should not merely ask the jury to "render a fair verdict," "do justice," or "do the right thing." Rather, he should conclude by asking unequivocally for a verdict in his client's favor on each of the claims or counts of the indictment. As is true throughout the trial,[58] concluding remarks are no place for modesty or understatement.

Moreover, an argument that does not ask for a ruling in the advocate's favor invites the following response:

> Significantly, my opponent did not ask for a verdict in his favor. He simply asked you to do what is "just" without saying which verdict would be the just one. I, on the other hand, submit unequivocally that there is only one just verdict in this case—a verdict in favor of my client.

There is no reason to invite this kind of reply.

Many advocates, in preparing closing argument, include comments designed to arouse sympathy for their client's position or antipathy towards their opponent. While such remarks may be considered proper if they have a foundation in the evidence,[59] the advocate must understand the sponsorship costs of arguments based on emotion. Most significantly, because of the cost of overtrying, when an advocate makes arguments based on sympathy, the jury is apt to give less weight to the advocate's arguments based on the cold facts.[60] In our view, comments based on emotion should be employed cautiously, if at all, and only after a careful analysis of the applicable sponsorship costs. These costs are apt to be at their lowest when the advocate's case is weak on the merits. By contrast, these costs are apt to be very high when the advocate's evidence is compelling.

Rebuttal Arguments

In General

This section provides guidance on how to rebut the opponent's closing argument. This guidance applies not only to prosecutors and plaintiffs' attorneys, who in many jurisdictions are afforded a formal opportunity to

58 *See* pages 17 to 20; pages 135 to 136; and page 197, *supra.*

59 *See, e.g.,* J. Stein, *Closing Argument* § 22, at 1-58 (Callaghan & Co. 1989) (arguments appealing to the jury's "sympathy" are permissible if based on the evidence).

60 An advocate's excessive reliance on emotional appeal permits the following well-known argument by his opponent (attribution unknown):

When you don't have the facts, you pound the law. When you don't have the law, you pound the facts. And when you don't have either, you pound the table.

deliver a rebuttal argument, but also to defense lawyers, who must rebut their opponent's contentions in the defense summation.

General Principles

An important implication of sponsorship analysis is that an advocate must rebut all of the opponent's substantial arguments if he can. The jury will be waiting to hear the advocate's response, and his failure to give one may lead it to conclude that the contention was unanswerable and thus conceded.[61] Although this point may seem obvious, a number of commentators give just the opposite advice.[62]

A few points bear special emphasis. First, it is extremely important for the advocate to anticipate what the opponent will argue during the summation. When an advocate fails to focus in advance on the opponent's likely argument, he may find that the best rebuttal remarks do not occur to him until after the trial is over. If the advocate has faithfully recorded the opponent's opening remarks and questions on direct and cross-examination, a careful reading of these notes will frequently enable the advocate to predict what the opponent will say in his summation.

Second, while the advocate should be reluctant to concede anything in his own argument relating to the disputed issues, he should seize upon any such concession by the opponent. In addition, he should correct any misstatements of law or fact that might affect the jury's verdict.

Finally, where appropriate, the advocate should explain why the opponent's arguments do not help resolve the case in his favor. The use of the phrase, "Imagine what he'd be saying if..." is often an effective way to preface such an attack. For instance, if the opponent argues that, because the advocate's witnesses corroborate each other so well, the advocate's case is "too strong, too neat—they obviously got their story together,"[63] the advocate can respond as follows: "Imagine what he'd be saying if my witnesses had contradicted each other." By the same token, if the opponent criticizes the advocate's case for inconsistencies in testimony, the advocate can respond, "Imagine what he'd be saying if they all matched perfectly. He'd say, 'It's too strong, too neat.'" It is surprising how often this technique

61 *See* page 188, n. 17, *supra*.

62 *See, e.g.*, J. Sonsteng, R. Haydock, & J. Boyd, *The Trial Book* § 10.6, at 337 (West 1984) ("It is not wise to spend significant portions of the closing argument responding to the opponent's issues, positions, and argument.").

63 *See, e.g.*, Bailey & Rothblatt, *supra* n. 28, § 22:4, at 498 (suggesting an "attack [of the prosecutor's case] for its perfection and strength").

can be employed to neutralize or even belittle the opponent's contentions. This technique works, however, only where (1) the opponent is relying on certain facts to prove a point (in the above example, consistency in the testimony of several witnesses to show their lack of veracity), and (2) the absence of those same facts could plausibly be argued to prove the same point (the *inconsistencies* in the testimony of the witnesses to show their lack of veracity). An advocate should, of course, test his own arguments before making them to see if they can survive the "imagine what he'd be saying if" test.

Countering the Opponent's Criticism for Not Introducing Harmful Evidence

It is a textbook argument to attack the opposing advocate for failing to bring out evidence unfavorable to his case. Consider, for example, an advocate's failure to bring out his client's prior murder conviction. The opponent could argue along the following lines:

> Ladies and Gentlemen of the Jury, do you recall how I had to bring out the full facts on cross-examination? The fact of the matter is: if I hadn't brought out the defendant's murder conviction, you never would have heard about it. Evidently that's how my opponent wanted it—why else would he have omitted evidence of his client's conviction in his presentation? Perhaps his strategy was a recognition that you would not render a favorable verdict if you heard all of the evidence. Plainly, consideration of the *full* story—*all* of the evidence—requires a verdict in my client's favor.

This can be a powerful argument. Many would use such an argument to make the opposing counsel look unfair or, at the very least, to highlight the opponent's apparent efforts in omitting the evidence.[64] Whatever its rationale, this criticism for omitting harmful evidence is presumably a major reason why the conventional wisdom advises an advocate to introduce evidence harmful to his case.

If the advocate has adhered to sponsorship principles in *omitting* a

64 *See, e.g.*, Bailey & Rothblatt, *supra* n. 28, § 22.3, at 498 ("[A] reason for highlighting favorable cross-examination is to show the unfairness of the case against the defendant. Argue that it was up to the prosecution to present the entire picture. Instead you had to coax the prosecution witness to reveal the whole truth . . . .").

harmful item, he will have concluded that the decision was warranted notwithstanding any loss of attorney credibility or any "sting" resulting from his apparent efforts to omit the matter.

Of course, the advocate cannot ignore the criticism. He must respond, justifying the omission and, if he can, taxing his opponent with the sponsorship costs his opponent incurred in eliciting the matter.

For example, in the case of a defense lawyer who did not bring out his client's prior criminal conviction, that lawyer could argue as follows:

> Ladies and Gentlemen of the Jury, my opponent has suggested that the fact that I did not bring out my client's prior criminal conviction somehow suggests that I didn't think you'd render a verdict in my favor if you heard it. That is simply wrong. I wasn't trying to *hide* something from you. I obviously knew that my opponent could bring it out if I didn't. I didn't bring it out because it's a cheap shot. The prosecutor wouldn't be making such a big deal out of my client's past if he had a solid case for conviction *this* time.[65]

As the above discussion reveals, the defense attorney who does not volunteer a harmful matter in his client's case can argue with credibility that the matter is not important to the verdict. By contrast, the conventional wisdom's approach of volunteering weaknesses would leave the defense in a troublesome situation. The prosecutor could argue:

> Even the defense lawyer concedes that his client's prior conviction is important to his credibility. Why else would he bring it out instead of waiting for me to do so?

Since the jury assumes that an advocate puts on only his best case, it will likely agree with the prosecutor's suggestion that the defense counsel's tactic was unusual. And if the jury does agree, it will be apt to give the weakness heightened weight. The best the defense lawyer could say in response would be:

> That conviction has nothing to do with this case. I just wanted you to hear all of the evidence so you would see that, even with

65 As the actual courtroom example recounted in Chapter One reflects, many juries will agree that eliciting such a prior conviction is a "cheap shot." *See* page 4, n. 2 *supra*, citing Allison, *Witness Preparation from the Criminal Defense Perspective,* 30 Tex. Tech. L. Rev. 1333, 1339 (1999).

> the prior conviction, the only reasonable verdict in this case is "not guilty."

This type of argument will not help the defense. The jury will most likely see two messages contained in such an argument: (1) that defense counsel is conceding the harmfulness of the conviction, and (2) that he is urging that his evidence is nonetheless sufficient to support a verdict of not guilty. As predicted by sponsorship analysis, the jury will be apt to credit the former and heavily discount the latter.

As this chapter has revealed, closing argument is the key to capitalizing on the principles of sponsorship analysis. If the advocate's opponent has failed to follow sponsorship doctrine, he will learn the hard way—as a result of the advocate's summation—that every ill-advised question or comment and every item of less-than-strong evidence has its costs. At the same time, if the advocate has followed sponsorship principles in presenting his own case, he will minimize his exposure to damaging arguments from the opponent.

Epilogue

This book has demonstrated that sponsorship principles permeate all aspects of a jury trial. At bottom, the purpose has been to explain how the sponsorship method can win trials. The book has also shown that the sponsorship of almost any item of evidence has a cost. Similarly, there is no such thing as a "free" argument, objection, or question. By understanding sponsorship principles, an advocate will be able to eliminate less-than-strong evidence and keep the focus of his presentation on the points that matter.

It should be no secret that the utility of the sponsorship method is not limited to the trial setting. The same detailed principles can, in varying degrees, serve to guide the appellate attorney, the negotiator, the salesman, and the politician. More generally, the sponsorship principles identified in this book dominate the rhetoric of *any* interested speaker, regardless of whether he faces an opponent. This is because any interested speaker is ultimately viewed as an effort-minimizing advocate striving to make his best presentation.

Significantly, however, sponsorship principles apply not only to the rhetoric of the *interested* advocate but also to that of the *disinterested* speaker. For instance, because of the listener's assumption of effort-minimization, the disinterested speaker stands to reap significant *benefits* of efforts by using favorable evidence. After all, a speaker who has no personal stake in the outcome is not apt to go out of his way to sponsor something unless it was "worth the effort." In short, this book's teaching, which recognizes the effects of sponsorship, reaches all rhetoric.

It is important for the courtroom advocate to understand that the sponsorship method is not a panacea. Obviously, the most important factor in any case is the strength of the evidence. An attorney with a compelling case who is employing the conventional wisdom may prevail over an attorney with a weak case who is employing sponsorship. Accordingly, there is no substitute for thorough investigation and fact-finding to uncover all evidence that is helpful to the advocate's case.

Moreover, these sponsorship techniques assume a grasp of the basics of logical argumentation as a means of persuasion. Such facility at argumentation is treated as a point of departure.

In addition, on rare occasions juries will decide cases on wholly irrational grounds, such as the personalities of the attorneys. And juries in different parts of the country may react differently to the same type of case. Where such factors predominate, sponsorship may have reduced impact.

For many of the above areas—such as strength of the case and personalities of the lawyers—the advocate has little or no control. For example, once the advocate has completed a thorough factual investigation, he is "stuck" with his facts. Similarly, the advocate cannot change his personality or ensure against a runaway jury. The one aspect of trial strategy he *can* control, however, is whether to apply the sponsorship method. And we have found that the benefits from applying that method are considerable.

Most significantly, even weak cases can be won using sponsorship principles. Similarly, such principles can serve as an insurance policy to ensure that a strong case is not needlessly lost because of an unnecessary strategy blunder, such as overtrying the case.

While the application of the sponsorship method can reap immediate benefits for the advocate, it might also have a salutary effect on our judicial system as a whole. If advocates were to apply sponsorship techniques on a widespread basis, trials would be shorter and more to the point. Advocates would understand the costs of overtrying cases. Marginal and irrelevant witnesses would be dispensed with. Elaborate but irrelevant exhibits would not be prepared and used. In addition, because trials would be less cluttered and more focused, the length of jury deliberations would inevitably decrease. Moreover, since each advocate's purpose would be to show the jury his client's best case and the opponent's worst case, a major goal of the adversary system—to promote the search for truth—would be advanced.

Bibliography

Books

American Bar Association, Standards Relating to the Prosecution Function and the Defense Function (1971)

American Bar Association, Standards for Criminal Justice (2d ed. 1980)

Amsterdam, A., B. Segal & M. Miller, *Trial Manual for the Defense of Criminal Cases* (Amer. Law. Inst. 1984)

Appleman, J., *Preparation and Trial* (Coiner Pub., Ltd. 1967)

Appleman, J., *Successful Jury Trials* (Coiner Pub., Ltd. 1952)

Aristotle, *The Rhetoric, translated in The Complete Works of Aristotle,* Barnes ed. (Princeton Univ. Press 1984)

Aron, R., J. Fast & R. Klein, *Trial Communication Skills* (Shephard's/McGraw-Hill, Inc. 1986)

Bailey, F. & H. Rothblatt, *Successful Techniques for Criminal Trials* (Lawyers Co-op Pub. Co. 1985)

Bentham, J., *Rationale of Judicial Evidence* (Bowring ed. 1827)

Berger, M., J. Mitchell & R. Clark, *Trial Advocacy: Planning, Analysis & Strategy* (Little, Brown & Co. 1989)

Bergman, P., *Trial Advocacy* (West 1979)

Broun, K., G. Dix, E. Imwinkelried, D. Kaye & R. Mosteller, *McCormick on Evidence* (West 6th ed. 2006)

Busch, F.X., *Law and Tactics in Jury Trials* (Bobbs-Merrill Co., Inc. 1959)

Carlson, R. & E. Imwinkelried, *Dynamics of Trial Practice: Problems and Materials* (West 3d ed. 2002)

Carlson, R., *Successful Techniques for Civil Trials* (Lawyers Co-op Pub. Co. 1992)

Caro, R., *The Years of Lyndon Johnson: The Path to Power* (Alfred A. Knopf 1983)
Castiglione, B., *The Book of the Courtier* (Penguin Classics 1976)
Clark, J., *Preparation of Cross-Examination* (P.L.I. 1946)
The Collected Works of Abraham Lincoln (R. Basler ed. 1953)
Cover, R., O. Fiss & J. Resnik, *Procedure* (Foundation Press, Inc. 1988)
Criminal Jury Instructions, District of Columbia (2002 ed.)
Decof, L., *Art of Advocacy: Opening Statement* (LexisNexis 2006)
Demosthenes' Public Orations (Everyman's Library 1966)
Dixit, A.K., *Optimization in Economic Theory* (Oxford Univ. Press 1976)
Dombroff, M., *Unfair Tactics* (Wiley Law Pub. 2d ed. 1988)
Dombroff on Direct and Cross Examination (Wiley Law Pub. 1985)
Drussel, D. & J. Wade, *Plaintiff's Proof of a Prima Facie Case* (Callaghan & Co. 1982 & 2005 Supp.)
Elliott, B. & W. Elliott, *The Law of Evidence* (Bobbs-Merrill Co. 1904)
Fontham, M., *Trial Technique and Evidence* (LexisNexis 2d ed. 2002)
Frederick, J., *The Psychology of the American Jury* (The Michie Co. 1988)
Fricke, C., *Planning and Trying Cases* (West rev. ed. 1957)
Fuller, L., "The Adversary System," reprinted in H. Berman, ed., *Talks on American Law* (Vintage Books 1961)
Gazan, S., *Encyclopedia of Trial Strategy and Tactics* (Prentice-Hall, Inc. 1962)
Gianna, D. & A. Julien, *Opening Statements 2d: Winning in the Beginning by Winning the Beginning* (Thomson West 2004)
Goldberg, S., *The First Trial: Where Do I Sit? What Do I Say?* (West 1982)
Graham, M., *Federal Rules of Evidence* (West 1986)
Hamlin, S., *What Makes Juries Listen Today* (Glasser LegalWorks 1998)
Hegland, K., *Trial and Practice Skills* (West 2d ed. 1994)
I *Corinthians* 14:8, *The Living Bible*
Imwinkelried, E., *Evidentiary Foundations* (LexisNexis 2002)
Jackson, T., *The Perfect Resume* (Anchor Press Doubleday 1981)
Jeans, J., *Trial Advocacy* (West 1993)
Jebb, R., *The Attic Orators from Antiphon to Isaeus* (Russell and Russell, Inc. 1962)
Jones on Evidence (Lawyers Co-op Pub. Co. 6th ed. 1972)
Julien, A., *Opening Statements* (West 2002)
Kamisar, Y., W. LaFave & J. Israel, *Modern Criminal Procedure* (West 11th ed. 2005)

Kaplan, B., "Trial By Jury," *reprinted in* H. Berman, ed., *Talks on American Law* (Vintage Books 1961)

Keeton, G.W., *Harris's Hints on Advocacy* (Stevens & Sons, Ltd. 18th ed. 1943)

Keeton, R., *Trial Tactics and Methods* (Little, Brown & Co. 2d ed. 1973)

Kennedy, G., *The Art of Persuasion in Greece* (Princeton Univ. Press 1963)

Kennedy, G., *The Art of Rhetoric in the Roman World* (Princeton University Press 1972)

Kestler, J., *Questioning Techniques and Tactics* (Shepard's/McGraw-Hill, Inc. 1982)

Kruger, A., *Modern Debate: Its Logic and Strategy* (McGraw-Hill 1960)

LaFave, W., J. Israel & N. King, *Criminal Procedure* (Thomson West 4th ed. 2004)

Lake, L.W., *How to Cross-Examine Witnesses Successfully* (Prentice-Hall 10th ed. 1970)

Landsman, S., *The Adversary System: A Description and Defense* (American Enterprise Institute 1984)

Lane, F., *Goldstein Trial Technique* (Thomson West supp. 2005)

Lempert, R. & S. Saltzburg, *A Modern Approach to Evidence* (West 2d ed. 1982)

Lesley, C., *Remembered Laughter: The Life of Noel Coward* (Alfred Knopf 1976)

Mauet, T., *Fundamentals of Trial Techniques* (Little, Brown & Co. 2d ed. 1988)

Mauet, T., *Trial Techniques* (Aspen Publishers 7th ed. 2007)

McCarty, D., *Psychology and the Law* (Prentice-Hall 1960)

Merriam Webster's Collegiate Dictionary (10th ed. 1997)

Moers, E., *The Dandy* (Viking Press 1960)

Moore's Federal Practice 3d (LexisNexis 2006)

Morgan, E., *Some Problems of Proof Under the Anglo-American System of Litigation* (Columbia Univ. Press 1956)

Morrill, A.E., *Anatomy of a Trial* (C.P.I. 1968)

Morrill, A.E., *Trial Diplomacy* (C.P.I. 1971)

Mueller, C., & L. Kirkpatrick, *Federal Evidence* (Lawyer's Co-op Pub. Co. 1994)

Nolan, J., *Trial Practice: Cases and Materials* (West 1981)

O'Malley, K., J. Grenig & W. Lee, *Federal Jury Practice and Instructions* (West 5th ed. 2000)

Orations of Demosthenes (Colonial Press 1900)
Palmer, B., *Courtroom Strategies* (Prentice-Hall, Inc. 4th ed. 1966)
Pearson, L., *The Art of Demosthenes* (Scholars Press 1981)
Posey, A. & L. Wrightman, *Trial Consulting* (Oxford University Press 2005)
Reed, J., *Conduct of Lawsuits* (Little, Brown 2d ed. 1912)
Schweitzer, S., *Cyclopedia of Trial Practice* (Lawyers Co-op Pub. Co. 2d ed. 1970)
Sidgwick, A., *Fallacies: A View of Logic from the Practical Side* (D. Appleton & Co. 1884)
Smith, L. & L. Malandro, *Courtroom Communication Strategies* (Kluwer Law Book Publishers, Inc. 1985)
Sonsteng, J., R. Haydock & J. Boyd, *The Trial Book—A Total System for the Preparation and Presentation of a Case* (West 1984)
Spellman, H., *Direct Examination of Witnesses* (Prentice Hall 1968)
Stanhope, Philip Dormer, *Lord Chesterfield's Letters to His Son and Others* (Everyman's Library 1969)
Stein, J., *Closing Argument* (Callaghan & Co. 1989)
Stryker, L., *The Art of Advocacy* (Zenger Pub. Co., Inc. 1979)
Tanford, J., *The Trial Process: Law, Tactics & Ethics* (LexisNexis 3d ed. 2002)
Traver, R., *Anatomy of a Murder* (St. Martin's Press 1958)
Trial Techniques with Irving Younger (R. Oliphant ed. 1978)
Turow, S., *Presumed Innocent* (Farrar Straus Giroux 1987)
Twiss, T., *Life of Lord Eldon, reprinted in* E. Frost-Knappman and D. Schrager, *The Quotable Lawyer* (Facts on File, Inc. rev. 1998)
Waicukauski, R., P. Sandler & J. Epps, *The Winning Argument* (A.B.A. 2001)
Wellman, F., *Day in Court* (MacMillan Co. 1926)
Wigmore, J., *Evidence* (Little, Brown & Co. Chadbourn rev. 1979)
Wouk, H., *The Caine Mutiny* (Doubleday 1952)
Wright, C. & A. Miller, *Federal Practice and Procedure* (West 1995)
Wyse, W., *The Speeches of Isaeus* (Cambridge Univ. Press 1904)
Younger, I., *The Art of Cross-Examination* (A.B.A. Monograph Series 1976)
Zipf, G.K., *Human Behavior and the Principle of Minimum Effort* (Addison-Wesley Press, Inc. 1949)

Newspapers and Periodicals

Alexander, D., *Preparing for More Effective Closing Argument,* 17 Me. Bar J. 194 (2002)

Allison, *Witness Preparation from the Criminal Defense Perspective,* 30 Tex. Tech. L. Rev. 1333, 1339 (1999)

Alschuler, *Courtroom Misconduct by Prosecutors and Trial Judges,* 50 Tex. L. Rev. 629, 636 (1972)

Annotation, 5 A.L.R. 2d 893 (1949)

Brogdon, *Inoculating Against Bad Facts: Brilliant Trial Strategy or Misguided Dogma?,* 63 Tex. B.J. 443 (May 2000)

Brown, *A Juryman's View,* 2 Ga. B.J. 225, 227, 229 (1965)

Buchanan, P.J., "Keep up the Pressure, George," reprinted in *San Diego Union,* Aug. 30, 1988, B7

Eannace, J., *An Art—Not a Science: A Criminal Lawyer's Perspective on Opening Statements,* 11-DEC NBA Nat'l B. Ass'n Mag. 41–42 (1997)

Evans, R. & R. Novak, "The Tower Scorecard," reprinted in *Washington Post,* Mar. 15, 1989, A23

Gladwell, Malcolm, "The Spin Myth," *New Yorker,* July 6, 1998, 66

Greenfield, Jeff, "Your Own Man Says So!," *Time,* July 8, 1996, 27

Jefferson, *Declarations Against Interest: An Exception to the Hearsay Rule,* 58 Harv. L. Rev. 1, 8 (1944)

Klonoff, R. & P. Colby, *A Trial Lawyer's Roadmap for Handling Bad Facts: The Role of Credibility,* 16 Trial Diplomacy Journal 139, 140 (1993)

Klonoff, R. & P. Colby, response to Brogdon, *Innoculating Against Bad Facts,* 63 Tex. B.J. 754 (Sept. 2000)

Kozinski, *Humor: How You Too... Can Lose Your Appeal,* 23 Montana Lawyer 5, 22 (Oct. 1997)

Kronius, J., "Mario Buatta's Unstuffy Style," *Washington Post,* Mar. 21, 2002, H4

Ladd, *Impeachment of One's Own Witness—New Developments,* 4 U. Chi. L. Rev. 69, 79 (1936)

Lambert, Elizabeth, "Wiltshire Perspectives, The Quiet Aesthetic of Designer Robert Kime," *Architectural Digest* 150 (January 1995)

Markus, *A Theory of Trial Advocacy,* 56 Tul. L. Rev. 95, 102–103, 105 (1981)

Nelson, J., "Her Life is Her Job," *Washington Post,* June 12, 1988 (Magazine) 35

New York Times, Oct. 6, 1988, B22

Note, *Drawing an Inference from the Failure to Produce a Knowledgeable*

Witness: Evidentiary and Constitutional Considerations, 61 Cal. L. Rev. 1422, 1424 (1973)

Rice & Leggett, "Insight: Empirical Study Results Contradict Sponsorship Theory," *Inside Litigation* 20 (1993)

Robinson, P., *Rough Edges in the Alignment of Legal Systems at the ICTY,* 3 J. Int'l Crim. Just. 1037, 1056–57 (2005)

Rutan, *Comment, Procuring the Right to an Unfair Trial: Federal Rule of Evidence 804(b)(6) and the Due Process Implications of the Rule's Failure to Require Standards of Reliability for Admissible Evidence,* 56 Am. U. L. Rev. 177, 198 (2006)

Seymour, W., *Why Prosecutors Act Like Prosecutors,* 11 Record of NYCBA 302, 312–313 (1956)

Sward, *Values, Ideology, and the Evolution of the Adversary System,* 64 Ind. L.J. 301, 313–316 (1989)

Thomas, *The Rule Against Impeaching One's Own Witness: A Reconsideration,* 31 Mo. L. Rev. 364 (1966)

Trial Preparation: An Interview with Louis Nizer, 2 Trial Dip. L.J. 6, 11 (1979)

Washington Post, Feb. 23, 1989, A1, col. 3

Washington Times, May 16, 1997, A1

Cases

Allard v. United States, 464 F.3d 529, 535 (5th Cir. 2006)

Arnold v. United States, 511 A.2d 399, 416 (D.C. 1986)

Austin v. United States, 382 F.2d 129, 138 (D.C. Cir. 1967)

Bahna v. United States, 68 F.3d 19, 22 (2d Cir. 1995)

Bernard v. United States, 625 F.2d 854, 857 (9th Cir. 1980)

Blood v. United States, 806 F.2d 1218 (4th Cir. 1986)

Boyles v. State, 175 N.W.2d 277 (Wisc. 1970)

Brady v. Maryland, 373 U.S. 83 (1973)

Bruton v. United States, 391 U.S. 123, 139–140 (1967)

Burke v. United States, 781 F.2d 1234, 1239 (7th Cir. 1985)

Cargill v. Turpin, 120 F.3d 1366, 1379 (11th Cir. 1997)

Carter v. Kentucky, 450 U.S. 288 (1981)

Cooper v. United States, 415 A.2d 528, 533 (D.C. 1980)

Curley v. United States, 160 F.2d 229, 232–233 (D.C. Cir.), *cert. denied,* 331 U.S. 837 (1947)

Currier v. United States, 454 F.2d 835, 839 (1st Cir. 1972)
Dent v. United States, 404 A.2d 165, 170 (D.C. 1979)
Doman v. Baltimore & O.R. Co., 22 S.E.2d 703 (W.Va. 1942)
Dreitzler v. United States, 577 F.2d 539, 553 (9th Cir. 1978), *cert. denied,* 440 U.S. 921 (1979)
Edward J. Sweeney & Sons, Inc. v. Texaco, Inc., 478 F. Supp. 243, 254 (E.D. Pa. 1979), *aff'd,* 637 F.2d 105 (3d Cir. 1980)
Estrella-Ortega v. United States, 423 F.2d 509, 510 (9th Cir. 1970)
Evans v. Multicon Const. Corp., 6 Mass. App. 291, 375 N.E.2d 338 (1978)
Freeman v. Commercial Union Assurance Co., 317 S.W.2d 563, 568 (Tex. Civ. App. 1958)
Griffin v. California, 380 U.S. 609 (1965)
Hurwitz v. United States, 459 F.3d 463, 481 (4th Cir. 2006)
Illinois Central Railroad Co. v. Staples, 272 F.2d 829, 834 (8th Cir. 1959)
Inglett & Co. v. Everglades Fertilizer Co., 255 F.2d 342, 349 (5th Cir. 1958)
Insco v. United States, 365 F. Supp. 1308, 1311 (M.D. Fla. 1973)
Jones v. Barnes, 463 U.S. 745 (1983)
Karnes v. United States, 531 F.2d 214, 217 (4th Cir. 1976)
Kean v. Comm'r of Internal Revenue, 469 F.2d 1183 (9th Cir. 1972)
Lakeside v. Oregon, 435 U.S. 333, 340 n. 10 (1978)
Leslie v. United States, 542 F.2d 285, 288–289 (5th Cir. 1976)
Lockett v. Ohio, 438 U.S. 586, 594–595 (1978)
Lokos v. State, 434 So.2d 831, 835 (Ala. 1983)
Lopez v. United States, 575 F.2d 681, 686 (9th Cir. 1978)
Lumpkin v. United States, 448 F.2d 1085, 1093 (D.C. Cir. 1971)
Luttrell v. United States, 320 F.2d 462, 464 (5th Cir. 1963)
Mallis v. United States, 467 F.2d 567, 569 (3d Cir. 1972)
Manson v. Brathwaite, 432 U.S. 98, 127 (1977)
McLhinney v. Lansdell Corp. of Maryland, 254 A.2d 177 (Md. App. 1969)
Mid America Title Co. v. Kirk, 867 F. Supp. 673, 679 (N.D. Ill. 1994), *aff'd* 59 F.3d 719 (7th Cir. 1995)
Miranda v. Arizona, 384 U.S. 436, 469 (1966)
Onufer v. Seven Springs Farm, Inc., 636 F.2d 46, 48 (3d Cir. 1980)
Oscanyan v. Arms Co., 103 U.S. 261, 263 (1880)
Patton v. Rambo, 20 Ala. 485 (1852)
People v. Cajina, 26 Cal. Rptr.3d 171 (Cal. App. 4th 2005)
People v. McClellan, 457 P.2d 871, 877 (Cal. 1969)

Pointer v. Pointer, 251 S.W.2d 334, 338 (Mo. App. 1952)
Portuondo v. Agard, 529 U.S. 61 (2000)
Resurrection Gold Mining Co. v. Fortune Gold Mining Co., 129 F. 668, 675 (8th Cir. 1904)
Riggi v. United States, 951 F.2d 1368, 1375 (3d Cir. 1991)
Robinson v. United States, 485 U.S. 25 (1988)
Sblendorio v. United States, 830 F.2d 1382, 1392 (7th Cir. 1987)
Shurman v. United States, 233 F.2d 272, 275 (5th Cir. 1956)
Silkwood v. Kerr-McGee Corp., Civ. No. 76-0888 (W.D. Okla. May 14, 1979)
State v. Kemp, 896 So.2d 349, 357 (La. App. 2d Cir. 2005)
Terry v. United States, 187 F.3d 650 (9th Cir. 1999)
Thomas v. United States, 447 A.2d 52, 57 (D.C. 1982)
Wesley v. United States, 422 F.3d 509, 516 (7th Cir. 2005)
White v. United States, 116 F.3d 903, 918 (D.C. Cir. 1997)
Williams v. State, 251 Ga. 749, 312 S.E.2d 40 (1983)
Young v. United States, 463 F.2d 934, 940 (D.C. Cir. 1972)

Statutes and Rules

Federal Rules of Appellate Procedure
Federal Rules of Civil Procedure
Federal Rules of Criminal Procedure
Federal Rules of Evidence
Model Code of Professional Responsibility
United States Code

Websites

"Mission Accomplished," remark, CommonDreams.org News Center, http://www.commondreams.org/headlines04/0927-24.htm

Index

References are to pages.

www.ingramcontent.com/pod-product-compliance
Lightning Source LLC
LaVergne TN
LVHW080649011026
849160LV00014B/1371
* 9 7 8 1 6 0 1 5 6 0 2 8 5 *